The Pentateuch in the
Twentieth Century

The Pentateuch in the Twentieth Century

The Legacy of Julius Wellhausen

ERNEST NICHOLSON

CLARENDON PRESS · OXFORD
1998

Oxford University Press, Great Clarendon Street, Oxford OX2 6DP
Oxford New York
Athens Auckland Bangkok Bogota Bombay
Buenos Aires Calcutta Cape Town Dar es Salaam
Delhi Florence Hong Kong Istanbul Karachi
Kuala Lumpur Madras Madrid Melbourne
Mexico City Nairobi Paris Singapore
Taipei Tokyo Toronto Warsaw
and associated companies in
Berlin Ibadan

Oxford is a trade mark of Oxford University Press

Published in the United States
by Oxford University Press Inc., New York

© E. W. Nicholson 1998

British Library Cataloguing in Publication Data
Data available

Library of Congress Cataloging in Publication Data
The Pentateuch in the twentieth century: the legacy of
Julius Wellhausen / Ernest Nicholson.
Includes bibliographical references and index.
1. Bible. O.T. Pentateuch—Criticism, interpretation, etc.
2. Documentary hypothesis (Pentateuchal criticism). 3. Wellhausen,
Julius, 1844–1918—Contributions in Biblical interpretation. I. Title.
BS1225.2N53 1998 222'.1066—dc21 97–35695
ISBN 0–19–826958–7

1 3 5 7 9 10 8 6 4 2

Typeset by Hope Services (Abingdon) Ltd.
Printed in Great Britain
on acid-free paper by
Biddles Ltd.,
Guildford & King's Lynn

PREFACE

There are problems in biblical studies which are so complex that they seem never to find an agreed resolution, yet which are so fascinating that scholars never give up the quest. Such is the 'Synoptic Problem' in the study of the Gospels; and such also is the question of the origins of the Pentateuch. Despite innumerable studies from at least the time of the Reformation, it was not until little more than a century ago that one hypothesis, the so-called 'Documentary Theory' formulated by Julius Wellhausen, established itself as the point of departure for all subsequent study of this topic. And even that represented only a pause for reflection, for it was not long before new approaches first supplemented, and then threatened to oust Wellhausen's great theory.

This book is an attempt to re-evaluate the Documentary Theory in the light of the vast literature that has appeared on the Pentateuch since it was first put forward. The first three chapters examine the work of form critics and traditio-historical critics who sought to build on Wellhausen's achievement but asked new questions about (for example) the oral traditions underlying the four 'sources' (JEDP) identified by Wellhausen, and the process by which they came to be incorporated into written documents. This material is familiar to scholars, but it will be useful for students of the Old Testament, and in any case is necessary if the newer developments surveyed in subsequent chapters are to be properly understood. For, as these chapters go on to show, in the last twenty-five years the study of the Pentateuch has been once more in turmoil. Rather than attempting to supplement Wellhausen's hypothesis, recent studies have either endeavoured to investigate the Pentateuch from scratch, or else to challenge almost every conclusion to which Wellhausen and those who followed him came concerning the date, origin, integrity, and nature of the sources. Not only are modern works of the origins of the Pentateuch challenging and provocative, however; they are usually also long, densely technical, and often in German. One intention of the present book is to make these discussions available in a clear and readable way to students of the Old Testament.

But the objective is not to provide merely a neutral 'state of the art' report. The book arises from conviction that much in current Pentateuchal research needs to be subjected to rigorous scrutiny and that much, indeed, is radically mistaken. The work of Wellhausen, for all that it needs revision and development in detail, remains the securest basis for understanding the Pentateuch. As the reader will see from the conclusions, however, this is not a mere call to go 'back to Wellhausen', for much in the intervening debate has significantly modified his conclusions, as well as asking questions that were not on his agenda. But the Documentary Hypothesis should remain our primary point of reference, and it alone provides the true perspective from which to approach this most difficult of areas in the study of the Old Testament.

A number of colleagues and friends have helped and advised me in writing this book. I am specially grateful to Hugh Williamson and John Barton for the interest they have taken throughout its preparation and for reading and commenting on various drafts. Their support has been invaluable. My thanks are due also to James Barr who read through the final typescript and made numerous helpful suggestions for its improvement. I enjoyed the benefit of many conversations with Graham Davies about various topics discussed in the book. His help too has been indispensable. Simon Hornblower, Fellow in Ancient History at Oriel College, has been a constant source of encouragement, and I am especially indebted to him for advice in the discussion of Israelite compared with Greek historiography. William Johnstone, John Day, and John Emerton have also come to my help in a number of key topics of debate, and I express my thanks to them also. I am very considerably indebted to the Librarian at the Faculty of Theology in Oxford, Susan Lake. I have also had the invaluable assistance here at Oriel College of Yvonne Scott, Anita Dean, and Lynn Ellwood.

Ernest Nicholson

Oriel College, Oxford
Easter 1997

CONTENTS

ABBREVIATIONS

AThANT	Abhandlungen zur Theologie des Alten und Neuen Testaments
ATD	Das Alte Testament Deutsch
BBB	Bonner biblische Beiträge
BKAT	Biblische Kommentar: Altes Testament
BN	*Biblische Notizen*
BWANT	Beiträge zur Wissenschaft vom Alten und Neuen Testament
BZ	*Biblische Zeitschrift*
BZAW	Beihefte zur Zeitschrift für die alttestamentliche Wissenschaft
EvTh	*Evangelische Theologie*
FRLANT	Forschungen zur Religion und Literatur des Alten und Neuen Testaments
HAT	Handbuch zum Alten Testament
HKAT	Handkommentar zum Alten Testament
HUCA	Hebrew Union College Annual
IBS	*Irish Biblical Studies*
ICC	International Critical Commentary
IDB	*Interpreters' Dictionary of the Bible*
JBL	*Journal of Biblical Literature*
JR	*Journal of Religion*
JSOT	*Journal for the Study of the Old Testament*
JTS	*Journal of Theological Studies*
KAT	Kommentar zum Alten Testament
LXX	The Septuagint
MT	Massoretic Text
OBO	*Orbis biblicus et orientalis*
OTS	Oudtestamentische Studiën
RB	*Revue Biblique*
RGG[1]	Die Religion in Geschichte und Gegenwart, 1st edn., Tübingen 1909–13
RGG[2]	Die Religion in Geschichte und Gegenwart, 2nd edn., Tübingen 1927–32

RTL	Revue Théologique de Louvain
SBL	Society of Biblical Literature
SVT	Supplements to Vetus Testamentum
TLZ	*Theologische Literaturzeitung*
ThPh	*Theologie und Philosophie*
ThR	*Theologische Rundschau*
ThStKr	*Theologische Studien und Kritiken*
TvT	*Tijdschrift voor Theologie*
ThZ	*Theologische Zeitschrift*
VT	*Vetus Testamentum*
WMANT	Wissenschaftliche Monographien zum Alten und Neuen Testament
ZAW	*Zeitschrift für die alttestamentliche Wissenschaft*
ZThK	*Zeitschrift für Theologie und Kirche*

PART I

From Julius Wellhausen to Martin Noth

1

The Documents of the Pentateuch

I

Julius Wellhausen (1844–1918) did not regard the investigation of the composition of the Pentateuch as an end in itself. Rather, it was a means to solving a larger and for him more urgent problem—the history and development of Israelite religion. More specifically, the problem was the place of the Pentateuchal law in the history of Israelite religion. Ostensibly the law lay at the foundation of Israel's religion, having been mediated by Moses to the people at Sinai. In reality, however, little or nothing of the law seems to have been known in the pre-exilic period, and the literature deriving from that period records and reflects customs and practices at odds with its demands. Neither the period of the Judges nor the monarchical period shows the faintest awareness 'of a sacred unifying constitution that had formerly existed', or displays any tendency towards the hierocracy envisaged in the detailed Priestly legislation in the middle books of the Pentateuch. In short: 'The religious community set up on so broad a basis in the wilderness, with its sacred centre and uniform organization, disappears and leaves no trace as soon as Israel settles in a land of its own, and becomes, in any proper sense, a nation.'[1]

In an autobiographical note in the 'Introduction' to his *Prolegomena to the History of Israel*[2] Wellhausen describes the difficulty he encountered in attempting to reconcile the traditional priority of the Pentateuchal law with the religious customs and institutions reflected in the historical and prophetic literature of the pre-exilic period:

[1] J. Wellhausen, *Prolegomena zur Geschichte Israels*, 5; the quotation is from the English translation, 5. (For details see next note.)
[2] This work was first published as *Geschichte Israels*, i (Berlin 1878) and was renamed in subsequent editions as *Prolegomena zur Geschichte Israels*. The English translation was made from the second edition (*Prolegomena zur Geschichte Israels* (Berlin 1883)) and published as *Prolegomena to the History of Israel* (Edinburgh 1885). References here are to the 2nd German edn., and quotations are from the English translation.

In my early student days I was attracted by the stories of Saul and David, Ahab and Elijah; the discourses of Amos and Isaiah laid strong hold on me, and I read myself well into the prophetic and historical books of the Old Testament. Thanks to such aids as were accessible to me, I even considered that I understood them tolerably, but at the same time was troubled with a bad conscience, as if I were beginning with the roof instead of the foundation; for I had no thorough acquaintance with the Law, of which I was accustomed to be told that it was the basis and postulate of the whole literature. At last I took courage and made my way through Exodus, Leviticus, Numbers, and even through Knobel's *Commentary* to these books. But it was in vain that I looked for the light which was to be shed from this source on the historical and prophetical books. On the contrary, my enjoyment of the latter was marred by the Law; it did not bring them any nearer me, but intruded itself uneasily, like a ghost that makes a noise indeed, but is not visible and really effects nothing. Even where there were points of contact between it and them, differences also made themselves felt, and I found it impossible to give a candid decision in favour of the priority of the Law. Dimly I began to perceive that throughout there was between them all the difference that separates two wholly distinct worlds. Yet, so far from attaining clear conceptions, I only fell into deeper confusion . . . At last, in the course of a casual visit in Göttingen in the summer of 1867, I learned through Ritschl that Karl Heinrich Graf placed the Law later than the Prophets, and, almost without knowing his reasons for the hypothesis, I was prepared to accept it; I readily acknowledged to myself the possibility of understanding Hebrew antiquity without the book of the Torah.[3]

Others before the publication of Graf's work[4] had arrived at the same hypothesis. Indeed, Graf (1815–69) had learnt it already in 1833 when he studied at Strasbourg where he attended lectures by the French scholar Edouard Reuss (1804–91) who taught first at the seminary there and subsequently became professor at the university. In 1835, and independently of Reuss and of each other, Johann Friedrich Leopold George (1811–73) and Wilhelm Vatke (1806–82) also argued it.[5] Reuss, George, and Vatke in turn were indebted to

---

[3] *Prolegomena*, 3–4; Eng. trans., 3–4.

[4] K. H. Graf, *Die geschichtlichen Bücher des Alten Testaments* (Leipzig 1866, but said to have appeared already in 1865; see J. W. Rogerson, *Old Testament Criticism in the Nineteenth Century* (London 1984), 258). Graf was never appointed to a professorship and remained a schoolteacher throughout his life.

[5] J. F. L. George, *Die älteren Jüdischen Feste mit einer Kritik der Gesetzgebung des Pentateuch* (Berlin 1835); W. Vatke, *Die biblische Theologie wissenschaftlich dargestellt*, i. *Die Religion des Alten Testamentes* (Berlin 1835). On George and Vatke and their contributions see Rogerson, *Old Testament Criticism in the Nineteenth Century*, chs. 3 and 4 respectively.

Wilhelm Martin Leberecht DeWette (1780–1849). DeWette's most important achievement was his development of the method of historical criticism expansively applied in his epoch-making work *Contributions to Old Testament Introduction* (1806–7),[6] 'the first work of Old Testament scholarship to use the critical method in order to present a view of the history of Israelite religion that is radically at variance with the view implied in the Old Testament itself'.[7] He was convinced that the various law codes in the Pentateuch were not delivered by Moses at Sinai but were the result of different stages of development in the history of Israelite religion. As Wellhausen put it, he was 'the first clearly to perceive and point out how disconnected are the alleged starting-point of Israel's history and that history itself'.[8] The main obstacle to such a view was the history of the Chronicler according to which the Mosaic law complete with sacrificial system and hierarchic establishment had been practised from the beginning and was fully in evidence from the time of David onwards. Against earlier scholars who had defended the historical reliability of the books of Chronicles, DeWette showed that their author's use of the earlier historical books of Samuel and Kings was tendentious, that he was motivated by a partiality towards Judah and a hatred of northern Israel, that, in short, the picture he presented of Israelite religion and cult in the pre-exilic period was anachronistic and a doctrinaire reading back into earlier times of the religious and cultic practice of the second Temple. The books Joshua–Kings provided evidence of a different picture. By comparing the demands of the various law codes in the Pentateuch with actual practice as reflected in these books, DeWette showed how incompatible was the belief in the Mosaic origin of the Pentateuchal laws with historical practice. Thus, for example, one of Deuteronomy's main demands is the centralization of worship, but such figures as Samuel, Saul, David, and Solomon evidently knew nothing of such a law. Or again, Samuel's hesitation in allowing the institution of monarchy would have been incomprehensible if the law of kingship in Deuteronomy 17: 14–20

---

[6] W. M. L. DeWette, *Beiträge zur Einleitung in das Alte Testament*, 2 vols. (Halle 1806–7). A fuller description in English of DeWette's contribution is provided by Rogerson, *Old Testament Criticism in the Nineteenth Century*, ch. 2, and in his admirable intellectual biography of DeWette, *W. M. L. de Wette Founder of Modern Biblical Criticism: An Intellectual Biography*, JSOT Supplement Series, 120 (Sheffield 1992).

[7] Rogerson, *Old Testament Criticism in the Nineteenth Century*, 29.

[8] *Prolegomena*, 4 ff.; Eng. trans., 4 f.

had been known at that time. Similarly, DeWette argued that the description of the Tabernacle in Exodus 25–8 was based upon the Temple built by Solomon and was therefore no earlier than this period, and that the distinction between priests and Levites in the Priestly sections of the Pentateuch was unknown until a late time in Israelite history.

DeWette's cogent dismissal of the historical dependability of the Chronicler, nowadays commonplace in Old Testament scholarship, was crucial for the subsequent study of Israelite religion and for understanding the emergence of the Pentateuch. What was necessary, however, was for criticism to turn aside from the historical problem identified by DeWette and others in order, in the first instance, to come to some sort of clear understanding of the composition of the Pentateuch.

II

A number of advances had already been made. Critical insights gained during the seventeenth and eighteenth centuries into the complexities of the literature of the Pentateuch gave rise to a number of theories about its composition and growth. On the basis of (1) the usage of the divine names *Elohim* and *Yahweh* in Genesis as well as (2) differences in style between narratives where such differences seemed unwarranted by the subject matter, and (3) the presence of duplicate narratives such as the two accounts of creation in Genesis 1–2, Jean Astruc (1684–1766), a medical doctor in Paris, and Johann Gottfried Eichhorn (1752–1827), professor of oriental languages at Jena University, recognized two main sources in that book (a number of further minor sources were also isolated) which were later to be designated by the sigla E (the Elohist source) and J (the Yahwist source). In 1798 Karl David Ilgen (1763–1834), Eichhorn's successor at Jena, argued that the Elohist material was itself composite and derived from two originally separate sources,[9] but this discovery did not find recognition among scholars until it was freshly argued by Hermann Hupfeld in 1853 (see below).

[9] K. D. Ilgen, *Die Urkunden des Jerusalemischen Tempelarchivs in ihrer Urgestalt als Beytrag zur Berichtigung der Geschichte der Religion und Politik, i. Die Urkunden des ersten Buches von Mose* (Halle 1798). On Ilgen's work and achievement see B. Seidel, *Karl David Ilgen und die Pentateuchforschung im Umbreis der sogenannten Älteren Urkundenhypothese*, BZAW 213 (Berlin 1993).

Against this so-called 'Older Documentary Theory' Alexander Geddes (1737–1802), a Scottish Roman Catholic priest, in 1792 advanced the view that the Pentateuch and the book of Joshua—he believed that the latter was not only a continuation of the story of the Pentateuch but also of its literary sources[10]—were composed of numerous originally separate fragments which had been combined by a redactor. This 'Fragment Theory' was subsequently introduced into Germany by Johann Severin Vater (1771–1826) where it was espoused by a number of other scholars,[11] among them DeWette, though not without reservation and modification. DeWette found evidence of an original document, a national 'epos of the Hebrew theocracy', in Genesis and Exodus to which the remaining parts or 'fragments' of the Pentateuch were gradually added. His theory thus tended towards a 'Supplementary Theory'. Heinrich Ewald (1803–75), who was one of Wellhausen's teachers and has been described as 'one of the greatest critical Old Testament scholars of all time',[12] later outlined such a Supplementary Theory, arguing that a basic source (*Grundschrift*), the Elohist source beginning at Genesis 1, runs through the Pentateuch and into Joshua, and that an editor expanded this with insertions derived from a second originally separate J source.[13] The theory was subsequently more expansively developed with the difference that the secondary insertions into an original *Grundschrift* were attributed not to an independent literary source but to the editor himself.[14]

Of these three main theories it was the approach represented by the Documentary Theory that in a much more developed and elaborated form—the so-called 'Newer Documentary Theory'—gradually prevailed among nineteenth-century scholars, that is, the view that the Pentateuch is the result of editorial combination of originally independent extensive narrative sources. The notion of a Supplementary

[10] A. Geddes, *The Holy Bible or the Books accounted Sacred by Christians and Jews: otherwise called the Books of the Old and New Covenants: faithfully translated from corrected texts of the originals with Various Readings, Explanatory Notes and Critical Remarks*, i (London 1792). 'To the Pentateuch I have joined the book of Joshua, both because I conceive it to have been compiled by the same author, and because it is a necessary appendix to the history contained in the former books' (p. xxi).

[11] J. S. Vater, *Commentar über den Pentateuch*, i–iv (Halle 1802–5).

[12] See Rogerson, *Old Testament Criticism in the Nineteenth Century*, ch. 6 (the quotation is on p. 91).

[13] H. Ewald in *ThStKr* 4 (1831), 595–606. (Review article of J. Stähelin, *Kritische Untersuchungen über die Genesis* (Basel 1830).)

[14] See especially F. Tuch, *Commentar über die Genesis* (Halle 1838).

Theory continued to play a role, however, in so far as the advocates of the Documentary Theory found that the main literary sources of the Pentateuch had undergone editorial expansion both before and after their combination. We shall see later that forms of a Supplementary Theory and of a Fragment Theory have been newly argued during recent years.

The path from the so-called 'Older Documentary Theory' to Wellhausen's work has often been described and need not be retold in detail here.[15] Briefly the main stages were as follows.

In his *Contributions* and already in a short doctoral treatise published a year earlier in 1805[16] DeWette argued that Deuteronomy was the latest book of the Pentateuch. His work confirmed the view already adumbrated by earlier scholars that part of the book of Deuteronomy was none other than the 'book of the law' found in the Temple in the reign of Josiah and the source of the reforms described in 2 Kings 22–3. It also served to emphasize the distinctiveness of Deuteronomy as an originally independent source in the Pentateuch. In terms of the emerging 'Newer Documentary Theory' this meant that three distinct and originally independent sources had been identified in the Pentateuch: the E source, which formed a framework into which two others, the J source and Deuteronomy (D), had been incorporated.

A further major advance was achieved in 1853 by Hermann Hupfeld (1796–1866),[17] professor at Halle University and an ardent disciple of DeWette though he had never been one of his students.[18] This concerned the E source to which hitherto the non-J passages in Genesis had substantially been attributed. Hupfeld now independently rediscovered what Ilgen had earlier argued, that the Elohist source in Genesis comprises two originally separate sources, an

---

[15] See e.g. R. J. Thompson, *Moses and the Law in a Century of Criticism since Graf*, SVT 19 (Leiden 1970); Rogerson, *Old Testament Criticism in the Nineteenth Century*. Very useful also, with an extensive bibliography, is E. Osswald, *Das Bild des Mose in der kritischen alttestamentlichen Wissenschaft seit Julius Wellhausen*, Theologische Arbeiten, 18 (Berlin 1962).

[16] *Dissertatio Critico-Exegetica qua Deuteronomium a prioribus Pentateuchi libris diversum alius cuiusdam recentioris auctoris opus esse monstratur* (A Critical-Exegetical Dissertation in which it is Demonstrated that Deuteronomy is Diverse from the Earlier Books of the Pentateuch and Derives from a Later Author) (Jena 1805).

[17] For a brief description about Hupfeld's life and work see Rogerson, *Old Testament Criticism in the Nineteenth Century*, ch. 9.

[18] H. Hupfeld, *Die Quellen der Genesis und die art ihrer Zusammensetzung* (Berlin 1853).

earlier Elohist (E^1) and a later Elohist (E^2). Thus Hupfeld's work on Genesis made possible the identification of four originally separate documents which had gradually been combined to form the Pentateuch and which, to give them their modern sigla, are P (the Priestly document, Hupfeld's E^1), E (his E^2), J, and D—*in this order*.

The next decisive step came with the work of Graf who in 1865, as noted above, on the basis of a suggestion made to him by his teacher Edouard Reuss at Strasbourg as far back as 1833, argued that P was not the earliest of the Pentateuchal sources, as had hitherto been generally agreed, but the latest.[19] Initially he limited this judgement to the legislative sections of this source in Exodus, Leviticus, and Numbers. Taking the original core of Deuteronomy as his pivot—he believed it to have comprised chapters 4–26 and 28 of the present book—he showed that its author presupposed the combined J and E sources (where E still included what Hupfeld in the meantime had shown to be both E^1 and E^2). On the other hand the author of Deuteronomy did not know the Priestly legislation in Exodus, Leviticus, and Numbers which was thus to be dated later than Deuteronomy's appearance in the seventh century. Almost immediately, however, Graf was persuaded by the Dutch scholar and professor at the University of Leiden, Abraham Kuenen (1828–91), who himself had already been moving towards such a view, that the Priestly narrative in Genesis (Hupfeld's E^1) could not be separated from the Priestly legislation in Exodus, Leviticus, and Numbers and that accordingly it also was late.[20] As a result Graf in 1869 argued that the Priestly material as a whole was the latest of the Pentateuchal documents to have been composed.[21] As we have seen, Graf's views were seized upon by Wellhausen as providing not only the solution to the problem of the composition of the Hexateuch but also the key to the understanding of the development of Israelite religion. In a number of articles in 1876–7 he lucidly and compellingly set out the new understanding of the growth of the Hexateuch.[22]

[19] K. H. Graf, *Die geschichtlichen Bücher*; see Rogerson, *Old Testament Criticism in the Nineteenth Century*, 258.

[20] According to Wellhausen (*Prolegomena*, 11 n. 1; Eng. trans., 11 n. 1), Graf already acknowledged this in a letter to A. Kuenen in 1866. For a recent assessment of Kuenen's contribution, see P. B. Dirksen and A. Van Der Kooij (eds.), *Abraham Kuenen (1828–1891): His Major Contributions to the Study of the Old Testament*, OTS 29 (1993).

[21] K. H. Graf, 'Die sogenannte Grundschrift des Pentateuchs', in A. Merx (ed.), *Archiv für wissenschaftliche Erforschung des Alten Testaments* (Halle 1869), 466–77.

[22] 'Die Composition des Hexateuchs', *Jahrbücher für Deutsche Theologie*, 21 (1876), 392–450, 531–602, and 22 (1877), 407–79. The articles were subsequently reprinted in

Wellhausen's conclusions were briefly as follows (more detail is offered in the following sections of this chapter). The earliest sources, J and E, were combined by a redactor (R^{JE}) whom he designated the 'Jehovist'. The Jehovist was no mere compiler, however, but in many places freely reshaped the sources he inherited, and, indeed, in a number of texts (for example the Sinai pericope) was an author. Wellhausen thus emphasized that the manner of the combination of the sources was by no means a mechanical 'scissors and paste' process. So closely have the sources been combined and reworked that in places it is no longer possible to separate J from E. In the *Prolegomena* Wellhausen rarely goes behind the work of the Jehovist to refer to J and E passages. In effect, he regarded the Jehovist as the creator of the Hexateuch. At a later stage of redaction the book of Deuteronomy, the core of which was composed in the seventh century BC, was combined with JE. An originally independent Priestly narrative, which he designated 'Q' (= *Quatuor foederum liber*, 'the book of the four covenants')[23] and which he dated to the early post-exilic period, was further expanded by the inclusion of a mass of Priestly legislation. This 'Priestly Code', as he referred to the expanded Q source, was subsequently worked into the already existing JED to form the Hexateuch substantially as we have it. That the Priestly Code was incorporated into the Hexateuch after the combination of JED is evidenced by the fact that the narrative sections in the book of Deuteronomy reflect a knowledge of JE but not of the P material in the Pentateuch.

No one more than Wellhausen emphasized how complex a process the composition of the Hexateuch was. He pointed to evidence, for example, that both the J and E sources had gone through more than one stage of expansion before being united by the Jehovist (see below). He frankly acknowledged passages, especially in the second half of Numbers and in Joshua, that could not be assigned to any of the main sources or their redactors.[24] He found indications that the

his *Skizzen und Vorarbeiten*, ii (Berlin 1885). A second edition with a supplement revising some earlier conclusions as well as further reflection on various Pentateuchal texts in the intervening years was published in *Die Composition des Hexateuchs und der Historischen Bücher des Alten Testaments* (Berlin 1889). References here are to the latter edition.

[23] The four covenants are those with Adam, Noah, Abraham, and the Sinai covenant.

[24] *Die Composition des Hexateuchs*, 208. He was subsequently persuaded by Kuenen that such passages were additions in the style and spirit of P by an author who was also influenced by JED, and he welcomed such a suggestion as further evidence against any notion of a mechanical fitting together of the original sources (ibid. 314f.).

Jehovist's work had also been subject to secondary additions before being united with Deuteronomy. Both Deuteronomy and the Priestly material had likewise undergone a complex process of growth. In short, Wellhausen was in no doubt that many hands at many times had contributed to the growth and final form of the Hexateuch.

Such was his recognition of the complexities of this literature that although subsequent generations acknowledge his work as the climax of nineteenth-century Pentateuchal research, he himself was in no doubt that his study should be viewed rather as the beginning of yet further research, and in his concluding remarks to his investigation he wrote that in so far as he hoped for a reward for his labours it should be 'discussion and contradiction'.[25] The result was a period of intensive further research and debate. The leads his work gave for further investigation were followed, and refinements of other aspects of the theory proposed, and although there was disagreement on details the theory in all its main essentials gained the support of the majority of leading scholars not only in Germany but also in Great Britain and in America.[26] A brief outline of this further research is provided in the remaining sections of this chapter. But 'contradiction' there also was, and issues were raised that have remained live ever since and, indeed, in some measure lie behind the current reopened debate about the Pentateuch. These too will be noted in the following pages.

III

The Yahwist and Elohist Sources

Almost immediately the view, which Wellhausen had already adumbrated, that neither of the two older sources in the Hexateuch, J and E, was homogeneous, received further attention. He had pointed to two distinct layers of J material in the primeval history and to other inconsistencies in J as well as E throughout the Hexateuch. At the end of his analysis he had also suggested that a closer investigation

---

[25] In the first edition of *Die Composition des Hexateuchs* (*Skizzen und Vorarbeiten*, 208) Wellhausen wrote: 'Wenn ich für die langwierige und undankbare Arbeit einen Lohn hoffe, so ist es Diskussion und Widerspruch.'

[26] See, e.g., R. J. Thompson, *Moses and the Law*, ch. 6, 'The Victory of Grafianism', and Rogerson, *Old Testament Criticism in the Nineteenth Century*, ch. 20, 'England from 1880: The Triumph of Wellhausen'; C. Houtman, *Der Pentateuch: Die Geschichte seiner Erforschung neben einer Auswertung* (Kampen 1994), ch. 3.

would reveal that both J and E, before they were combined, had developed through various stages which could be represented by the sigla J¹, J², J³, E¹, E², E³, adding that a 'supplementary theory' was thus in some measure still valid.[27] In 1883 Karl Budde (1850–1935), then professor at Bonn university, examined Genesis 1–11 in greater detail and argued that the J material here was based upon two originally separate sources, a primeval history without a flood narrative (J¹) and one which was based upon this earlier history but incorporated a flood narrative (J²).[28] Both sources were later combined by a redactor who himself belonged to the J 'school'. Kuenen similarly found evidence of two such layers of J material in these chapters but argued that the J² elements were the result of secondary expansion of the earlier J¹ stratum.[29] He also found evidence of such secondary expansion in the J material in the patriarchal narratives in Genesis, and further suggested that the J material in Exodus, Numbers, and Joshua could scarcely have remained untouched by such a redactor, though the many alterations through which the material in these books had passed rendered more exact discernment of this no longer possible.

Notwithstanding its sparser presence in the Hexateuch when compared with the material preserved from J, E also was believed by Kuenen to have developed in a similar manner to J. Otto Procksch (1874–1947) also, for example, in a detailed monograph on the Elohist source, maintained that an original E document, which he too designated as E¹, had subsequently been utilized and expanded into a later form, E².[30]

This trend to find more and more layers of material in both J and E led its adherents to refer no longer to a Yahwist or an Elohist author but rather to a J 'school' and an E 'school'. Such further division did not, however, go unopposed. For example, Otto Gruppe (1851–1919), who worked mainly in classical mythology and philology, already in 1889 argued against Budde that the unevenness in the

---

[27] *Die Composition des Hexateuchs*, 207.

[28] K. Budde, *Die biblische Urgeschichte, Genesis 1–12.5 untersucht* (Giessen 1883). See also, for example, C. Bruston, 'Les Quatre Sources des lois de l'Exode', *Revue de Théologie de Lausanne* (1883), and 'Les Deux Jehovistes: Études sur les sources de l'histoire sainte', *Revue de Théologie de Lausanne* (1885); 'Les Cinq documents de loi mosaïque', *ZAW* 12 (1892), 177–211; B. Stade, 'Beiträge zur Pentateuchkritik', *ZAW* 14 (1894), 250–318.

[29] A. Kuenen, *Historisch-kritisch Onderzoek*, i (2nd edn., Leiden 1885).

[30] O. Procksch, *Das nordhebräische Sagenbuch. Die Elohimquelle* (Leipzig 1906).

J material in Genesis 1–11 was the result of the use by one author of traditional material of diverse origin[31]—an anticipation of what was later to be more widely believed when the oral, preliterary stages in the history of the Pentateuchal sources received greater attention and emphasis. Others later offered a still different explanation of variations within the J source.[32]

The scope of both J and E was further considered at this time and the view argued that these sources continue not only into the book of Joshua but into the remaining books, the Former Prophets, at least as far as the beginning of 1 Kings.[33] As we shall see, this view was to receive further elaboration in subsequent research.[34]

The question which of the two older sources in the Pentateuch, J and E, was the earlier and the period to which each was to be dated was much discussed. This was made more difficult by the trend to find different layers of composition in each. Concerning their relative chronology, the dominant view before Wellhausen had been that E was prior to J. In 1878, however, Wellhausen expressed the view that J was the earlier and this soon became the majority view.[35] It was argued, for example, that J's more naïve and anthropomorphic narration pointed to an earlier time than E's less anthropomorphic and more theologically advanced presentation. It was also argued, for example, that the so-called 'ethical decalogue' in Exodus 20, which was assigned to E, with its almost total emphasis on moral norms, represented a later stage of development than the J decalogue or dodecalogue in Exodus 34 which, it was maintained, still reflects the more cultically oriented, earlier stage in the development of Israelite religion.

Opinions also varied on whether E was dependent upon J. The attempt was made by some, for example Kuenen, on the basis of a detailed examination of their respective vocabularies to show that E borrowed from J in such parallel narratives as Genesis 26: 6–12 (J)

---

[31] O. Gruppe, 'War Genesis 6, 1–4 ursprünglich mit der Sintflut verbunden?', *ZAW* 9 (1889), 135–55.

[32] The so-called 'Newest Documentary Theory'. For this, see below, Ch. 2.

[33] Cf. C. H. Cornill, 'Ein Elohistischer Bericht über die Entstehung des israelitischen Königtums in I Samuelis i–xv aufgezeigt', *Zeitschrift für kirkliche Wissenschaft und kirkliches Leben*, 6 (1885), 113ff.; 'Zur Quellenkritik der Bücher Samuelis', *Königsberger Studien*, i (1887), 23–59; 'Noch einmal Saule Königswahl und Verwerfung', *ZAW* 10 (1890), 96–109; K. Budde, *Die Bücher Richter und Samuel: Ihre Quellen und ihr Aufbau* (Giessen 1890).

[34] See below, Ch. 2.

[35] In his *Geschichte Israels*, i. 370f.; cf. *Prolegomena*, 383; Eng. trans., 361.

and Genesis 20 (E). In the nature of the case, however, such compar-
isons were too slenderly based to offer any sure foundation for such
an argument. Scholars therefore remained divided on this question.
It may be noted, however, that Heinrich Holzinger (1863–1944), in
his comprehensive presentation and defence of the Documentary
Theory, argued that both J and E were independently based upon a
common original source, and maintained that this offered a better
explanation of the distinctive emphases, religious, national, and
otherwise, which each author sought to make, and that it also
explained why E apparently did not know J's account of the primeval
history in Genesis 1–11 in which no E material was present[36]—a view
that was to be freshly argued and widely accepted at a later time, especially by Martin Noth.[37]

Concerning the more precise dating of J and E, Wellhausen did not
go beyond a general dating of both to the monarchical period and
before the appearance of the book of Deuteronomy which he
ascribed to the late seventh century.[38] Whilst some argued for an
earlier date of J and E—notably Eduard König (1846–1936) who
dated E to c.1200 BC and J to c.1000 BC—most scholars assigned both
sources to the monarchical period and not usually earlier than the
ninth century.[39] A date for J in the second half of the ninth century
was widely favoured, whilst a date for E about a century later was also
widely agreed. August Dillmann (1823–94), however, from 1880
onwards successively professor at Kiel, Giessen, and Berlin, tena-
ciously held to the view that E was as early as the first half of the ninth
century and assigned J to the first half of the eighth century.[40]

In the discussion of the provenance of these two sources it was generally acknowledged that neither J nor E provided any overt parti-
sanship, whether for the Northern Kingdom or for Judah. There was
general agreement that E originated in northern Israel. More contro-
versial was the question of the origin of J. A strong body of opinion,
of which Kuenen was a representative, pointed to the interest of J in
such important northern sanctuaries as Bethel and Shechem as well
as in the transjordanian sanctuaries of Mahanaim and Penuel which

---

[36] H. Holzinger, *Einleitung in den Hexateuch* (Freiburg 1893), 219.
[37] See below, Ch. 3.   [38] *Prolegomena*, 9; Eng. trans., 9.
[39] An exception was Budde in *Die biblische Urgeschichte* who allowed for a date as
early as the tenth century for his J¹ source; he assigned his J² to the later ninth or possibly the eighth century, and the Yahwistic redactor who combined these two earlier J
sources to not later than the eighth century.
[40] A. Dillmann, *Die Genesis* (6th edn., Leipzig 1892), p. xix.

had no relation to Judah. Even Beersheba, it was pointed out, was a place of pilgrimage for northern Israelites as late as the time of Amos (Amos 5: 5). This together with other considerations was taken as evidence that J was a northern Israelite work. Most scholars agreed, however, that it originated in Judah. It was argued in favour of this, for example, that the patriarchal narratives in J locate Abraham in the southern sanctuary of Hebron of which E knows nothing; that J records the overthrow of Sodom and Gomorrah of which again E shows no knowledge; that the Abraham–Lot stories, peculiar to J, are southern in origin; that in the Joseph narrative J ascribes the leading role to Judah whilst E ascribes it to Reuben; that the story of Tamar in Genesis 38 (J) displays a favourable attitude towards the tribe of Judah; etc.

IV

The Book of Deuteronomy

The view that the 'book of the law' discovered in the Temple in Jerusalem in 621 BC (2 Kgs. 22–3) is to be identified with Deuteronomy, at least in an earlier stage of its composition and growth, was of central importance for the Graf–Wellhausen theory. Opposition to it was maintained by a number of scholars, the so-called Gramberg school, who challenged the historicity of the narrative in 2 Kings 22–3 and dated Deuteronomy to the exilic period,[41] as others were to argue later.[42] Most scholars, however, supported the close association between Deuteronomy and Josiah's reformation. The only matter of dispute concerned how much of the present book constituted 'the book of the law' referred to in the narrative in 2 Kings, and opinions varied between limiting the original core to the central law section in chapters 12–26 and assigning much of the book as we now have it to the time of Josiah. Wellhausen, for example, believed chapters 12–26 to have been the original limits of the book, allowing for some secondary revision, and argued that two separate editions of the book had subsequently appeared, each with its own hortatory and historical framework, one comprising chapters 1: 1–4: 44 + 12–26 + 27, the

---

[41] C. W. P. Gramberg seems to have been the first to argue this view in his *Kritische Der Religionsideen des Alten Testaments*, i (Berlin 1829), 153 f., 305 f.
[42] For a review see E. W. Nicholson, *Deuteronomy and Tradition* (Oxford 1967), 4 ff.

other 4: 45–11: 32 + 12–26 + 28–30. A subsequent redactor combined them both and the remaining chapters were still further additions.[43] More conservatively, on the other hand, for example, Samuel Rolles Driver (1846–1914), Regius Professor of Hebrew at Oxford, held that the so-called 'first introduction' in 1: 1–4: 40 belonged to the original book which also contained chapters 5–26 together with a superscription in 4: 41–9 and a conclusion in chapter 28, with 27: 9–10 possibly being the original connection between chapters 26 and 28.[44] Various stages in between these views were also argued.

A different criterion for understanding the composition and growth of the book was suggested in the 1890s. This is the frequent transition in the book from a singular to a plural form of address, Israel sometimes being addressed as 'thou' and 'thee' and sometimes as 'you'. In 1891 Carl Heinrich Cornill (1854–1920) regarded some laws as secondary on account of their use of the plural instead of the more usual singular,[45] and a few years later several studies were published offering detailed analyses of Deuteronomy based upon this changing form of address.[46] In his detailed but also very complex analysis Karl Steuernagel (1869–1958), for example, argued that separate editions of the book using the singular and plural form of address respectively had once existed and were subsequently combined. More recently the 'you-plural' passages in the book have been more widely regarded as having arisen from secondary redactional supplementation rather than deriving from a separate edition of it.[47]

Opinion was also divided on the question of how long before 621 BC the original book of Deuteronomy had been composed. There was little support among critical scholars for a date prior to the reign of Hezekiah in the late eighth century BC and few were prepared to date it as early as this. The reign of Manasseh, described in 2 Kings 21 as notoriously apostate, was favoured by some as the background to the composition of the book which is so characterized by its passionate

[43] *Die Composition des Hexateuchs*, 186–93.

[44] S. R. Driver, *An Introduction to the Literature of the Old Testament* (Edinburgh 1891). References here are to the 9th edn. (1913), 93 ff.

[45] C. H. Cornill, *Einleitung in das Alte Testament* (Tübingen 1891). For a review see Nicholson, *Deuteronomy and Tradition*, 22 ff.

[46] W. Staerk, *Das Deuteronomium. Sein Inhalt und seine literarische Form* (Leipzig 1984); C. Steuernagel, *Der Rahmen des Deuteronomium. Literar-kritische Untersuchung über seine Zusammensetzung und Entstehung* (Halle 1894); id., *Die Entstehung des deuteronomischen Gesetz* (Berlin 1895; 2nd edn., 1901).

[47] For more discussion see A. D. H. Mayes, *Deuteronomy*, New Century Bible (London 1979), 34–55.

drive for cultic purity. Many, however, argued that the book was composed during Josiah's reign. Sometimes associated with this was the view that its 'discovery' in the eighteenth year of Josiah was no accident but a 'pious fraud'. That is, it was argued that the book was composed by members of the Jerusalem priesthood, shortly before its discovery as a reformation programme, and that its authors had to resort to this deception of its supposed loss and discovery in order to have the book and its demands accepted and implemented by the state authorities.[48]

Finally, it was generally agreed that the authors of Deuteronomy knew J and E, but it was disputed whether these narrative sources were known and used separately or as already combined and supplemented by the so-called Jehovist. This question was further complicated by the different views, noted above, concerning what parts of the present book of Deuteronomy constituted its original core (*Urdeuteronomium*), since, for example, Deuteronomy 1–11 or even 5–11, if these belonged to the original book, show some knowledge of the combined JE.

V

The Priestly Source

Like J, E, and D, the Priestly source in the Hexateuch was also widely agreed not to be all of one piece but to have developed in different stages. Here too, therefore, scholars spoke of a Priestly 'school'. Wellhausen distinguished between two main stages in the development of the Priestly source: an original narrative, which he designated Q, and a considerable amount of material, almost entirely legislative, which derives from the secondary redaction of this original document. Though Q takes the form of a history similar to that of J and E, the history it records serves primarily as a framework on which to arrange the legislative material. This dominant characteristic of Q was further enhanced by the inclusion of the abundant secondary material inserted into it so that the Priestly source as a whole is aptly described as 'the Priestly Code'.

---

[48] Wellhausen seems to have supported this view. See *Prolegomena*, 24 f.; Eng. trans., 25 f.

That an original document of this nature can be isolated in the Priestly source as a whole was widely accepted, though there was disagreement on its precise scope (see below), the siglum P^G (*Grundschrift* = 'basic document') being more generally preferred for it than Wellhausen's term Q. At the same time the attempt was made to be more precise about the secondary redaction of this original document into the Priestly source as we now have it. One major block of material regarded as belonging to the secondary expansion of P^G was identified as Leviticus 17–26. Wellhausen argued that these chapters constituted an originally independent legal corpus, and in 1877 August Klostermann (1837–1915) further emphasized this and designated them 'the Holiness legislation' (H) on account of the frequent occurrence in them of the formula 'you shall be holy, for I, the Lord your God, am holy'.[49] For the redactor who incorporated this 'Holiness Code' into P^G the siglum P^H was henceforth widely employed, some additional material outside these chapters frequently being assigned to this redactor if not to H itself. The remaining secondary or supplementary material in P was variously designated, the siglum P^S (= P supplementa) being frequently used, however, as a sort of 'umbrella' term for it when taken as a whole.

That P^G forms the framework of the Pentateuch in its present form was widely agreed: the Pentateuch begins with P's account of the creation (Gen.1: 1–2: 4a) and ends with its record of the death of Moses (Deut. 34: 1a, 7–9)—hence the use of the term *Grundschrift* to describe this original Priestly narration. Its overall concern was to narrate the origin and foundation of the Israelite theocracy and its ordinances and institutions. The P^G material in Genesis describes the prehistory of the rise of the theocracy, mostly in concise, at times tabulated manner (e.g. the tables of 'genealogies'); narratives proper are provided only when, as for example in the case of Genesis 17, a particular theocratic institution (in this case the rite of circumcision) is being described. Greater use of narrative proper is in evidence when it comes to the period of the bondage and exodus, since here the more immediate beginnings of the theocracy are being described. The narrative elements recede again when Israel arrives at Sinai at which point in the P^G material in Exodus 19–Numbers 10 the all-important giving of the manifold legislation which is to govern the life of the theocracy very largely predominates. Thereafter, in the P^G material in

---

[49] A. Klostermann, 'Beiträge zur Entstehungsgeschichte des Pentateuchs', *Zeitschrift für die gesamte Lutherische Theologie und Kirche*, 38 (1877), 401–45.

the remainder of Numbers, is recorded the departure from Sinai, the sending out of spies (as in JE) to survey the promised land, and other preparations for the journey to the land. As already noted, P^G in the Pentateuch ends with the record of the death of Moses, the death of Aaron having been recorded in Numbers 20: 22 ff.

Opinion was divided on whether P^G went beyond the death of Moses and recorded the entry into the land of Canaan. Wellhausen argued that it ended with the record of Moses' death in Deuteronomy 34. There are but the sparsest fragments of P material in Joshua 1–11. The P material in the remainder of Joshua, which concerns the division of the land between the tribes, cannot have belonged to P^G since a division of the land without a prior record of a conquest of the land rather hangs in the air. Wellhausen therefore argued that the P material in Joshua 12–24 already presupposes the combined JED material in Joshua and is to be assigned to a later Priestly editor and not to P^G.

Others, however, contended that the original Priestly narrative did contain a record of the entry into the land under Joshua. It was argued, for example, that the whole movement of the narrative of P^G in the Pentateuch pointed to and demanded completion in the entry into the land where the theocracy would achieve full realization. Further, the divine commissioning of Joshua as Moses' successor, which is recorded by P in Numbers 27: 12 ff., itself points to the impending role of Joshua as leader of the people into the land. That there are only sparse elements of P in Joshua 1–11 was therefore understood as an indication that P^G contained only a summary presentation of the settlement.

There was the beginning also of controversy about whether the Priestly material in the Pentateuch had ever been an independent document on the analogy of J or E or whether it originated as redactional supplementation of an already existing Pentateuchal corpus. The former of these two possibilities was the majority opinion, but the latter view was argued as early as 1880 by Siegmund Maybaum (1844–1919), whose main research focused upon the origin of Jewish institutions.[50] His work on P received a sharp response from Budde[51] and remained without influence. As we shall see, however, this understanding of the origin of P was freshly argued later and has received influential support in more recent years.

---

[50] S. Maybaum, *Die Entwicklung des altisraelitischen Priesterthums* (Breslau 1880).
[51] Budde, *Die biblische Urgeschichte*, 276–80.

As to the period in which it was composed, there remained those who argued that it originated before Deuteronomy, Dillmann being the strongest representative of this view.[52] But most scholars accepted Graf's insight, subsequently so cogently advocated by Wellhausen, that P post-dates D. Amongst these there was also agreement that the plans for the restored community in Ezekiel 40–8, believed to have been composed by Ezekiel in the earlier part of the exilic period, represent the midpoint, so to speak, between D and P[G]. Since this 'temple blueprint' in Ezekiel shows no knowledge of P[G] and in a number of important respects is strikingly different from it, the latter cannot have been in existence when it was drawn up.

An example is provided by Ezekiel 44: 6–16, which was of special importance for Wellhausen in his reconstruction of the history of the priesthood in Israel.[53] According to this chapter, only the Levites of Jerusalem, the sons of Zadok, are to be priests in the newly constructed Jerusalem. All other Levites are deprived of the full priestly rights in punishment for the apostasy they committed alongside the people. Henceforth they are to be only servants and assistants of the sons of Zadok. The background to what Ezekiel here sets out is the centralization of worship to Jerusalem and the abolition of the local sanctuaries with consequent loss of employment for the levitical priests who had ministered at them from time immemorial. Though Deuteronomy sought to provide for these country Levites to continue their ministry at the central sanctuary (Deut. 18: 6 f.), the priests in Jerusalem, whose privileges this threatened, refused to admit them to the full priestly rights which they had historically enjoyed (cf. 2 Kgs. 23: 9). In this situation Ezekiel, 'a thorough Jerusalemite', 'drapes the logic of facts with the mantle of morality' and in his plans for the newly constituted cult in the new Jerusalem decrees that the sons of Zadok, who had been unsullied by the apostasy of the pre-reform period, are alone to minister at the altar of Yahweh, while the remainder of the Levites are to be their assistants and servants performing the menial tasks in the cult. In the Priestly legislation in the Pentateuch, however, the distinction between priest and Levite which Ezekiel introduces and justifies has always existed (Num. 3). 'That the prophet should know nothing about a priestly law with whose tendencies he is in thorough sympathy admits of only

---

[52] A. Dillmann, *Die Bücher Numeri, Deuteronomium und Josua* (2nd edn., Leipzig 1886), 593–690.

[53] See ch. 4, 'The Priests and the Levites', in his *Prolegomena*.

one explanation—that it did not then exist. His own ordinances are only to be understood as preparatory steps towards its own exact-ment.'[54]

The upper limit for the composition of P^G was therefore generally agreed to be the late exilic period. It was also widely accepted that the lower limit was the year 458 BC. It was then that Ezra returned to Jerusalem—this was the prevalent view of the date of Ezra's mission at that time—bringing 'the book of the law of Moses, which the Lord had commanded to Israel' which was read to a solemn assembly of the people in Jerusalem some years later (444 BC). Wellhausen and some other scholars argued that Ezra's law book was the Pentateuch substantially as we have it. Others argued, however, that it comprised only P^G into which the 'Holiness Code' (H), which was dated to the exilic or early post-exilic period, had already been incorporated. The remaining Priestly material (P^S) was subsequently worked into P^{G+H} and the combination of the Priestly code as a whole with JED fol-lowed, the completed or at least substantially completed Pentateuch being dated to about 400 BC and in any event not later than the Chronicler in the fourth century BC.

To summarize, according to the Wellhausen 'school' the docu-ments were dated as follows:

J: *c*.840 BC
E: *c*.700
D: *c*.623
P: *c*.500–450

Dillmann and his supporters concluded as follows:

E: 900–850
J: 800–750
P: 800–700
D: 650–623

VI

The Combination of the Sources

The predominant view concerning the combination of the main Pentateuchal sources was that J and E were first united, that JE was

---

[54] *Prolegomena*, 129; Eng. trans., 124.

then edited by a Deuteronomic redactor who incorporated Deuteronomy into it, and that a still later redactor worked P into JED. A different order was advocated by Dillmann who, as already noted, placed the composition of P^G before Deuteronomy and argued for the priority of E over J. According to him, the first stage of redaction combined P^G + E + J and the resulting P^{G}EJ was subsequently combined with D in a second stage. The first stage may have taken place in the period between about 700 BC and the appearance of Deuteronomy or, at the latest, during the two or three decades preceding the exile. He dated the second stage to the exilic period. In a third stage of redaction most of the remaining Priestly material, including P^H, was incorporated. This took place between *c.*536 and 444 BC, though he allowed for still further supplementation in the period after Ezra.

The representatives of the Graf–Wellhausen theory had no difficulty in exposing the weaknesses of Dillmann's reconstruction. They were able to show that, for example, the author(s) of Deuteronomy 5–11 (especially chapters 5, 9, 10) evidently presupposed the JE material in Exodus 19–34 but not the P material in these chapters, Wellhausen himself having drawn particular attention to this.[55] The same was found to be true, again by Wellhausen, of Deuteronomy 1–4 where, for example, the record of the sending of spies to Canaan presupposes the JE narrative in Numbers 13–14 but not that of P in these chapters (p. 197). It was also argued that where Deuteronomic redactional material could be discerned in the Pentateuch, it was in the JE material and had not affected the P material. The latter must therefore have been incorporated subsequently into the Deuteronomic redaction of JE. That J and E had been combined independently of the incorporation of P was argued on the grounds, first, that these two sources are much more closely and intimately woven together with each other than with the P material in the Pentateuch and, secondly, that the contributions of the redactor who combined J and E (R^{JE}) show no influence of P.

So closely have J and E been united that it is impossible in many places to isolate them from each other. They can be separated more easily in Genesis, but in the bondage–exodus narrative as in the Sinai narrative in Exodus 19–24, 32–4 much less so. Indeed, in the case of the description of the Sinai events, Wellhausen claimed that the

---

[55] *Die Composition des Hexateuchs*, 205 ff.

Jehovist is to be thought of as an author and not merely a compiler (pp. 94 ff.). Here he has employed the received material from his sources J and E to construct his own presentation of the Sinai events. Significant reworking of the J and E accounts of the bondage–exodus was also attributed to the Jehovist. Sufficient material in the Hexateuch directly from the Jehovist was found to enable scholars to list vocabulary and phraseology peculiar to this redactor, and to assign particular passages to his hand. For example, the psalm in Exodus 15: 1–18 was ascribed by some to the Jehovist. Various divine speeches, for example, Genesis 15: 13–26, were also attributed to the Jehovist.[56]

Sufficient unevenness was, however, found in the material belonging to R^JE to suggest that this redaction was not all of one piece but was the work of several hands. Some scholars therefore spoke of a Jehovist 'school' after the analogy of the postulated J 'school' or E 'school'. There was widespread agreement that in style the Jehovist redaction displays affinities with the Deuteronomic 'school'.[57] Some went so far as to suggest that those responsible for JE belonged to this 'school'. Such a view did not find widespread support, however, but it was suggested by Holzinger (p. 491) that the Jehovist and the Deuteronomic redaction may have belonged to the same wider process of redaction, the Jehovistic redaction of J and E gradually leading to the Deuteronomic redaction. The affinities of the Jehovist with the Deuteronomic style were taken as indicating that the combination of J and E took place in the Deuteronomic period, either not long before the appearance of Deuteronomy or not long after it.[58]

The next stage of redaction was the incorporation, by a Deuteronomic redactor, of Deuteronomy together with insertions into, and some significant revision of, JE.

There was little support for the view of John William Colenso (1814–83), more famously known as the Anglican Bishop of Natal who was tried for heresy, that extensive insertions from the Deuteronomic redactor are to be found in Genesis. He argued that no less than one hundred and seventeen verses from R^D are to be found in this book,[59] where most scholars found only a modest presence of this redactor's hand, some indeed limiting it to as little as 26: 5,

---

[56] See e.g. Holzinger, *Einleitung in den Hexateuch*, 482 f.   [57] Ibid. 490.
[58] For details see ibid. 491.
[59] J. W. Colenso, *The Pentateuch and the Book of Joshua Critically Examined*, 7 vols. (London 1862–79).

others adding a few other brief insertions. Brief insertions were also found here and there in Exodus 1–18 and in Numbers, though again there was disagreement in detail. It was widely accepted, however, that this redactor made not only many insertions into the Sinai narrative in Exodus 19–24, 32–4 but also substantially revised these chapters. Thus much or all of Exodus 19: 3b–8 was ascribed to R^D as also was some of the hortatory material in E's decalogue in Exodus 20. The J decalogue or dodecalogue in Exodus 34 was also believed to have been subjected to a certain amount of revision and amplification by this redactor. The 'book of the covenant' as it now stands (Exod. 20: 22–3: 33) was attributed by many to the Deuteronomic redactor who was also believed to have given it its present position in the Sinai narrative.

The original book of Deuteronomy was also believed to have been expanded by R^D, though again, as we have seen, there was disagreement on what was secondary material in the book as it now stands. A marked presence of the work of R^D was found in the book of Joshua; chapters 1 and 23 were regarded as purely Deuteronomic compositions and many other shorter passages and insertions were also attributed to this stage of redaction. The hand of the same editors was likewise found throughout the remaining books of the Former Prophets. Once again, however, the Deuteronomic redaction of the Pentateuch and Former Prophets was generally believed not to have been carried out all at one sitting, so to speak, but to be the result of a longer process, the work of the Deuteronomic 'school'. This process of redaction was held to have taken place substantially during the exilic period, allowance being made for some further Deuteronomic redaction in the early post-exilic period.

The third and final major redaction of the Pentateuch was the combination of JED with P, the Priestly redaction (R^P). As already noted, there was disagreement on whether this had taken place, at least substantially, before Ezra's mission so that the 'book of the law' read in 444 BC already comprised JEDP, or whether Ezra's law consisted only of P material and was only subsequently combined with JED. It was widely agreed, however, that though the legislation of P superseded that of JED, the latter had already acquired a position of some authority. P was therefore combined with JED in order to secure for it a similar authority. This in turn was seen to have governed the method of the Priestly redaction which, though clearly carried through in the interests of P and from its standpoint, strove to leave

JED as much intact as possible. Thus the legislation of JED, even what was incompatible with P's, was preserved, the older JED material in Exodus 19–24; 32–4 being retained alongside the Priestly material in Exodus 25–31; 35–40; Numbers 1–10. In addition, many narratives of JED were retained alongside P's own version of them, for example the creation story in Genesis 2: 4b ff. alongside P's narrative in 1: 1–2: 4a; the narrative of the covenant with Abraham in Genesis 15 alongside P's in chapter 17; the call of Moses in Exodus 3–4 alongside P's version of it in chapter 6; the commissioning of Joshua as Moses's successor in Deuteronomy 31 alongside P's record of it in Numbers 27; etc. Nevertheless, P was made the framework into which JED was placed. This is already seen in the way that the Pentateuch begins and ends with P material, as noted earlier.

The chronological framework of P's narration of the history, seen especially in its fondness for genealogies, provided a ready basis for the redactor's work. There was general agreement also that, notwithstanding the conservatism of R^P with regard to JED, this redactor did not hesitate in places to abandon some of the material this older corpus had contained. Thus Wellhausen argued that, for example, an account by J of the appearance of the rainbow after the flood was deleted by R^P in favour of P's own record of this in Genesis 9. Also believed to have been omitted by P from the older material was, for example, the record of Abraham's arrival in Canaan, the narrative of the birth and naming of Ishmael, the death of Sarah and Abraham, the record that it was at the people's request that spies were sent to reconnoitre the promised land as Deuteronomy 1: 22, considered to be based upon an older JE account, records. At the same time R^P was also believed to have omitted some material from P in favour of already existing JED material. Wellhausen again, for example, pointed to the absence of the beginning of P's history of Abraham in favour of J's narrative in Genesis 12: 1 ff. Similarly, no P narrative of the birth of Isaac and Esau has been preserved, Genesis 25: 19–26 being largely from J. In the case of the book of Exodus it was considered that, for example, R^P has omitted P's account of the introduction of Moses before 6: 2. It was also conjectured that P must originally have included an account of the 'Testimony' containing the ten commandments, since Exodus 25: 21 seems to point to this.

Thus R^P was regarded as having been responsible for the Pentateuch substantially as we now have it, though once again scholars generally understood R^P not as an individual but as a 'school' and the redaction itself to have been carried out in different stages. A distinction was drawn, however, between the Priestly redaction of the Pentateuch and that of the book of Joshua. Thus Holzinger, for example, argued that Ezra's law book by its nature could not have included P's narrative of the settlement in the land; it would have been confined to the Priestly narrative and legislation ending with the death of Moses.[60] As a result the Pentateuchal period became at the time of Ezra the authoritative period and the book of Joshua was henceforth disjoined from it. The work of R^P proper was confined to the Pentateuchal period in JED; the Priestly redaction of Joshua was carried out quite separately. This is evidenced, it was argued, by the greater freedom with which the Priestly redaction is carried out in Joshua as compared with that of the Pentateuch. Thus very little of P is found in Joshua 1–12 and even in the second half of the book where P material is much more in evidence it has in no way been made the framework for the JED narrative as it has been in the Priestly redaction of the Pentateuch. The description of the division of the land in JED has apparently been favoured and retained by the Priestly redactor, as is evidenced by 18: 1 which must once have prefaced P's account of the division of the land at Shiloh but which has now been relegated to a secondary stage in the allotment of the tribal territories. A somewhat different view was advanced by, for example, J. E. Carpenter (1844–1927) and G. Harford (1860–1921) in their thorough and detailed work. Although they too agreed that the Priestly redaction of Joshua was carried out separately from the redaction of the Pentateuch by R^P, they argued that this arose because Joshua had already been disjoined from the Pentateuch at the stage of the Deuteronomic redaction of JE. That is, they believed that the Deuteronomic redaction of Joshua was also implemented separately from R^D's redaction of the JE Pentateuch.[61]

VII

It needs to be stressed that the wisest among those who supported the 'New Documentary Theory' were, like Wellhausen himself, aware that they were dealing in probabilities and not certainties. Thus, for

---

[60] Holzinger, *Einleitung in den Hexateuch*, 500.

[61] J. E. Carpenter and G. Harford, *The Composition of the Hexateuch* (London 1902), 343 ff.

example, due caution was expressed about isolating J from E, so closely had they been combined. It was also fully acknowledged that so fragmentary is the E material that its origin as an independent narrative source must remain at best only probable rather than a so-called 'assured result'.[62] The unevenness or 'seams' within the sources themselves were seen as further evidence that the origin and growth of each of them was virtually as complex as the composition of the Pentateuch as a whole, whether because such 'seams' indicated the successive work of a 'school' of authors and redactors over a protracted period of time or, alternatively, the diverse origin of traditional material incorporated into the individual sources. As we have also seen, there was no small amount of disagreement among scholars about details. In short, what their researches showed above all was the complexity of the process that led to the final form of the Pentateuch, and that many hands at varying times over a protracted period contributed to its composition. That the theory won their support was not therefore because one could write 'Q.E.D.' below it, but because it offered a more cogent and comprehensive explanation than its rivals of the problems that an analysis of the text yields, even though it made no claim to solve all of them.

Subsequent research, as we shall see, proposed refinements to the theory. For example, debate continued concerning the relationship between the Former Prophets beyond Joshua and the Pentateuchal sources, eventually leading to a new understanding of the composition both of Deuteronomy and of Joshua–Kings. Some argued a new version of the theory, the so-called 'Newest Documentary Theory', finding evidence of a fifth main source, variously defined, which could be isolated from J. Opposition to the theory also continued unabated. Old objections to it were freshly argued, and new ones added. The late dating of P, for example, one of the cornerstones of the theory, continued to be contested in favour of an earlier, pre-exilic origin. The question was raised whether the Priestly narrative (P[G]; Wellhausen's Q) had ever existed as an independent source or whether P as a whole originated as editorial supplementation of an already existing Pentateuchal corpus. That the E material derived from an independent narrative source was also challenged, and new theories of the origin of this material suggested. The very credibility

---

[62] See the cautious remarks on this by Driver, *Introduction to the Literature of the Old Testament*, 116.

of the presuppositions and of the method employed in arriving at the theory was challenged.

These and other issues remain debated to the present day, as we shall see. Of more immediate interest at this stage, however, are significant new developments that emerged in the last years of the nineteenth century. These centred on the question whether it was possible to penetrate behind the sources, especially the older sources J and E, to uncover earlier, preliterary stages in the formation of the literature and of the traditions it embodied, and to determine what light this might shed on the origin of the Pentateuch itself. It was of course already commonly agreed that the authors of the sources inherited traditional materials. But the focus of attention was hitherto upon the work of the authors in composing their narratives, and it was not thought possible to uncover the sources they employed, whether oral or written, since these would have been creatively reworked and reshaped by the authors. As we shall now see, however, already in the closing years of the nineteenth century the quest that was undertaken for the oral stages in the transmission of the diverse materials which the Pentateuch comprises, as well as for the origin and development of Israelite traditions that form the substance of the Pentateuch, began an important new stage in the investigation of the origin and formation of the Pentateuch. The focus upon the 'documents' of the Pentateuch and their authors now shifted to an investigation of the stages in the history of the literature and traditions that had taken place in the centuries before these authors wrote. It is to a description of this research that we now turn.

2

Behind the Documents of the Pentateuch

The focus of the Documentary Theory was upon the composition of the Pentateuch as a literary corpus. The method employed was 'literary-critical' or 'source-critical' in the sense that the different sources and the redactional material which now unites them were separated from each other on grounds of style, vocabulary, and the like, as well as the distinctive theological and religious outlook and interest which could be discerned in each source. The emphasis was accordingly upon the creativity of the separate authors or 'schools' of authors who composed the original documents and upon the contributions of the various redactors who gradually combined them. In other words, it was believed that it is at this level of source-critical analysis that the problem of the origin and composition of the Pentateuch is to be solved.

As a result of this, little importance was credited to the 'pre-compositional' stage or stages in the development of the literature. That the authors of the various documents were frequently dependent upon inherited oral tradition was generally conceded. Now and again attention was drawn to the antiquity of the subject matter of a passage over against the relatively late literary expression of it by the authors of the Pentateuchal sources.[1] But no serious attempt was made by Wellhausen and his followers to elevate the investigation of the pre-compositional stage in the emergence of the literature to a subject for research in its own right. Quite the contrary was the case. Wellhausen himself held a low estimate of the significance of the pre-compositional stage and spurned the task of investigating it as of no more than antiquarian interest and outside the scope proper of the

---

[1] Thus S. R. Driver commented: 'The date at which an event, or institution, is first mentioned in writing, must not, however, be confused with that at which it occurred, or originated: in the early stages of a nation's history the memory of the past is preserved habitually by tradition; and the Jews, long after they were possessed of a literature, were still apt to depend much upon tradition.' (*An Introduction to the Literature of the Old Testament*, 125.)

theologian and exegete. The work of creative planning, arrangement, and composition of the diverse materials in the sources of the Pentateuch was the accomplishment of the authors of these sources; it was they who gave order to, and wove connections between, whatever medley of disconnected oral materials they had inherited. Thus he wrote: 'Oral tradition among the people includes only individual stories which surely come from the same circle of thought yet which are not organized into a planned totality. The recorder of the individual narratives is the one who initiates the plan and the connections.'[2] And again: 'From the mouth of the people there comes nothing but the detached narratives, which may or may not happen to have some bearing on each other: to weave them together in a connected whole is the work of the poetical or literary artist. Thus the agreement of the sources in the plan of the narrative is not a matter of course, but a matter requiring explanation, and only to be explained on the ground of the literary dependence of one source on the other.'[3]

Further consequences of this emphasis upon a purely literary-critical approach to the Pentateuch manifested themselves when scholars sought to use the results achieved by it for describing the early history of Israel and the nature and development of early Israelite religion. This exclusive emphasis upon the literary or compositional stage meant that the Pentateuchal documents, written centuries after the events they describe, were seen to yield useful information about the periods in which they themselves came into existence but very little about the history and religion of Israel they ostensibly describe. Thus, for example, Wellhausen maintained concerning the patriarchal narratives that from them 'we attain no historical knowledge of the patriarchs, but only of the time when the stories about them arose in the Israelite people; this later age is here unconsciously projected, in its inner and outward features, into hoar antiquity, and is reflected there like a glorified mirage.'[4] No consideration is here given to the origin and history of the patriarchal traditions; the emphasis is placed upon the final literary expression of them at the hands of the Pentateuchal authors at the relatively late time in which they worked. It was not considered that a study of the pre-literary stage in the history of these traditions or a closer

[2] Wellhausen, *Die Composition des Hexateuchs*, 8.
[3] *Prolegomena*, 311; Eng. trans., 296.
[4] *Prolegomena*, 336, cf. 382; Eng. trans., 318 f., cf. 360.

investigation of the nature of individual stories about the patriarchs
or of the possible interconnections which may have emerged between
such stories in the pre-literary stage might yield rather different
results. The same was true of the way in which the Pentateuchal
narratives concerning the Mosaic period were handled. Certainly
Wellhausen was somewhat more positive here and believed that a
skeletal outline of history could be derived from the J and E documents which display a common historical framework. Once again,
however, it was not seriously entertained that an investigation of the
pre-literary history of these Pentateuchal traditions might yield a different picture; it was not envisaged that the development of these traditions in the pre-literary stage may have been a major creative force
in the formation of the Pentateuch, including the very historical
framework which it now displays. Much less was it thought that a
study of the way in which these traditions developed and were inter-
related in the pre-literary stage, and of the possible theological moti-
vations underlying such a process, might shed light upon the early
history of Israel and of Israelite religion with which these scholars
were so much concerned.

Not surprisingly, therefore, already in the closing years of the nineteenth century there emerged a movement of scholars who rejected as
inadequate the preoccupation of Wellhausen and his followers with a
purely literary-critical and source-critical approach, and who were
confident that rich results were to be gained by just such a study of
the pre-compositional stage in the history of Pentateuchal traditions
and literature.

I

The movement in question is known as *Die religionsgeschichtliche
Schule* ('The History of Religion School'). Its earliest members
attributed its foundation to Albert Eichhorn (1856–1926), professor
of church history at Halle from 1885, though perhaps it would be
more accurate to say that a number of scholars were responsible for
its emergence but on the basis of his ideas and inspiration.[5] At any

---

[5] See H. Gressmann, *Albert Eichhorn und die Religionsgeschichtliche Schule*
(Göttingen 1924). Douglas Knight has offered a detailed description of development
of traditio-historical research in his book, *Rediscovering the Traditions of Israel*, SBL
Dissertation Series, 9 (Missoula, Mont. 1975).

rate among its founding generation were such scholars as William
Wrede (1859–1906), Wilhelm Bousset (1865–1920), Johannes Weiss
(1863–1914) in New Testament studies, the systematic theologian
Ernst Troeltsch (1865–1923), and Hermann Gunkel (1862–1932) and
later Hugo Gressmann (1877–1927). The latter two were its most
notable representatives in Old Testament studies, though Gunkel was
the pioneer here and the more influential of the two.[6]

Within the field of biblical studies the emphasis of this movement,
as its name indicates, was upon the historical development of religion, whether that of ancient Israel or of Judaism or of Christianity.
Such an undertaking was not in itself new. Earlier generations of
scholars had been concerned with this; one has only to think of
Wellhausen's *Prolegomena* in the field of Israelite religion for an
example of such an attempt. What was new were the method and the
insights which these scholars now brought to bear on the task, and
the deeper dimensions they endeavoured to uncover in the origin and
historical development of biblical religion. Thus amongst a series of
'theses' laid down by Albert Eichhorn in 1886 was, for example: 'Any
interpretation of a myth which does not consider the origin and
development of the myth is false'.[7] Eichhorn regarded the preoccupation of scholars with a purely literary-critical handling of the biblical materials inadequate for a full investigation of the origin and
development of biblical religion. It would not do simply to separate
the sources from each other, arrange them chronologically and then
solely on this basis attempt to depict the history and development of
the religion. One must focus attention upon the *substance* and *ideas*
of the texts and seek to trace the origin, development, and transformation of these in the period before they found final expression in the
relatively late literary documents in which they are now contained. In
short, with Eichhorn 'the attention of modern scholarship became
directed to the period of tradition development'.[8] Thus entered what
has become known as the traditio-historical method of enquiry into
the biblical literature.

As already indicated, in the field of Old Testament studies it was
Hermann Gunkel who pioneered these new ideas. His first major
work, published in 1895, was *Creation and Chaos in the Beginning and*

[6] See W. Klatt, *Hermann Gunkel. Zu seiner Theologie der Religionsgeschichte und zur Enstehung der formgeschichtlichen Methode*, FRLANT 100 (Göttingen 1969).
[7] Cited in Gressmann, *Albert Eichhorn und die Religionsgeschichtliche Schule*, 8.
[8] Knight, *Rediscovering the Traditions of Israel*, 71.

at the End of Time: A Religio-Historical Investigation of Genesis 1 and Revelation 12, which was dedicated to Albert Eichhorn and could be said to be a working out, with regard to the biblical creation myths from Genesis 1 to Revelation 12, of Eichhorn's 'thesis' noted above.[9]

Gunkel's preliminary remarks concerning his approach are directed specifically against Wellhausen's handling of Genesis 1. Wellhausen drew a sharp contrast between the nature of this chapter and that of the creation-paradise narrative which follows in chapters 2–3. In the case of the latter 'we are on the ground of marvel and myth'; the materials for this narrative came from 'the many-coloured traditions of the old world of Western Asia. Here we are in the enchanted garden of the ideas of genuine antiquity; the fresh early smell of earth meets us in the breeze'.[10] But Genesis 1 is quite unlike this: 'It would be vain to deny the exalted ease and the uniform greatness that give the narrative its character. The beginning especially is incomparable: "The earth was without form and void, and darkness lay upon the deep, and the Spirit of God moved upon the water. Then God said: Let there be light, and there was light." But chaos being given, all the rest is spun out of it: all that follows is reflection, systematic construction; we can easily follow the calculation from point to point' (p. 298).

Certainly, Gunkel agrees, Genesis 1 as it lies before us is not to be considered ancient: 'the manifold colours of the old myth are completely absent; the monotone greyness, known to us also from elsewhere in the Priestly Code, points us to the time when reasoned reflection has replaced the old poetic way of contemplating nature.'[11]

Nevertheless, argues Gunkel, this does not mean that Genesis 1 is nothing more than the invention of its author. In considering such a narrative 'we must differentiate strictly between a narrative as it lies before us and its prehistory. In dealing with the narratives in Genesis it is the task of research, after the literary facts have been ascertained, to raise the question—often much more important—whether perhaps something can be stated concerning the earlier history of the narrative. By doing so it will not infrequently be seen that, though handed down to us in a later revised condition, there is here subject-matter from a period in Israel long before that of the extant record of it' (pp. 5–6). By this he means: 'It is the common fate of older

---

[9] H. Gunkel, *Schöpfung und Chaos in Urzeit und Enzeit. Eine religionsgeschichtliche Untersuchung über Gen 1 und Ap Joh 12* (Göttingen 1895).

[10] *Prolegomena*, 320; Eng. trans., 304.   [11] *Schöpfung und Chaos*, 5.

narratives conserved in a younger form, that certain features, which once had good meaning in the earlier context, are transmitted in a new association to which they have in the meantime lost connection. Such old features—fragments of an earlier whole, without connection in the present account and hardly understandable in the intellectual situation of the narrator—betray to the researcher the existence as well as individual features of an earlier form of the present narrative' (p. 6).

This latter statement describes succinctly what lies at the heart of the traditio-historical method, and Gunkel proceeds to draw attention to the sort of features he has in mind in considering the narrative in Genesis 1. Thus the notion of 'chaos' itself, as Wellhausen conceded, was inherited by the author from much more ancient mythology. Other features point in the same direction, for example the idea that in the beginning there was darkness and water. Such an idea was certainly not the invention of the Priestly author; it originated in an ancient myth. Or again, the term *tᵉhom* ('deep') without the definite article betrays itself as having come down from a much more ancient myth. Similarly, an ancient mythological conception is echoed in the depiction of 'the Spirit of God' 'brooding' upon the face of the deep. Thus one after another Gunkel draws attention to features in this narrative which its author inherited from a more ancient source and on account of which Gunkel gave the second chapter of his work the title 'Genesis 1 is not a free composition of the author'.

Gunkel then finds evidence which points to ancient Mesopotamia as the original home of a myth displaying such features as these. The notion that at the beginning water covered the face of the earth points to the sort of climatic conditions which prevailed in Babylon rather than in Palestine. The contrast in this matter between Genesis 1 and the narrative in Genesis 2 is striking. In the latter water is the friend without which the soil cannot yield its fruits; it is thus the creation and gift of God. By contrast, in Genesis 1 water is the enemy which God overcomes in creating the world. The contrast points, in the case of Genesis 2, to a Palestinian background, where the much-needed water was in short supply, and in the case of Genesis 1 to Babylon where annually water became a threat. Thus Gunkel was able to conclude that Genesis 1, though a relatively late literary composition, reflects a much more ancient tradition, the origin of which is in all probability to be traced to ancient Babylon where it centred upon the primeval battle between the creator god Marduk and the representative of chaos, the goddess Tiamat whose very name lies behind the Hebrew word *t^ehom* in the narrative in Genesis 1. He argues that this ancient Babylonian myth found its way to Palestine at an early time whence it was passed on orally to Israel.

Gunkel also ranged over other allusions to, or features of, ancient myths which are preserved in the Old Testament and which echo the same myth discernible behind Genesis 1 or variant forms of such a myth referring to the primeval sea-monster Rahab, Leviathan, etc. His purpose was not merely to trace the origins of such mythical material; he was more concerned to investigate the ways in which such ancient material was adapted and transformed within the development of Israel's own religion. By such means something of the very distinctive differences between Israelite religion, most notably its monotheism, and that of ancient Babylon are brought into relief. As the title of his work itself indicates, Gunkel further traced the history of this mythological material down to Revelation 12 which he regarded as the final manifestation of the long history of the use of this ancient material in Israel and Judaism.

II

Here then was an example of the results that could be achieved from a careful investigation of possible traditional elements preserved within literary documents of a much later period. Notwithstanding the continued opposition of Wellhausen,[12] Gunkel's work became increasingly influential as establishing the viability of investigating the history of Israelite traditions in the pre-literary stage of development. In the hands of later scholars, as we shall see, this traditio-historical method was intensively employed in an attempt to extend our knowledge of the origins and history of Israelite religion and of the origin and growth of the Pentateuchal materials beyond what a purely literary-critical approach was able to achieve.

But a further step remained to be taken by Gunkel. In *Creation and Chaos* he was predominantly concerned with tracing the history of tradition with, for the most part, only incidental attention to the forms and means whereby ancient traditional material was transmitted and developed in the course of Israelite history. With the

---

[12] Cf. Knight, *Rediscovering the Traditions of Israel*, 72–5.

publication of his commentary on Genesis[13] Gunkel gave much more attention to the 'types' or 'forms' (*Gattungen*) of Hebrew literature; that is, he now concentrated not only on the history of traditions but on 'literary history' (*Literaturgeschichte*) about which he wrote, in addition to his introduction to the commentary on Genesis, a number of shorter contributions.[14]

By 'literary history' Gunkel did not mean the sort of treatment of the books of the Old Testament to be found in standard works of 'Old Testament Introduction'. Much valuable work of this nature had already been achieved, though there would always remain limitations on the amount we can find out about such questions as the dating and authorship of individual books. Gunkel had in mind, however, a history of Hebrew literature in a different sense. We have to remember, he argues, that in literature such as that of ancient Israel, the personalities of the individual authors are of far less importance than in literature of later ages.

In the Psalms, for instance, we find an extraordinary sameness of content—in different Psalms we find the same thoughts, moods, forms of expression, metaphors, rhetorical figures, phrases. Even the very greatest writers in Israel, the prophets, frequently exhibit the most striking uniformity. This is due to the fact that in antiquity the power of custom was far greater than it is in the modern world, and besides, like everything else connected with religion, religious literature . . . is very conservative. Therefore a history of Hebrew literature, if it is to do justice to its subject-matter, has comparatively little concern with the personality of the writers. That has, of course, a place of its own, but Hebrew literary history should occupy itself more with the literary type that lies deeper than any individual effort. Hebrew literary history is therefore the history of the literary types practised in Israel, and it is perfectly possible to produce such a history from the sources that are available . . . We must take the writings of the Old Testament, and, as many of these are collections of writings, we must take their constituent parts out of the

---

[13] H. Gunkel, *Genesis, übersetz und erklärt*, HKAT (Göttingen 1901). (Quotations below will be cited as *Genesis*.) The 'Introduction' to the Commentary was translated into English by W. H. Carruth and published in 1901 as *The Legends of Genesis* and reprinted by Schocken Books (New York 1964). (Quotations below, from the latter, which will be cited as *Legends*.)

[14] H. Gunkel, 'Fundamental Problems of Hebrew Literary History', in *What Remains of the Old Testament* (London 1928), 57–68, originally published as 'Die Grundprobleme der israelitischen Literaturgeschichte', *Deutsche Literaturzeitung*, 18 (1906), 1797–1800, 1861–6, reprinted in *Reden und Aufsätze* (Göttingen 1913), 29–38; 'Literaturgeschichte', *RGG* iii (2nd edn.; Tübingen 1929), cols. 1677–80; 'Sagen und Legenden II. In Israel', *RGG* v (1931), cols. 49–60; *Das Märchen im Alten Testament* (Tübingen 1913); Eng. trans., *The Folktale in the Old Testament* (Sheffield 1991).

order in which they happen to appear in our Canon and in which 'Old Testament Introduction' usually studies them, and then rearrange them according to the type to which they belong.[15]

Many such types had already been identified by scholars: myths, folk-tales, popular stories, cultic legends, historical narratives and, in poetic literature, dirges, love songs, taunt songs, thanksgiving psalms, psalms of praise, distinctive types of prophetic oracles, etc. It is the task of literary history to study them systematically in order to show the materials with which each type deals and the form it necessarily assumes. It will be found that each type originally belonged to a quite definite setting in the life of Israel (*Sitz im Leben*); that is, the particular literary form which a subject-matter assumed was itself dictated by the particular setting in life to which it was addressed. Thus in studying such literary types 'we must in each case have the whole situation clearly before us and ask ourselves, Who is speaking? Who are the listeners? What is the *mise en scène* at the time? What effect is aimed at?'[16] Such a study will also reveal, Gunkel further maintained, that with few exceptions such types were originally not written but oral compositions.

The importance of this method of 'type criticism' or, as it was later to become more familiarly known, 'form criticism' (*Formgeschichte*) is as follows. First, since different sorts of subject-matter found expression in different literary types or forms, by isolating the original individual literary units the scholar is able to penetrate behind the present larger literary context of the material to an earlier stage in its formation and transmission. Type or form criticism thus reveals itself as an essential handmaid of the traditio-historical quest; that is, an investigation of the form in which, and the process whereby, a particular subject-matter has been transmitted illuminates the origin and development of what has been so transmitted. Secondly, however, the isolation of such original literary units enables the scholar to uncover the earlier stages in the history and growth of the literature itself. In this way, for example, the extent to which the Pentateuchal materials had already taken shape during the long period before the work of the Yahwist and the Elohist would be illuminated.

---

[15] *Reden und Aufsätze*, 31; the quotation is from 'Fundamental Problems of Hebrew Literary History', 58 f.
[16] *Reden und Aufsätze*, 33; 'Fundamental Problems of Hebrew Literary History', 62.

When Gunkel applied this method of form criticism in his study of Genesis he found a great variety of such types: myths such as are found in Genesis 1–11; stories about individual patriarchs; ethnological legends explaining the origin of the relationship between different tribes or peoples; aetiological stories explaining some custom or institution; cultic legends telling of the foundation of a particular sanctuary; etymological stories explaining how someone or some place acquired his name; etc.

Of the great antiquity of many of these Gunkel was in no doubt. They are much older than the Pentateuchal literary sources in which they are now found. He pointed out, for example, that the tribal and race names which many of them preserve are almost forgotten in other Old Testament literature; 'we know nothing of Shem, Ham, and Japhet, of Abel and Cain, of Esau and Jacob, nothing of Hagar and scarcely anything of Ishmael, from the historical records of Israel'.[17] The great age of such stories is also indicated by, for example, 'the primitive vigour of many touches that reveal to us the religion and morality of the earliest times, as for instance, the many mythological traces, such as the story of the marriages with angels, of Jacob's wrestling with God, and the many stories of deceit and fraud on the part of the patriarchs, and so on'.[18] It is also evident, Gunkel claimed, that not a little of this material was inherited by Israel from its ancient Near Eastern neighbours; the discussion of the origin of the creation myths in the Old Testament in his *Creation and Chaos* had already exemplified this. He argued that it is probable that most of the stories concerning the patriarchs were in circulation before Israel entered Canaan. In particular, the religion displayed in these legends, containing here and there as they do the names of the pre-Yahwistic gods (El Olam, El Bethel, El Shaddai, etc.), points to their non-Israelite origin. He saw it as one of the most brilliant achievements of the Israelites that they were able to take over such ancient material and adapt it to their own national religion and ethos.[19]

It is already clear from these observations that Gunkel believed the authors of the Pentateuchal sources to have been heirs of an already existing mass of much older material. In just what shape, however, did it come to them? Here we recall the statement of Wellhausen quoted earlier: 'Oral tradition among the people includes only individual stories which surely come from the same circle of thought yet

---

[17] *Legends*, 23; *Genesis*, p. xi.   [18] *Legends*, 88; *Genesis*, pp. xl–xli.
[19] *Legends*, 95; *Genesis*, p. xliii.

which are not organized into a planned totality. The recorder [by this Wellhausen of course means the authors of J, E, etc.] of the individual narratives is the one who initiates the plan and the connections.'

Gunkel accepted that popular stories such as Genesis contains originally existed as independent units; even in their present form they provide clear evidence of this. For example, Abraham is commanded to sacrifice his son Isaac (Gen. 22). This he sets about doing, but at the last moment divine intervention preserves Isaac's life: 'Then they returned together to Beersheba'. The narrative has a clear beginning and ends with the resolution of the complication which has arisen: 'no one can ask, What followed?'.[20] Gunkel further argued that the unity of the separate stories is also shown in the fact that they are in each case filled with a single harmonious sentiment: in the story just mentioned, the sacrifice of Isaac, emotion is predominant; in that of Jacob's deception of Isaac, humour; in the story of Sodom, moral earnestness; in the story of Babel, the fear of Almighty God. He added that the effect of many of the stories is spoiled by being followed immediately with new ones which drive the reader suddenly from one mood to another.[21]

We may note in passing that in such observations as these Gunkel had already gone beyond the relative vagueness which Wellhausen often displayed in his handling of the impress these stories retained from their oral past. More important, however, was Gunkel's view that in many instances such stories were already joined together at the oral stage of transmission and that it was not left to the authors of the Pentateuchal sources to initiate 'the plan and the connections', as Wellhausen had argued. In other words, already at the oral stage individual stories concerning the same individual or dwelling upon a similar theme were attracted to each other and were thus combined to form 'cycles of legends' (*Sagenkränze*).[22] According to Gunkel, one such 'cycle' comprises the stories of Abraham and Lot (Gen. 12: 1–8; 13; 18: 1–16: 19: 1–28; 19: 30–8). Abraham and Lot migrate from Haran and journey to Bethel where they separate, Lot moving to the Jordan valley to Sodom, Abraham dwelling at Hebron. A story about Abraham is then taken up, narrating the visit to him of three men who promise him the birth of a son and announce that they will

---

[20] *Legends*, 43 f.; *Genesis*, p. xx.   [21] *Legends*, 44; *Genesis*, p. xx.
[22] Though not wholly satisfactory, the translation 'legend' for the German word *Sage* (plur. *Sagen*) is preferable to 'saga', which connotes a more extensive narration (e.g. the Icelandic sagas) than the brief narratives in Genesis about the patriarchs.

return within a year. The scene turns to Sodom where Lot receives the men in friendship but the citizens of the city dishonour them. Rescued by the divine visitors from the destruction of Sodom, Lot flees to the mountains with his daughters. By this means it is indicated where both ancestors have their homeland: Abraham remains in Hebron whilst Lot dwells henceforth in the mountains of Moab. Originally the cycle would have come to a conclusion by telling of the birth of sons to each of these two ancestors and thus of the origin of the two peoples, Israel, the descendants of Abraham, and Moab and Ammon, the descendants of Lot. Extant, however, is only the record of the birth of Lot's sons; that concerning Abraham is now missing. The overall purpose in the creation of this 'cycle' was thus to answer the question of the origin of the peoples named after Abraham and Lot and how they came to possess their ancestral lands.[23]

Gunkel also drew attention to a Jacob–Esau–Laban 'cycle' of stories in Genesis 25–33. It arose from the combination of two originally separate, smaller cycles, one concerning Jacob and Esau, the other concerning Jacob and Laban.[24] For the purposes of combining the two, the Jacob–Esau 'cycle' has been divided into two parts to form a framework for the inclusion of the Jacob–Laban 'cycle'. At the end of the first part it is narrated that Jacob fled from Esau to Laban (Gen. 27). This then facilitated the insertion of the Jacob–Laban cycle. In due course, however, Jacob is forced to flee from Laban (31: 1–32: 1) back home. This has facilitated the inclusion of the remainder of the Jacob–Esau 'cycle'.

Gunkel also regarded the Joseph narrative in Genesis 37–50 as a 'cycle'. Here, however, the original legends have been much more artistically and skilfully woven together than in the 'cycles' referred to above. A considerably greater unity thus characterizes this Joseph 'cycle'; only in a few places are there slight breaks in the flow of the narrative. It is thus to be considered as the highest achievement of narrative art in Genesis, a clear advance upon the other less tightly woven 'cycles' and displaying a fully developed narrative art as against the much older briefly told legends. So much so is this, that although Gunkel believed it possible to discern originally independent legends in the Joseph narrative, he regarded it as more of a *novelle* than a 'cycle' of legends.[25]

---

[23] Cf. *Genesis*, 146 ff.   [24] Ibid. 265 ff.   [25] Ibid. 356 ff.

III

Gunkel's investigation of the long period of development through which so much of the material in Genesis passed led him to a very distinctive understanding of the role of those responsible for the Pentateuchal documents. He accepted the view that neither J or E constitute complete unities deriving from two individual authors; they are the product of 'schools'. But he now raised the question whether these documents are literary unities in any sense or whether, on the contrary, they are not more accurately described as collections, codifications of oral traditions, and whether their composers are not to be called *collectors* rather than *authors*.[26]

Gunkel argued that they are correctly described as collectors and not authors. This is evidenced, first, by the fact that they have each adopted such heterogeneous materials: 'J contains separate legends and legend-cycles, condensed and detailed stories, delicate and coarse elements, primitive and modern elements in morals and religion, stories with vivid antique colours along with those quite faded out . . . It is much the same with E . . . This variety shows that the legends of E, and still more of J, do not bear the stamp of a single definite time and still less of a single personality, but that they were adopted by their collectors essentially as they were found'.[27] Secondly, it is evidenced by the variants of both documents of which J very frequently has the older version, though often the younger version. This also indicates, he argued, that there is no literary connection between J and E; where both sources agree, it is because they employed a common original. Thirdly, however, Gunkel believed that the manner in which the stories have been brought together in the documents indicates that we are dealing with collections which cannot have been completed at one given time but developed over a longer period. For example, he discerned three hands to have been at work in the creation of the Abraham–Lot 'cycle'. First came the 'cycle' of stories referred to above into which a second hand introduced other elements, such as the story of Abraham in Egypt and the flight of Hagar 'probably from another book of legends', whilst still a third hand has added certain details, such as the appeal of Abraham on behalf of Sodom. Thus Gunkel concludes that J and E were not individual authors or

---

[26] *Legends*, 124 ff.; *Genesis*, p. lvi ff.   [27] *Legends*, 125; *Genesis*, p. lvi.

editors of older and consistent writings, but were 'schools of narrators'.

As such, these collectors were 'not masters, but rather servants of their subjects'[28] and have faithfully recorded a great deal of what had been handed down to them. At the same time alterations, a certain amount of smoothing out of material, omissions of some older features in order to make room for the introduction of something new and different, would have been made by them. They would also have been influenced by the religious and ethical outlook of their own time. But it is not always easy to discern between what changes they implemented and what had already taken place at the earlier, oral stage of transmission and development.

A further important consequence followed from this concerning the way in which the Pentateuchal sources J and E had hitherto been regarded. Amongst the representatives of the Wellhausen school the attempt was frequently undertaken, once the sources had been separated from each other, to describe the theology and religious outlook of the author or 'school of authors' of each. Examples of this are to be found in such works as those of Holzinger or Carpenter and Harford. Such an undertaking was only possible when those responsible for the sources J and E were conceived of as authors to whom could be attributed what they wrote. When, however, they are viewed as collectors such an undertaking becomes much less viable. These collectors, urged Gunkel, were 'not masters, but rather servants of their subjects'. The contrast in this respect between J and E on the one hand and P on the other illustrates this.[29] P was indeed the work of an author; he dealt 'very arbitrarily with the tradition as it came down to him'.[30] He had no conception of the fidelity of the older collectors responsible for J and E who 'merely accumulated the stone left to them in a loose heap', whilst P 'erected a symmetrical structure in accordance with his own taste'.[31] P, unlike the collectors of J and E, was a genuine author who reworked thoroughly the traditional material handed down to him.

With regard to dating, Gunkel argued that both J and E belonged to the same general period, though J was the earlier of the two. He dated the formation of the individual legends to about 1200 BC with a subsequent remodelling of them in the period of the early monarchy. This remodelling was carried on into the period of the collection

---

[28] *Legends*, 130; *Genesis*, p. lviii.   [29] Cf. *Legends*, 145 ff.; *Genesis*, pp. lxiv ff.
[30] *Legends*, 153; *Genesis*, p. lxviii.   [31] *Legends*, 153; *Genesis*, p. lxviii.

itself, that is, during the period of the activity of the J and E collectors. He rejected the then current view that the influence of the great prophets could be discerned in the work of J and E and concluded that the collections took shape in all essentials before their time, though he allowed for some prophetic influence upon the very latest portions of the collections, for example Abraham's plea to God concerning Sodom. He thus placed J in the ninth century and E in the first half of the eighth century. The redactor who combined J and E (the Jehovist) he dated to the end of the monarchical period. Following Wellhausen, he dated P to the period *c.*500–444 BC and also agreed that this document, like J and E, was not completed all at once.

IV

In the decades following Gunkel's pioneering works Pentateuchal studies pursued two separate lines of enquiry and debate. On the one hand Gunkel's insights gave the impulse for further research into the pre-compositional stages in the history of both the literature and the Pentateuchal traditions. As a result, the methods introduced by him were further tested and refined and their potential exemplified in a number of other areas of the literature as well as in Genesis itself to which he had so productively devoted himself. On the other hand 'classical' source analysis continued to receive much attention: the presence of still further documents in the Pentateuch in addition to J, E, D, and P was argued, whilst at the same time some of the most fundamental claims of the literary-critical and source analysis described in the preceding chapter were vigorously challenged.

(1) To begin with this further discussion of the literary sources, we saw in the preceding chapter that further investigation of the classical sources found evidence of more and more layers of material in these sources so that, for example, neither J nor E was any longer referred to as the work of a single author but as the products of 'schools' of authors designated in some such manner as J^1, J^2, J^3; E^1, E^2, E^3. Such further division of the sources did not go unopposed at the time. O. Gruppe, for example, already in 1889 argued against Budde that the unevenness in the J material in Genesis 1–11 was the result of the use by one author of traditional material of diverse origin and composition—an anticipation of the sort of results Gunkel's study of the

'literary history' of the legends of Genesis yielded.[32] The issue was tackled afresh, however, by Rudolph Smend (1851–1913) in his influential work published in 1912.[33] He defended the unity of E and whilst agreeing that J was not homogeneous argued that it comprised not one basic source which had been secondarily expanded, but two originally independent documents, J[1] and J[2]. He thus posited five main sources in the Hexateuch in the order J[1], J[2], E, D, and P.

This 'Newest Documentary Theory', as Smend's view came to be termed, was favourably received by a number of scholars. Walther Eichrodt supported it in his monograph on the sources of Genesis published in 1916.[34] Otto Eissfeldt adopted it, with modifications, in his *Synopsis of the Hexateuch* in 1922[35] but gave Smend's J[1] the siglum L (= *Laienquelle*, 'Lay Source') partly to re-emphasize that it was originally a separate document and not merely expansions to J, and partly to indicate its nature as the least theological of the Hexateuchal sources and also at the opposite end of the spectrum to the Priestly document. He dated it in the century 950–850 BC. In 1927 Julian Morgenstern also argued for a further source in addition to J, E, D, and P in the Hexateuch.[36] This is his proposed Kenite source (K) which he dated to c.900 BC and traced, as its designation indicates, to the Kenite region in southern Palestine. Only fragments of it have been preserved; it began, he believed, with the birth of Moses, reached its climax with an account of the revelation of the Kenite god Yahweh to Israel (Exod. 33 and 34), and concluded with an account of the settlement of Israel and the Kenites in southern Palestine (Num. 10; Judg. 1). In 1930, Robert Pfeiffer also argued for an additional source, in this case in Genesis, which he designated S (= Seir) and traced, as its designation indicates, to south-eastern Palestine.[37] He dated it towards the end of the tenth century and believed that it was combined with the other Pentateuchal sources during the fifth century. Though belonging to a later period, mention may here be

[32] O. Gruppe, 'War Genesis 6, 1–4 ursprünglich mit der Sintflut verbunden?', *ZAW* 9 (1889), 135–55.

[33] R. Smend, *Die Erzählungen des Hexateuchs auf ihre quellen untersucht* (Berlin 1912).

[34] W. Eichrodt, *Die Quellen der Genesis von neuem untersucht*, BZAW 31 (Giessen 1916).

[35] O. Eissfeldt, *Hexateuch-Synopse* (Leipzig 1922).

[36] J. Morgenstern, 'The Oldest Document of the Hexateuch', HUCA 4 (1927), 1–138.

[37] R. H. Pfeiffer, 'A Non-Israelite Source of the Book of Genesis', *ZAW* 48 (1930), 63–73. See also his *Introduction to the Old Testament* (New York 1948), 159–67.

made also of the work of Cuthbert Simpson which followed the lines laid down by Smend, but regarded J^2 as having arisen from a revision and expansion of J^1.[38] Still later, Georg Fohrer adopted Smend's analysis, again with modifications, but preferred the siglum N for this fifth source in the Pentateuch on account of the nomadic character which he believed it displays.[39]

(2) In addition to this continued literary-critical analysis of the Hexateuch itself, fresh consideration was now also given to the view that the two (or three) oldest Hexateuchal documents J and E (or J^1, J^2, E) continue beyond Joshua into Judges, Samuel, and Kings. That these books had undergone Deuteronomic editing was already widely accepted. In the late nineteenth century, however, Carl Heinrich Cornill and Karl Budde argued that the documents J and E can be traced as far as 1 Kings 2.[40] It was this view which now received more attention in a number of publications in the 1920s. Thus in 1921 Immanuel Benzinger argued that J continues as far as 2 Kings 17: 3–4 and E as far as the account of Josiah's reign in 2 Kings 22–3, E thus having been completed by 609 BC, the year of Josiah's death, and J about a century earlier.[41] In the same year Smend argued that his Hexateuchal sources J^1, J^2, and E continue into Samuel with further traces of them in Kings.[42] Eissfeldt likewise found both J and E as well as his source L in these books.[43] Best known of all from this time, since it was followed by two later detailed studies, is Gustav Hölscher's long contribution in 1923[44] in which he argued that J can be traced to the division of the kingdom in 1 Kings 12, whilst E continues to 2 Kings 25, an exilic rather than a pre-exilic dating for the composition of E thus being indicated.

Sustained opposition to such a 'documentary theory' of the composition of Judges, Samuel, and Kings came most notably from

---

[38] C. A. Simpson, *The Early Traditions of Israel* (Oxford 1948).

[39] G. Fohrer, *Überlieferung und Geschichte des Exodus*, BZAW 91 (Berlin 1964).

[40] Cornill, 'Ein Elohistischer Bericht über die Entstehung des israelitischen Königtums in I Samuelis i–xv aufgezeigt'; 'Noch einmal Sauls Königswahl und Verwerfung'; Budde, *Die Bücher Richter und Samuel*.

[41] I. Benzinger, *Jahwist und Elohist in den Königsbüchern*, BZAW 27 (Giessen 1921).

[42] R. Smend, 'JE in den geschichtlichen Büchern des Alten Testaments', *ZAW* 39 (1921), 181–217.

[43] O. Eissfeldt, *Die Quellen des Richterbuches* (Leipzig 1925), and *Die Komposition der Samuelbücher* (Leipzig 1931).

[44] G. Hölscher, 'Das Buch der Könige, seine Quellen und seine Redaktion', in *Eucharisterion für Gunkel*, FRLANT 18 (Göttingen 1923), 158–213. See also his later studies *Die Anfänge der hebräischen Geschichtsschreibung* (Heidelberg 1942), and *Geschichtsschreibung in Israel* (Lund 1952).

Rudolph Kittel who argued instead that these books were composed on the basis of numerous smaller literary units and complexes, though he conceded that some of these were probably related to the Hexateuchal sources J and E.[45] Further support for the sort of analysis proposed by Kittel came, for example, from Leonard Rost who made a special study of the books of Samuel and argued that they comprise a number of originally separate literary compositions such as an 'ark narrative' in 1 Samuel 4–6; 2 Samuel 6 and, most notably, a narrative of the succession of Solomon in 2 Samuel 7, 9–20 which is concluded in 1 Kings 1–2.[46] None of these sources was in any way related to either J or E. As we shall see, it was this approach to the analysis of these books which later became more widely accepted through Martin Noth's important work in 1943.[47]

(3) Returning to the Hexateuch proper, the Priestly material here was also subjected to fresh literary-critical analysis during this period. Instead of the subdivision of this material into an original narrative (P^G) to which the remaining Priestly material was added in successive stages, Gerhard von Rad in 1934 argued that P comprises two originally separate narratives, P^A and P^B, the former of which was simpler and less complex than the latter which has a more priestly character.[48] Both were historical narratives, though this was more pronounced in the case of P^A. Both also presupposed an earlier Priestly 'book of generations' vestiges of which can still be traced in Genesis 5: 1; 6: 9, and elsewhere. So alike were P^A and P^B that they gradually merged together in the course of their transmission in the same Priestly circle. Von Rad still left room, however, for the secondary incorporation of much other Priestly material such as, for example, the Holiness Code in Leviticus 17–26 and indeed most of the remainder of Leviticus.

Meanwhile, however, the nature of the Priestly material in the Hexateuch had been quite otherwise assessed by a number of scholars who, whilst not denying the presence of such material in these books, argued that it did not derive from an originally separate, continuous document such as J. Already in 1880 S. Maybaum had argued

---

[45] R. Kittel, *Die Heilige Schrift des Alten Testaments*, 4th edn., ed. A. Bertholet (Tübingen 1922), 367–492. Cf. also his earlier contribution, 'Die pentateuchischen Urkunden in den Büchern Richter und Samuel', *ThStKr* 65 (1892), 44–71.

[46] L. Rost, *Die Überlieferung von der Thronmachfolge Davids*, BWANT 3/6 (Stuttgart 1926); Eng. trans., *The Succession to the Throne of David* (Sheffield 1982).

[47] See below, Ch. 3.

[48] G. von Rad, *Die Priesterschrift im Hexateuch*, BWANT 4/13 (Stuttgart 1934).

this.[49] He maintained that a codex of Priestly ritual legislation, composed by an author who belonged to the circle of Ezekiel's disciples, was subsequently worked into JED by a redactor who at the same time composed and inserted the P-narrative material. In other words, there never was a Priestly *Grundschrift* (Q or P^G). Maybaum's work received a sharp response from Budde[50] and remained without influence. From a different standpoint, August Klostermann in 1893 challenged the view that any such separate documents as J, E, or P ever existed.[51] The admittedly diverse Pentateuchal materials developed rather through successive stages of agglomeration centring on the Sinaitic law and within the context of cultic recital. He thus anticipated, as we shall see, an approach which was to gain wider favour in more recent discussion. Influenced by Klostermann's conclusions though differing widely from him in other respects, the conservative scholar James Orr in 1906 also rejected any suggestion that P once constituted an independent narrative document.[52] He saw the fragmentary nature of the P material as a strong argument against the prevailing view: 'In truth, anything more fragmentary, broken, incomplete, or generally unsatisfactory as a connected narrative, it would be hard to imagine' (p. 342). So closely interwoven are J, E, and P that they belong to the same period and must be seen as the product of a closely co-ordinated plan carried out by admittedly different authors. Subsequent repudiation of the original independence of P came from Bernardus Eerdmans and Johannes Dahse who proposed a different solution to the literary problems of the composition of the Pentateuch as a whole.[53] Rejections of their views came especially from John Skinner and Walther Eichrodt,[54] but in 1924 Eerdmans's understanding of P was supported by Max Löhr.[55] Löhr himself later found a strong ally in Paul Volz in a work published the year before von Rad's study of P referred to above.[56] Since in more recent years

---

[49] S. Maybaum, *Die Entwickelung des altisraelitischen Priesterthums* (Breslau 1880).

[50] In *Die biblische Urgeschichte* (Giessen 1883), 276 ff.

[51] A. Klostermann, *Der Pentateuch* (Leipzig 1893; 2nd edn. 1907).

[52] J. Orr, *The Problem of the Old Testament* (London 1907).

[53] B. D. Eerdmans, *Die Composition der Genesis* (Giessen 1908); J. Dahse, *Textkritische Materialen zur Hexateuchfrage I* (Giessen 1912).

[54] J. Skinner, *The Divine Names in Genesis* (London 1914); Eichrodt, *Die Quellen der Genesis von neuem untersucht*.

[55] M. Löhr, *Untersuchung zum Hexateuchproblem*, i. *Der Priesterkodex in der Genesis*, BZAW 38 (Giessen 1924).

[56] P. Volz, 'Anhang. P ist kein Erzähler', in P. Volz and W. Rudolph (eds.), *Der Elohist als Erzähler. Ein Irrweg der Pentateuchkritik?*, BZAW 63 (Giessen 1933), 135–42.

the independence of P has been freshly questioned, notably by F. M. Cross and E. Blum, we shall leave discussion of this until a later stage.[57]

(4) A further challenge to the prevailing Documentary Theory concerned the dating of Deuteronomy which, as we have seen, was of crucial importance for that theory as a whole. The views of the so-called Gramberg school[58] during the nineteenth century that the narrative of Josiah's reformation in 2 Kings 22–3 was unreliable and that Deuteronomy was an exilic or post-exilic composition found renewed support among a number of scholars in the twentieth century such as Robert Kennett and Gustav Hölscher.[59] Hölscher, for example, argued that Deuteronomy, especially with regard to its demand for the centralization of the cult, was a utopian programme of a group of priests living in exile and divorced from the realities of life in Palestine where such a demand would have been impossible to enforce. Quite contrary to this late dating of Deuteronomy, however, a number of other scholars, most notably Theodor Oestreicher and Adam Welch, argued that the book does not demand centralization or at least did not do so originally and that it was composed as early as the tenth century BC.[60] Different theories of how the book assumed its present form continued, with much discussion of the relevance for this question of the you-plural and you-singular passages in the book. A new phase in the discussion of the provenance of the book now began with Welch's argument that it originated in northern Israel and not, as hitherto widely believed, in Judah or in Jerusalem itself. In these various ways the programme for the investigation of Deuteronomy for a generation to come was largely determined by the debate at this time, a debate which made Deuteronomy more than any of the other Pentateuchal documents the 'storm-centre' of Pentateuchal study in the years following the end of the First World War.[61]

(5) The years between the wars saw the beginning of yet another challenge to the Graf–Wellhausen Documentary Theory, and again one which has retained support to the present time. Just as the original independence of P was questioned, so now the nature and origin

---

[57] See below, Ch. 7.	[58] See above, Ch. 1, p. 15.

[59] R. H. Kennett, 'The Date of Deuteronomy', *JTS* 7 (1905), 161–86; *Deuteronomy and the Decalogue* (Cambridge 1920); G. Hölscher, 'Komposition und Ursprung des Deuteronomiums', *ZAW* 40 (1922), 161–255.

[60] T. Oestreicher, *Das Deuteronomische Grundgessetz* (Gütersloh 1923); A. C. Welch, *The Code of Deuteronomy: A New Theory of its Origin* (London 1924).

[61] For a review see my book, *Deuteronomy and Tradition* (Oxford 1967).

of the E material came in for reassessment. Volz's work referred to above in connection with P was mainly devoted to a rejection of the view that the E material in Genesis ever existed as a separate continuous document. Wilhelm Rudolph, who collaborated with Volz in this work—he contributed the discussion of the Joseph narrative— subsequently extended the analysis to the remaining books of the Hexateuch.[62] Both scholars argued that the E material was the result of redactional additions to J. Earlier, in 1930, the Norwegian scholar Sigmund Mowinckel (1884–1966), who ranks among the most creative Old Testament scholars of this century, in an article adumbrated his own assessment of E which he later worked out in greater detail.[63] He argued that the E material emerged gradually as the result of a traditio-historical process based upon the material in J. J itself was the work of an author who belonged to the scribal circle attached to the Temple and court in Jerusalem. It was composed about 800 BC. But the material which this author collected and employed continued to develop in the course of its transmission and use so that alongside J there emerged J^V (= J *variatus*). The Elohist, properly understood, he argued, was the person who revised the venerable work of J by incorporating into it the younger J^V material which had developed orally, at least to begin with, subsequent to the composition of J.

It will be seen from this that Mowinckel adopted the partnership between literary criticism and the traditio-historical method which had characterized the approach of Gunkel whose pupil he had been. In this, however, Mowinckel was at odds with a number of his fellow Scandinavian scholars who rejected outright a literary-critical method as a 'bookish' approach born of a modern, Western way of regarding literature and quite alien to the manner in which the ancient literature of the Old Testament came into existence. For a proper understanding of the latter only a thoroughgoing traditio-historical approach with a strong emphasis upon the role of oral tradition is appropriate.

---

[62] W. Rudolph, *Der 'Elohist' von Exodus bis Joshua*, BZAW 68 (Berlin 1938).
[63] S. Mowinckel, 'Der Ursprung der Bil'āmsage', *ZAW* 48 (1930), 233–71; *Erwägungen zur Pentateuch Quellenfrage* (Universitetsforlaget, Trondheim 1964), 59–118.

V

The beginnings of such an approach took place during the period
here under review and at the hands of the Danish scholar Johannes
Pedersen (1883–1977), though, as far as the Pentateuch is concerned,
it received its best known expression in the Swedish scholar Ivan
Engnell's traditio-historical introduction to the Old Testament in
1945.[64] Two articles published by Pedersen in the 1930s were particularly significant in setting the direction for this approach. In the
first, published in 1931,[65] he argued that Wellhausen's description of
the development of Israelite religion betrays a predetermined evolu-
tionist conception derived from Hegel's philosophy via the biblical
scholar Wilhelm Vatke whose work Wellhausen admired. The specifically Hegelian terminology is absent in Wellhausen's presentation,
but the net result is none the less the same as in Vatke's. Thus the
sources are separated from each other and chronologically arranged;
each represents a specific period in Israel's history and thus a stage-
by-stage evolution of the religion is depicted, an evolution which,
Pedersen argued, is determined by the struggle of the antithesis
between nature and spirit in which the spirit asserts itself gradually
until the antithesis is resolved in the period after the exile (p. 171).
Thus, it is claimed, Wellhausen's literary-critical source analysis went
hand-in-hand with his evolutionary conception of Israelite religion.[66]
The method is thus to be rejected just as much as the results, for while
'his source-critical method undoubtedly has its validity, even for
antiquity, when it is a matter of determining events and external facts,
it has severe limitations when it is a matter of describing the culture
of a people. Once we are clear about that, we shall also see that the
neat separation of the various Pentateuchal sources and their assign-

---

[64] I. Engnell, *Gamla Testamentet. En traditionshistorisk inledning*, i (Stockholm
1945). For a comprehensive survey and assessment of the debate on these issues among
Scandinavian scholars see Knight, *Rediscovering the Traditions of Israel*, pt. 2.

[65] J. Pedersen, 'Die Auffassung vom Alten Testament', *ZAW* 49 (1931), 161–81.

[66] L. Perlitt, *Vatke und Wellhausen. Geschichtsphilosophische Voraussetzungen und
historiographische Motive für die Darstellung der Religion und Geschichte Israels durch
Wilhelm Vatke und Julius Wellhausen*, BZAW 94 (Berlin 1965) has shown decisively
how untenable this claim is about the supposed influence upon Wellhausen of the phi-
losophy of Hegel as mediated by Vatke. See also John Barton, 'Wellhausen's
Prolegomena to the History of Israel: Influences and Effects', in Daniel Smith-
Christopher (ed.), *Text and Experience: Towards a Cultural Exegesis of the Bible*
(Sheffield 1995), 316–29.

ment to specifically designated points of time is problematic with respect to history' (p. 175). The material in the Pentateuch represented by the sigla J, E, D, and P cannot be regarded in the way proposed by Wellhausen. Rather, they designate 'collections which received their present form in post-exilic times and each of which contains subject-matter deriving from or rooted in ancient times. They do not admit of being arranged in exact order according to an evolutionary scheme; rather, they are parallel and together serve to yield a picture of the many-coloured variety of Israelite culture' (p. 178). Thus he claimed: 'All the Pentateuchal sources are as well pre-exilic as post-exilic . . . the neat and organized arrangement of the various strata and of their redaction, such as Wellhausen and his generation aimed at carrying through, is based upon an illusion' (p. 179).

In a second article, published in 1934,[67] Pedersen demonstrated his abandonment of the literary-critical method and its results in his study of Exodus 1–15. He found the key to the origin and development of these chapters in Exodus 12 which describes the institution of the Passover. He argued that this corpus as a whole arose in connection with, and is the product of, a centuries-old cultic drama in which Israel relived the deliverance in the exodus. These chapters are not to be understood as comprising literary strata composed by authors and subsequently combined by redactors such as the regnant Documentary Theory posited. 'Such a festival legend was not created all at once; it was again and again remodelled over centuries, what was old being transformed and what was new being added. That many unevennesses should have arisen is only to be expected. It is scarcely possible to trace this process in a literary manner; it is not achievable by the source-critical hypothesis' (p. 175). Its kernel, discernible in some of the data it contains and reflected in some of the actions it describes, belongs to the earliest period in Israel's history, whilst the corpus as we have it reflects conditions in the post-exilic Temple community in Jerusalem.

Pedersen's outright rejection of the source-critical method in favour of an exclusively traditio-historical approach found support among a number of Scandinavian scholars of whom we may mention the Swedish scholar Henrik Nyberg[68] but especially Engnell who

---

[67] J. Pedersen, 'Passahfest und Passahlegende', *ZAW* 52 (1934), 165–75.
[68] H. S. Nyberg, *Studien zum Hoseabuche. Zugleich ein Beitrag zur Klärung des Problems der alttestamentlichen Textkritik* (Uppsala 1935). See Knight, *Rediscovering the Traditions of Israel*, 233–9.

became its most enthusiastic champion. Such an extreme position with regard to literary criticism was rejected, however, by scholars at large including other Scandinavian scholars, notably Mowinckel who led the opposition to it.[69] Instead, the lines already laid down by Gunkel were widely followed: that literary criticism, though with full acknowledgement of its limitations, is an indispensable companion to the methods of form criticism and traditio-historical research. It is this latter view which has prevailed, even in cases where the results of the literary-critical analysis of the Pentateuch outlined in the previous chapter have been rejected.

An increasing number of scholars, however, shared Pedersen's emphasis upon the cult as an important means of transmitting and shaping Israelite traditions. Closely related to this was a new interest in the nature of Israel's annual cultic festivals, especially the autumn feast of Tabernacles. In this, Mowinckel's epoch-making *Studies in the Psalms*,[70] especially the second volume published in 1922, was widely influential.[71] There he argued that Israel's most important annual festival was the feast of Tabernacles celebrated in the autumn. It was a new year festival and centred on the dramatic portrayal of Yahweh's kingship, his creation of the world, and his election of Israel as his people. Mowinckel related a specific group of psalms to the liturgy of this festival (Pss. 47; 93; 95–100) but found its basic ideas reflected in many others. Part of this festival, he maintained, took the form of a renewal of the covenant between Yahweh and Israel; psalms 50 and 81 reflect this aspect of the festival. Mowinckel returned to this in his book on the origin of the decalogue in 1927.[72] Here he argued at greater length that the narratives of J and E in Exodus 19–24 concerning the making of the covenant at Sinai were nothing other than descriptions in the language of historical myth of a cultic festival still celebrated in Jerusalem at the time when these authors wrote. Underlying these narratives can be seen the various parts of that festival: the preliminary sanctification of the assembled congregation, a procession to the accompaniment of horn and trumpet, the offering of sacrifice, perhaps the performance of a blood-rite;

---

[69] See especially his *Prophecy and Tradition: The Prophetic Books in the Light of the Study of the Growth and History of Tradition* (Oslo 1946). Cf. Knight, *Rediscovering the Traditions of Israel*, 221–4, 250–9.

[70] S. Mowinckel, *Psalmenstudien*, i–vi (Kristiana 1921–6).

[71] Id., *Der Thronbesteigungsfest Jahwäs und der Ursprung der Eschatologie* (Kristiana 1922).

[72] Id., *Le Décalogue* (Paris 1927).

in short, a festival in honour of God who manifested himself in order to conclude a covenant and who disclosed his name, his nature, and his will (pp. 120–1). It was within the context of such a festival that Yahweh's law, in the form of a series such as is represented by the decalogue (but not the decalogue itself which Mowinckel dated to the late monarchical period), had its original setting.

The role of ancient Israel's cultic festivals in the shaping and transmission of tradition, especially the Pentateuchal traditions, was to receive increasing attention in subsequent decades. As we shall see in Chapter 3, it received special emphasis in the influential studies by Gerhard von Rad and Martin Noth.

Pedersen's understanding of Exodus 1–15 as reflecting the cultic legend and the 'cultic drama' of the Passover festival therefore mirrored an important trend in Old Testament studies that had newly emerged at that time. His claim that Exodus 1–15 had been shaped within the context of the Passover festival found acceptance among many scholars, though not always without modification. Thus Noth, for example, pointed out pertinently that taken as a whole these chapters reach their climax not in the institution and celebration of the Passover, which is what we would expect if they constitute the Passover legend, but in the deliverance of the Israelites at the Red Sea. He therefore accepted Pedersen's thesis only in a reduced form, limiting the theory to the story of the Egyptian plagues up to and including the destruction of the firstborn and the Passover ceremony itself.[73] It is to be noted also, however, that Noth did not find such an appraisal of these chapters in Exodus in any way incompatible with a literary analysis of them in terms of the Documentary Theory.

VI

More directly in line than Pedersen with Gunkel's methods and results were the contributions of Hugo Gressmann and Albrecht Alt. Both illustrate the growing confidence of scholars, as a result of Gunkel's pioneering work, to investigate the pre-compositional stages of the documents of the Pentateuch and uncover information about Israelite history and religion at much earlier times than had hitherto been considered possible. What Gunkel sought to achieve in

[73] M. Noth, *Überlieferungsgeschichte des Pentateuch* (Stuttgart 1948), 71–7; Eng. trans., *A History of Pentateuchal Traditions* (Englewood Cliffs, NJ 1972), 66–71.

his study of the narratives of Genesis, Gressmann attempted for those relating to Moses in the succeeding books of the Pentateuch.[74] Like Gunkel, he insisted on the necessity of literary criticism as the first stage in the analysis he desired; amongst other things it enables us to determine the final stages in the history of the formation of the literature. His understanding of J, E, and P was the same as that of Gunkel; the former two are the work of collectors—he dated J to *c.*850 BC and E to *c.*750 BC—whilst P, though containing ancient material, is more the work of an author. His main concern, however, was to penetrate behind these late collections to earlier stages in the formation of the literature. In his detailed analysis of the many stories about Moses and the Mosaic period (ch. I) layer after layer is peeled off in an endeavour to recover the earliest form of the legends and trace their subsequent development, including their combination into 'cycles' of stories. On this basis Gressmann in his second chapter described the results of his analysis for a literary history of these legends. In his third chapter he drew conclusions concerning the history of the Mosaic period. None of the material here involved is history-writing but legends (*Sagen*). Nevertheless some of the oldest of these legends yield a certain amount of historical information about the period with which they are concerned. Like Wellhausen before him, Gressmann accepted that a skeletal history of Israel during this period could be derived from this material. In his fourth and final chapter he discussed the light shed by his findings upon early Israelite religion, cult, and morality.

In one important respect Gressmann's conclusions fell short of what later research suggested.[75] He accepted as historically reliable the main outlines provided by the Pentateuch concerning the time of Moses. It was not until the work of Gerhard von Rad and especially Martin Noth that the possibility was investigated that even the outlines, which Wellhausen and earlier scholars had also accepted as historically reliable, were themselves the creation of the interweaving of originally separate traditions.

The claim is justified that next only to the work of Gunkel the contributions of Albrecht Alt (1883–1956) during the period here under review were of far-reaching significance for the future of Pentateuchal

[74] H. Gressmann, *Mose und seine Zeit. Ein Kommentar zu den Mose-Sagen*, FRLANT 18 (Göttingen 1913).
[75] For this and a fuller description of Gressmann's research see Knight, *Rediscovering the Traditions of Israel*, 84–7.

research. It is no exaggeration to say that Alt's research provided the foundation and in significant ways the framework for the study of early Israel and the origin and history of the Pentateuchal traditions during the middle decades of this century, especially at the hands of his two most distinguished pupils, Martin Noth and Gerhard von Rad. In a series of brilliant studies published in the 1920s and 1930s he illuminated such topics as the nature and origin of the forms of law in the Pentateuch, the settlement of the Israelites in Palestine, and the nature of patriarchal religion.[76] Two of these are of special significance for our purposes here, *The God of the Fathers* and *The Settlement of the Israelites in Palestine*. The latter provided the basis for a new understanding of pre-monarchic Israel as a confederation of tribes which subsequent research regarded as the context in which the Pentateuchal traditions were shaped and developed and, indeed, in which the formative stages in the creation of the Pentateuch took place. The former was also subsequently widely influential, especially the conclusions it argued concerning the origin of the divine promises to the patriarchs in Genesis. As we shall also see, these promises have more recently become the focus of a prominent new theory of the origin of the Pentateuch. For this reason too, therefore, it is worth reminding ourselves briefly of Alt's conclusions.

Alt was primarily a historian and saw a major result of the new methods and direction in research stimulated by Gunkel that 'the prehistory of Israel now seemed as a whole to grow more important and easier to understand than in research of the previous generation'.[77] He discerned in the patriarchal narratives evidence of the pre-Yahwistic religion of Israel's ancestors which the introduction of the worship of Yahweh among the tribes had not entirely obliterated. Two types of deities are evidenced in these stories. On the one hand there are the Elim, 'gods', recognizable in the titles El Bethel of Bethel (Gen. 31: 13; 35: 7), El Olam of Beersheba (Gen. 21: 33), El Roi at a sanctuary further south (Gen. 16: 13), and, without indication of

---

[76] A. Alt, *Die Landnahme der Israeliten in Palästina* (Leipzig 1925), repr. in his *Kleine Schriften zur Geschichte des Volkes Israel*, i (Munich 1953), 89–125; Eng. trans., 'The Settlement of the Israelites in Palestine', in *Essays and Old Testament History and Religion* (Oxford 1966), 133–69; *Der Gott der Väter*, BWANT 3/12 (Stuttgart 1929), repr. in *Kleine Schriften*, i. 1–78; Eng. trans., 'The God of the Fathers', *Essays in Old Testament History and Religion*, 1–66; *Die Ursprünge des Israelitischen Rechts* (Leipzig 1934), repr. in *Kleine Schriften*, i. 278–332; Eng. trans., 'The Origins of Israelite Law', *Essays in Old Testament History and Religion*, 79–132.

[77] Alt, 'Der Gott der Väter', *Kleine Schriften*, i. 4; Eng. trans., 6.

their location, El Elyon (Gen. 14: 18 ff., etc.) and El Shaddai (Gen. 17: 1, etc.). The Book of Judges adds El Bᵉrith or Ba'al Bᵉrith of Shechem (Judg. 9: 4, 46). As a rule, Alt suggested, the original purpose of the legends in which they are mentioned was the legitimation of the sanctuaries where they were worshipped. These Elim were local Canaanite deities whom the Israelites worshipped during and after their settlement in the area where they were acknowledged.[78] This means that these deities cannot have been worshipped by the Israelites before their settlement in Canaan.

At this point Alt drew attention to a distinctive element in these stories hitherto unexplored by scholars, that is, the frequent references to 'the god of my (your, etc.) father' and he argued that it is in these references that we come upon the ancestral cults of the diverse Israelite clans before their settlement in Canaan. He adduced evidence of such cults from Nabataean and Palmyrene inscriptions from a much later time (*c.*100 BC to the fourth century AD). The gods in question were not related to a specific sanctuary, as in the case of the Elim referred to above, but originated in personal revelations to the semi-nomadic patriarchal figures by whom they were first worshipped. Thus, when texts refer to 'the god of my father', for example, 'the god of Abraham' or 'the god of Isaac', what was originally meant was the god first worshipped by these individuals. Hence 'the mighty one of Jacob' ('*abīr 'ya'akōb*) designated the god originally worshipped by Jacob and his clan; 'the fear of Isaac' (*pahad yishāq*) was the god originally worshipped by Isaac and his clan. The relationship between these gods and their worshippers embodied two promises directed to the needs of such clans, first the promise of descendants and second the promise of land. The first expresses the concern of such clans for their continued maintenance and increase in their semi-nomadic wanderings; the second represents the claim of settlers to their land.[79] The first promise originated before the entry into the land, the second in Palestine itself.

When, after their permanent settlement in the land, these various clans adopted the worship of the Elim at the local sanctuaries, the ancestral gods were identified with them. Thus it has come about that the patriarchal figures, originally the recipients of divine revelations in the pre-settlement period, are now described in the legends as recipients of revelations from these local deities. At a later stage when

---

[78] Alt, 'Der Gott der Väter', *Kleine Schriften*, i. 4; Eng. trans., 7–8; Eng. trans., 9.
[79] Ibid. 66; Eng. trans., 65.

the worship of Yahweh was introduced it gradually penetrated the older sanctuaries and imposed itself as the newest stratum upon the cults hitherto practised at them. In this way the patriarchal traditions advanced to the Yahwistic stage in which we now find them in J and E. The identification of the ancestral gods of the fathers with Yahweh was facilitated, according to Alt, by the similarity in character between them: 'What the gods of the Fathers were to the smaller communities, he was to the whole confederation of the tribes'.[80]

Originally the cultic traditions associated with each patriarch existed separately from each other at different major sanctuaries. How then did the relationships between these patriarchs familiar to us from the Pentateuchal narrative come about? This was not due to the authors of the Pentateuchal sources but, argued Alt, took place in the pre-literary stage and was the result of pilgrimages by groups of worshippers from one sanctuary to another. Thus we know of pilgrimages by people from the territory of the House of Joseph in northern Israel, where the traditions concerning Jacob had their original home, to Beersheba in southern Palestine where those concerning Isaac were located. In this way the traditions about Jacob and Isaac became associated with each other. The patriarch Abraham was originally associated with Mamre in the territory of Judah, but pilgrims from this area would have journeyed to Beersheba relatively nearby. Thus the figures of Abraham and Isaac became related. The sanctuary of Beersheba thus played a key role in the formation of the relationships between the traditions associated with each of the three patriarchs. Alt was able to conclude, therefore, that a 'line can be traced from the names of the patriarchs to their introduction into the cultic legends (*Sagen*) of sanctuaries in Palestine, from their separate existence among bodies of worshippers drawn from a single tribe or region to the point where they were brought together and the genealogy formed'.[81]

Alt's work on the patriarchs was in part made possible by the particular understanding of Israelite origins which he had arrived at just a few years earlier in his monograph *The Settlement of the Israelites in Palestine*.[82] There he argued that Israelite origins are to be traced to semi-nomadic people who dwelt on the desert fringes of Palestine whence they migrated annually into the sown land in search of summer pastures for their herds. Over a protracted period numerous of

---

[80] Ibid. 62; Eng. trans., 60.   [81] Ibid. 58; Eng. trans., 57.
[82] See above, n. 76.

these semi-nomadic clans settled permanently in the land where initially they inhabited the sparsely populated areas well away from the
centres of Canaanite population; it was only at a later stage of territorial expansion that conflict took place between them and the
indigenous Canaanite city-states.

It was left to Alt's distinguished pupil Martin Noth (1902–68) in
one of his earliest works to complete what he had begun in this study,
and Noth achieved this in his monograph *The System of the Twelve
Tribes of Israel*[83] in which he argued that pre-monarchical Israel took
the form of a twelve-tribe sacral confederation whose worship of
Yahweh and the various institutions related to this were crucially formative for the future history of Israel and the peculiar development
of Israelite religion. On the analogy of the city-state leagues later
attested in Greece and known to the Greeks as 'amphictyonies' (sing.
'amphictyony'), Noth described the Israelite tribal confederation as
an 'amphictyony'. This understanding of early Israel became almost
universally accepted among scholars for a generation to come. It was
also the presupposition of the most influential research into the
origin of the Pentateuch in the decades that followed, providing a
picture of the social and religious context for an investigation of the
growth of the Pentateuchal traditions that earlier research could
scarcely have considered possible.

According to Noth, Israel, properly understood, originated as a
sacral union or confederacy of twelve tribes on the soil of Canaan in
the pre-monarchic period. This tribal league came into existence only
after numerous separate clans and groups of semi-nomads had made
their entry into the land and were there gradually bound together
into separate tribes which eventually together constituted Israel. It is
therefore impossible, according to Noth, to investigate the history of
Israel before the settlement, since by definition there was no Israel
before the emergence of the twelve-tribe league in Canaan. All that
we can say of the period before this is that there were disparate semi-
nomadic clans and groups of clans each of which led its own separate
existence and maintained its own traditions. Noth argued that the
separate tribes of Israel did not exist as such before the settlement,
since most of them assumed the tribal form in which we encounter
them in the Old Testament only after the settlement. That is to say,
the tribes which went to make up Israel came into existence for the

---

[83] M. Noth, *Das System der zwölf Stämme Israels*, BWANT 4/1 (Stuttgart 1930).

most part as the result of the consolidation of originally separate clans which after they had entered the land occupied a common region or area there.

The settlement of the clans and their formation into tribes was a protracted process and can be reconstructed only in general terms. On the basis of a number of observations, especially concerning ancient traditions about the tribes and collections of old aphorisms relating to them such as are contained in Genesis 49, Noth concluded that the first to have settled were the tribes Reuben, Simeon, Levi, Judah, Issachar, and Zebulun, which are grouped together in the earliest traditions and referred to as 'the sons of Leah'. It was at a later time that the clans which constituted the tribe of Benjamin came in, to be followed subsequently by 'the house of Joseph'. Joseph and Benjamin are referred to in the Old Testament as 'the sons of Rachel' and Noth suggested that the basis of this relationship was the proximity of these tribes to one another in central Palestine, and also possibly because Benjamin was connected in some way with the settlement of Joseph. As for the other tribes, the so-called concubine tribes Asher, Dan, Naphtali and Gad, the latter may have entered at the same time as Joseph, whilst the other three probably settled at an earlier stage.

A most important feature in the traditions concerning early Israel is the constancy of the number twelve as the number of the tribes; in spite of changes in the fortunes of the tribes—Levi, most notably, seems to have ceased to be a 'secular' tribe at an early stage—this number is maintained. This constancy in the number of the tribes was accounted for by Noth in his well-known theory that early Israel took the form of a tribal league on the analogy of the city-state 'amphictyonies' later attested in Greece and Italy.

Of the institutions of this early Israelite 'amphictyony', the most prominent was the central sanctuary, the oversight and upkeep of which was the responsibility of each tribe for one month of the year. In Israel the Ark was the common cultic object of the tribes and the various sanctuaries in which it was located from time to time were each in turn the central sanctuaries of Israel. According to Noth, Shechem was the first of these central shrines and was succeeded by Bethel, then Gilgal, and finally Shiloh. It was primarily their communal worship of Yahweh at the central sanctuary which formed the focal point and binding factor in the life of the Israelite confederation. We can no longer ascertain the precise form of the amphictyonic cultic observances, but there is some evidence, Noth argued, that the most important cultic occasion was an annual festival at which each of the tribes was officially represented and which probably centred mainly on a confession of faith in Yahweh together with a proclamation of the divine law and a covenant-making ceremony. This much Noth derived from the narrative in Joshua 24 which, he believed, reflects a regularly recurring cultic event in early Israel. It was this proclamation of the divine law which gave Israel's worship its distinctive character, since it was the authority of this law in the ordering of tribal life that marked Israel off from the surrounding peoples. It is especially in connection with this proclamation of divine law that an office of 'judge' can be discerned and understood (cf. Judg. 10: 1–5; 12: 7–15).

As to the foundation of the twelve-tribe 'amphictyony' of early Israel, Noth found evidence of this also in Joshua 24. Scholars before him had already drawn attention to the importance and antiquity of some of the material in this chapter, and it had been pointed out that the occasion described seems to presuppose the presence at Shechem of two separate groups: on the one hand Joshua and his 'house' and on the other those who are here called upon to abandon the worship of the gods which their fathers had served 'beyond the river' and to serve Yahweh (Josh. 24: 14 f.). Noth suggested that it was under the leadership of the house of Joseph, represented by Joshua, that the twelve-tribe 'amphictyony' was established at Shechem. Properly understood, the name Israel designates this twelve-tribe confederation; its later use to connote the Northern Kingdom of Israel as against the southern state of Judah is secondary.

Increasingly this theory of an early Israelite 'amphictyony' and its institutions, especially its cultic institutions and calendar, became the presupposition and framework in which scholars sought the origin and development of the Pentateuchal traditions and, indeed, the very form of the Pentateuch itself. This was especially so in the case of Noth himself and, no less, of his contemporary Gerhard von Rad. Their work led the way and in large measure set the agenda for research for decades to come. Indeed, in several respects their writings may legitimately be described as marking the climax of Pentateuchal research this century. I describe their achievement briefly in the next chapter. We shall see in subsequent chapters that in significant ways it has been in engagement with, and reaction to, their work that the current new phase in Pentateuchal research has emerged.

3

From Tradition to Literature

The main achievements of the generation of Pentateuchal research which began with Gunkel's work around the turn of the century lay less in the new results it could claim, important though many of these were, than in the new directions it opened up for research. Form criticism, though it yielded a rewarding first harvest, clearly created such possibilities for fresh advances that it required an extensive programme of research and application which would occupy scholars for decades to come. The accomplishments of traditio-historical investigation during these years were likewise of great significance, but the potential of this approach also remained to be more fully exploited.

Alongside the promising advances being made on the basis of these new methods, this period was scarcely less notable for its continuation of the task of source criticism which was considered to have been by no means exhausted, notwithstanding the almost exclusive attention which had been devoted to it by preceding generations. As we have seen, the 'Newer Documentary Theory', which was one of the crowning achievements of nineteenth-century research, was now revised by some into the 'Newest Documentary Theory'. Much effort was at the same time devoted to tracing the continuation of the Hexateuchal sources beyond Joshua into the remaining books of the Former Prophets. Further, old controversies concerning the criteria of the documentary hypothesis continued, with, indeed, fresh impetus, whilst some of its hitherto least contested results were now shaken by fresh questioning. Such was what may be described as the upheaval in Pentateuchal study and the methods to be employed that it is no exaggeration to say that research since then has been largely occupied with the new tasks and problems it posed.

What gave the more immediate impulse for the beginning of the period of research which followed, however, and to which I now turn was, first, the necessity to pursue further the possibilities which had been opened up for investigating the pre-compositional stages in the history of the literature and the traditions, and, second, a sense of frustration with what was seen as the failure of the preceding period to concern itself adequately with the final form of the literature from which attention had been more and more drawn away by a pre-occupation with its individual parts and with its pre-compositional history.

It might appear that these two interests which this new period of research took up, the one concerned with the pre-compositional history of the literature and the other with the compositional stage proper, were pulling scholars in quite opposite directions. But that was not the intention or the case. What was now called for was an attempt to pursue the entire history of the literature and of the Pentateuchal traditions, from their beginnings through successive stages of development up to their incorporation in the extended literary sources of the Pentateuch and beyond this to the redactional interweaving of these sources to yield the literature in its final form. Properly carried out, an investigation of the pre-compositional history of the literature and the traditions would not only illuminate our understanding of the development of Israelite religion and theology, but would also shed new light upon the contribution of those who stood at the end of this whole process, that is, those who were responsible for the composition of the Pentateuchal documents.

For this reason I have chosen as a title for this chapter 'From Tradition to Literature', for it was with this that the period now to be surveyed was largely concerned. However, lest such a title should give the impression that this period narrowly concerned itself with the mere process of how this corpus of literature and religious traditions came into being, it must be added that much of what was attempted was theologically motivated and yielded theological insights which played a major role in the wider study of Old Testament theology that came into such prominence in this same period. In this way too this period, with its renewed interest in the study of the theology of the Pentateuchal literature, displays a marked contrast to the more historically and history-of-religions orientation of the period surveyed in the preceding chapters.

The works of two scholars dominated this period, Gerhard von Rad (1901–71) and Martin Noth (1902–68), and a very great deal of Pentateuchal research that followed their works was directly dependent upon them, whether by way of further development of the methods and insights they advanced or by way of critical reaction to them. Further, the current fresh debate about the Pentateuch, which will be our concern in the second part of this book, in several important respects takes its basic points of orientation from the works of these two scholars. In view of this, the present chapter will offer a somewhat detailed account of the contributions of these two scholars.

I

Gerhard von Rad

This new period had an auspicious beginning with the publication in 1938 of Gerhard von Rad's famous monograph *The Form-Critical Problem of the Hexateuch*.[1] It was von Rad who most effectively sounded the protest against what was viewed as a process of fragmentation in Hexateuchal studies which had set in at that time. He wrote in his opening paragraphs of younger scholars being 'weary of research in Hexateuchal studies', and of the reason for this: the main lines of investigation being pursued had

led inevitably further and further away from the final form of the text as we have it. A process of analysis, doubtless almost always interesting but nevertheless highly stylised has run its course, and a more or less clear perception of its inevitability handicaps many scholars today. Indeed, even those who are fully prepared to recognise that it was both necessary and important to traverse these paths cannot ignore the profoundly disintegrating effect which has been one result of this method of Hexateuchal criticism.On almost all sides the final form of the Hexateuch has come to be regarded as a starting-point barely worthy of discussion, from which the debate should move away as rapidly as possible in order to reach the real problems underlying it.[2]

It was from this 'disquieting situation', as he referred to it, that von Rad's work took its origin.

In keeping with his concern with the Hexateuch in its final form, von Rad began with a brief recapitulation of its contents, the story it narrates from creation to the entry into the promised land, and he characterized what is recounted as 'purely and simply a "history of

---

[1] G. von Rad, *Das formgeschichtliche Problem des Hexateuch*, BWANT 26 (Stuttgart 1938), repr. in his *Gesammelte Studien zum Alten Testament* (Munich 1958), 9–86 (references below are to the latter which will be cited as *GS*); Eng. trans., 'The Form-Critical Problem of the Hexateuch', in *The Form-Critical Problem of the Hexateuch and Other Essays* (Edinburgh 1965), 1–78. Quotations here are from the latter.

[2] *GS*, 9; Eng. trans., 1.

redemption". We might equally well call it a *creed*, a summary of the principal facts of God's redemptive activity.'[3] It is this basic idea of God's redemptive activity that underlies the 'truly immense compilation' which the Hexateuch constitutes. 'The intricate elaboration of the one basic idea into this tremendous edifice is no first essay, nor is it something which has grown of its own accord to the proportions of classical maturity. Rather . . . it is something pressed to the ultimate limits of what is possible and of what is readable.'[4] In other words, von Rad saw the Hexateuch as a grand elaboration of a basic form, a 'creed' of God's redemptive activity, and the task he set himself was that of uncovering the earliest formulation of this creed and its contents and the later appropriation of this credal confession of early Israel as the organizing principle in the formation of the Hexateuch together with the development and elaboration it underwent in the process.

At this point von Rad drew attention to Deuteronomy 26: 5b–9, which is a short prayer or confession prescribed for a worshipper offering at the altar a gift of the first-fruits of the harvest. It expresses briefly the principal facts of God's redemptive activity. Though it occurs in the relatively late book of Deuteronomy, this confession, he maintained, is very much older: 'one might even be so bold', he suggested, 'as to remove the traces of the deuteronomic editor's retouching and to attempt a reconstruction of the original formula'.[5] The rhythmical and alliterative character of the opening phrases of the passage (*'ᵃrāmī 'ōbēd 'ābī*), he added, reveals its antiquity. Von Rad classified this passage as a creed, regarding it, indeed, as probably the earliest example of its kind. Such a creed would have expressed briefly the traditional way in which Israel's faith was presented at an early time and, further, such a credal formulation of that faith would have had its setting in a recurring cultic occasion.

Conspicuously absent from Deuteronomy 26: 5b–9, however, is any reference to the revelation of Yahweh at Sinai and the making of the covenant there, events which have such an important place in the narrative of the Hexateuch. How is this to be explained? That it is not a chance omission is indicated, von Rad argued, by a similar absence of any reference to the Sinai events in two other examples of his genre of credal confession, Deuteronomy 6: 20–4 and Joshua 24: 2b–13. Its absence in the latter passage is all the more striking, since here the redemptive history is presented in somewhat more detail than in

---

[3] *GS*, 10; Eng. trans., 2.   [4] Ibid.   [5] *GS*, 12; Eng. trans., 4.

either of the other two terser formulations. Evidently, all three passages were compiled according to the same basic plan, a plan which,
though it permitted the addition of many details, as in Joshua 24:
2b–13, was fixed with regard to its essential ingredients and did not
allow for such a fundamental alteration as would have been occa-
sioned by the inclusion of a reference to the Sinai events. This
conclusion is reinforced by a number of 'free adaptations of the creed
in cult-lyrics' (Exod. 6: 15; 1 Sam. 12; Pss. 78, 105, 135, 136) where
likewise there is no mention of the revelation and covenant at Sinai.[6]

On the basis of these observations von Rad argued that the Sinai tradition had once existed quite independently of the celebration and formulation of the redemptive history represented by these old credal
statements or, as he defined it, the 'settlement' (*Landnahme*) tradition.
This conclusion concurred with the view already arrived at by earlier
literary analysis of the Pentateuch that the Sinai narrative had been
secondarily imposed upon an earlier form of the narrative which knew
nothing of the journey to Sinai and the events which took place there.[7]

With regard to the Sinai pericope in Exodus 19–24, the theophany
and the making of the covenant are the dominant elements which
'from the point of view of both content and structure . . . form a fixed
and complete cycle of tradition'[8] in which we search in vain for any
mention of the elements of the redemptive acts of God in the exodus
and the wilderness traditions. Further, in passages elsewhere that are
variants of the Sinai tradition there is a similar lack of reference to
the elements of the settlement tradition (e.g. Deut. 33: 2, 4; Judg. 5:
4 f.; Hab. 3: 3 ff.).

Von Rad then argued, here adopting the view already arrived at by
Mowinckel which we noted earlier,[9] that the narrative of the Sinai
events in Exodus 19 ff. reflects a cultic festival the contents and liturgical procedures of which have been 'translated into the language of
literary mythology'. The parts of the festival can be clearly discerned
underlying the narrative: exhortation and recital of the events at Sinai
(Exod. 19); reading of the law (decalogue and the book of the
covenant); promise of blessing (Exod. 23: 20 ff.) sealing of the
covenant (Exod. 24). He found the same pattern in the book of
Deuteronomy as a whole: historical presentation of the events at
Sinai (1–11); the reading of the law (12: 1–26: 15); the sealing of the

---

[6] *GS*, 16 ff; Eng. trans., 8 ff.
[7] Wellhausen especially has argued this. Cf. *Prolegomena*, 362 ff.; Eng. trans., 342 ff.
[8] *GS*, 25; Eng. trans., 18.   [9] See above, pp. 52–3.

covenant (26: 16–19); blessings and curses (27–8). On the basis of Deuteronomy 31: 10–11 he maintained that the festival in question was celebrated at the feast of Tabernacles in the autumn, whilst a number of texts, notably Deuteronomy 27 and Joshua 24, provide evidence that it took place at the ancient sanctuary at Shechem which was an important Israelite centre in the pre-monarchical period, as Noth and others had demonstrated.

For his point of departure for a discussion of the cultic festival in which the settlement tradition had its *Sitz im Leben*, von Rad returned to Deuteronomy 26 where the ancient creed there preserved is related to the presentation of the first-fruits thus providing a clue to the occasion in Israel's annual calendar when this tradition of redemptive history was celebrated. The cultic calendars in the Old Testament all make provision for a festival which included the presentation of the produce of the earth: the feast of Weeks in early summer referred to in Numbers 28: 26 specifically as 'the day of the first-fruits' and in Exodus 23: 16 as 'the harvest festival of the first-fruits which you have made' (cf. Exod. 34: 22; Lev. 23: 15 ff.; Deut. 16: 9 f.). Von Rad thus concluded that the creed in Deuteronomy 26: 5 ff. was the cult legend of the feast of Weeks; it contains those elements of Israelite faith which were celebrated at that festival.

According to the old traditions underlying Joshua 3–4 Israel after crossing the Jordan journeyed to Gilgal which became the base, the camp, from which the tribes went out on their conquering exploits and to which they returned afterwards (Josh. 9: 16; 10: 6, 9, 15). More significant still, however, is the tradition that it was at Gilgal that Joshua made the apportionment of the promised land to the tribes (Josh. 14: 6–14; 18: 2–10).[10] Since therefore the credal tradition represented by Deuteronomy 26: 5b–9 celebrated above all the *gift of the land*, it is plausible to conclude, von Rad argued, that it was at the old sanctuary at Gilgal, so closely related in the tradition with Israel's occupation of the land, that the festival in question was celebrated in pre-monarchic Israel.

II

How and when did these traditions, originally bound up with Israel's annual cultic life, find literary expression in the Hexateuch? What was

[10] According to von Rad we should read 'Gilgal' and not 'Shiloh' in Josh. 18: 9, 10.

involved in the process 'from tradition to literature'? It is here, von Rad claimed, that the work of the Yahwist was of such epoch-making significance. He rejected any suggestion that we should abandon the view that J derived from the hand of a collector and author and posit instead a long process of anonymous growth, beginning with a nucleus in the settlement tradition which was developed through the accretion of layer upon layer of traditional materials over many generations.[11] On the contrary: 'One plan alone governs the whole, and a gigantic structure such as this, the whole conforming to one single plan, does not grow up naturally of its own accord. How could such heterogeneous materials as those embraced by the Yahwist have cast themselves in this form of their own accord?'[12]

The Yahwist is not to be regarded, however, merely as a collector in the manner suggested by Gunkel. In making this judgement of the Yahwist's work Gunkel had failed to take into account 'the co-ordinating power of the writer's overall theological purpose, and the gathering of separate materials around a very small nucleus of basic concepts'.[13] These basic concepts were provided for the Yahwist by the settlement tradition as exemplified in credal formulation in Deuteronomy 26: 5b–9 and elsewhere. It was this that the Yahwist employed as his 'outline plan', and all was subordinated to this basic plan. Notwithstanding the multifarious traditional materials which he employed, the credal plan remains paramount. Thus the Yahwist is rediscovered by von Rad as an author and theologian, one who spoke to his contemporaries 'out of a concern for the real and living faith, not as a more or less detached story-teller committed to nothing more than an ancient fund of traditions'.[14]

The Yahwist had at his disposal a mass of traditional materials many of which lent themselves readily and without difficulty to his overall plan. Von Rad cited as an example of this the narrative of Exodus 1–15, here following Pedersen's view that this material forms a complete whole which derived from the Passover ceremony. It was a genuine exodus tradition distinct from the settlement tradition but easily included because of its closely related subject matter. Another example is afforded by the Balaam story which was relatively easily harmonized with the scheme of the settlement tradition. The inclusion of other traditions, however, was considerably less easy

---

[11] *GS* 58 f.; Eng. trans. 51 f.
[13] *GS* 58; Eng. trans., 51.
[12] *GS* 59; Eng. trans., 52.
[14] *GS* 77; Eng. trans., 69.

and 'strained the original plan almost to bursting point, and resulted in a forcible broadening of its formerly rather narrow theological basis'.[15] Von Rad saw this at three points: in the interpolation of the Sinai tradition, in the development of the patriarchal tradition, and in the introductory addition of the primeval history.

(1) The fusion of the Sinai tradition with the tradition of the redemptive history shows all the signs of having been the result of a purely literary process. It had its own cultic setting quite distinct from the settlement tradition in early Israel. It was the Yahwist who united them. In order to incorporate the Sinai tradition into his work the Yahwist had to disrupt the Kadesh tradition. But the gain was significant, argued von Rad, for

> by the absorption of the Sinai tradition the simple soteriological conception of the settlement tradition gained new support of a powerful and salutary kind. Everything which the Yahwist tells us, as he unfolds the plan of his tradition, is now coloured by the divine self-revelation of Mt. Sinai. This is true above all with regard to the underlying purpose of that tradition, which now became the record of the redemptive activity of One who lays upon man the obligation to obey his will, and calls man to account for his actions. The blending of the two traditions gives definition to the two fundamental propositions of the whole message of the Bible: Law and Gospel.[16]

(2) From the opening phrase of the old creed in Deuteronomy 26 it is clear that from the earliest times the settlement tradition took the patriarchal period as its starting-point in narrating the redemptive history and began with a reference to Jacob, the 'wandering Aramaean' (cf. 1 Sam. 12: 8). It is, however, clearly a far cry from this bare reference in the creed to the elaborate patriarchal history in Genesis concerning not only Jacob but Abraham and Isaac. What was the Yahwist's contribution to this?

Von Rad based his discussion of this upon the findings of both Gunkel and Alt. Gunkel's analysis of the patriarchal narratives had isolated the separate 'cycles' of stories which had already taken shape in the pre-compositional stages of development and which the Yahwist would have inherited among the diverse materials he collected. Alt had demonstrated among other things that already in the pre-compositional stages the genealogy which now links the three patriarchal figures would have emerged as the result of pilgrimages between the major sanctuaries where the original traditions concern-

---

[15] *GS* 50; Eng. trans., 53.   [16] *GS* 62; Eng. trans., 54.

ing each had their home. In these ways, therefore, the Yahwist had no need to be an innovator but was dependent upon an already developed literature and tradition. Nevertheless, according to von Rad the Yahwist made his own distinctive and considerable contribution to the formation and presentation of the patriarchal history.

Thus the Yahwist's handiwork is discernible in Genesis 15 with, on the one hand, its emphasis upon the divine promise to Abraham and, on the other, the way in which it introduces a tension arising from human reluctance to believe the promise. The same is true of Genesis 12: 10 ff., where the promise is threatened by disbelief, and also of Genesis 16: 1 ff., where likewise lack of faith leads to a complication in attempting to force the promise. Thus von Rad concluded that the strong theological interest which gives cohesion to the stories about Abraham as we have them is certainly traceable to the Yahwist.[17] He found similar evidence of the Yahwist's distinctive theological contribution in the Jacob stories, the prayer in Genesis 32: 10 ff. being particularly significant here; it 'is indicative of the whole course of Jacob's life-history'.[18] Finally, von Rad pointed to the Yahwist's use of the Joseph narrative, a work which he inherited already finished in all essentials. It has been used as a means of describing Israel's growth to nationhood in Egypt and thus forms a bridge from the patriarchal period to that of the bondage and exodus. But it suited the Yahwist's purpose in another way also: it is a story witnessing to God's providential care. As such the Yahwist was able to incorporate it into this work whilst at the same time preserving its autonomy.

The most significant contribution of the Yahwist to the formation of the patriarchal history, however, was his integration of it with the settlement tradition. The promise of land to the patriarchs originated in the pre-Israelite period, as Alt had shown; it had to do with the permanent settlement of the erstwhile semi-nomadic clans in the land. It knew nothing of the idea that the descendants of these patriarchal figures would yet have to leave the land and only subsequently find the realization of the promise. The Yahwist did not therefore create this promise but inherited it as an already fixed element in the traditions which came to him. But by incorporating it into the settlement tradition he altered the nature and purpose of the original promise which is now understood as referring to the settlement that became a reality only in the time of Joshua: 'Thus the relationship of

---

[17] Cf. *GS* 66; Eng. trans., 59.   [18] *GS* 67; Eng. trans., 59.

the patriarchs to the land in which they dwell now appears to be merely provisional, and their present situation but a temporary one . . . The whole patriarchal period has ceased to be regarded as significant in itself; it is now no more than a time of promise pointing to a fulfilment outside itself, a fulfilment spoken of only at the very end of the Yahwist's work.'[19] The Yahwist thus showed the promise to have been fulfilled in a way that goes far beyond what was originally understood and formulated.

(3) According to von Rad, the Yahwist made a further major contribution in the formation of the Hexateuch by prefacing the whole with a presentation of the primeval history to which the settlement tradition exemplified in the old creed in Deuteronomy 26 makes no reference. For this he had at his disposal a variety of old stories which he brought together and made to serve one purpose: a description of the growing power of sin in the world. In addition, however, the Yahwist in this presentation of the primeval history also emphasized a hidden growth of grace alongside the increasing gulf between God and humanity narrated in Genesis 2–11: God forgives and sustains at the same time as he punishes, as in the case of the Fall, of Cain's crime against Abel, and of the Flood. Although the story of the Tower of Babel appears to be concerned only with judgement, it is at this point that the pre-patriarchal history is linked with the history of redemption: Abraham is called and the promise given that all the nations would be blessed through him (Gen. 12: 1–3). In this way the opening words of the patriarchal history at one and the same time bring to an end the primeval history and provide the key to it. Here the Yahwist proclaimed that 'the ultimate purpose of the redemption which God will bring about in Israel is that of bridging the gulf between God and the entire human race'.[20] This promise of blessing, the formulation of which is due to the Yahwist himself, is thereby made normative for the whole of the redemptive history he narrates.

To what period in Israel's history is the Yahwist to be dated? As we saw earlier, most scholars since Wellhausen had dated the J document, or at least its beginning, to the middle of the monarchical period, that is, *c*.850 BC. Against this, however, von Rad argued that the purpose and achievement of the Yahwist were much more directly related to David than scholars hitherto had been willing to recognize. The Yahwist employed a wealth of materials which had their original home in the cult but which have now been 'historicized': 'their inner

---

[19] *GS* 69; Eng. trans., 62.　　　　　　　　　　　[20] *GS* 69; Eng. trans., 66.

content has actually been removed bodily from its narrow sacral context into the freer atmosphere of common history.'[21] In the work of
the Yahwist faith in Yahweh no longer understands God's activity to
be tied to Israel's time-honoured sacral institutions in the cult, the
ark, charismatic leaders such as those of the period of the Judges, and
so on; rather

*the main emphasis in God's dealings with his people is now to be sought outside
the sacral institutions* . . . God's activity is now perhaps less perceptible to the
outward sight, but it is actually perceived more fully and more constantly
because his guidance is seen to extend equally to every historical occurrence,
sacred or profane, up to the time of the settlement. The Yahwist bears witness to the fact that history is directed and ordered by God. The providence
of Yahweh is revealed to the eye of faith in every sphere of life, private and
public.[22]

At this point von Rad pointed to the narrative of Solomon's succession to the throne of David (2 Sam. 9–20; 1 Kgs. 1–2) the author of
which, as Leonard Rost had shown, 'stands, with some reservations,
in opposition to the cult, and recognises the divine activity in the
course of history'.[23] It was to this author, whom Rost placed in the
early reign of Solomon, that the new conception of the nature of
God's activity in history owed its origin. Von Rad placed the Yahwist
in the same period, arguing that the achievements of David were the
background to the Yahwist's work, specifically his territorial achievements which were now seen to mark the fulfilment of Yahweh's
ancient promise to Israel concerning the land:

The events of David's reign could forthwith acquire a profound religious significance. Age-old decrees of Yahweh were recalled, and David was seen to
be the agent of God's will. Such would have been the joyful realisation which
swept over the contemporaries of David and their immediate successors.
Doubtless they found it surprising, for the days were long past when
Yahweh's deliverance of Israel might still be known in actual experience. In
the call of Saul, Yahweh's help had once more been revealed in the ancient
manner, in a holy war; but then for several decades the faith of Israel had
experienced nothing further of that kind. It seemed that Yahweh had with-
drawn from the field of history. Then came David's great feats, and with
them, almost overnight, the fulfilment of God's ancient decrees. So Yahweh
was still with Israel: He had not allowed his purpose to lapse. None the less,

[21] *GS* 75; Eng. trans., 68.   [22] *GS* 78; Eng. trans., 71.
[23] L. Rost, *Die Überlieferung von der Thronnachfolge Davids*, BWANT 3/6 (Stuttgart
1926), 136; Eng. trans., *The Succession to the Throne of David* (Sheffield 1982), 115.

his activity had not been such as had been known formerly in the holy wars of old. It was more secret, unsensational, almost hidden under the cloak of secular affairs, visible only to the eye of faith.[24]

In this connection von Rad drew attention to the lists in Judges 1, which he regarded as the conclusion of the Yahwist's work, and suggested how relevant these apparently 'remote memoranda' would have been for David's contemporaries and their successors: 'No one could read these stereotyped descriptions of the as yet unoccupied territories without reflecting that God had not in fact left the matter in this state of semi-fulfilment. He had continued his care for Israel and had kept all his promises, even though it was not in the time of Joshua, but not until the time of David that this was seen. That is what the Yahwist's restrained mode of presentation actually invites us to read between the lines at the end of the work.'[25]

As the title of his monograph already indicates, von Rad was not concerned with the question of the composition and growth of the Hexateuch as a whole but only with the investigation of the plan which governs the whole. This, as we have seen, he believed to have been the achievement of the Yahwist during the latter part of the tenth century who took as his basic outline the elements of the settlement tradition and in his grand elaboration of them incorporated the Sinai tradition, ordered and expanded the patriarchal history, and prefaced the whole with the primeval history. It is therefore to the Yahwist that the Hexateuch owes its overall plan: 'The Elohist and the priestly writer do not diverge from the pattern in this respect: their writings are no more than variations upon the massive theme of the Yahwist's conception, despite their admittedly great theological originality.'[26] He concluded his study with some observations upon both E and P in the light of his form-critical conclusions about the Yahwist's work as follows.

(1) The ancient settlement tradition contained no mention of pre-patriarchal history and the expansion of its scheme by the Yahwist was 'a very great theological liberty' on his part. It was not a liberty that the Elohist wished to emulate; rather, he evidently felt himself to be under an obligation to adhere more closely in this respect to the form which had been hallowed by centuries of tradition in Israel. Von Rad's form-critical findings were thus seen by him as offering an explanation why the Elohist, as literary criticism had already con-

[24] *GS* 80; Eng. trans., 72 f.   [25] *GS* 81; Eng. trans., 73.   [26] *GS* 82; Eng. trans., 74.

cluded, began his narrative with the patriarchal period and not, as in the case of J, with the primeval history.

(2) Von Rad rejected Noth's view that the collector of the Gilgal stories in Joshua is not to be identified with the writer of one of the Pentateuchal sources and that the literary problems of the book of Joshua require analysis independently of the results of Pentateuchal source-criticism.[27] Von Rad argued that the ancient aetiological interests of these stories have been brushed aside and that they are now 'simply held together by the one common factor of relationship to the settlement tradition'. Since therefore this ancient material has been subordinated to the settlement tradition, it cannot reasonably be claimed, he argued, that this literary composition has a separate identity distinct from the Pentateuchal sources. In other words, the literary problem of the book of Joshua cannot be isolated from the overall problem of the Hexateuch, whose sources constitute one single whole from the point of view of form; they conform to a particular genre, the settlement tradition. He accepted the view of literary analysis that the Elohist source can be discerned through Genesis to Deuteronomy and, this being so, the Elohist's settlement story would have had its own conclusion in Joshua unless we are to prefer Rudolph's theory of the E material as merely redactional supplementation here and there in the literature.

(3) The Priestly writer was bound to the recognition of the purposeful activity of God in history which characterizes the Yahwist's work, including the Yahwist's arrangement of the materials. But there is a fundamental difference in the approach of the two authors. The Yahwist inherited a situation in which the old cultic materials were being loosed from their ancient setting, and he carried this process further with the result that he portrayed God's activity in history in an 'almost secular manner'. The Priestly writer, by contrast, strove for the validation of sacral institutions: 'He provides the theological guarantee of these institutions, important as they are for his own day; and he does so by making a historical survey, in the course of which he gives an account of those revelations and ordinances connected with the history of redemption which correspond to the rites, usages and beliefs he wishes to validate. The whole tradition, with all its constituent elements, is thus brought back by P within the ambit of the cultus.'[28] This is not to say, however, that P reverts to the mode of

---

[27] For Noth's view, see below. [28] *GS* 84; Eng. trans., 76 f.

thought concerning the ancient cultic traditions which prevailed in the early, pre-J period and before the Yahwist took up and utilized them. Rather, a new mode of 'sacerdotal cultic thought' characterizes P: 'To put the matter crudely, the priestly writings are distinguished from [the ancient cultic traditions] by the absence of any kind of religious naïveté. The material has been worked over in the light of a theological conception of truly great proportions, and the whole picture from the creation of the world to the erection of the tabernacle at Shiloh [Josh. 8: 1] has been included in its purview.'[29]

III

Martin Noth

Both in its method and in its conclusions von Rad's monograph was programmatic for much of what he himself subsequently wrote, for example his commentary on Genesis and, most notably, his monumental *Old Testament Theology*.[30] It also directly set the agenda for many works which sought to build upon its insights, whilst in not a few instances even those who arrived at distinctly different conclusions were not without significant debt to one or other of its main claims. Noth's work, to which we now turn, was also indebted to von Rad's monograph, but was by no means simply epigonic, for although it adopted some of von Rad's conclusions, in several major respects it differed markedly from them. The work in question is his *A History of Pentateuchal Traditions* which was published in 1948.[31] Noth defined the task he set himself in this work as follows:

The growth and formation of the large body of traditions now found in the extensive and complicated literary structure of the Pentateuch was a long process, nourished by many roots and influenced by manifold interests and

[29] *GS* 84 f.; Eng. trans., 77.
[30] G. von Rad, *Das erste Buch Moses, Genesis*, ATD 2–4 (5th edn., Göttingen 1958); Eng. trans., *Genesis* (London 1961); id., *Theologie des Alten Testaments:* i. *Die Theologie der geschichtlichen Überlieferungen Israels* (Munich 1957); Eng. trans., *Old Testament Theology*, i. *The Theology of Israel's Historical Traditions* (Edinburgh 1962); id., *Theologie des Alten Testaments*, ii. *Die Theologie der prophetischen Überlieferungen Israels* (Munich 1960); Eng. trans., *Old Testament Theology*, ii. *The Theology of Israel's Prophetic Traditions* (Edinburgh 1965).
[31] Noth, *Überlieferungsgeschichte des Pentateuch*; Eng. trans., *A History of Pentateuchal Traditions*. (Quotations are from the latter. The abbreviation *ÜGP* will be used when referring to the German original.)

tendencies. In the course of this development, traditions which doubtless were circulated and transmitted orally at first were probably written down in time, for reasons that are no longer known to us and to an extent that can no longer be determined with certainty. In any event, later on they were brought together in large literary works and these in turn, through the purely literary labours of so-called redactors, were finally compiled into the large corpus of the transmitted Pentateuch. It is the task of a 'history of Pentateuchal traditions' to investigate this whole process from beginning to end.[32]

Noth set a limit, however, to his own investigation of this process: his main concern was to be with the pre-literary history of the traditions rather than with the final literary stages, that is, the well-known documents of the Pentateuch. He gave two reasons for his. First, in comparison with the attention which had hitherto been devoted to the final literary stages, the pre-literary history of the Pentateuchal traditions had been widely neglected. There had of course been the important contributions of Gunkel and Gressmann on Genesis and the narratives relating to Moses respectively. But these had focused mainly upon *individual materials*, on their prehistory and origin and had left many wider issues unconsidered. The major task which had now to be undertaken was

to ascertain the *basic themes* from which the totality of the transmitted Pentateuch developed, to uncover their roots, to investigate how they were replenished with individual materials, to pursue their connections with each other, and to assess their significance. Thus the task is to understand, in a manner that is historically responsible and proper, the essential content and important concerns of the Pentateuch—which, from its manifold beginnings, variously rooted in cultic situations, to the final stages in the process of its emergence, claims recognition as a great document of faith.[33]

The second reason which Noth gave was that 'the decisive steps on the way to the formation of the Pentateuch were taken during the pre-literary stage, and the literary fixations only gave final form to material which in its essentials was already given. Therefore, to understand properly the structure and content of the Pentateuch as a whole and in its details, one must attempt to penetrate into the early stages of the history of its traditions.'[34] Thus Noth, quite in keeping with the protest sounded by von Rad which we noted earlier, was concerned with the formation of the totality of the Pentateuch. The difference was, that whilst for von Rad the Yahwist played the decisive

[32] *ÜGP* 1; Eng. trans., 1. [33] *ÜGP* 3 f.; Eng. trans., 3. [34] *ÜGP* 1 f.; Eng. trans., 1 f.

role in this, for Noth the formative stages had been completed before the Yahwist took up his pen, though, as we shall see, Noth did assign a specific theological intention to the Yahwist.

Essential for an understanding of Noth's investigation of, and conclusions concerning, the pre-literary history of the formation of the Pentateuch is a knowledge of his view as to the nature and social form of Israel in the pre-monarchic period in which he places the decisive stages of this process, that is, the so-called twelve-tribe 'amphictyony'.[35] Equally important, however, was his assessment of the source analysis of the Pentateuchal literature which is in some respects distinctively different from the prevailing view up to that time and which, especially in its conclusions concerning the relationship between the Pentateuch and the Former Prophets, became widely influential.

The literary-critical problem of the Pentateuch

Noth's discussion of this in his *History of Pentateuchal Traditions*[36] was anticipated by important conclusions already arrived at in two earlier works. The first of these was his commentary on Joshua, published in the same year as von Rad's monograph.[37] Whereas von Rad still thought in terms of a Hexateuch, Noth broke radically with such a view and argued that the literary history of the book of Joshua is not to be understood in connection with the Pentateuchal sources. Rather, it was a creation of a Deuteronomistic author who employed older sources, none of which can be related to the J, E, or P documents of the Pentateuch. The original book of Joshua comprised chapters 1–12 and 23 of the present book; the remaining material (chapters 13–22 and 24) was added in subsequent stages of expansion. The presence of P material was limited to chapter 21 and a few other brief additions, but these were redactional additions to an already existing book and cannot be regarded as part of the original Priestly narrative of the Pentateuch. In a subsequent work, *The Deuteronomistic History* published in 1943,[38] Noth went further and denied the presence of any P material in Joshua. In this book he

---

[35] See above, pp. 58–60.　　　　[36] *ÜGP* 4–44; Eng. trans., 5–41.
[37] M. Noth, *Das Buch Josua*, HAT 1/7 (Tübingen 1938).
[38] Id., *Überlieferungsgeschichtliche Studien* (Tübingen 1943); Eng. trans., *The Deuteronomistic History*, JSOT Supplement Series, 15 (Sheffield 1981).

argued his well-known view that the corpus Deuteronomy–2 Kings is the work of a Deuteronomist author who lived during the exilic period in Judah and wrote his history of Israel on the basis of numerous sources which he assembled and knit together with his own literary insertions. Contrary to the prevailing view hitherto, therefore, Noth denied that there ever was a Hexateuch; the sources J, E, and P do not continue beyond the end of Deuteronomy.

Does this mean that neither J nor E nor P originally contained an account of the settlement of Israel in Canaan? In an appendix to his work of 1943 Noth argued that P did not contain such an account and that the Priestly author ended his narrative with the record of the death of Moses in Deuteronomy 34: 1, 7–9.[39] None of the material between Numbers 27: 12–23 (P) and Deuteronomy 34: 1, 7–9, some of which concerns preparation for entry into the land, can be ascribed to P. The passage describing the appointment of Joshua as Moses's successor (Num. 27: 15–23) says nothing of Joshua's role in the future settlement and the division of the land among the tribes. Such passages in Numbers 10–26 as can be ascribed to P show a similar lack of real interest in the settlement. In several passages, for example Numbers 13–14 and 20: 1–13, punishment for offences is described in terms of non-entrance to the promised land. But this cannot be regarded as a positive interest in the settlement as such. In short, it seems that for the original Priestly narrative, the climax of God's dealings with his people was reached at Sinai and it is on the revelation at Sinai that P is most expansive. The narrative ended with a record of the death of the two main figures of the Sinai revelation, Aaron (Num. 20: 22–9) and Moses (Num. 27: 12 ff. + Deut. 34: 1, 7–9) with no positive interest in the events of the settlement which followed.

On the other hand, the older Pentateuchal material (JE) was certainly greatly interested in the entry into and possession of the promised land. This can be seen in, for example, the dominant place which the promise of the land occupies in the J and E material in Genesis. Further, material belonging to these older sources in the book of Numbers (e.g. 14: 23, 24; 21: 21–32; 32: 1, 2, 5, 16, 39–42) is concerned with preparation for the settlement in the land. That we no

---

[39] Id., 'Die "Priesterschrift" und die Redaktion des Pentateuch', in *Überlieferungsgeschichtliche Studien*, 180–216; Eng. trans. in *The Chronicler's History*, JSOT Supplement Series, 50 (Sheffield 1987), 107–47.

longer have either the Yahwist[40] or the Elohist accounts of the settlement has arisen from the stage at which these (already combined)
sources were united with P. In this, P, which did not share their interest in the settlement, was used as the framework. Hence the combined
JEP ended with the record of the death of Moses in Deuteronomy 34:
1, 7–9, just as it began with the Priestly account of creation in Genesis
1. That the P record of the death of Moses in Deuteronomy 34: 1, 7–9
is now at the end of this book arose at the stage when the Deuteronomistic corpus was united with the already existing JEP corpus.
According to Noth, therefore, the stages in the redaction of the
Pentateuch were somewhat different from what most earlier commentators had believed. That J and E were first combined is agreed;
but the next stage was not the combination of JE with D (R^{JED}) but
R^{JEP} and subsequently the combination of this with the Deuteronomistic History in Deuteronomy–2 Kings. It may be added, however, with regard to this final stage, that Noth did not subscribe to the
concept of a Deuteronomistic redaction of the material in JEP, but
described a number of additions to this material as being in the *style*
of the Deuteronomistic corpus.[41]

That P formed the framework for the redaction of JE was taken up
and freshly emphasized by Noth in his discussion of the literary criticism of the Pentateuch in his *History of Pentateuchal Traditions*,
which in this respect adds nothing essentially new to the conclusions
he had already arrived at in his commentary on Joshua and *The
Deuteronomistic History*. He also emphasized, however, that P was a
narrative work the main interest of which was a portrayal of the establishment of the legitimate cult at Sinai (Exod. 25–31; 35–40; Lev. 8–9)
and the constitution of the community of the twelve tribes (Num.
1–9). A careful distinction is therefore to be maintained between this
original P narrative and the great amount of secondary material
which has been added secondarily to it, some of it having been added
not simply to P but to the completed Pentateuch. The siglum P^S
should be reserved for material which can be shown to have been
added strictly to the *independent* P narrative; it is quite inaccurate to
describe the many other later passages in the style of P with this

---

[40] Noth also rejected the view that Judges 1 preserves a J account of the settlement
or part thereof. Cf. his *Überlieferungsgeschichtliche Studien*, 211; Eng. trans. in *The
Chronicler's History*, 140. Cf. also *ÜGP* 35 n. 127; Eng. trans. 33 n. 127.

[41] Cf. *ÜGP* 32 f. and Eng. trans., 30 f. nn. 106, 109, 112, 113, 114; *ÜGP* 35 and Eng.
trans., 32 f. n. 126.

siglum.[42] Noth also rejected the attempts to find separate stages in
the prehistory of the composition of P, such as von Rad had proposed
with his P[A] and P[B]. 'The various kinds of structural irregularities
must be traced rather to the fact that frequently traditions which were
more or less firmly formed previous to the P narrative itself have been
absorbed into it.'[43] Viewed as a whole and in its parts 'such an entity
[the P narrative] resists separation into several, originally independent narratives and presents itself rather as the work of one man with
a definite plan and distinct views, who integrated the appropriated
Vorlagen into the total work and used them as materials subordinated
to his purposes. It is quite in keeping with the usual practice in the
narrative literature of the Old Testament that secondary materials
were added to this entity from time to time.'[44]

Though he adhered to the view that J and E once existed as independent documents with much in common in both structure and content, Noth rejected any suggestion that the one was composed in
direct dependence upon the other; the many differences between
them render this improbable. Rather, the resemblances between them
are to be explained by postulating a common basis (*Grundlage*) from
which both drew the nucleus of their content independently of one
another.[45] This *Grundlage* (= G) came into existence in the pre-
monarchic period and in it the really decisive stages in the formation
of the Pentateuch were accomplished.

The Origin of the Pentateuch

The creation of G was not due to an 'author' or series of 'authors';
rather, it emerged, developed, and was transmitted through the
mouths of 'narrators' in the amphictyonic period and primarily on
those occasions when the tribes through their representatives and pilgrims were assembled at the cultic centres. By this means originally
local traditions pertaining to this or that individual tribe or clan
acquired an 'all-Israelite orientation'. Noth left open the question
whether G was written or oral. That it did not contain any primeval
history is already evident from the fact that no E material can be
detected in Genesis I–II. But the remaining major 'themes' of the
Pentateuch were brought together in the process of the creation of

[42] *ÜGP* 9 and Eng. trans., 10 n. 15.
[44] *ÜGP* 10 f.; Eng. trans., 11.
[43] *ÜGP* 9; Eng. trans., 10.
[45] *ÜGP* 40–3; Eng. trans., 38–41.

G. These 'themes' are, in the order in which Noth believed them to have been united, the Guidance out of Egypt, the Guidance into the Arable Land, the Promise to the Patriarchs, the Guidance in the Wilderness, the Revelation at Sinai. Each 'theme' had its basis in an essential core of traditions—for example, the theme 'Guidance out of Egypt' in originally hymnic confessions that Yahweh brought Israel forth from the land of Egypt—which became elaborated in narrative form. This in turn led to the incorporation of other traditional elements which had not been directly related to the core tradition or only loosely so. By such means each 'theme' was filled out and enriched. Finally, these 'themes' were gradually interwoven. In some more detail, the process which led to the creation of G was as follows.[46]

Its crystallization point was the confession that Yahweh brought Israel forth from Egypt; this confession existed from the earliest times in hymnic form and is found in such form in numerous different contexts. The nucleus of this tradition was, according to Noth, the 'miracle at the sea' and the previous actions of God against the Egyptians formed but the prelude to this final decisive action. How did this tradition become an 'all-Israelite' tradition? Noth rejected the frequently made suggestion that the central Palestinian tribes Joseph and Benjamin were those which had been in bondage in Egypt. The dominant role of these tribes in the Pentateuchal narrative is due only to the way in which the emerging Pentateuchal narrative G was moulded very largely by these latter tribes in whose territory the central sanctuaries of the tribal confederation of Israel lay. Those who had been in Egypt did not constitute any one or two particular tribes; rather, they were absorbed throughout the tribes as a whole as these emerged and took shape on the soil of Canaan. After their escape from Egypt, the clans which had been enslaved there made their way to the borders of Canaan, there to rejoin the semi-nomadic clans with whom they may have been previously connected. They brought with them the news of their miraculous deliverance which so moved those with whom they met up that the story was passed on everywhere and transmitted to their descendants. In this way this basic confession was already the common property of the numerous clans which subsequently came together to constitute Israel. That is, this confession acquired an all-Israelite orientation at the earliest possible moment.

[46] For details see *ÜGP* 48–67; Eng. trans., 46–62.

Besides its formulation in hymnic style, this confession would have been elaborated into an extended narrative, especially on occasions of cultic assemblies when men skilled in narrative art would have recited the substance of this faith over and over again. In addition to its main subject—the destruction of the Egyptians at 'the Sea'—the sojourn of the Israelites in Egypt, their subjection to slave labour and their eventual flight from bondage would also have belonged to the indispensable and fixed stock of narrative motifs, which could be further enriched according to the skill of the particular narrator. Thus the exodus narrative became the first stage in the emergence of G.

Noth pointed to many texts in which the confession that Yahweh brought Israel forth from Egypt is followed by the statement that he led them into the land of Canaan (e.g. Lev. 25: 38; Deut. 4: 38; 6; 23; 26: 9; Josh. 24: 8; Judg. 2: 1; 6: 19; etc.). The exodus confession would itself have prompted the addition of this theme, for the entry into, and occupation of, the land in which the tribes now lived would have been viewed as the goal of the deliverance from Egypt.

Originally individual tribes or groups of tribes within Israel would have had their own occupation traditions recalling the particular manner and route in which they each came into possession of the territory in which they now dwelt. The confession that Yahweh guided them into the land would have been related in a rather general way to the celebration of the first-fruits at the feast of Weeks.[47] But the development of the theme of the settlement in the land would have required an all-Israelite tradition. Such a tradition is presupposed by the JE material. It is the same tradition as is presupposed in the first half of the book of Joshua, that is, the tradition of a route leading through southern transjordan and then across the lower Jordan. This tradition, reflected in the old aetiological stories in Joshua 2–9, initially belonged to the tribe of Benjamin. At a subsequent stage it was appropriated also by the House of Joseph which became closely associated with Benjamin in the life of the 'amphictyony', and then, because of the dominant influence of these central Palestinian tribes in the history of the tribal league, it would have become an all-Israelite tradition. Once again, cultic assemblies at the central sanctuaries would have been the occasion for the narration of this theme.

The next theme in the development of G was the inclusion of the

---

[47] Cf. *ÜGP* 55; Eng. trans., 52.

theme 'Promise to the Patriarchs'. The patriarchs in question are of
course Abraham, Isaac, and Jacob, though in accordance with his
understanding of Israelite origins Noth believed it probable that
there were originally other patriarchs; that is, many of the separate
clans and tribes would have had their own ancestral traditions. The
reason only these three have come to occupy a dominant place in the
Israelite tradition was due to the manner in which the original
Pentateuchal *Grundlage* was developed. Further, these three patriarchs were originally unrelated to each other. Their present relationships as father, son, and grandson arose because the traditions
relating to each of them acquired an all-Israelite orientation.

Following Alt, Noth believed the individual patriarchs to have
been clan leaders who were the recipients of divine promises of land.
Initially the descendants of these patriarchs who settled permanently
in Palestine celebrated the fulfilment of such promises, especially at
the sanctuaries in the territories where they settled. Thus the traditions concerning Abraham appear to have been located at the sanctuary at the 'terebinth of Mamre' in Hebron (cf. Gen. 13: 18; 18: 1 ff.),
those concerning Isaac at Beersheba (cf. Gen. 21: 22 ff.; 26: 23 ff.; 46:
1 ff.), and those concerning Jacob at Shechem (cf. Gen. 35: 4) and
Bethel (cf. Gen. 28: 11 ff.; 35: 1, 3, 6 ff.). At a later time such traditions
were adopted by the Israelite tribes which settled in the vicinity of
these sanctuaries and who believed the promises to these patriarchs
to have been fulfilled in their own occupation of the land. Thus the
divine promises given to these ancestors by their own clan deities
came to be associated with Yahweh. In a further stage of development these traditions acquired an all-Israelite significance. This
would have taken place when these traditions became associated with
the tradition of the occupation of the land by all Israel. This development was effected initially by the central Palestinian tribes, which
accounts for the fact that the figure of Jacob, the traditions about
whom were native to central Palestine and had their home at the
sanctuaries of Bethel and Shechem, became the father of Israel.
Initially, therefore, Jacob would have been the sole representative of
the patriarchs in the emergence of G.[48] Subsequently, however, the
figures of Abraham and Isaac were included. Noth suggested that
this probably came about when the southern Palestinian tribes,
among whom the traditions relating to Abraham and Isaac had their
home, began to influence the further development of G.

[48] *ÜGP* 60; Eng. trans., 56 f.

The addition of this theme had important consequences for the development of the Pentateuch. Most notably, it introduced the significant thread of 'promise and fulfilment' which binds together the entire work and thus provided a basis for theologizing its contents so that it became the witness to God's purposeful saving activity.

The fourth theme to be included in the developing Pentateuchal narrative G was that of the 'Guidance in the Wilderness'. In several summaries of the saving acts of Yahweh the wandering in the wilderness is included (e.g. Deut. 29: 4f.; Jer. 2: 6; Amos 2: 10; Ps. 136: 16). This theme arose simply from a desire to describe what happened to Israel after the exodus and before the settlement in the land. Hence the all-Israelite traditions of exodus and entry into Palestine are presupposed by this theme. According to Noth, it found a place in G under the influence of the southern tribes who lived in proximity to the desert and for whom therefore an interest in Israel's journey through the desert, with all the perils this would have entailed, would have been natural.

Noth accepted von Rad's view, on the basis of Deuteronomy 26: 5b–9 and related texts, that the Sinai tradition was developed and transmitted independently of the other major traditions of the Pentateuch and was not combined with them until a relatively late time. But he rejected von Rad's claim that its incorporation was the achievement of the Yahwist and argued instead that it was already united with the other themes in the formation of G.

According to Noth, the decisive revelation of Yahweh which formed the nucleus of the Sinai tradition may have taken place in the course of a pilgrimage by some semi-nomadic clans to Yahweh's holy mountain of Sinai. When, at a later time, the descendants of these clans became part of Israel, the Sinai tradition was handed down within the context of an all-Israelite covenant festival celebrated periodically at the central sanctuary of the 'amphictyony', initially at Shechem (cf. Josh. 24). In this way the Sinai tradition acquired an all-Israelite significance at a very early stage in the history of the confederacy.

Why was it then that a tradition of such fundamental importance for Israel did not find a place in G until the final stages of the development of this narrative? Noth argued as follows:

The evidence adduced suggests that the theme 'revelation at Sinai' comes out of a situation which, in a later era, seemed removed to a somewhat misty and distant past, for the reason that new events, institutions, and conceptions had pushed decisively to the fore in the meantime and now virtually dominated the field . . . It [sc. the Sinai tradition] remains so far in the background because the comparatively more recent themes of the 'guidance out of Egypt' and the 'guidance into the arable land' had such a strong attraction as the basis of faith and election and, being newer, held the field.[49]

In view of the probability that the southern tribes influenced the development of the later stages in the emergence of G, it was probably under their influence that the Sinai theme was added to it.

The development of G comprised not merely the narrative formulation of these themes alongside each other, but also their elaboration and enrichment by the incorporation of a great diversity of traditional materials in the course of the repeated narration of the themes over the years, and also the gradual growing together of the themes. To the process of elaboration and enrichment belonged, for example, the inclusion of the plagues narratives, further materials concerning the patriarchs, episodes concerning the conquest, stories about thirst, hunger and enemies in the wilderness, the desert murmurings of the people, and so forth. The development of materials concerning, for example, the figure of Moses also belonged to this process, so that Moses, the original tradition concerning whom was that of his grave, became associated first with the theme of guidance into the land and then with the themes of guidance out of Egypt, guidance in the wilderness, and the revelation at Sinai. With regard to the gradual merging of the themes with each other, the presence of Moses in four of them would have been a significant contribution. Important too were various genealogies and itineraries. In addition Noth pointed to processes of 'bracketing' whereby these themes became merged. For example, with the story of Moses's flight to the Midianites (Exod. 2: 11 ff.), and his subsequent initial encounter with God there (Exod. 3: 1 ff.), later themes immediately enter very significantly into that of the guidance out of Egypt. What is foreshadowed here is the story of the meeting with the Midianites at the 'mountain of God' (Exod. 18), which belongs to the theme of guidance in the wilderness, and probably also the theme of revelation at Sinai, for it was probably because this 'mountain of God' was at a secondary stage identified with Sinai that the joining of the theme of revelation at Sinai with that of the guidance in the wilderness was facilitated.

The theme of 'promise to the patriarchs', however, shows evidence of having been much less blended with those that follow in the Pentateuch. In fact it is only in the traditio-historically late passage

---

[49] *ÜGP* 65 f.; Eng. trans., 61.

Genesis 15 that such a blending is to be seen. 'The blending of themes is present here to the extent that the event of covenant making, together with the phenomena of fire and smoke indicating the presence of God and probably the whole idea of a covenant between God and man, are derived from the Sinai theophany.'[50] This can only mean, according to Noth, that Genesis 15 presupposes the completion of the basic structure of G, the last stage in the creation of which was the incorporation of the theme of revelation at Sinai.

The story of Joseph and his brothers is also traditio-historically a latecomer into G.[51] It already presupposes the tradition of Jacob's migration to Egypt with his family and thus the two themes of promise to the patriarchs and guidance out of Egypt. But it is only very loosely connected with each of these, for it has no substantive relations to the patriarchal theme proper, whilst its connection with the theme of guidance out of Egypt consists merely in the statement in Exodus 1: 18 that there arose a king in Egypt who did not know Joseph. That Joseph is the central figure in this story is to be explained on the grounds that it originated in the House of Joseph; that is, we have here a further instance of the influence of the central Palestinian tribes upon the formation of G. Within the context of G the Joseph narrative functioned as a connecting piece between the themes of promise to the patriarchs and guidance out of Egypt.

The Documentary Sources of the Tetrateuch

In accordance with his intention to investigate the whole process of the origin and development of the Pentateuch, Noth returned in the final parts of his work to the literary sources J, E, and P. With these sources the Pentateuchal narrative attained final formulations, in each case in a particular individual linguistic and stylistic form. This means that each of these sources was the work of one single author. Noth rejected the older view that these sources are the works of 'schools' of narrators, arguing that such a view made great demands on the formal consistency of the works of individual authors and did not take into account sufficiently the fact of their dependence upon longer and more complex older tradition.[52] Because of the fragmentary nature of the E material which has been preserved, it is of course impossible to demonstrate with any certainty that it derived from a

[50] *ÜGP* 218; Eng. trans., 200.   [51] *ÜGP* 226–32; Eng. trans., 208–13.
[52] Cf. *ÜGP* 245 and Eng. trans., 208 n. 601.

single author; we can only assume it on the analogy of the two other sources. But in the case of J, 'this is true beyond any doubt in view of the unique theological grounding and structure of the whole . . . and it is likewise true in the case of P'.[53]

From the foregoing survey it is clear that Noth did not share von Rad's view of the creative contribution of the Yahwist. Though the interweaving of the themes brings us close to the stage of the oldest literary fixations, it remains the case that this process took place very largely at the preliterary stage. Thus the Yahwist cannot be credited with the incorporation of the Sinai tradition and the further working out of the patriarchal traditions, as von Rad proposed, since this had already been accomplished in the formation of G. Noth agreed with von Rad, however, that the Yahwist was responsible for prefacing his narration of the saving history with the primeval history, which 'involves a tremendous expansion of the horizon through the alignment of Israel's prehistory with the grand sweep of the history of mankind as a whole'.[54] It is above all the theological portrayal of mankind as alienated from God and in his whole being disobedient to God that runs through the primeval history.

This portrayal then constitutes the appropriate background for the overall interpretation of the transmitted material of the Pentateuchal narrative as given in the introductory verses Gen. 12: 1–3, a passage formulated by J. Here the Pentateuchal narrative is viewed as a 'history of salvation' (*Heilsgeschichte*), that is, the narration of a concrete divine action in history which aims toward a still future blessing of 'all the clans of the inhabited earth,' in other words, the whole of mankind, and which employs Israel as the instrument of that saving action.[55]

Thus 'the entire weight of the theology of J rests upon the beginning of his narrative . . . It sufficed for him to have said plainly at the beginning how he intended to understand everything beyond that' (ibid.).

Noth accepted the usual view that J originated in Judah, but saw difficulties in determining its time of origin with any certainty. It is possible that it was composed in the Davidic–Solomonic period; the flowering of cultural and spiritual life of that time would certainly have provided a matrix for the theological achievement of the Yahwist. Nevertheless, the lack of any clear references to this period in J's narrative counsels caution and thus the possibility remains that J derived from a later period.

---

[53] *ÜGP* 245; Eng. trans., 228.   [54] *ÜGP* 256; Eng. trans., 237.
[55] *ÜGP* 256 f.; Eng. trans., 237.

That there are no E elements in the primeval history shows that its author adhered more strictly than the Yahwist to the tradition as shaped in G. The fragments that remain of E afford only a partial glimpse of its author's theology, but some texts afford a glimpse of what this might have been. Texts such as Genesis 15: 13–16* and 50: 20b suggest at least one basic theme essential for E. This is 'that God had directed the prehistory of Israel, from the migration of Abraham into the promised land and on, toward the goal of the Israelite tribes' occupation of the land with an overruling purpose which surpassed the often shortsighted intentions and ideas of the persons involved. And God had indicated this purpose at the outset to the chosen Abraham in a mysterious manner without mention of any concrete names.'[56] The E narrative could have been committed to writing relatively late, notwithstanding its close adherence to G, which would still have been transmitted even in the period of literary fixations. On the other hand, cogent arguments against dating it to the Davidic–Solomonic period are lacking. The customary view that E was of north Israelite provenance is not as well founded as is usually supposed. For example, the inclusion in it of such distinctly southern Palestinian materials as Genesis 22 and Exodus 18 suggest a southern provenance.

That P was composed in the period after Deuteronomy was regarded by Noth as firmly established. The first part of the exilic period provides the upper limit for its composition; this would explain, for example, the importance P attached to such non-cultic observances as the Sabbath and circumcision (Gen. 2: 2 f.; 17: 10 ff.). But how much later than the exile P was composed must remain open, again for lack of any concrete indications. Noth subscribed to the view that it was composed among southern circles, but whether in the Judaean home-land itself or in Babylon must also remain an open question. P has shaped the whole Pentateuchal narrative anew from the standpoint of his particular intentions. Noth considered it strongly probable that the author of P had before him a form of the J narrative, which had already been expanded by the incorporation of elements from E. A further important literary *Vorlage* of this author was a 'Toledoth Book', a collection of genealogies which originally probably extended from Adam to the sons of Jacob and Esau. From these two *Vorlagen*, the JE narrative and this 'Toledoth Book', was derived the skeleton of the P narrative and on this basis the author planned his narrative and formulated it in his own distinctive literary manner.

[56] *ÜGP* 256; Eng. trans., 236.

According to Noth this author set a new limit for the narrative by omitting the theme 'Guidance into the Arable Land' which was evidently of no importance for him. Although the customary designation of this source as the 'Priestly Narrative' is justified and it seems likely that its author was a priest, 'this should not mislead us into regarding P as a distinctly priestly work'.[57] The 'spirit of his literary work is not unconditionally priestly, if it may be assumed that one of the characteristic marks of the priestly spirit is that an existing scheme of cultic institutions and orders is regarded as something absolutely legitimate, sacrosanct, and therefore inviolable and unchangeable' (ibid.). Noth argues that P is not in fact exclusively oriented toward a historically given body of cultic matters. 'Rather, from the standpoint of particular basic theological conceptions, he envisions an "ideal" cultic order by portraying it as having been realized at one time in remote antiquity', that is, at Sinai the revelation at which marks the climax of the Priestly narrative.[58]

IV

Notwithstanding the differences between their conclusions, the contributions of von Rad and Noth remain the most comprehensive attempt to account for the origins and composition of the Pentateuch.[59] Their deployment and refinement of form-critical and traditio-historical research carried further the labours of earlier scholars such as Gunkel and Alt to such an extent as to transform our understanding of the origin and growth of the Pentateuch and of the transmission and development of the distinctive religious and theological traditions that gave rise to it and which it reflects. What they achieved was not only widely influential but set the agenda for further research during the subsequent decades. They themselves contributed significantly to this. From von Rad came his commentaries on Genesis and Deuteronomy,[60] and his substantial discussion of the theology of the Hexateuch in his *Old Testament Theology*. Noth

---

[57] *ÜGP* 260; Eng. trans., 240.   [58] *ÜGP* 260 ff.; Eng. trans., 240 ff.

[59] On this see the comments of Douglas Knight, 'The Pentateuch', in Douglas A. Knight and Gene M. Tucker (eds.), *The Hebrew Bible and its Modern Interpreters* (Chico, Calif. 1985), 263–96 (see esp. 265 ff.).

[60] G. von Rad, *Das fünfte Buch Mose, Deuteronomium, übersetz und erklärt*, ATD 8 (Göttingen 1964); Eng. trans., *Deuteronomy* (London 1966). See also his earlier monograph *Deuteronomium-Studien*, FRLANT 58 (Göttingen 1947); Eng. trans., *Studies in Deuteronomy* (London 1953).

wrote commentaries on Exodus, Numbers, and Leviticus,[61] and published his *History of Israel*[62] which reflects the results he had achieved in his Pentateuchal research. Von Rad's association of the Yahwist with the period of the united monarchy, and thus a dating of a century or so earlier than most scholars had hitherto suggested, gained further support and widespread acceptance. His view of the theology of the Yahwist stimulated other studies of the 'kerygma' not only of J, but of the Elohist and the Priestly writer.[63]

From the early 1960s, however, critical re-examination and rejection of vital aspects of the work of both von Rad and Noth gathered momentum with the result that the synthesis which their combined research offered gradually collapsed. Increasingly, for example, it was agreed that the so-called 'little historical creeds' in such passages as Deuteronomy 26 and Joshua 24 were not the ancient formulations that von Rad had argued, but were most likely Deuteronomic compositions of the late pre-exilic or the exilic period presupposing an already well-developed Pentateuchal tradition. That is, such brief recapitulations of the story of Israel's origins probably stand much more towards the end of the development of the Pentateuch than at its beginnings.[64] The undermining of von Rad's theory of an ancient

---

[61] M. Noth, *Das zweite Buch Mose, Exodus, übersetz und erklärt*, ATD 5 (Göttingen 1959); Eng. trans., *Exodus* (London 1962); id., *Das dritte Buch Mose, Leviticus, übersetz und erklärt*, ATD 6 (Göttingen 1962); Eng. trans., *Leviticus* (London 1965); id., *Das vierte Buch Mose, Numeri, übersetz und erklärt*, ATD 7 (Göttingen 1959); Eng. trans., *Numbers* (London 1968).

[62] M. Noth, *Geschichte Israels* (Göttingen 1950); Eng. trans., *The History of Israel* (2nd edn., London 1958).

[63] Cf. H. W. Wolff, 'Das Kerygma das Jahwisten', *EvTh* 24 (1964), 73–93, repr. in his *Gesammelte Studien zum Alten Testament* (Munich 1964), 345–73, and see also W. Brueggemann and H. W. Wolff, *The Vitality of Old Testament Traditions* (Atlanta 1978), which also includes an English translation of Wolff's article.

[64] Significant discussions of the so-called 'creed' in Deuteronomy 26: 5b–9 and related passages came from C. H. W. Brekelmans, 'Het "historische Credo" van Israel', *TvT* 3 (1963), 1–11; L. Rost, 'Das kleine geschichtliche Credo', in his *Das kleine Credo und andere Studien zum Alten Testament* (Heidelberg 1965), 11–25; W. Richter, 'Beobachtungen zur theologische Systembildung in der alt. Literature anhand des "kleinen geschichtlichen Credo"', in L. Scheffczyk (ed.), *Wahrheit und Verkündigung, Festschrift für M. Schmaus* (Paderborn 1967), 191–5; J. P. Hyatt, 'Were there an Ancient Historical Credo in Israel and an Independent Sinai Tradition?', in H. Thomas Frank and W. L. Reed (eds.), *Translating and Understanding the Old Testament: Essays in Honour of H. G. May* (New York 1970), 152–70; N. Lohfink, 'Zum "kleinen geschichtlichen Credo" Dtn. 26: 5–9', *ThPh* 46 (1971), 19–39. These scholars argued that the passage is either entirely or substantially a late composition from a Deuteronomic author. For a discussion see E. W. Nicholson, *Exodus and Sinai in History and Tradition* (Oxford 1973), 20–6.

Israelite 'credo' as the framework of the Yahwist's work has not been the least among the impulses towards the current new chapter in Pentateuchal research which has also been critical of other important aspects of von Rad's work, especially his early dating of the Yahwist.[65]

Most significant, however, was the eventual abandonment of Noth's theory of Israelite origins and, closely related to this, of pre-monarchical Israel as a so-called 'amphictyony'.[66] The importance of such a picture of early Israel for Pentateuchal research during the middle decades of this century can scarcely be overstated. It also contributed significantly to the continuing consensus on the Documentary Theory, since the Pentateuchal sources, especially the earliest documents J and E, could be seen in important ways to be the deposit of traditions, whether written or oral or both, of the pre-monarchical period. This had the additional effect of vindicating the dating of these sources to an early period in the pre-exilic period, and also lent added credibility to von Rad's assignment of the work of the Yahwist to a time as early as the reign of Solomon in the tenth century. The abandonment of the theory of an 'amphictyony', however, removed the matrix in which, it was widely believed, the Pentateuchal traditions developed and, indeed, as Noth and von Rad in their different ways argued, the very form of the Pentateuch or Hexateuch itself took shape. With this has also come a distinct waning in the attempt to penetrate behind the text of the Pentateuch to the history of the traditions it embodies or to the oral stages of the transmission of individual narratives or 'cycles' of narratives. Recent research, as we shall see, has been predominantly concerned with the literary history of the Pentateuch.

There have been more direct influences towards the current renewed debate about the Pentateuch among which special mention must be made of Lothar Perlitt's incisive study *Covenant Theology in the Old Testament*,[67] which reversed opinion on the early origin of the

---

[65] It may also be noted that the so-called 'Biblical Theology Movement' of the post-war years found the documentary theory very 'user-friendly' (cf. e.g. G. E. Wright and Reginald Fuller, *The Book of the Acts of God* (London 1960)). The demise of this movement is also part of the background to the new period of Pentateuchal research.

[66] For a discussion of the main issues see e.g. A. D. H. Mayes, *Israel in the Period of the Judges* (London 1974).

[67] L. Perlitt, *Bundestheologie im Alten Testament*, WMANT 36 (Neukirchen 1969). Cf. A. de Pury and T. Römer, 'Le Pentateuque en question: Position du problème et brève histoire de la recherche', in A. de Pury (ed.), *Le Pentateuque en question: Les origines et la composition des cinq premiers livres de la Bible à la lumière des recherches récentes* (Geneva 1989), 49–50.

covenant, tracing its formulation instead to Deuteronomic circles of the late pre-exilic period. From the point of view of our present purpose, the significance of Perlitt's work was in bringing into the foreground once more the contribution of Deuteronomic and Deuteronomistic editors to the composition and redaction of the Tetrateuch. Although a number of scholars had already reopened this issue,[68] his work served to put it still more decidedly on the agenda of Pentateuchal research and, as we shall see, it has become a marked feature of recent studies.

It is against this background that a number of distinguished scholars during the past thirty years or so have reopened in a vigorous manner the question of Pentateuchal origins, challenging not only earlier results but also the methods employed in arriving at them, and offering new approaches and solutions.[69] No new consensus has emerged and no theory has yet attracted such support as to constitute a new 'school'. The debate seems wide open, and the methods employed and the results achieved are in some cases irreconcilable.

Pentateuchal research since Wellhausen has never been at rest, and each generation has debated new theories and defended old ones. In an essay more than seventy years ago on 'The Present Position of Old Testament Criticism' J. E. McFadyen wrote: 'today less than ever can the Pentateuchal problem be considered as closed'.[70] Twenty-five years later C. R. North echoed this of the period he was reviewing.[71] The same statement can be made without qualification or fear of dissent in the 1990s. There is a difference today, however, for

---

[68] Notably N. Lohfink, *Das Hauptgebot. Eine Untersuchung literarischer Einleitungsfragen zu Dtn 5–11*, Analecta Biblica, 20 (Rome 1963), 121–4; C. H. W. Brekelmans, 'Die sogenannten deuteronomischen Elemente in Genesis bis Numeri. Ein Beitrag zur Vorgeschichte des Deuteronomiums', SVT 15 (1966), 90–6; 'Éléments Deutéronomiques dans le Pentateuque', *Recherches Bibliques*, 8 (Bruges 1967), 77–91.

[69] For comprehensive surveys and bibliographies see Herbert Schmid, *Die Gestalt des Mose: Probleme alttestamentlicher Forschung unter Berüchsichtigung der Pentateuchkrise*, Erträge der Forschung, 237 (Darmstadt 1986); S. J. De Vries, 'A Review of Recent Research in the Tradition History of the Pentateuch', in SBL Seminar Papers (1987), 459–502; de Pury and Römer, 'Le Pentateuque en question', 9–80. C. Houtman, *Inleiding in de Pentateuch* (Kampen 1980); *Der Pentateuch: Die Geschichte seiner Erforschung neben einer Auswertung* (2nd edn., Kampen 1994). More general but helpful is J. Blenkinsopp, *The Pentateuch: An Introduction to the First Five Books of the Bible* (London 1992), ch. 1.

[70] J. E. McFadyen, 'The Present Position of Old Testament Criticism', in A. S. Peake (ed.), *The People and the Book* (Oxford 1925), 183–219 (the quotation is on pp. 194 f.).

[71] C. R. North, 'Pentateuchal Criticism', in H. H. Rowley (ed.), *The Old Testament and Modern Study* (Oxford 1951), 48–83 (see esp. p. 48).

whereas both these scholars and other reviewers of Pentateuchal research up to relatively recently[72] could justifiably claim that the Documentary Theory in its essentials remained fundamentally unshaken, contemporary research is characterized by a call for an abandonment or at best a radical revision of its main features. Such are the varied and conflicting new theories and the new 'paradigms' of Pentateuchal origins that, to use a further quotation from McFadyen's essay, 'Everywhere uncertainties abound, and, like the dove after the Deluge, we seem to find no solid ground anywhere for the sole of our foot' (p. 218).

In Part II of this book, which now follows, I offer a critical review of this recent research.

---

[72] For example, R. E. Clements, 'Pentateuchal Problems', in G. W. Anderson (ed.), *Tradition and Interpretation: Essays by Members of the Society for Old Testament Study* (Oxford 1979), 96–124.

PART II

The Problem of the Pentateuch
in Current Research

4

The Theory Under Attack: Rolf Rendtorff's
New Paradigm of the Origin of the Pentateuch

As late as the early 1970s, that is, virtually a century after Wellhausen's presentation of it, the Documentary Theory of the composition of the Pentateuch remained firmly in place among the majority of Old Testament scholars. There were still dissenting voices, as there always had been. For example, in 1965, Frederick Winnett, in his presidential address to the Society of Biblical Literature in New York, declared his conviction that 'much of what is told us about the Pentateuch in *Introductions to the Old Testament* stands in need of considerable revision', and he went on to outline ways in which he believed this to be so.[1] Writing a few years later, however, a leading British Old Testament scholar, Ronald Clements, in his contribution to a volume of essays under the auspices of the Society for Old Testament Study, could confidently reaffirm as the *opinio communis* that 'the analysis of the Pentateuch into its constituent literary sources has remained a primary feature of study, so that fresh insights and methods of approach must be regarded as supplementing, rather than replacing, it'. That was in 1974.[2] By the end of the decade, however, and continuing throughout the 1980s and into the present decade, one major study after another, like a series of hammer blows, has rejected the main claims of the Documentary Theory and the criteria on the basis of which they were argued. Winnett's view,[3] for which he expected few if any converts (p. 19), is now in the driving-seat, so to speak, and those who adhere to the

---

[1] F. V. Winnett, 'Re-examining the Foundations', *JBL* 84 (1965), 2. This article contains modifications to Winnett's earlier study *The Mosaic Tradition* (Toronto 1949) in which he had already moved away from the Documentary Theory, for example, in rejecting the view that E was an originally independent source.

[2] Clements' survey was written in 1974, though various mishaps delayed the publication of the volume in which it is included until 1979: 'Pentateuchal Problems', in G. W. Anderson (ed.), *Tradition and Interpretation: Essays by Members of the Society for Old Testament Study* (Oxford 1979), 96–124. The quotation is on p. 99.

[3] See below, Ch. 5, pp. 132–4.

Documentary Theory are very much on the defensive. As a result, Pentateuchal research since the mid-1970s has become a mirror image of what it was in the years following the publication of Wellhausen's study of the composition of the Pentateuch in the mid-1870s: whereas at that time the Documentary Theory which he had so persuasively argued was in the ascendant, commanding ever increasing support, today it is in sharp decline—some would say in a state of advanced *rigor mortis*—and new solutions are being argued and urged in its place.

We cannot speak of a 'school', however, for though some recognize mutual debts to each other, there are fundamental differences between them both in method and in results. Rolf Rendtorff, Gerhard von Rad's successor at Heidelberg and one of the leading German Old Testament scholars during the second half of this century, presses for a thorough traditio-historical approach, that is, the investigation of the gradual growth from smaller units to larger and still larger complexes (e.g. the patriarchal narrative in Genesis 12–50) which were united only at a final stage, when each individual complex was virtually complete in itself, to form the Pentateuch.[4] On this understanding of the formation of the Pentateuch, the earlier notion of expansive narratives composed by individual creative authors such as the 'Yahwist' is ruled out.

In contrast to Rendtorff, however, stand such scholars as John Van Seters, Sven Tengström, and Norman Whybray who have re-emphasized the creative role of authors in the formation and composition of the Pentateuch. They reject not only the concept of the formation of a Pentateuchal *Grundlage* that evolved gradually through 'narrators' at cultic assemblies, such as Noth suggested, but also Rendtorff's similar notion of the piecemeal emergence of tradition complexes. Such an approach to the formation of the Pentateuch as he has argued cannot realistically account for the sort of intellectual and

---

[4] R. Rendtorff, *Das überlieferungsgeschichtliche Problem des Pentateuch*, BZAW 147 (Berlin 1977); Eng. trans., *The Problem of the Process of Transmission in the Pentateuch*, JSOT Supplement Series, 89 (Sheffield 1990). An earlier outline of his approach and conclusions was published as 'Der "Yahwist" als Theologe. Zum Delemma der Pentateuchkritik', SVT 28 (1975), 158–66; Eng. trans., 'The "Yahwist" as Theologian? The Dilemma of Pentateuchal Criticism', *JSOT* 3 (1977), 2–10; id., *Das Alte Testament: Eine Einfuhrung* (Neukirchen-Vluyn 1983), 166–74; Eng. trans., *The Old Testament: An Introduction* (London 1986), 157–64. Rendtorff has received some limited support from E. Blum (see below), *Die Komposition der Vätergeschichte*, WMANT 57 (Neukirchen 1984).

creative endeavour necessary for the writing of such literature.[5] Rather, according to Van Seters and Whybray, whether in the case of the Tetrateuch or the Deuteronomistic History a more illuminating 'model' for understanding their composition is provided by the work of the Greek historians such as Herodotus.

Van Seters, Tengström, and Whybray are by no means at one, however, in their conclusions. Van Seters and Tengström argue a 'supplementary' theory—each differing widely from the other, however, in what is considered to be the original narrative that has been supplemented—whilst Whybray's view is that the Tetrateuch substantially as we have it was composed by a single author who employed many different sources at his disposal to which he added material composed by himself. That is, Whybray seems to argue something approaching a 'fragment' hypothesis.

With few exceptions, the predominant trend has been to date the beginnings of the composition of the Tetrateuch to the exilic period or even later.[6] The main impetus for this has come from Hans Heinrich Schmid's influential monograph, *The So-called Yahwist*,[7] which combines a critique of von Rad's dating of the Yahwist to the period of the so-called 'Solomonic Enlightenment' with a detailed examination of a number of key contexts in the Yahwist's narrative which, he argues, show the influence of literary forms and theological developments of much later times, for example the call narratives of the writing prophets of the eighth century onwards, the notion of the making of a covenant at Sinai, and especially various distinctive features of the Deuteronomistic corpus. As a result, Schmid brings the composition of J into proximity with that of the Deuteronomistic History in the exilic period. On this issue Van Seters, Whybray,

---

[5] J. Van Seters, *Abraham on History and Tradition* (New Haven 1975); id., *In Search of History. Historiography in the Ancient World and the Origins of Biblical History* (New Haven 1983); id., *Der Jahwist als Historiker* (Zürich 1987); id., *Prologue to History: The Yahwist as Historian in Genesis* (Louisville, Ky. 1992); id., *The Life of Moses: The Yahwist as Historian in Exodus–Numbers* (Kampen 1994); S. Tengström, *Die Hexateucherzählung. Eine literaturgeschichtliche Studie*, Coniectanea Biblica, Old Testament Series 7 (Lund 1976); R. N. Whybray, *The Making of the Pentateuch: A Methodological Study*, JSOT Monograph Series, 53 (Sheffield 1987).

[6] The main exceptions are S. Tengström, op. cit., who argues for an eleventh-century origin of a *Grunderzählung* which he believes can be isolated from Genesis–Joshua, and K. Berge, *Die Zeit des Jahwisten: Ein Beitrag zur Datierung jahwistischer Vätertexte*, BZAW 186 (Berlin 1990) who, concentrating on the patriarchal narratives, returns to a tenth-century dating for the Yahwist.

[7] H. H. Schmid, *Der sogenannte Jahwist: Beobachtungen und Fragen zur Pentateuchforschung* (Zürich 1976).

Hermann Vorländer (*The Origin of the Jehovistic History*)[8] and Martin Rose (*Studies in the Relationship between the Yahwistic and Deuteronomistic Writings*)[9] join ranks with Schmid, Whybray attributing the Tetrateuch substantially as we have it to this period. Hans-Christoph Schmitt, on the basis of a study of the story of Joseph (*The Non-priestly Joseph Story*),[10] suggests that an Elohistic author during the exilic period reworked disparate literary complexes from the pre-exilic period and that this work was subsequently supplemented by a Yahwistic editor ('Late J'). Somewhat similarly, more recently Christoph Levin in his book *The Yahwist*[11] has argued that the Yahwist is best understood as an exilic collector and redactor of pre-exilic *written* sources. The Dutch scholar Cees Houtman *Introduction to the Pentateuch*[12] argues that three originally independent components—Genesis, Exodus–Numbers, and Deuteronomy—each with its own prehistory were worked together in the sixth century BC to form the Pentateuch as part of a history which extended to the end of 2 Kings. Erhard Blum, who was a pupil of Rendtorff and, as we shall see, lends some support to the latter's conclusions, in his two monumental studies of the Pentateuch, *The Composition of the Patriarchal History* and *Studies in the Composition of the Pentateuch*,[13] argues that a Deuteronomistic redactor of the early post-exilic years reworked a pre-exilic 'history of the time of Moses', joining it with a (pre-Priestly) narrative of the patriarchs. This Deuteronomistic work (K^D) subsequently underwent a Priestly redaction (K^P) which gave us the Pentateuch substantially as we have it. For Blum, therefore, as for Rendtorff, the notion of continuous and originally independent sources such as J, E, and P must be abandoned.

Some of these scholars also argue that the pre-Priestly narrative of the Tetrateuch—in conventional terms, JE—was composed as a sort of prologue to the Deuteronomistic History, thus reversing the com-

---

[8] H. Vorländer, *Die Entstehungszeit des jehowistischen Geschichtswerkes* (Frankfurt am Main 1978).

[9] M. Rose, *Deuteronomist und Jahwist. Untersuchungen zu den Berührungspunkten beider Literaturwerke*, AThANT 67 (Zürich 1981).

[10] H.-C. Schmitt, *Die Nichtpriesterliche Josephsgeschichte: Ein Beitrag zur neuesten Pentateuchkritik*, BZAW 154 (Berlin 1980).

[11] C. Levin, *Der Yahwist*, FRLANT 157 (Göttingen 1993).

[12] C. Houtman, *Inleiding in de Pentateuch* (Kampen 1980); 2nd edn., *Der Pentateuch: Die Geschichte seiner Erforschung neben einer Auswertung* (Kampen 1994).

[13] E. Blum, *Die Komposition der Vätergeschichte*, WMANT 57 (Neukirchen 1984); id., *Studien zur Komposition des Pentateuch*, BZAW 189 (Berlin 1990).

mon view hitherto that the authors of Deuteronomy and of the Deuteronomistic History knew and presupposed JE. The majority opinion among them is also that neither the Elohistic or Priestly texts in the Pentateuch derive from originally independent narrative documents but are the work of editors and redactors.[14]

The main issues arising are thus a mixture of old and new, for example, the credibility of the well-known criteria for isolating the sources of the Pentateuch; whether E and P were originally discrete documents or derive from redactors; the nature and extent of Deuteronomic or Deuteronomistic redaction of JE; whether the notion of continuous sources such as are designated by J, E, P arises only from an ill-considered method and should now be abandoned in favour of a new approach; and whether the pre-P Tetrateuch was known to the Deuteronomic and Deuteronomistic writers or was composed subsequent to their work.

A convenient way of illustrating the results of recent research is in terms of the new 'paradigms' it has advanced of how the Pentateuch was composed.[15] In broad terms, two main paradigms have each been widely supported hitherto:

(1) According to the first, the sources J, E, and D continue beyond the Pentateuch into Joshua. That is, scholars favouring this analysis think in terms of a Hexateuch. Clearly, Wellhausen's conclusions favour this paradigm. We also include for convenience here, however, the view argued variously by others that to some extent at least these sources continue beyond Joshua into Judges, Samuel, and Kings.

(2) The second paradigm derives from Noth's influential work arguing that Deuteronomy and the Former Prophets are the work of a Deuteronomistic historian on the basis of numerous independent sources, that this corpus presupposed a JE narrative from creation to the settlement, but that the JE account of the settlement was excised when this narrative was subsequently combined with the Priestly narrative which, it is argued, never contained a settlement narrative.

---

[14] S. Tengström has devoted a separate monograph attempting to demonstrate this afresh in the case of P, *Die Toledotformel und die literarische Struktur der priesterlichen Erweiterungsschicht im Pentateuch*, Coniectanea Biblica, Old Testament Series 17 (Lund 1981). See below, Ch. 7.

[15] For this see S. Boorer, *The Promise of the Land as Oath: A Key to the Formation of the Pentateuch*, BZAW 205 (Berlin 1992), 7–33.

Recent research has added two further paradigms:

(3) There never was an independent Tetrateuch. Rather, the pre-P Tetrateuch was composed after, and perhaps as a 'prologue' to, the Deuteronomistic History, extending the story of Israel back from the eve of the settlement to the patriarchal age and providing also a primeval history beginning with creation. The Tetrateuch was thus composed as an extension of the Deuteronomistic History.

(4) The fourth paradigm is suggested by Rendtorff's conclusions: the Pentateuch is the creation of a Deuteronomic redactor who combined originally independent tradition complexes, arranging them sequentially into a history of Israel from the patriarchs to the settlement, a Priestly writer subsequently adding the primeval history.[16] On this view, the composition of the Pentateuch is best understood on the analogy of Deuteronomistic History, that is, the result of a combination and redaction of originally independent narratives.

It is with the theory represented by this latter paradigm that I begin a review, in this and the following chapters, of recent Pentateuchal research. It is not only a new but a radical theory, advocating the abandonment of the notion of continuous sources in the formation of the Pentateuch and rejecting the method and criteria on which these were based, and calling for a new approach based on a thorough form-critical investigation of the literature. According to Rendtorff, a proper understanding of the growth of the Pentateuch has been frustrated by a failure to perceive the unbridgeable differences between traditional literary criticism, which yielded the notion of continuous sources in the creation of the Pentateuch, and a form-critical approach to the literature. Scholars have been misled, he argues, into imagining that form criticism is simply an extension of the older method. Rather, the two methods are opposed to one another both in their starting-point and in their statement of the question. It is because scholars have failed fully to appreciate this distinction that the potential of form criticism for our understanding of the origin and composition of the Pentateuch has not been fully exploited.

---

[16] See also his 'L'histoire biblique des origines (Gen. 1–11) dans le contexte de la rédaction "sacerdotale" du Pentateuque', in A. de Pury (ed.), *Le Pentateuque en Question* (Geneva 1989), 83–94. Cf. also F. Crüsemann, 'Die Eigenständigkeit der Urgeschichte. Ein Beitrag zur Diskussion um den "Jahwisten"', in J. Jeremias and L. Perlitt (eds.), *Die Botschaft und die Boten. Festschrift für H.-W. Wolff* (Neukirchen-Vluyn 1981), 11–29.

Since Rendtorff's approach calls for a new appreciation of the potential of the form-critical method introduced by Gunkel, and takes up some of his findings, which were outlined in Chapter 2 above, and since he also regards the contributions by von Rad and Noth, outlined in the foregoing chapter, as fundamentally flawed, a consideration of his work falls naturally at this stage.

I

Rendtorff contrasts the methods of literary criticism and form criticism as two fundamentally different approaches to the study of the Pentateuch; they are 'opposed to each other in their starting point and in their statement of the question'.[17] The literary-critical method in the classical form it has followed since Wellhausen takes as its point of departure the completed Pentateuch, and seeks to trace continuous literary sources running through it. The form-critical method, however, begins as it were from the opposite end, that is, with the smallest, originally independent, individual units, and traces the process of their development up to their final written form. That is, the larger contexts in which each individual text now stands are not the initial concern of form criticism.

It is a major shortcoming of research, Rendtorff argues, that scholars in general have failed to appreciate this fundamental difference between the two approaches and thus the proper relationship between them. The reason is that those who made use of form criticism and traditio-historical enquiry adhered 'almost without exception to literary source division. Consequently, one could speak quite frankly of "an extension of the methods by means of form criticism"[18] without realizing clearly or even mentioning that it is in fact not a matter of an extension, but of a fundamental alteration of the statement of the question' (p. 1; Eng. trans., 11).

The consequence of this is that the form-critical approach and the closely related investigation of the history of traditions has not yet

---

[17] Rendtorff, *Das überlieferungsgeschichtliche Problem des Pentateuch*, 1; Eng. trans., *The Problem of the Process of Transmission in the Pentateuch*, 11. Quotations are generally from the English translation, but in some places I supply my own translation.

[18] Rendtorff cites as an example K. Koch, *Was ist Formgeschichte* (Neukirchen 1964; 2nd edn., 1974), esp. ch. 2; Eng. trans., *The Growth of the Biblical Tradition: The Form-critical Method* (London 1969).

been fully developed. Rendtorff's work is aimed at showing the reasons for this and exemplifying the gains to be achieved in Pentateuchal research by a more systematic application of form criticism. He seeks also to bring out more strongly than hitherto the limitations of the literary-critical source division of the Pentateuch which he believes are inherent in the different methodological approach offered by form criticism.

Rendtorff's thesis is that the Hexateuch was formed by the combination of a number of originally separate complexes of tradition which developed independently of each other and were united only at a final stage, when each was virtually complete in itself. These tradition complexes are the primeval history in Genesis 1–11, the story of the patriarchal age in the remainder of Genesis, the complex of narratives centring upon Moses and the exodus, the Sinai tradition, the narratives recounting Israel's sojourn in the wilderness, and finally those narrating Israel's entry into, and occupation of, the land of Canaan. Each of these larger units has its own distinctive profile and character, and each is assembled from various elements of tradition and presents itself now as a more or less self-contained unit. Research has acknowledged these individual complexes, and many studies have been devoted to them. Almost always, however, such studies either presuppose or are concerned with showing that the present coherence and unity of these complexes is due to their belonging to a larger literary context, the Pentateuchal sources. What is required, Rendtorff contends, is a more systematic and thorough form-critical analysis of these larger units, tracing their growth and development from the smallest discernible units through successive stages of development and combination to the emergence of these larger complexes as we have them. As things stand, research so far has left a 'gaping cleft' between the study of the smallest units and concern for the final literary stage in the composition of the Pentateuch.

In his commentary on Genesis Gunkel concerned himself primarily with isolating the smallest literary units and investigating their *Sitz im Leben*. As a further step he also drew attention to the secondary uniting of such units into 'cycles' of stories. Gressmann attempted a similar task in his study of the stories about Moses. The work of both Gunkel and Gressmann pointed to a further though even more complicated stage of investigation, that is, a study of the larger complexes of tradition which the Pentateuch comprises. This is implied in their assessment of the work of the Yahwist and Elohist as 'collectors' who were 'not masters, but rather servants' of what they inherited, faithfully recording a great deal of what had been handed down to them. Both these scholars also believed that the manner in which the stories have been brought together in the documents indicates that we are dealing with collections which cannot have been completed at one given time but developed over a longer period at the hands of 'schools of narrators'. But neither Gunkel nor Gressmann attempted to trace the process of growth of the literature beyond individual 'cycles' of stories to an investigation of the larger complexes of narratives to which they now belong.

Von Rad's monograph *The Form-Critical Problem of the Hexateuch* certainly represents an advance by going beyond the treatment of individual small units or 'cycles' of stories, which featured so prominently in the works of Gunkel and Gressmann, to a concern for the larger tradition complexes to which he gave much greater prominence than they had. Notwithstanding this, however, and his acknowledgement of the many so to speak 'ready-made' units of tradition which the Yahwist inherited, there is a distinct return to the position of Wellhausen as against that of Gunkel—von Rad's emphasis upon the creative, authorial contribution of the Yahwist in handling, and in important respects reshaping, the materials he inherited. That is, von Rad did not make sufficient allowance for a much greater development and combination of traditional materials in the formation of the larger tradition complexes before these were assembled and united to form the Hexateuch. The reason for this was his adherence to the generally acknowledged notion of source division of the Pentateuch and the special theological role he attributed to the Yahwist: 'The Yahwist depicts a side of Israel's experience which we see continually repeating itself in the spiritual history of many nations: ancient and often very scattered traditions are brought together around one central co-ordinating conception, and by some massive *tour de force* achieve literary status.'[19]

Rendtorff makes a similar criticism of Noth's detailed study *A History of Pentateuchal Traditions*. Noth rightly saw 'the growth and gradual formation of the larger blocks of tradition which lie before us today in the extensive and complicated literary shape which is the Pentateuch' as a long process, leading from the formation in oral

---

[19] G. von Rad, 'Das formgeschichtliche Problem des Hexateuch', *Gesammelte Studien*, 55; Eng. trans., 'The Form-Critical Problem of the Hexateuch', in *The Form-Critical Problem of the Hexateuch and Other Essays* (Edinburgh 1965), 48.

tradition, across the written record, up to the purely literary redaction. He then defined the task of a history of Pentateuchal traditions
as being 'to trace this process from beginning to end'. Such a programme, Rendtorff comments, 'should have suggested a treatment of
the path from the smallest units to the larger complexes of tradition
so as to arrive at a coherent picture of the whole process'.[20]
But Noth's investigation largely concentrates on the union of the
major themes and their 'filling out' with disparate traditional material. Then, after some considerations concerning 'bracketings',
'genealogies' and 'itineraries' he 'jumps to the end of the process of
formation and occupies himself with the traditional "Pentateuchal
sources" without having given any consideration to the various stages
of the intermediate literary shaping and process of tradition'.[21] Thus
the path from the smallest units to the larger complexes has not yet
been methodically trodden and examined.

It is thus a serious deficiency in the work of both von Rad and
Noth that they failed to realise that the form-critical approach inaugurated a completely new approach to the problem of the growth of
the Pentateuch. Neither carried through 'the task of the traditio-
historical method which builds on the form-critical statement of the
question . . . to pursue the whole of the formation of the tradition
right up to the present final literary stage'.[22] A main reason for this is
their adherence to the literary-critical source analysis of the
Pentateuch. This is not to say that literary criticism as such is to be
rejected. Literary criticism enables us to isolate different materials
within the completed Pentateuch and thus provides a first step towards
a form-critical enquiry. But the literary-critical *method* must not be
confused with the *theory* of different expansive literary sources and
their combination into the present Pentateuch. Literary-critical questions must be put at all phases of the traditio-historical enquiry, but

they must be related on each occasion to the stage of the formation of the tradition and limited thereby. Only at the end of the inquiry into the process of
the history of the tradition can the question of the literary-critical judgment
of the final shape be put. From the standpoint of the traditio-historical
approach, one is only justified in accepting continuous 'sources' in the
Pentateuch when, at the end of the traditio-historical inquiry, the source theory offers the most plausible answer to the questions which arise from the
final shape of the text.[23]

[20] *Problem*, 8; Eng. trans., 20.   [21] Ibid. 8; Eng. trans., 19.
[22] Ibid. 12; Eng. trans., 24.   [23] Ibid. 12; Eng. trans., 24.

But the existence of the extensive Pentateuchal sources designated by the sigla J, E, P should not be presupposed. It is Rendtorff's contention that a traditio-historical investigation of the growth of the larger tradition complexes does not, however, lead us back to the discovery of these extensive literary sources. Rather, it bypasses them. He finds that the large tradition complexes such as the primeval history or the patriarchal history developed to a very considerable extent independently of each other and were 'stitched' together only in the final stage of the creation of the Pentateuch. These larger tradition complexes

> are a synthesis, forming a new unit, of texts which form-critically and because of their origin are often to be judged very differently. The larger units that are thus formed distinguish themselves clearly over against others in which the traditions belonging to other cycles of themes have been brought together in like manner. One can in many cases recognize more or less clearly the means by which the collectors or authors have shaped and brought together into a unity the originally independent and often quite disparate material. This procedure must be studied in closer detail in order to close the gap in the study of the history of the origin and growth of the Pentateuch.[24]

It is to this task, Rendtorff urges, that Pentateuchal research must now turn. He chooses as an example for detailed study the patriarchal complex of stories in Genesis 12–50:

> The different stages of the pro cess of the formation of the tradition can be clearly discerned in them: the independent individual narratives, the formation of individual 'cycles of stories', the gradual collecting of the narratives about the individual patriarchs, and finally, the putting together of stories about the patriarchs so as to form a larger unit. This makes clear the means used in the course of formation of the individual stories and the comprehensive larger units and the theological intentions at work in the process of assembling and reworking them.[25]

II

On the basis of earlier research, especially that of Gunkel, Rendtorff points to a number of smaller, originally independent complexes of material within the patriarchal material in Genesis 12–50 as a whole:

(1) The Joseph narrative (Gen. 37–50), which has a character of its own and is best described as a *novelle*.

---

[24] Ibid. 19; Eng. trans., 32. [25] Ibid. 20; Eng. trans., 32 f.

(2) A complex of Jacob narratives comprising an originally separate Jacob–Esau 'cycle' (25: 19–34; 27–8; 32–6) and a Jacob–Laban 'cycle' (29–31), together with other material relating to Jacob such as the notices about the birth of his children (29: 31–30: 24; 35: 16–20) and various 'cult legends' or fragments thereof (Bethel 28: 10–22; 35: 1–8, 14; Mahanaim 32: 2 f.; Penuel 32: 23–33; Shechem 33: 18–20).

(3) The Isaac material in Genesis 26 which was an originally independent unit. Following Noth, Rendtorff argues that the Isaac variants of the stories related elsewhere to Abraham are traditio-historically the older.

(4) The Abraham complex. Here too originally separate 'cycles' of stories can be discerned, such as an Abraham–Lot complex (12: 1–8; 13; 18: 1–16aα; 19: 1–28; 19: 30–8). Just as Gunkel had described 12: 1–8 as the 'motto' for the Abraham complex, so Rendtorff argues that it belongs to the phase of the overall combination of the Abraham complex as a whole. A further group of Abraham traditions may be recognized in Genesis 20–2, designated by Kessler as a 'Negeb group' on account of the location with which they are associated.[26]

(5) A number of narratives which are loosely related to their context. Rendtorff cites these as Genesis 14, 16, 17, 23, and also 12: 10–20. He argues that Genesis 24 is relatively late and presupposes the entire Abraham tradition. Matters are somewhat more difficult in the case of Genesis 15. Both sections of this chapter (vv. 1–6 and 7–21) presuppose in various ways the topics of the Abraham tradition as a whole. It was not composed with its present context in mind but presents rather a peculiarly independent development of the basic themes of the Abraham tradition.

The process whereby these complexes concerning Abraham, Isaac, and Jacob developed and were combined to form the patriarchal complex as a whole took place in different stages and by means of different theological interpretations. Of primary importance in the editing (*Bearbeitung*) of each individual tradition complex and of the subsequent combination of such complexes were divine promise speeches. In the Abraham complex these speeches are more closely related to their context than in the Jacob complex, whilst in the Isaac complex in Genesis 26 the two divine speeches (vv. 2–5 and 24) in no

---

[26] The reference is to R. Kessler, *Die Querverweise im Pentateuch. Überlieferungs-geschichtliche Untersuchung der expliziten Querverbindungen innerhalb des vorpriester-lichen Pentateuchs*, unpub. diss., Heidelberg 1972, 69 ff.

way arise from the Isaac traditions but have been added to provide a theological framework for them.

Following Claus Westermann,[27] Rendtorff identifies the promises in question as the promise of land, of numerous descendants, and of blessing, to which he himself adds the promise of guidance. Of these, the promise of blessing was not an originally independent promise; it is always found in connection with other promise themes, usually with the promise of numerous descendants. The other promises are found alone but also to varying extent and in different ways in combination with each other, though they were originally independent of each other. In addition, Rendtorff finds evidence of several stages of development in the promise of land, of an earlier and a later formulation of the promise of blessing for others through the descendants of the patriarchs, and of two mutually independent groups of formulations of the promise of numerous progeny.

He argues that the promise of the land was originally directed to the individual patriarch himself ('*to thee* I will give it', Gen.13: 17; 15: 7). It was subsequently extended by the addition of 'and to thy seed' (13: 15; 28: 13). That this is a secondary development is evident, he argues, from the insertion of 'and to thy seed' (ולזרעך) after the verb. The formulation in 35: 12 in which the verb is repeated is also seen as particularly clear evidence of the secondary nature of the combination of the words 'to thee' and 'and to thy seed'. A further stage of development is to be found, he maintains, in formulations in which the words 'to thee' and 'and to thy seed' have been brought together either before or after the verb (17: 8; 26: 3; 28: 4). In a final stage of development the promise is directed solely 'to thy seed' (12: 7; 15: 18; 24: 7 (reported in a narrative context); 26: 4; 48: 4 (again reported in a narrative context)).

The earlier of the two formulations of the promise of blessing for others employs the *niph'al* of the verb 'to bless' and refers to 'all the families of the earth' (12: 3; 28: 14). The later formulation (22: 18; 26: 4) employs the *hithpa'el* and refers to 'all the nations of the world'. Chapter 18: 18, which employs the *niph'al* and refers to 'all the nations of the world', is regarded by Rendtorff as an intermediate stage between the earlier and the later formulations.

Two separate groups of formulations of the promise of numerous progeny are found. One refers to the increase of the 'seed' and occurs

---

[27] C. Westermann, 'Arten der Erzählung in der Genesis', in his *Forschung am Alten Testament* (Munich 1964), 9–91, esp. 11–34.

in several texts without the use of any metaphor describing how numerous the descendants will be (16: 10; 21: 12; 26: 24), in several with such a metaphor (15: 5; 26: 4; 13: 16; 28: 14; 32: 13), and in one where several such metaphors are used (22: 17). The other group does not employ the word 'seed'. In 17: 2 and 48: 16 it is stated that the descendants will become many, whilst in a number of other formulations they are spoken of as becoming a 'people', 'peoples', 'nations', or an 'assembly' (12: 2; 17: 4, 5, 6, 16, 20; 18: 18; 21: 13, 18; 28: 3; 35: 11; 46: 3; 48: 4).

In its briefly expressed form ('I will be with thee', 'I am with thee', 'I will do thee good', and the like) the promise of guidance occurs only in material relating to Isaac and Jacob (26: 3, 24; 28: 15; 31: 3, 5; cf. 28: 20; 31: 42; 32: 10, 13; 35: 3; 48: 21). But although such formulae do not occur in the Abraham material, there are here statements which in content stand in immediate proximity to them. Genesis 12: 1 'Get thee out of thy country, and from thy kindred, and from thy father's house, unto the land *that I will show thee*' is cited by Rendtorff in this connection; except for its omission of 'I am with thee', it is similar to 31: 3. Rendtorff also includes here 13: 17 and 22: 2. In these texts Abraham is described as undertaking journeys at the direction of God, even though the guidance formulae employed in the Isaac and Jacob narratives are not found. He suggests that the theme of guidance in the Abraham material, witnessed to in 13: 17 and 22: 2, may have given rise to the guidance formulae themselves which were then used in the Isaac and Jacob material.

III

These various ways in which the divine promises are expressed are evidence, according to Rendtorff, of different stages in the growth of the patriarchal traditions. The same is true, it is then argued, of the varying ways in which these promises have been combined.

For example, in 28: 13–15 there occur four promises, that of the land, followed by that of numerous progeny and of blessing for others, then the promise of guidance. According to Rendtorff the promise of guidance was the earliest to be included here. By means of it (v. 15) the dream of Jacob at Bethel is connected with the larger Jacob tradition. Subsequently the promise of the land was added (v.

13), the phrase 'the land on which you lie' linking it with the context. He argues that initially this promise of land concerned only the patriarch himself. At a further stage the word 'and to thy seed' was added. The key-word 'seed' then attracted the further addition of the promise of numerous 'seed' and with it the promise of blessing for others (v. 14). Accordingly, we have evidence of a step-by-step development which arose from the context of the story itself.

Rendtorff argues a similar development in the case of 13: 15–17. Here too the promise of guidance represents the earliest stage; verse 17 belongs more directly to the context (cf. v. 14). Subsequently verse 15, with its key-word 'seed', was added and this in turn attracted the further addition of the promise of numerous 'seed' in verse 16. The metaphor used to describe how numerous the seed will be is the same in 13: 16 and 28: 14.

Matters are different, however, in those texts where the promise of numerous descendants is followed by the inclusion of the promise of the land (17: 8; 28: 4; 35: 12; 48: 4b). In these passages the promises of descendants do not contain the key-word 'seed' which could have acted as a stimulus for the addition of the promise of the land to that of the 'seed'. Unlike 13: 15 ff. and 28: 13 ff. there is here no step-by-step development but simply the combination of two quite independent elements which have been brought together, evidently because by this stage in the development of the patriarchal traditions they were considered as belonging together. These passages thus evidence, Rendtorff argues, a later stage of development than that represented in 13: 15 ff. and 28: 13 ff. Genesis 17 provides a good example of this. The promise of the land (v. 8) has been included because by this stage the promise of descendants was not felt to be complete without it.

According to Rendtorff the promise of guidance played a particularly important role in providing each of the three patriarchal complexes with its framework. Thus it occurs in both divine speeches in the Isaac complex, the one at the beginning (26: 3) and the other toward the end (26: 24). In the Jacob complex it occurs at the beginning when Jacob is fleeing to Haran (28: 15), at the turning point when he is commanded by God to return to his homeland (31: 3), and finally in 46: 2–4 when he is commanded to go down to Egypt. Similarly, in the Abraham complex, the theme of guidance, though not expressed in the formulae used in the other two complexes, occurs at the beginning (12: 1) and at the end (22: 2): 'The command, which

becomes divine guidance because of Abraham's obedience, stands at
the beginning and the end of the Abraham narrative'.[28]

These divine promise speeches by which each of the three patriarchal complexes was developed through different stages were also,
Rendtorff argues, the means whereby the three complexes were combined into the larger patriarchal complex as a whole. Though other
aspects of these speeches contributed to this, the way in which all
three were combined is most clearly in evidence in the promises of
blessing for others. These are found at the beginning and end of the
Abraham complex (12: 3 and 22: 18, with a reference to it in 18: 18),
and at the beginning of the Isaac complex (26: 4) and of the Jacob
complex (28: 14).

Rendtorff finds evidence in this of two phases whereby the separate
complexes were combined. In the case of the promise of blessing for
others at the beginning of the Abraham complex (12: 3) and in the
Jacob complex (28: 14) the formula used employs the *niph'al* of the
verb and refers to 'all the families of the earth'. In the divine speech
to Abraham in 22: 18, however, and in the promise to Isaac (26: 4) the
hithpa'el is employed and the accompanying phrase is 'all the nations
of the world'. According to Rendtorff the formula in 12: 3 and 27: 14
is earlier than that used in 22: 18 and 26: 4. Further evidence that the
latter two are later than the former two is that in 12: 3 and 28: 14 the
blessing for others is promised through the patriarch himself ('in
thee'), whereas in 22: 18 and 26: 4 it is promised through the patriarch's 'seed'. On this basis Rendtorff argues that the Abraham and
Jacob complexes were the first to be united. In a second phase came
the inclusion of the Isaac complex which employs the same formula
and takes up the reference to the divine oath to Abraham referred to
in 22: 16 (cf.26: 3). Other similarities between 22: 16–18 and 26: 3–5
are also evident.

IV

From all this Rendtorff concludes that the patriarchal complex in
Genesis 12–50 developed through several stages of theological editing and interpretation into substantially the large tradition complex
it now is. The question now arises whether the same single process

[28] *Problem*, 59; Eng. trans., 76. Rendtorff (see *Problem*, 59 n. 1; Eng. trans., 77 n. 1)
regards Gen. 23 and 24 as an appendage to the Abraham complex.

which yielded the patriarchal complex also embraces the other large tradition complexes which the Pentateuch comprises. Rendtorff argues that the answer to this is emphatically no. The promise speeches, so prominent in the patriarchal corpus, have nothing corresponding to them in the subsequent books of the Pentateuch. The contents of the promise speeches are not even expressed in some other form. It is particularly surprising, he argues, that the promise of the land to the patriarchs is not taken up in the exodus material. When the land is here first mentioned (Exod. 3: 8), it is referred to as though the promise of the land to the patriarchs is completely unknown.[29] It is only the late Priestly stratum that first refers to God's oath to the forefathers concerning the land (Exod. 6: 2 ff. See below). Thus he concludes:

It can hardly be demonstrated more clearly that the patriarchal stories are not combined with the subsequent theme complexes in a common, comprehensive work of theological editing. If there had been a 'Yahwist' who was responsible for the compilation and theological editing, then surely the traces of his work must have been recognisable here. It is absolutely unthinkable that a theologian of such rank as the 'Yahwist' must have been, according to the prevalent view, should have displayed the promise speeches so prominently in the patriarchal stories, and then later on not have mentioned them at all. The fact that the Exodus from Egypt is not represented as a return to the land of the patriarchs, leads to only one conclusion—namely, that the two accounts were conceived and theologically edited independently of one another—and also that they were not brought into relation to one another theologically before the phase of the final, priestly redaction. Clearly, there is no room here for the idea of the 'Yahwist' as a theologian. There is no such person . . . Anyone who wants to grasp the theological intentions which stand behind the collection and editing of the material of the Pentateuch must rather examine these editorial traces in very exact detail. In this way one will come across various important theological statements, but he will not meet the authors of the 'sources' as understood in the classical documentary hypothesis.[30]

What is here said of the Yahwist is claimed also in the case of the P material. This material does not derive from an originally independent narrative encompassing the main themes of the Pentateuch from the primeval history onwards. The passages usually assigned to P are

[29] Rendtorff, *Problem*, 66; Eng. trans., 85.
[30] R. Rendtorff, 'Der "Yahwist" als Theologe. Zum Delemma der Pentateuchkritik', SVT 28 (1975), 66; Eng. trans., 'The "Yahwist" as Theologian? The Dilemma of Pentateuchal Criticism', *JSOT* 3 (1977), 9 f.

better understood as editorial additions to an existing text. In the patriarchal narratives in Genesis some fragments are attributed to P but without sound reason (e.g. 31: 18aβb; 33: 18a; 35: 6a). Only the barest fragments of P have been found in the Joseph narrative. Further, it is surely surprising, Rendtorff argues, that if P was the extended narrative it is supposed to have been, it does not deal with Isaac. In the case of Abraham, chapter 17 is indeed from P, but it does not provide evidence that it originally belonged to an extended narrative. For example, the circumcision element so prominent in it is not found again in the patriarchal material with the exception of 21: 4. Rendtorff further argues that Genesis 23 cannot be considered a composition of the Priestly writer. It is a 'secular story' which nowhere mentions God—surely something not to be expected of such a writer. There is nothing in all this to suggest that the material which can be ascribed to P is anything more than further editorial work on an already existing complex. Three passages in the Jacob material particularly evidence this (27: 46–28: 5; 35: 9–13; 48: 3 f.). These occur at those points in the narrative where the promise of guidance occurs. Rendtorff argues that they derive from an editor who was concerned to expand and add further emphasis to an already existing complex at these particular junctures.

Rendtorff acknowledges that Exodus 2: 23–5 and 6: 2–9 are P texts referring back to the patriarchal traditions, especially to Genesis 17, and that these two texts thus indicate a deliberate connection of the patriarchal tradition with that of the exodus. But in the course of the ensuing presentation no further such references back are to be found. The exodus events, the wandering in the wilderness, and the settlement narratives give no indication that the land, the goal of Israel's journey, was the land promised by God to the forefathers. These two texts do not yield evidence of a comprehensive P redaction of the entire Pentateuch but only of a late connection of the patriarchal tradition with the exodus tradition under the aspect of the covenant of Yahweh with the fathers.

By what means, then, were the originally independent and already substantially developed individual complexes which the Pentateuch comprises finally linked together to form the Pentateuch? Rendtorff here points to a number of texts which he believes to have been inserted at decisive points and which have effected this combination (Gen. 50: 24; Exod. 13: 3–10, 11; 32: 12; 33: 1–3a; Num. 11: 11–15; 14: 22–4; 32: 11). Of these, he argues, Genesis 50: 24 and Exodus 33: 1–3a are particularly important. These two texts join the patriarchal stories with the traditions which narrate the journey of the Israelites from Egypt back to the promised land. They thereby 'clamp together all Pentateuchal traditions under one all-embracing theme: YHWH has given the land to the Israelites'.[31] According to Rendtorff the editorial stratum which these texts constitute is Deuteronomic, more specifically 'proto-Deuteronomic' or 'early Deuteronomic'.

To employ terms from the history of Pentateuchal research, Rendtorff's understanding of the composition of the Pentateuch may thus be described as a modern version of the 'fragment theory'. His understanding of the composition of Genesis 12–50 may be similarly described: this narrative complex is substantially the result of the editorial joining together of originally discrete 'smaller literary units'.

V

Rendtorff's analysis of the development of the promise speeches in the patriarchal complex is of fundamental importance for his thesis as a whole, since it is in these speeches that he finds evidence not of the combination of different continuous literary sources such as the older Pentateuchal source theory posited, but of a process of editing (*Bearbeitung*) which took place in different stages and by means of which originally independent promises were built up and combined with each other. By the term *Bearbeitung*, which is used frequently throughout his book, Rendtorff appears to mean an editorial activity carried out in a number of stages on existing texts. As we have seen, he attempts to demonstrate these different stages in the development of the promise speeches. According to Rendtorff it was by such multi-staged editorial work upon received traditional material concerning each of the patriarchs that the patriarchal complex developed substantially into its present form.

As examples of his procedure we may look at his analysis of Genesis 13: 15–18 and 28: 13–15. It will be recalled that in the case of the latter he finds evidence that verse 15, containing the promise of guidance, was the earliest promise to be associated with this context. He argues that it belongs more immediately to the substance of this chapter. Subsequently, he suggests, verse 13, containing the promise of land to Jacob *himself*, was added and then, in a further stage of

[31] *Problem*, 79, Eng. trans., 99.

editing, this promise was extended by the insertion of 'and to thy seed' which follows the verb. The word 'seed' later attracted the further addition of the promise of numerous 'seed' and the promise that in the patriarch and in his 'seed' all the families of the earth will be blessed. Thus this short passage is no longer seen as a literary unit deriving from the hand of a single author or editor but is believed to have been built up in several stages of editing. A similar analysis is proposed in the case of Genesis 13: 15–18.

Rendtorff's analysis of these two passages is unconvincing. To deal first with 28: 13–15, his criterion for finding different stages of development in these verses is highly questionable. It is by no means clear that the word 'and to thy seed' (ולזרעך) is a secondary addition in verse 13 simply because it follows the verb. Constructions of the same kind are found elsewhere, for example, in Numbers 18: 8, 11 and Deuteronomy 1: 36. Of these, the latter is all the more striking since it concerns a promise of land, in this instance to Caleb. Here Caleb precedes the verb whilst the word 'and to his children' follows it: 'To him I will give the land that he has trodden upon, and to his children'. There is surely no justification for regarding the Hebrew word here (ולבניו 'and to his children') as a later addition. The same is true of the promise concerning Aaron and his sons in Numbers 18: 8, 11. The position of the word ולזרעך 'and to thy seed' at the end of Genesis 28: 13 offers no evidence that it is a secondary addition to this verse.[32] One may add that it is possible that the author placed 'and to thy seed' after the verb in verse 13 precisely because he wished to make a further statement about the 'seed', in this case about how numerous it would be, in verse 14; that is, it is normal Hebrew syntax.[33] If Genesis 28: 14 is a secondary addition to v. 13, this would have to be argued on other grounds. What of verse 15? Can it be regarded as having been placed in this context prior to verses 13–14? This is possible,[34] but in my opinion unlikely. It is difficult to see what the second half of this verse refers to—'for I will not leave thee, until I have performed that of which I have spoken to thee'—if not to the promise announced in verse 13. In short, there are no compelling reasons for doubting that this short passage was composed by one and the same author.

[32] This remains so even if the promise in v. 13 is regarded as original in this context.
[33] Cf. J. A. Emerton, 'The Origin of the Promises to the Patriarchs in the Older Sources of the Book of Genesis', *VT* 32 (1982), 25.
[34] Cf. ibid. 22.

Rendtorff's argument concerning Genesis 13: 14ff. is equally doubtful. Here too, as in 28: 13 ff., there are no compelling arguments for believing that these verses developed in the editorial stages suggested by him. That the word 'and to thy seed' follows the verb is because in view of its accompanying phrase 'for ever' it is syntactically better in this position. As for the view that verse 17 belongs to an earlier stage of editing, it is arguably this verse which is a secondary addition to this short passage. In this verse Abraham is commanded to '*journey* throughout the land, to the length of it and to the breadth of it'. Yet in verse 18 he journeys simply to Mamre. It might be argued that verse 18 is more compatible with verse 14 where the patriarch is told to *look* from where he stands, to the north and to the south, etc. Here also, therefore, with the possible exception of verse 17, there are no sound reasons for doubting that this short passage is the work of one author. Just as there is no reason for believing that the word ולזרעך 'and to thy seed' is an addition in 13: 15; 28: 13 simply because it follows the verb, so also it is unconvincing to find in this formulation an earlier stage of development than those formulations in which the patriarch and his 'seed' are placed together either before or after the verb.

What then of Rendtorff's suggestion that the formulations in which the promise is spoken of with reference to the 'seed' alone represent the latest and final stage in the development of this promise and thus provide evidence of different editorial strata in the patriarchal complex? A difficulty surely arises for such a view from the formulations of this promise contained in the passages ascribed by him to the P stage of editing. Here one finds no uniformity in the formulations employed. In two of them (Gen. 17: 8; 28: 4) the promise is of the type 'to thee and to thy seed', in a third it is formulated with reference to the 'seed' alone (48: 4), whilst in a fourth (35: 12) it is different again: 'to thee I will give it [the land], and to thy seed after thee will I give the land'. This editor evidently did not limit himself to just one type of formulation. This being so, what reason is there for insisting that an earlier editor or author could not have employed the same flexibility? John Emerton's comment on the significance Rendtorff attaches to these different formulations is apt: 'there is no necessary antithesis between the promise to give the land to a patriarch and the promise to give it to him and his seed or simply to his seed. To promise the land to a patriarch implies promising it to his descendants too, and the writer could allow himself variety in the wording

of the promise without intending an essential difference of meaning
. . . Rendtorff makes much of a distinction that is probably unimportant.'[35]

In short, there are no compelling reasons for believing that these
promise speeches were composed in the step-by-step manner proposed by Rendtorff. Nevertheless, a modified form of Rendtorff's
view has been argued by Blum who, whilst not accepting such a step-by-step growth of these promise speeches, agrees with him that they
were the editorial means of uniting originally discrete narratives. He
agrees also with Rendtorff that these promise speeches are evidence
that the patriarchal narrative was composed independently of the
bondage–exodus–wilderness narrative that follows and was only secondarily united with it.

VI

Blum has dealt extensively with the patriarchal narratives in the
first of two monumental works on the composition of the Pentateuch,
The Composition of the Patriarchal History.[36] This is an impressively
scholarly study the detailed arguments of which as well as its many
excurses and degressions on aspects of Genesis 12–50 and on the history of research defy summarizing in the space here available. We
must confine ourselves to its main conclusions. In the briefest outline
these are as follows.

(1) Blum isolates from Genesis 25–33 an originally independent
narrative about Jacob (*Die Jakoberzählung*) comprising the cult foundation legend of Bethel in Genesis 28: 10–19* (without the promises
in vv. 13–15) and the Jacob–Esau–Laban narrative in chapters 25:
19 ff.; 27–33*. This latter narrative had a prior development of its
own and was united with 28: 10 ff.* by means of Jacob's vows in 28:
20–2 and the theme of reconciliation between Jacob and Esau. The
historical background of this Jacob narrative was the formation of
the northern state of Israel under Jeroboam I (pp. 175–84). The narrative served to legitimize important elements in the political consolidation of the new state. For evidence of this Blum points to the

---

[35] J. A. Emerton, 'The Origin of the Promises to the Patriarchs in the Older Sources
of the Book of Genesis', *VT* 32 (1982), 26.

[36] The second volume is his *Studien zur Komposition des Pentateuch*. See below,
Ch. 6.

significance attached in this narrative to Bethel, chosen by Jeroboam as a state sanctuary, and Penuel, an important centre of the new state, and Shechem (cf. 1 Kgs. 12: 25 ff.), as well as the tendency (cf. especially chapter 33) to elevate Joseph among the sons of Jacob (Jeroboam was an Ephraimite, and northern Israel was already known collectively as 'the house of Joseph'(cf. 2 Sam. 19: 21; 1 Kgs. 11: 28)).

(2) This story about Jacob was expanded into a still larger narrative (*Die Jakobsgeschichte*) by means of a series of notices which joined it with the originally independent Joseph narrative in Genesis 37–50* which, he suggests, may have been composed in the eighth century BC. Thus an account of Jacob's life from birth to death is narrated in Genesis 25–50*. Subsequently, probably after the fall of Samaria in 721 BC, this northern Israelite complex was given a Judaean orientation by the incorporation of chapters 38 (the story of Tamar) and 49 (the blessing of Jacob) both of which give prominence to Judah among the sons of Jacob.

(3) In Part II Blum investigates the further expansion of this originally northern Israelite 'history of Jacob' into the patriarchal history in Genesis 12–50 substantially as we have it. He first isolates an originally independent Abraham–Lot narrative in Genesis 13*, 18–19*, which he describes as a self-contained composition centring upon the origins of the people descended from Abraham and Lot and the ancestral relationships between them. According to Blum the original beginning of this narrative is no longer extant. It is not to be found in Genesis 12: 1–9: the theme of an 'exodus' from Haran in this passage, and of the sort of symbolic taking possession of the land by Abraham, as well as the stringing together of notices about the patriarch's itinerary in the land go thematically beyond the more homogeneous content of the Abraham–Lot narrative (pp. 285 f.; 331 ff.). The passage[37] presupposes a larger picture of the patriarchal history and belongs to the second main stage in the formation of Genesis 12–50 (see below). The Abraham–Lot narrative would also have included a record of the birth of Isaac, promised in chapter 18, but this has evidently been replaced by 21: 1–7.

This Abraham–Lot narrative was combined with the expanded Jacob narrative in 25–50* by means of the promises in 13: 14–17 and

---

[37] Blum ascribes vv. 4–5 to a still later Priestly editor.

28: 13–15 and this constituted the first stage of the completion of the patriarchal history as a whole. He dates this to the period between the fall of the Northern Kingdom in 721 BC and the destruction of the state of Judah in 586 BC, the period to which he also traces the origin of the promise speeches in Genesis.[38] This narrative was further expanded during the exilic period by the addition of a number of originally independent stories about Abraham (12: 10–20; 16; 21: 8–21; 22) and the Isaac narrative in chapter 26. At the same time the theme of the promises to the patriarchs was extended to other contexts in Genesis 12–50. A Deuteronomistic editor subsequently added chapters 15 and 24 and other smaller additions, and at this stage also the patriarchal complex was connected with the other major tradition complexes of the Pentateuch. There followed a Priestly redaction which added, among other texts, the 'tables of the generations' and other chronological notices.[39]

VII

Although the title of Rendtorff's book describes his study as 'the Traditio-Historical Problem of the Pentateuch', what he engages in is primarily an investigation of the editorial joining together of *already existing narratives* to form Genesis 12–50 substantially as we have it. This is not *Überlieferungsgeschichte* in any usual sense of the word.[40] Rather, he deals with stages in the formation of Genesis 12–50 close to the fixation of the Pentateuch which produced our extant text. Whatever may have been the content, nature and purpose of the individual patriarchal stories or 'cycles' of such stories in the oral stages of their history—and there has been much speculation about this[41]— it is with the literary contours and content they had attained at the stage or stages when the patriarchal history proper in Genesis 12–50 was being put together that Rendtorff is concerned. We are taken only a step or two back, so to speak, from Genesis 12–50 to its supposed already formed 'smaller literary units', and the focus of interest is on the editorial process whereby they were combined to yield

---

[38] *Die Komposition der Vätergeschichte*, 293–6.

[39] For Blum's discussion of the P material, see below, Ch. 7.

[40] See the perceptive comments on this by W. McKane in his review of Rendtorff's monograph in *VT* 28 (1978), 379 f.

[41] For a detailed review and discussion of this see W. McKane, *Studies in the Patriarchal Narratives* (Edinburgh 1979).

the extant patriarchal history, with a brief consideration (pp. 75–9; Eng. trans., 94–100) of how this was then stitched together, by means of a handful of brief editorial touches, with the other major narrative complexes to form the Pentateuch.

The matter is left in no doubt in Blum's work. He is unconcerned with the remoter, oral origins and transmission of the patriarchal stories and focuses instead on the composition and subsequent history of written texts, as the use of the word *Komposition* in the title of his book already indicates. His investigation is wider than Rendtorff's, since he attempts not only to identify the smaller literary units in Genesis 12–50 but also to trace their composition and combination to more or less specific backgrounds in Israel's history and to suggest what purpose their authors and editors may have had in mind in composing and combining them. That is, the smaller units which Genesis 12–50 comprises are the work of authors and cannot be described as 'cycles of stories' (*Sagenkränze*) which emerged in the course of oral transmission. Rather, they are newly created literary compositions by authors employing traditional materials.[42] Put differently, the genre description of the smaller units is different: no longer *Sagenkränze* but 'the Abraham–Lot *narrative*', 'the Jacob history (*die Jakobsgeschichte*)', etc.

At this literary level with which both Rendtorff and Blum are concerned, however, the evidence suggests that the narrative sequences they reconstruct from the extant text presuppose and complement each other in such significant ways as to render it highly unlikely that they were composed in isolation from each other and only secondarily linked together.

Consider, for example, the pronounced aetiological element to which Blum draws attention both in the Abraham–Lot narrative and in the Jacob narrative. These aetiologies define the genealogical relationships between Israel's ancestors and those of the neighbouring peoples—Aram, Ammon, Moab, Edom—and by this means the origins of these nations as understood by Israel. At the same time they also trace the allocation of the land occupied by each of these nations to the period of origins (p. 289). Further, it seems clear, as Blum points out (pp. 289 f.), that the narratives recounting how both Esau and Lot left Canaan were partly intended to show how the land of Canaan was thereby left for Israel to occupy.

---

[42] Blum, *Die Komposition der Vätergeschichte*, 288 f.

On Blum's hypothesis, the southern, Abraham–Lot narrative provides an aetiology of the origin of two of Israel's transjordan neighbours, the Moabites and the Ammonites, both of whom are portrayed as descendants of Lot, Abraham's nephew, whilst the northern, Jacob narrative in addition to narrating the kinship between Israel and Aram also includes an aetiology of the origin of the Edomites, who are portrayed as the descendants of Esau, the brother of Jacob/Israel. If, as Blum argues, however, the narratives in Genesis about the two patriarchs Abraham and Jacob developed independently of each other during the monarchical period, it is surely strange that the Judaean Abraham–Lot narrative makes no mention of Edom, Judah's southern neighbour, whilst the Jacob narrative includes an aetiology of the origin of the people of Edom with whom, as far as we know, neither the northern Israelite state nor the northern tribes had any close dealings. Stranger still, on Blum's hypothesis we also have to accept as a remarkable coincidence that the two independently composed narratives about Abraham and Jacob happened to cover without overlap the aetiologies of all of Israel's neighbouring nations so that when they were united they conveniently complemented one another in this important matter. In addition, both Abraham and Jacob, who are the subject of the two narrative complexes, are 'all-Israelite' figures, and the narratives about them are told from an 'all-Israelite' perspective. For example, Abraham builds altars at important sanctuaries both in Judah and in northern Israel, including Shechem and Bethel. The stories also presuppose the sequence Abraham→Isaac→Jacob. All this surely suggests that the connections and complementarity between the 'smaller units' belong to their substance and cannot plausibly be accounted for in terms of a secondary editorial linking together of independent narratives composed in isolation from one another. Put differently, in so far as we can discern or conjecture originally independent stories (*Sagen*) or 'cycles' of such stories in Genesis 12–37, they have evidently been thoroughly worked over to create a continuous and cumulative story of Israel's ancestors.

In terms specifically of Rendtorff's emphasis upon the promise speeches as the means of uniting the supposed 'smaller literary units', or of Blum's modified proposal of this that an originally independent Abraham–Lot narrative was editorially united with the Jacob narrative by means of the promise speeches in 13: 14–17 and 28: 13–15, these promises are by no means the only linkage between the narratives about the patriarchs. Although they contribute to the continuity between these narratives they are not essential to it.

This takes us only so far, however, and does not address the still more significant conclusion arrived at by Rendtorff and Blum—that the patriarchal history in Genesis 12–50* was originally independent of the narrative complexes that follow it in the Pentateuch. According to Rendtorff the patriarchal history was joined to them only at a late stage by a number of secondary editorial texts from a Deuteronomic redactor (Gen. 50: 24; Exod. 13: 3–10, 11; 32: 12; 33: 1–3a; Num. 11: 11–15; 14: 22–4; 32: 11). For a particularly graphic illustration of the original independence of the patriarchal history from the bondage–exodus narrative, he draws special attention to Yahweh's address to Moses in Exodus 3: 8 where the land is referred to as though the promise of it to the patriarchs is completely unknown. Blum too attaches special significance to the promise speeches and allusions to them in Exodus/Numbers as editorial linking-texts between the patriarchal narrative and what follows (Gen. 15; 22: 15–18; 24: 7; 26: 3bβ–5, *24; Exod. 13: 5, 11; 33: 1; 32: 13; Num. 11: 12; 14: 16, 23).[43]

Blum's detailed study of the patriarchal complex in Genesis 12–50 has been followed by *Studies in the Composition of the Pentateuch*. Together, these two monumental volumes are the most comprehensive and detailed of recent times. As we shall see, whilst agreeing with Rendtorff concerning the original independence of the patriarchal history, Blum parts company with him on the composition of the remaining narrative complexes of the Pentateuch. The following comments concerning the wider aspect of Rendtorff's work will serve as an introduction to Blum's second volume.

VIII

Though he concentrates on the patriarchal narrative in Genesis 12–50 to exemplify his theory, Rendtorff considers briefly the evidence for the original independence of the complex of stories describing Israel's wandering in the wilderness.[44] It will be recalled that according to Noth this theme developed in dependence upon the exodus tradition as an answer to the question of what happened to

---

[43] *Die Komposition der Vätergeschichte* 371 ff., 396 ff.
[44] *Problem*, 73 f.; Eng. trans., 92 f.

Israel's ancestors between the exodus and the entry into the land. It was thus, on his theory, a relative latecomer into the developing Pentateuchal *Grundlage* (G). Rendtorff acknowledges that in particular the tradition of Israel's 'murmuring' in the wilderness, which is prominent in this complex, of necessity presupposes the bondage–exodus tradition, since it centres on a contrast between the plight of the Israelites in the desert and the relative security they had enjoyed in Egypt. He argues, however, that this does not mean that these two tradition complexes were originally related to each other: 'Apart from the mere reference back to the better situation in Egypt, the content of these texts shows no further connections with the traditions about the leading out from Egypt.'[45] Accordingly, all that we can say, he claims, is that the 'fact' of the exodus from the fruitful land of Egypt was one of the presuppositions for the development of this 'murmuring' tradition and that only in this limited sense was there a traditio-historical relation between the bondage–exodus tradition and the wilderness tradition. He further argues that the reference to the exodus in these 'murmuring' texts serves only as a means of drawing a contrast between Israel's situation in the wilderness and in Egypt, whilst the real significance of the exodus as the saving act of Yahweh on Israel's behalf is barely mentioned: 'It is scarcely possible to glean from the texts that the leading out of Eygpt was a saving action of YHWH for Israel.'[46]

Rendtorff is demanding more from this wilderness complex, however, than it was intended to provide. Even on his own view, the compiler who combined it with the exodus tradition complex did not feel it necessary to supplement the wilderness complex with additional references to the exodus; he evidently recognized that it was already closely enough related to the exodus complex whilst at the same time retaining its own distinctive emphases. Quite apart from this, however, Rendtorff's comments on the 'murmuring' theme fail to do justice to its purpose. Is its function merely to contrast the plight of the Israelites in the wilderness with the better conditions they had in Egypt? Is the people's 'murmuring' not also seen as a faithless response to Yahweh's saving action precisely in the exodus? Is their complaint not primarily viewed as 'unbelief which has called into question God's very election of a people'?[47]

[45] *Problem*, 73; Eng. trans., 92.   [46] Ibid. 73; Eng. trans., 93.
[47] Cf. B. S. Childs, *Exodus* (London 1974), 285.

Further, a prominent theme in the wilderness complex that is closely related to the 'murmuring' tradition is Yahweh's continuing saving help for the Israelites in the wilderness. Both of these themes— Israel's 'murmuring' and Yahweh's continuing saving help—are, however, embedded in the exodus complex. They are found together in the narrative of the deliverance at the sea (Exod. 14) which is both the climax of the exodus and also the beginning of Yahweh's saving help for Israel in the wilderness.[48]

Considerations such as these suggest a much closer relationship between the wilderness tradition and the bondage–exodus tradition than Rendtorff is willing to acknowledge. To claim that the wilderness tradition complex presupposes only the bare 'fact' of the exodus scarcely does justice to the evidence. That the wilderness narratives developed in close connection with the bondage–exodus complex still offers a more plausible explanation than Rendtorff's thesis.

What then of the various texts in Exodus and Numbers centring upon the oath to the patriarchs which Rendtorff regards as editorial linkages between the major literary complexes which the Pentateuch comprises (Exod. 13: 3–10, 11; 32: 12; 33: 1–3a; Num. 11: 11–15; 14: 22–4; 32: 11)? It is likely that each of them belongs to a context that is an addition to an earlier narrative.[49] However, that these texts were the means whereby an editor combined originally independent narrative complexes to form the Pentateuch seems questionable. They do not occur at the sort of literary junctures we might expect if Rendtorff's theory is to have plausibility. Two of them occur in the Sinai narrative, and neither is at the beginning or the end of it, and Numbers 32: 11 is not a direct reference to the oath to the patriarchs but occurs in a recollection of the rebellion in the wilderness described in Numbers 13–14. Rather, with the exception of Exodus 13: 3–16, these passages have been inserted into descriptions of crises which threatened the future of Israel as the people of Yahweh—apostasy at Sinai and rebellion in the wilderness. That is, it was the theology of the divine oath to the ancestors rather than a need for editorial linkages that motivated the editor or editors responsible for their insertion. An additional reason against Rendtorff's understanding of

---

[48] G. W. Coats, 'The Traditio-Historical Character of the Red Sea Motif', *VT* 17 (1967), 253–65.

[49] S. Boorer's book (see above n. 15) offers the most recent discussion of these texts and their relation to their contexts.

these texts as editorial linkages is the likelihood that they were not all included in their contexts at the same time.[50]

IX

Blum, whilst sharing Rendtorff's view of the original independence of the patriarchal history, parts company with him on the composition of the Pentateuchal narrative following Genesis. Like Rendtorff, however, he abandons the conventional sigla J, E, JE, and the literary sources they designate. Instead he argues that two main stages can be discerned in the composition of the Pentateuch, the first of which he terms the 'D-Komposition' (K[D]), and the second the 'P-Komposition' (K[P]). The former of these is of more immediate concern to us at this stage; I shall turn to the second stage later.[51]

The 'D-Komposition', K[D], derives from editors who worked under the influence of the Deuteronomistic authors and after the composition of the Deuteronomistic History. He dates K[D] to the generation immediately following the return from exile. The authors of K[D] inherited two main narrative complexes, an edition of Genesis 12–50* from the exilic period, and a narrative which may be described as a 'Life of Moses' from his birth to his death, that is, from the bondage to the end of the period of the wandering in the wilderness. This 'Life of Moses' was composed in the pre-exilic period sometime after the fall of the Northern Kingdom in 722 BC. It is to K[D] that we owe the promise texts in Genesis connecting the patriarchal history with Exodus and the remainder of the Pentateuch (Gen. 15; 22: 15–18; 24: 7; 26: 3bβ–5, 24*; Exod. 13: 5, 11; 32: 13; 33: 1; Num. 11: 12; 14: 16, 23). K[D] was composed subsequent to the Deuteronomistic History, but its distinctive literary nature rules out the notion currently favoured by a number of other scholars that it was consciously composed as a sort of 'prologue' to that corpus.[52]

Before the work of K[D] there was no literary connection between the patriarchal history and the bondage–exodus–wilderness narrative in Exodus/Numbers. Blum recognizes that aspects of, and individual passages in, the patriarchal history presuppose a knowledge of the bondage and exodus traditions, for example, the Joseph story. He

[50] See below, pp. 191 f.   [51] See below, Ch. 7.
[52] Blum, *Studien zur Komposition des Pentateuch*, 164 n. 276.

argues, however, that the widely accepted view among scholars that the Joseph story was itself originally an independent *novelle* is evidence that the mere knowledge in patriarchal narratives of other Pentateuchal traditions such as the exodus does not imply that they originally shared a common literary context with them.[53] Even a passage such as Genesis 46: 1–5a, which refers to a future exodus from Egypt and a re-entry into the land of Canaan, does not necessarily point to the narrative of bondage and exodus that follows. 'To be able to understand this, the hearer/listener needed no literary context, but only a knowledge of the outline of the saving history up to the settlement in the land.'[54] Blum also accepts as compelling the argument of Rendtorff that the references in Exodus and Numbers to the promises so prominent in Genesis derive from late Deuteronomic and Priestly editors and that this is strong evidence that originally the narrative complex beginning with Exodus was independent of Genesis 12–50.[55]

X

The Joseph narrative is surely a weak link, however, in the case for the original independence of the patriarchal history. Most scholars agree that this narrative was an originally independent story or *novelle*. It has a different character from either the Abraham–Lot narrative or the Jacob narrative in each of which we can still discern at least the outlines of originally individual stories and episodes that have secondarily been brought together. Viewed as an independent composition, the Joseph narrative has its own internal structure, a plot with complication and resolution—the enmity of Joseph's brothers resulting in Jacob's loss of his favourite son, the rise of Joseph to power in Egypt and the ensuing events that bring him and his brothers face to face again, their reconciliation and Jacob's reunion in old age with the son whom he had believed to be dead. It is an example of classic Hebrew narrative art at its best, with the general theme of the providential guidance of God.[56]

[53] *Die Komposition der Vätergeschichte*, 360.
[54] Ibid.   [55] Ibid. 361.
[56] That it was composed by specifically wisdom circles to embody wisdom teaching seems unlikely, as Stuart Weeks has now persuasively argued in his *Early Israelite Wisdom*, Oxford Theological Monographs (Oxford 1994), ch. 6.

What Blum fails to consider, however, is that when incorporated into the larger context of the patriarchal history, the story takes on a different narrative role. It is no longer an independent narration of an episode in the lives of Israel's ancestors. Rather, set within the larger narrative of Israel's first ancestors beginning with Abraham, it becomes reconstituted, so to speak, into a complication in that larger story the resolution of which lies beyond it. The larger context into which it has been incorporated describes the migration of Abraham from Mesopotamia to Canaan, God's promise of this land to him and his descendants (Gen. 12: 7),[57] the birth of his son and grandson and of the latter's twelve sons who are the eponymous ancestors of the twelve tribes. The Joseph narrative introduces a complication by describing a turn of events which brought about a further migration of these ancestors from Canaan to Egypt. At the same time, its account of the burial of Jacob in Canaan is no longer the dénouement it is in the Joseph story read as an originally independent tale, but has the effect of heightening the reader's/hearer's expectation of what followed next by signalling a destiny beyond this migration that would return Jacob's descendants to the land of Canaan which their ancestors had taken in possession as their homeland.[58]

In contrast to the Joseph story, the narrative of the patriarchs in Genesis 12–50 is manifestly an unfinished story—scarcely characteristic of Hebrew narrative art, one might justifiably add, if it was originally an independent narrative—and the argument that the tradition of what followed next would have been in the minds of its readers/hearers only underlines how unfinished a story it would have seemed to them. In other words, contrary to Blum's and Rendtorff's view, it is difficult to conceive of the inclusion of the Joseph narrative in the complex of patriarchal stories without at the same time an ensuing narrative, such as the book of Exodus offers, of the movement forward of the story beyond the burial of Jacob in the land of Canaan and the Pharaoh's accommodation of Joseph and his brethren in Goshen. That is, the Joseph story functions as a bridge between the narrative of the patriarchs and the bondage–exodus narrative. Whatever significance is attached to the secondary text Genesis 50: 24, it was scarcely needed to unite the Genesis narrative with what follows in the book of Exodus. Rendtorff's claim that this

[57] On the originality of this promise, see below, Ch. 5, p. 142.
[58] This remains the case even if a passage such as 46: 1–5a is a secondary editorial insertion.

verse provides a necessary link between the patriarchal story and the bondage–exodus which 'is not present in the two units of tradition themselves' (pp. 96 f.) is manifestly unjustified.

There is also a ring of implausibility about Blum's argument on this matter. His theory requires us to accept that there was a commonplace knowledge of the saving history from the patriarchs onwards which the author of the Joseph story, as well as other redactors of Genesis, could presuppose on the part of his hearers/readers, but that it did not occur to anyone to combine the story of the patriarchs with the bondage–exodus–wilderness narrative until the early post-exilic period. The authors of the Deuteronomistic History also knew both the oath to the patriarchs[59] and the saving history from the exodus to the settlement, yet their work too, *ex hypothesi*, preceded any combination of the latter with a story of Israel's patriarchs in a common literary context. We are bound to ask what idea pre-exilic Israel can have had of its own history if it had not yet joined together its memories of Abraham, Isaac, and Jacob with those of Moses and the exodus.

XI

There remains a further argument for the original independence of Genesis 12–50 from the narrative that follows to which both Rendtorff and Blum attach considerable importance, that is the absence in the narrative of the call of Moses of any reference to the oath promising the land to the patriarchs and their descendants which is so prominent a feature of Genesis 12–50. Exodus 3: 8 reads: 'I am come down to deliver them out of the hand of the Egyptians and to bring them up out of that land unto a good land and a large, unto a land flowing with milk and honey; unto the place of the

---

[59] T. Römer has argued that the identification of the 'fathers' in such texts as Deut. 1: 8; 6: 10; etc. with the patriarchs of Genesis derives from a late redactor, and that originally references to the 'fathers' had in mind the ancestors who escaped from Egypt (*Israel's Väter. Untersuchungen zur Väterthematik im Deuteronomium und in der deuteronomistischen Tradition*, OBO 99 (Freiburg 1990); 'Le Deutéronome: à la Quête des Origines', in P. Haudeberg (ed.), *Le Pentateuque: Débats et Recherches* (Paris 1992), 65–98). For a critique see N. Lohfink, *Die Väter Israels in Deuteronomium, mit einer Stellungnahme von Thomas Römer*, OBO 111 (Freiburg 1991); 'Deutéronome et Pentateuque: État de la Recherche', in P. Haudebert (ed.), *Le Pentateuque*, 35–64.

Canaanite, and the Hittite, and the Amorite, and the Perizzite, and
the Hivite, and the Jebusite.' Rendtorff comments:[60]

The land is introduced here as an unknown land, and more, as a land that is
the home of foreign nations; there is not a word which mentions that the
patriarchs have already lived a long time in this land and that God has
promised it to them and their descendants as a permanent possession.
Following the terminology of the promise of the land in Genesis, those
addressed here would be the 'seed' for whom the promise holds good. But
they are not spoken to as such.

Against Rendtorff, however, the passage is not as devoid of links
with the patriarchal age as his statement here claims. In addressing
Moses in this passage, God declares that he is 'the God of thy father,
the God of Abraham, the God of Isaac, and the God of Jacob', and
also refers to Israel as 'my people'. Such statements seem to presuppose a patriarchal story in which the three patriarchs have
already been associated as father, son, and grandson and in which
they and their descendants are the people of the God who thus
addresses Moses. There can therefore be no question of a
bondage–exodus narrative such as Rendtorff supposes, or of a 'Life
of Moses' such as Blum suggests, that did not presuppose, even if it
was not from a literary point of view linked to, a form of the story
of the ancestors of Israel who lived in the land of Canaan and were
the people of the same God as the God of Moses and his contemporary Israelites. That is, the God who now announces the imminent deliverance of his people from bondage is the God of the
patriarchs who had lived in the land of Canaan before their descendants became enslaved in Egypt. It follows from this that the problem which both Rendtorff and Blum find in God's announcement to
Moses in Exodus 3: 8 remains, whether or not the narrative is part
of a larger literary context that includes Genesis 12–50. That is, the
disjunction between what God declares to Moses in Exodus 3: 8 and
what is recorded in Genesis 12–50 did not arise because an editor
joined the latter with an originally independent bondage–exodus
narrative. The radical proposal of both Rendtorff and Blum that
Genesis 12–50 was not originally related to the Pentateuchal narrative that follows accordingly does not explain that disjunction. The
explanation for it must lie elsewhere than in the supposed separate
composition of these complexes.

[60] Rendtorff, *Problem*, 66; Eng. trans., 85.

A consideration of the references to the oath to the patriarchs in Exodus and Numbers (Exod. 13: 3–10, 11; 32: 12; 33: 1–3a; Num. 11: 11–15; 14: 22–4; 32: 11) may suggest an explanation. As noted above, these texts belong to passages that are usually regarded as secondary additions to their contexts and dependent upon Genesis 15 which itself is a secondary addition in Genesis.[61] They are secondary not only at the literary level, however, but also theologically. For the most part they are in contexts narrating or referring to crises in Israel's relationship with Yahweh at Sinai and during the journey from Sinai towards the land of Canaan. At Sinai (Exod. 32: 7–14; cf. 33: 1–3) and subsequently in the wilderness (Num.14: 11b–23a; cf. 32: 7–15) Yahweh threatens to abandon the people because of their apostasy and rebellion, but steps back from this on account of the oath to the patriarchs. In this way the promises to the patriarchs assume the dimension of Yahweh's primary and enduring commitment to Israel with a corresponding subordination of the exodus. Like the texts themselves, this is certainly a secondary development. It is only in relatively late texts that the exodus is subordinated in such a way (Deut. 4: 37; 7: 8; Ps. 105: 43). Elsewhere, the exodus stands on its own as the primary saving act of Yahweh and there is every reason for believing that it was the central confession of Yahweh's saving work on Israel's behalf. That the narrative of Yahweh's announcement to Moses in Exodus 3 makes no reference to the oath to the patriarchs is wholly in line with this. The exodus marks a new beginning for Israel, dependent solely upon a new initiative of Yahweh, rather than the outcome of an earlier promise.

The bringing together of the patriarchal traditions and the exodus tradition was bound to create the sort of disjunction to which Rendtorff and Blum draw attention. Elsewhere in the Old Testament the two traditions stand independent of one another, on the one hand such texts as Hosea 11: 1 (cf. 12: 10), Jeremiah 2: 2, Ezekiel 20: 5, which associate Israel's election with the exodus, and on the other texts such as Isaiah 41: 8 f., 51: 2, which refer to Israel as having been 'called' or 'chosen' in Abraham.[62] In my opinion, the tensions within the narrative of the call of Moses can be explained as arising from a clash of these traditions, and this accounts for the declaration of God as being 'the God of Abraham, the God of Isaac, and the God of Jacob' and of Israel being his people, whilst on the other hand

[61] See below, Ch. 5, pp. 141–3.
[62] Cf. also the secondary addition in Micah 7: 20.

making no mention of the promises to the patriarchs or of the land as having originally been promised and given to them.

XII

Thus the idea that the Pentateuch is composed of larger tradition complexes, rather than of distinct literary sources each of which runs through the whole work, does not do justice to the complexities of the material as it stands. Rather than separate blocks of material, each representing, so to speak, one episode in the story which the Pentateuch tells, there remains much merit in the older view that the text contains a basically single narrative thread running from Genesis 1 to Deuteronomy 34. None of the sources, as they currently survive in the final form of the Pentateuch, contains every stage in this narrative thread. All of them presuppose, however, that Israel from early times had a narrative account of its origins which was consecutive, and which contained stories of the patriarchs, the exodus, and the settlement in the land of promise. The attempt to divide the narrative into quite separate tradition complexes is no more successful in Rendtorff's work than were its anticipations in the work of Martin Noth. And Noth at least thought that the complexes had come together even before the monarchical period to form a continuous narrative (G), whether oral or written. Rendtorff's theory requires us to think that it was only at the stage of the Pentateuch's final composition that the blocks dealing with (say) the exodus and the patriarchs were joined together. We are bound to ask what idea pre-exilic Israel can have had of its own history if it had not yet joined together its memories of Abraham, Isaac, and Jacob with those of Moses and the exodus, or either of these with the settlement in the land. It seems much more likely that the material should be divided into sources each aware of Israel's past as a single whole, rather than horizontally, as it were, into blocks of material each dealing with a different period of Israel's history, yet not related to each other till very late in the process of the Pentateuch's composition.

Whatever we may think of Rendtorff's theory, however, it does have the merit of achieving what von Rad thought so desirable: it begins with the 'final form' of the Pentateuchal text, and tries to work out how that text can most naturally be broken down, rather than with a highly hypothetical theory of sources as though that were self-evident. In the work of Wellhausen and his immediate successors, the existence of sources was indeed not a dogma taken upon trust, but a hypothesis to be tested. But in any discipline one generation's hypotheses become the next generation's givens, and there is no doubt the Documentary Hypothesis had become, for many, almost synonymous with the Pentateuch itself, as if our Bibles actually marked passages as J, E, D, or P. Against this assumption, Rendtorff's work is a justified warning that we should always begin with the text, not with theories about it—just as Wellhausen himself did, we should add, producing a theory which may now look jaded to some, but was revolutionary in his day. That does not mean, however, that Rendtorff's own theory is correct, and we have seen good reason to criticize it.

More recent studies have continued to engage with the Documentary Theory, even while taking seriously Rendtorff's challenge to it. In particular, they have taken issue with the traditional dating (relative and absolute) of the sources. They have also questioned how far the sources were originally independent, free-standing documents, and asked whether P, in particular, might not represent a redactional strand rather than a source-document in its own right. It is to these questions that we turn in the remainder of the book.

5

Attempts to Redate the 'Yahwist'

One of the most striking shifts in recent Pentateuchal research has taken place in the study of what has hitherto been generally accepted as the oldest of its sources, that is, the so-called J document. First, there has been a mounting trend towards dating this narrative to the exilic period or even later. Detailed studies advocating this have come from Hans Heinrich Schmid, John Van Seters, Hermann Vorländer, Hans-Christoph Schmitt, Martin Rose, and Christoph Levin. Second, and closely associated with this, some have taken the further step to argue that this earlier material in the Tetrateuch was composed as a 'prologue' to the Deuteronomistic History and was not therefore, as usually believed, presupposed by the authors of the latter. Van Seters and Rose have especially sought to demonstrate this. On such a view D is no longer the mid-point between J(E) and P, but was rather the first stage in the emergence of the Pentateuch—a topsy-turvy view, indeed, from the perspective of the Documentary Theory.

Major studies by Van Seters and Schmid have led the way in the current move towards dating the Yahwist narrative to the exilic period, the former in a number of substantial contributions,[1] the latter in an influential monograph.[2] A significant forerunner, however, was Frederick Winnett whose short and bold outline of the case for such a dating of the Yahwist influenced both of these scholars, especially Van Seters whose teacher he was at the University of Toronto, and has continued to win followers.[3]

---

[1] J. Van Seters, *Abraham in History and Tradition* (New Haven 1975); id., *In Search of History. Historiography in the Ancient World and the Origins of Biblical History* (New Haven 1983); id., *Der Jahwist als Historiker* (Zürich 1987); id., *Prologue to History: The Yahwist as Historian in Genesis* (Louisville, Ky. 1922); id., *The Life of Moses: The Yahwist as Historian in Exodus–Numbers* (Kampen 1994).

[2] H. H. Schmid, *Der sogenanate Jahwist: Beobachtungen und Fragen zur Pentateuchforschung* (Zürich 1976).

[3] F. V. Winnett, 'Re-examining the Foundations', *JBL* 84 (1965), 1–19. Cf. also N. E. Wagner, 'Pentateuchal Criticism: No Clear Future', *Canadian Journal of Theology*, 13 (1967), 225–32.

I

Winnett argued that the book of Genesis (before the inclusion of the P material) is the work of an author whom he describes as 'Late J' and whom he dates to the early post-exilic period. The pre-P primeval history derives from this author who employed sources of diverse origin, mainly oral but possibly some written. The Joseph story as we now have it also derives from this author who reworked an earlier E story of Joseph, part of which he left untouched and part of which he recast to give a more prominent role to Judah. For the central section of Genesis, 'Late J' drew upon an earlier J document, probably of cultic origin, containing a series of stories about Abraham and Jacob which may have been composed as early as the reign of David. This J narrative had already been subjected to official revision by the edition of E supplements including, for example, Genesis 20–2. The editorial work of P represents an official revision of 'Late J' and was carried out about 400 BC. However, P not only supplemented 'Late J's' book of Genesis but prefixed it to an already existing 'Mosaic tradition' in the books of Exodus and Numbers, at the same time supplementing also these books. He also detached Deuteronomy from the Deuteronomistic History and appended it to the 'Mosaic tradition', thereby creating the Pentateuch as we have it. That is, according to Winnett 'Before P there was no Pentateuch' (p. 18).

For evidence of the post-exilic background to the work of 'Late J', Winnett points, for example, to the theme of universal blessing struck in Genesis 12: 2–3 as being influenced by the preaching of Deutero-Isaiah. He also argues that this late Yahwist anticipated a number of ideas found in P. For example, the references to the building of altars by Abraham and Isaac (Gen. 12: 8; 13: 4; 26: 5) indicate 'a deliberate avoidance of having the patriarchs take the next logical step, that of offering sacrifice. Instead they are said to have "called upon the name of YHWH", i.e. to have invoked God under the name of YHWH' (p. 11). From this Winnett concludes that the 'Late J' author cannot have lived long before the time of P who also avoids any reference to the offering of sacrifice by Israel's ancestors. Evidence of the lateness of this author is also provided by, for example, the references to 'Ur of the Chaldeans' in Genesis 11: 28, 31, since this presupposes a date after the rise of the Chaldean empire in the late seventh century. The strongest argument for a late date, however, is the author's universalist and monotheistic outlook, which is exemplified prominently in the primeval history: 'He views the universe as the creation of a one and only God, YHWH. In some of the old myths and legends surviving from the past he sees evidence that the original harmony of creation had been upset by the entry of sin into the world, by man's disobedience to the commands of God. Sin to him is not a nationalistic affair, the apostasy of the nation from YHWH, as it was to the eighth-century prophets; it is a universal, human phenomenon' (p. 4).

Winnett expected few converts to his thesis but modestly hoped that his 'somewhat radical views' would attract sufficient support to stimulate a more programmatic re-examination of the regnant theory of the composition of the Pentateuch and explore the sort of alternative which he had briefly outlined. He has gained more support than he anticipated, however, beginning appropriately with the extensive contributions of John Van Seters who was his pupil at Toronto and is now Professor of Biblical Literature in the University of North Carolina at Chapel Hill.

II

Van Seters, in his *Abraham in History and Tradition*, ch. 6, seeks to steer Pentateuchal research away from the quest for the history of its pre-compositional stages. In this he believes the doubts expressed by Wellhausen concerning the possibility of such a quest to be fully justified. Thus he rejects Noth's attempt to find a *Grundlage* upon which both the Yahwist and the Elohist are believed to have been dependent. Rather, he argues, here stating briefly his own approach, 'the whole elaborate system of redactors and groundworks is unnecessary if it can be shown that the various *writers* who succeeded one another (and who were admittedly also compilers and editors) were directly dependent upon the works of their predecessors and incorporated these works into their own' (p. 129).

He then sets out his own proposals for investigating the development of the Abraham narratives (ch. 7). He makes a number of observations on the nature of oral composition and contrasts its main characteristics with those of written or 'scribal' composition. In this he makes use of the influential study published early this century by the distinguished Danish folklorist A. Olrik on 'the epic laws of folk narrative',[4] and he argues that the key to understanding the origin and development of the Abraham narratives lies in a study of the well-known doublets among these narratives, for such a study will reveal whether these narratives are based upon independently transmitted oral tradition or whether the one version of a story was presupposed and used by the author of its doublet(s). A comparison of the doublets will then make it possible to formulate the basic characteristics of the tradition's development and its various sources, and to assign the remaining parts of the tradition to the appropriate source stratum.

Van Seters finally turns to a detailed consideration of the individual narratives concerning Abraham and includes also the material concerning Isaac in Genesis 26. He begins (ch. 8) with the story of the beautiful wife in a foreign king's court in Genesis 12: 10–20 and 20, both concerning Abraham and Sarah, and in 26: 1–11 where it is related to Isaac and Rebecca. He argues that the story as narrated in Genesis 12 is the earliest and that it corresponds closely to the folktale model as exemplified in Olrik's 'epic laws'. By contrast, the story as narrated in Genesis 20 does not display the characteristics of oral composition, but is a literary composition by an author who had before him the narrative in chapter 12: 10–20 which he has recast for specific theological and moral purposes. As for the story as told in Genesis 26: 1–11, neither is it an oral composition; rather, it is a literary composition by yet another author directly dependent upon both Genesis 12: 10–20 and 20. Indeed, the Isaac tradition in chapter 26 as a whole is a literary composition worked out by an author using as his sources not old oral tradition, as is often maintained, but elements and motifs from the Abraham narratives.

Van Seters's discussion of this thrice-told tale of 'the ancestress in danger' leads him to posit the first three stages in the development of the Abraham tradition as a whole. The primary stage is represented by the story in Genesis 12: 10–20 and the second by the narrative in chapter 20. These two 'pre-Yahwistic' stages were followed by the work of the Yahwist proper from whom Genesis 26: 1–11 derives. In the remaining chapters in his book Van Seters assigns the remaining material relating to Abraham in Genesis to each of these three stages to which he adds a fourth stage, that contributed by a Priestly

---

[4] A. Olrik, 'Epische Gesetze der Volksdichtung', *Zeitschrift für Deutsches Altertum und Deutsche Literatur*, 51 (1909), 1–12. An English translation is provided in A. Dundes (ed.), *The Study of Folklore* (Englewood Cliffs, NJ 1965), 129–41.

editor—he argues that the P stratum did not derive from an originally independent document—and finally a fifth stage comprising Genesis 14 with the exception of vv. 18–20 which are a still later addition.[5] His conclusions are as follows (p. 313):

1. A pre-J first stage comprising Genesis 12: 1, 4a, 6a, 7, 10–20; 13: 1–2; 16: 1–3a, 4–9, 11ab, 12; 13: 18; 18: 1a, 10–14; 21: 2, 6–7 (except the mention of Lot in 12: 4a and 13: 1). 'These references represent a small unified work with three episodes and a brief framework' (p. 313).

2. A pre-J second stage comprising Genesis 20: 1–17; 21: 25–6, 28–31a. 'This represents one unified story that originally came after the adventure in Egypt (13: 1), to which it was added. It was subsequently transposed to its present position by the Yahwist, who added 20: 1a ("From there . . . Negeb") as a transition' (p. 313).

3. Stage three represents the work of the Yahwist (J) proper who added brief secondary additions to stages 1 and 2: 12: 2–3, 6b, 8–9; 16: 7b, 10, 11c, 13–14; 20: 1aα; 21: 1; and larger episodic units 13: 3–5, 7–17; 15; 18: 1b–9, 15–19: 38; 21: 8–24, 27, 31b–34; 22; 24; 25, 1–6, 11; 26. 'All of these were skilfully incorporated into the older literary work with some new arrangement of the materials' (p. 313).

4. Additions by a Priestly editor: secondary genealogical and chronological additions (11: 26–32; 12: 4b–5; 13: 6; 16: 3b, 15–16; 21: 3–5; 25: 7–10) and the larger episodic units chapters 17 and 23.

5. A post-P stage consisting of Genesis 14 with the exception of verses 18–20 which are a later addition.

Van Seters argues that the Yahwistic narrative (his Stage 3) was composed in the late exilic period. Of prime importance for this conclusion is the narrative of the Abrahamic covenant in Genesis 15, which he regards as a unity composed by the Yahwist who used a variety of forms for its composition drawn from the royal court tradition, the cult, prophetic narrative conventions, and legal spheres (ch. 12). The reference to Ur of the Chaldeans is taken as presupposing the period of Chaldean dominance, that is, the neo-Babylonian period and specifically the reign of Nabonidus who favoured Ur and

---

[5] For a discussion of Van Seters's analysis of Genesis 14, see J. A. Emerton, 'Some Problems in Genesis XIV', SVT 41 (1990), 73–102.

Haran (p. 264. Cf. pp. 24 f., 34, 38).[6] The so-called self-introduction formula 'I am Yahweh who brought you from Ur of the Chaldeans to give you possession of this land' represents, he maintains, a significant shift in Israel's ancient election tradition, for here, in Genesis 15, 'from Ur of the Chaldeans' replaces 'from Egypt, from the house of bondage' in the earlier tradition. Whilst Jeremiah and Ezekiel still held to the theme of divine election through the exodus event and the promise of land to Israel at the time of the exodus, Deutero-Isaiah reflects a situation in which Israel's election was conceived of as coming through the forefathers (e.g. Isa. 41: 8 ff.): 'Here God's election and call of Abraham from a distant land is viewed as Israel's election also. And the relevance of this for the exiles is that God can again bring them from these same distant regions to the promised land' (p. 265). Again, whilst in the Deuteronomistic literature and in Jeremiah and Ezekiel the promise of the land was also closely tied to the conditions of the Sinai covenant, the crisis of the exile called for a new basis for a claim to the land that would supersede the older covenantal basis now forfeited. Hence, Van Seters argues, Abraham's question in Genesis 15: 8 'How can I be sure that I will inherit it?' is the question of the exiled community concerning the land: 'They had become uncertain because the previous covenantal basis was no longer valid as any grounds for hope in a restoration. Consequently, in what follows (vv. 9–10 and 17–21), there is a "new" covenant in the form of the strongest possible oath. It is a promise that is entirely unconditional' (p. 265).[7]

Other features of Genesis 15 are similarly viewed by Van Seters as presupposing the exilic period and as bearing close similarities to some features in Deutero-Isaiah. For example, Genesis 15: 1 ('Fear not, Abram . . . ') is taken as a prophetic word addressed to the exilic community and is compared with Isaiah 40: 9–10; 41: 10. Or again, the statement in Genesis 15: 6 'And he believed Yahweh and he reckoned it to him as righteousness' gains new significance when it too is viewed against an exilic background: 'One cannot read through Deutero-Isaiah without being convinced that his fundamental

[6] J. A. Emerton ('The Origin of the Promises to the Patriarchs in the Older Sources of the Book of Genesis', *VT* 32 (1982), 30) pertinently asks: 'Why should the favour shown by [Nabonidus] to these two cities have led a Jew to invent the idea that Abraham came from them?'

[7] See also his 'Confessional Reformulation in the Exilic Period', *VT* 22 (1972), 448–59, and 'The So-Called Deuteronomistic Redaction of the Pentateuch', SVT 43 (Leiden 1991), 58–77.

concern is with faith in God's desire and ability to restore his people once more. In this exilic context the statement about faith being reckoned as righteousness becomes most appropriate and Abraham, the sojourner, becomes the ideal of the Jew who lived in this hope' (p. 269). Similarly, Van Seters further suggests, Isaiah 54: 1–3 with its combination of the themes of numerous progeny for a barren individual, inheritance of the land, and extensive territory contains the themes of Genesis 15.

Van Seters has devoted a second volume to the book of Genesis under the title *Prologue to History: The Yahwist as Historian in Genesis*. Here and in his more general study of ancient historiography, *In Search of History*, he presents a detailed case for the view that the Yahwist was an antiquarian historian whose work can be compared with that of the ancient Greek historians, including Herodotus, and who, working among the exiles in Babylonia, combined an ancient Near Eastern historiographical tradition with a Western tradition. I shall consider Van Seters's arguments for this in the next chapter.

In his latest substantial volume, *The Life of Moses: The Yahwist as Historian in Exodus–Numbers*, the radical nature of Van Seters's work from a source critical point of view becomes still clearer. Here too he argues for a late exilic dating for the Yahwist's narrative, which he dates contemporary with Second Isaiah and to which he assigns virtually all of the material in the Tetrateuch which cannot strictly be assigned to P. Here too, as in *Abraham in History and Tradition*, he remains critical of attempts to uncover the preliterary stages in the history of the material. The main difference between his discussion of Exodus–Numbers is that, unlike Genesis, he can draw for comparison upon texts in the Deuteronomistic corpus which recount parallel versions of events narrated in these books. From such a comparison he concludes that, contrary to the regnant view of the priority of J, the Yahwist was dependent upon the Deuteronomist's work. He thus joins forces with Rose, who has dealt most extensively with these parallel texts.[8]

For example, from a comparison of the story of the spies in Deuteronomy 1: 19–2: 1 and its parallel in Numbers 13–14,[9] Van Seters argues that the association of Caleb with the story of the spies in Deuteronomy 1 is secondary. The abrupt reference to Caleb in

[8] M. Rose, *Deuteronomist und Jahwist. Untersuchungen zu den Berührungspunkten beider Literaturwerke*, AThANT 67 (Zürich 1981). See below and also Ch. 6.
[9] Van Seters, *The Life of Moses*, 370–9.

verse 36 is itself an indication of this, since he is not mentioned as having participated in the events narrated earlier. Originally, he had no part in the story of the spies here narrated. It was the Yahwist who, taking up the story in Deuteronomy 1, worked Caleb into his narrative in Numbers 13. Van Seters argues that in composing Numbers 13, J, on the basis of the reference to the Anakim in Deuteronomy 1 (cf. Josh. 15: 14), combined the Caleb tradition about the conquest of the Hebron region, the oldest version of which is contained in Joshua 15: 14–19, with the story of the spies in Deuteronomy 1, making Caleb one of the spies, substituting his encouragement of the people for that of Moses and making him an exception to the judgement. Once Caleb was associated with the spy story, the account in Deuteronomy had to be edited to include Caleb as an exception also (Deut. 1: 36).

A further example is provided by his analysis of the parallels between the Sinai pericope in Exodus and Deuteronomy.[10] He argues that the decalogue in Exodus 20: 1–17 with its introduction in 19: 20–5 is a Priestly addition taken over from Deuteronomy with some modifications, especially the sabbath law (p. 280). That is, though J was dependent upon the Deuteronomistic corpus and made use of Deuteronomy's narration of apostasy and renewal at Horeb/Sinai (Deut. 9–10), he omitted one of the most important features of Deuteronomy's narration of the events at Horeb/Sinai, the proclamation of 'the ten words' by God to Israel (Deut. 5).[11] Van Seters offers no explanation of this. Further, Williamson has pointed out that as a consequence of this, whilst there is a close correspondence between Exodus 34: 1–2, 4, 28–9 and Deuteronomy 10: 1–5, 10, Van Seters is obliged to maintain that J omitted precisely the phrase 'the ten words' from his *Vorlage* (Deut. 10: 4, at Exod. 34: 28), and that this phrase was then reintroduced by P at the very same point 'as a secondary gloss' (p. 331). As Williamson aptly comments (p. 432), 'This looks like a return to the kind of detailed literary dissection of a particular passage consequent upon a wider presupposition about composition about which Van Seters is elsewhere so critical, and it serves as a reminder that in the case of so complex a work as the Pentateuch we cannot always escape such consequences, whichever side of D we date J'.

[10] Ibid. p. 3.
[11] For the following comments, see H. G. M. Williamson's review of Van Seters's *Life of Moses* in *VT* 45 (1995), 431 f.

I shall comment further on Van Seters's and Rose's comparison of parallel narratives in the Tetrateuch and the Deuteronomistic literature later.[12] Returning to Van Seters's conclusions in *Abraham in History and Tradition*, the following comments may here be made:

(1) First, the distinction he draws between narratives which he believes display the features of oral composition and those which he maintains betray their origin as literary or 'scribal' compositions is untenable.[13] Recent reconsideration of Olrik's so-called 'epic laws' has shown that they do not provide sufficiently precise canons to enable such a distinction to be made. There is no way of determining that, for example, Genesis 12: 10–20 is a written version of an oral folktale. Thus, the criterion on which he constructs his Stage 1 in the emergence of the Yahwist's document is without foundation.

(2) Other questions arise concerning his proposed Stage 1. He offers only a vague indication of the date of its composition, and though he has much to say about its literary character, he gives no explanation of why it was composed, or for what possible purpose it was intended. It may also be asked whether it is the rounded, 'unified work' he believes it to be. It begins with the call of Abraham to journey to a land which Yahweh will show him and which he promises to give in possession to Abraham's descendants. Yet the narratives which follow centre very largely on the birth of Abraham's two sons, Ishmael and Isaac, whilst the theme of promise of the land, introduced at the beginning of the composition, is never again mentioned.

(3) There is an obvious difficulty in Van Seters's view that Genesis 20 was composed for the purpose of correcting the moral and theological shortcomings of the narrative in Genesis 12: 10–20: Why did the author of the former leave standing in his compilation of Stage 2 a narrative from Stage 1 which, *ex hypothesi*, he was so much concerned to correct by his own composition in Genesis 20? Would readers or listeners of the expanded story of Abraham not have understood the story in chapter 20 as relating a different incident to that narrated in chapter 12 rather than one intended to correct what the author of the new story found objectionable in the latter? I shall

[12] See below, Ch. 6, pp. 175–81.
[13] See P. G. Kirkpatrick, *The Old Testament and Folklore Study*, JSOT Supplement Series, 62 (Sheffield 1988). Cf. also R. C. Culley, *Studies in the Structure of Hebrew Narrative* (Missoula, Mont. 1976).

return later to a detailed consideration of the relevance of duplicate stories for the study of Pentateuchal origins.[14]

(4) That the traditions about Israel's patriarchs were of importance during the exilic period is unquestionable. Their significance is well attested in the literature of the period as Van Seters and others have pointed out. The 'kerygmatic' use of these traditions corresponds with that of other traditions during that period, including the exodus and wilderness traditions and those centring upon the Davidic dynasty and upon Zion.

The case argued by Van Seters concerning the significance of the promises of land and progeny to the patriarchs during the exilic period finds some support in texts in both Ezekiel and Deutero-Isaiah. Thus, in Ezekiel 33: 23 ff. the prophet inveighs against the appeal of those left in the land to Abraham's possession of the land as vindication of their claim that the land had been given to them: 'Abraham was but one man and he possessed the land. But we are many, and the land is given to us to possess'. The same promise-bearing name of Abraham is found also on the lips of Deutero-Isaiah later in the exilic period: the exiles are addressed as 'the descendants ("seed") of Abraham, my friend' (Isa. 41: 8. Cf. Gen. 18: 17), whilst in 51: 2 the prophet exhorts them to 'look unto Abraham your father, and unto Sarah that bare you: for when he was but one I called him, and I blessed him, and made him many'. In addition, there are grounds for agreeing with Van Seters that these promises may be much later than scholars such as Alt argued.

During the middle decades of this century and following the publication of Alt's study of them,[15] it was widely accepted that the promises of land and progeny were traceable to the oldest layers of tradition in Genesis.[16] Virtually the only dissenting voice was J. Hoftijzer whose monograph arguing that they originated at the literary level as late, secondary insertions into an existing Pentateuchal text gained few adherents.[17] The case remains a strong one, however, that these promises are secondary, or mostly so, in their contexts, and Hoftijzer's view has attracted increasing support in recent years.[18]

---

[14] See below, Ch. 8.   [15] See above, Ch. 2.
[16] For a history of the research see Boorer, *The Promise of the Land as Oath*, 38–99.
[17] J. Hoftijzer, *Die Verheissung an die drei Erzväter* (Leiden 1956). The most thorough discussion of the promises prior to Hoftijzer's was W. Staerk's *Studien zur Religions- und Sprachgeschichte des Alten Testaments*, i (Berlin 1899).
[18] For a cautious assessment see especially Emerton, 'The Origin of the Promises to the Patriarchs in the Older Sources of the Book of Genesis', 14–32.

Some of the promises are indisputably original: the promise of a son for Abraham and Sarah in 18: 10, 14, and for Hagar in 16: 11. There is also no need to reject 12: 7 as secondary and, indeed, it is possible that the other promises of land are dependent upon it and are developments of it. As Emerton argues, it is appropriate to the context: 'Abraham is told in xii 1 to travel to the land that Yahweh will show him, and he goes to Shechem (vv. 6–7), the region of Bethel (v. 8), and Hebron (xiii 18), and builds an altar in each place. Abraham thus visits some of the principal holy places in the land, and the context is concerned with the land to which Yahweh has led him; and so the promise of the land in xii 7 fits the context and is probably original' (p. 22). Genesis 15 contains promises in vv. 4–5 and 18. Though it is possible that vv. 1–6 are a secondary addition to this chapter, v. 18 is original. But there are good reasons for believing that this chapter is a secondary addition to its context. It is very probable also, however, that the remaining promises are secondary additions to their contexts.[19]

The evidence suggests that the promises are unlikely to have been composed before the late monarchical period. There are good grounds for believing that Genesis 15: 9–12, 17–21,[20] which is a key passage among them narrating a solemn oath of Yahweh pledging the land to Abraham's descendants,[21] is late and probably derives from a time close to Deuteronomy.[22] The late pre-exilic period and after the fall of the Northern Kingdom or the exilic period have both been argued. The crisis arising from the fall of the Northern Kingdom in 722 BC with its consequences of loss of land and deportation suggests itself as a plausible *terminus a quo*. Since the tradition of Yahweh's oath to the patriarchs is prominent in the Deuteronomistic History, its composition in the exilic period marks the *terminus ad quem*.[23]

---

[19] Emerton suggests (ibid. 22) that 28: 15 is original to the context, since it refers to guidance back to the land and so fits the context, and originally followed 13 or at least 13a. (He regards v. 14 as secondary.) Though rather vague, however, what does 15b refer to if not to the promises in vv. 13–14? The possibility that both v. 13b and v. 15 are original here cannot be ruled out. On the other hand, v. 16 may originally have immediately followed v. 12, and vv. 13–15 may be a secondary insertion by a J editor into this passage, which is usually assigned to E.

[20] vv. 13–15 are probably a secondary addition.

[21] For this see especially Hoftijzer, *Die Verheissung*, 17–23.

[22] For this see especially O. Kaiser, 'Traditionsgeschichtliche Untersuchung von Genesis 15', *ZAW* 70 (1958), 107–26.

[23] For a rejection of the view that the pre-P Tetrateuch was composed subsequent to the Deuteronomistic History, see below, Ch. 6.

Against Van Seters, therefore, although it may be agreed that most of the promise-speeches in Genesis and related texts in the Tetrateuch are late, perhaps as late as the exilic period, they seem also to be secondary insertions into an existing text. As such they are part of the problem of the origin and growth of the Tetrateuch rather than the key to its solution.

III

In his monograph *The So-called Yahwist*, H. H. Schmid, formerly Professor of Old Testament at the University of Zürich and now its Rector, argues the case for an exilic dating of J(E) on a broader basis than Van Seters. By the phrase 'so-called Yahwist' Schmid means that we should not think of the composition of the Tetrateuchal material designated by this term as the work of a single collector, author, and theologian. It was a retrograde step when scholars generally, following von Rad, moved away from the findings of earlier research that J is in fact a multilayered work and was not composed at one sitting, so to speak. Rather, J is the outcome of 'an (inner-) Yahwistic process of redaction and interpretation' of inherited traditions (p. 167). He explains that although the results he arrives at differ greatly from the usual picture of the Yahwist and the traditional source theory, he retains the term 'Yahwist' first, because he 'did not wish to sever completely the links with previous Pentateuchal study', and also because he 'wished to enquire, by means of this study, what is presumably the oldest total redaction of the Pentateuch'; thus 'the restrictive title "the so-called Yahwist" is meant to express both a continuity and a discontinuity with previous research'.[24]

Schmid ranges in detail over a number of key contexts in the material usually ascribed to J, and seeks to demonstrate that they presuppose a knowledge of the writing prophets of the pre-exilic period, and were directly influenced by Deuteronomic and Deuteronomistic literature and theology. Individual texts ánd pericopae examined include the call of Moses, the plagues of Egypt, the deliverance of Israel at 'the Sea', episodes in the wilderness, the making of the covenant at Sinai, and the promises to the patriarchs, and from a discussion of these he concludes that the Yahwist belonged to the same milieu as the Deuteronomistic authors, that is, the exilic period.

[24] H. H. Schmid, 'In Search of New Approaches in Pentateuchal Research', *JSOT* 3 (1977), 40.

Schmid argues that the Yahwist's work no less than the Deuteronomist's was composed to meet the crisis which the fall of the Judaean state and the exile raised not merely for the future of Israel as the people of Yahweh but for the future of Yahwism itself (pp. 176 ff.). Taking up traditions of varied age and origin and reworking them, the Yahwist composed his work as a theology of history to meet the crisis of the time, that is, whether Yahweh's will was any longer effective in history or whether history is in reality independent of his will, since in apparent contradiction of his purposes his people had now lost their statehood and had suffered exile at the hands of a triumphant enemy. Like the Deuteronomistic History, the Yahwist's theology of history has for one of its main themes Israel's guilt. At the same time the Yahwist also describes Yahweh's forbearance with his people whose guilt, though it has brought its own consequences upon the nation, is met and overcome by Yahweh's continued faithfulness to Israel, his 'indestructible nevertheless (*Dennoch*)' to his people (p. 179). By this 'nevertheless' the Yahwist's theology is thus a theology of hope that will enable Israel to survive the calamity of the time.

A few illustrations only can be briefly noted here of the case Schmid seeks to make. He insists, for example, that the call and commissioning of Moses in Exodus 3–4 (pp. 19–43) and the action he is commanded to carry out as narrated in the plague narratives presuppose the call-visions and role of the writing prophets from Isaiah onwards (pp. 44–53): the prophetic mission assigned to Moses as the messenger of Yahweh's will ('Go and say to . . . ': 3: 16; 7: 15–16, 26; 8: 16; 9: 1, 13); the announcement by Yahweh of the message to be delivered by the messenger (Exod. 3: 16 f.; 7: 16, 26; 8: 16; 9: 1, 13; 10: 3); the use of the messenger formula ('Thus says Yahweh . . . ': 7: 17, 26; 8: 16; 9: 1, 13; 10: 3); the characteristic protest of the one called (4: 1), and his authentication by means of signs (4: 2 ff.); and the function of Moses as intercessor (8: 4 ff., 24 ff.; 9: 28 f.; 10: 16 ff.).

Episodes in the narratives of the wandering in the wilderness provide further evidence of the influence of a well-attested Deuteronomistic literary form (pp. 61–82).[25] Thus, the structure of such J narratives as Exodus 15: 22–5a; 17: 1bβ–7; Numbers 11: 1–3; *11: 4–32; *12: 1–15; 21: 4b–9 describing (a) an offence by Israel (e.g. complaint against Moses and God) incurring (b) God's anger and punishment, followed by (c) plea/intercession for help, and (d)

[25] See also H. Vorländer, *Die Entstehungszeit des jehowistischen Geschichtswerkes* (Frankfurt am Main 1978), 361 f.

forgiveness and deliverance from affliction, display the influence of the use of this structure in the Deuteronomistic literature, most notably in the book of Judges with its familiar (a) offence of Israel; (b) defeat by and subjection to an enemy; (c) cry for help to Yahweh; (d) deliverance. The tradition of the making of a covenant at Sinai is likewise of Deuteronomic origin (pp. 83–118). The promises to the patriarchs are also most likely of exilic origin (pp. 119–53).

Schmid's lively and lucid book has been a major influence in current Pentateuchal research. More than any other recent study, his has undermined confidence in the early dating of the Yahwist's work so widely favoured since von Rad's monograph in 1938, whilst his arguments concerning the presence in J of literary forms and theological developments of a much later period in Israel's history have found increasing favour. Of special significance are his conclusions concerning the influence of the Deuteronomic/Deuteronomistic literature upon the Yahwist's narrative. Though he drew a distinction between the Yahwist and the Deuteronomistic writers, thinking in terms only of the influence of the latter upon J, his conclusions have been seen by others as evidence of a more direct involvement of Deuteronomistic writers in the composition of the pre-Priestly Tetrateuch. In particular, as we shall see, Erhard Blum's theory of a Deuteronomistic 'composition layer' (K^D) in the Tetrateuch is indebted to Schmid's conclusions.

But questions also arise concerning Schmid's conclusions, for example, whether the Yahwist's 'theology of history' necessarily presupposes an exilic context, or whether the general character of this narrative fits the same setting as the Deuteronomistic History and the other literature from the exilic period. Is the literary structure of such texts as Exodus 15: 22–5a; 17: 1bβ–7; Numbers 11: 1–3; *11: 4–32; *12: 1–15; 21: 4b–9 due to Deuteronomistic influence, or does the account of the commissioning of Moses in Exodus 3–4 necessarily reflect the *Gattung* of the prophetic call-vision? I shall return in Chapter 6 to these and other issues arising from Schmid's work. First, however, a further prominent trend in current research must receive our attention.

IV

Though Schmid concluded that the Yahwist's narrative derives from the same milieu as the Deuteronomistic literature, he did not consider a possible closer relationship between these two works. Others have suggested such a relationship, however, arguing that the Yahwist composed his work subsequent to the Deuteronomistic corpus and as a 'prologue' to it. Van Seters and Martin Rose, who was a pupil of H. H. Schmid and is now Professor of Old Testament at the University of Neuchâtel, have devoted special studies to this. In his *Prologue to History* Van Seters focuses upon the question of the genre of the Yahwist's narrative, finding in it a work of 'antiquarian historiography' on the analogy of examples of ancient Greek historiography.[26] He has followed this by his *The Life of Moses: The Yahwist as Historian in Exodus–Numbers* in which he deals extensively with the pre-P narrative in Exodus and Numbers, here adopting in part a method similar to that of Rose who has devoted special attention to parallel texts in JE and the Deuteronomistic corpus, concluding that the former are later than the latter.[27]

Some observations by Norman Whybray will serve as a preface to a consideration of Van Seters' more detailed studies. Whybray argues that the Tetrateuch in substantially its present form is the work of a single author of the exilic period who may have intended it as a supplement in the form of a 'prologue' to the Deuteronomistic History. This author had at his disposal a mass of materials which, adopting what Whybray refers to as 'the canons of the historiography of his time', he 'radically reworked . . . probably with substantial additions of his own invention'.[28] By 'canons of the historiography of his time' he means those of early Greek historiography. He writes that since the main Pentateuchal source, J, has usually been dated centuries before the earliest Greek historical works, a comparison between it and Greek historiography has not hitherto been considered worth while. If the date of the Yahwist is brought down to the sixth century, however, then 'his work would be almost contemporary with them' (p. 226). According to Van Seters the forms and methods employed in early Greek historiography provide a controlled and adequate means of understanding those of the writers of the early prose historiography of the Old Testament.[29]

[26] See especially his *In Search of History* and *Prologue to History: The Yahwist as Historian in Genesis*.

[27] Rose, *Deuteronomist und Jahwist*.

[28] R. N. Whybray, *The Making of the Pentateuch: A Methodological Study* (Sheffield 1987), 242.

[29] Van Seters, *In Search of History*, 17.

In his *In Search of History* he draws special attention to the relevance of early Greek history writings, notably Herodotus, for a proper appreciation of the literary techniques of the Old Testament historical narratives. In narrative style and technique, he argues, the Old Testament historical literature and Herodotus show many similarities. He points to their common use of parataxis and prolepsis as well as so-called 'ring composition', to the use by each of speeches placed on the lips of leading figures in the events narrated, the free composition of appropriate stories and anecdotes where their sources failed them, the insertion of editorial comment to introduce or sum up the theme of a unit, or to provide a transition to the next unit, the periodization of history with the dovetailing of eras, themes, and *logoi*, and the association of important themes with major figures (pp. 37–8, 358). By means of such literary devices these authors skilfully wove together and creatively structured the disparate materials, both written and oral, which they had collected, and gave a sense of unity to the long and complex works they wrote. The use of royal chronologies, genealogies, or genealogical chronologies as a way of ordering separate story units is common in early Greek history writing in general and in Herodotus in particular, and is also prominent in the Old Testament literature (p. 38).

Van Seters finds further similarities between Old Testament historical writings and Herodotus in prominent interpretative themes. For example, both Herodotus and the Deuteronomist show a dominant concern with divine retribution for unlawful acts as a fundamental principle of historical causality; that is, for both 'history is theodicy' (p. 40). Themes of 'divine providence, or retribution or salvation, and the use of the past as a mirror for present and future events in order to deal with the problem of change appear to be basic concerns addressed by both Herodotus and the Old Testament historiographic literature and constitute a major motivation for their existence' (p. 52). In scope of subject matter and the themes treated, nothing in the literature of the ancient Near East before the fourth century, he argues, so closely resembles the biblical histories as the Greek histories.

In his later volume, *Prologue to History*, Van Seters argues that the Yahwist[30] may appropriately be described as a historian, more specifically an 'antiquarian historian', whose work bears striking similarities to writings of the Greek 'antiquarian tradition' such as is

---

[30] For the reasons already outlined above, Van Seters includes the so-called E material as well as J in the work of this author.

represented by the so-called *Catalogue of Women*, an anonymous addition to Hesiod's Theogany from the mid-sixth century BC,[31] and by the writings of the early Greek historians and mythographers such as Acusilaus, Pherecydes, Hecataeus, Herodotus, Hellanicus.[32] He finds in the classification of the Yahwist's work as 'antiquarian history' the key also to the purpose for which J was composed, that is, as a prologue to the Deuteronomistic History which is also properly described as a work of ancient historiography. He believes that this solves the form-critical problem of the Hexateuch, providing a proper genre description of it, and clarifies the relationship of the Yahwist to the Deuteronomist.

Focusing on the Yahwist's narrative in Genesis, Van Seters argues that the Yahwist was indebted both to a 'Western', that is, Greek tradition of antiquarian historiography, and to an 'Eastern', Mesopotamian tradition. The 'Western' tradition includes within its treatment of the primeval or heroic age quite different themes and concerns, and it structures its presentation in a very different form or genre in which genealogical lists are employed as a framework into which all major traditions relevant to the particular history were fitted:

This western focus on the origin of peoples and tribes and on the first inventors of culture and the treatment of these by means of genealogical chronology is absent from the eastern tradition. By contrast, the eastern emphasis upon the creation of humankind, universal kingship and the flood as the end of the primeval age, and the structure of a king-list chronology play only a marginal and secondary role in the western tradition as late foreign elements. (*Prologue to History*, 98)

From his examination of the primeval history and patriarchal narratives, he finds parallels in *The Catalogue of Women* to such narratives in Genesis as the episode of the union of the sons of God with the daughters of mankind (Gen. 6: 1–4), the Table of the Nations (Gen. 10), the genealogical frameworks of the patriarchal narratives, and the stories about the eponymous ancestors of Israel and her neighbours and the lands they gained possession of for their descendants, for example, Lot, Ishmael, Esau. He believes that *The Catalogue of Women* was intended as a sort of 'prologue that leads up

[31] See M. L. West, *The Hesiodic Catalogue of Women: Its Nature, Structure and Origins* (Oxford 1985).

[32] See his *Prologue to History*, ch. 4, and 'The Primeval Histories of Greece and Israel Compared', *ZAW* 100 (1988), 1–22.

to the big event, the Panhellenic tradition of the Trojan War, to which
so many of the heroes of the various genealogies on both sides of the
hostilities are related'.[33] 'The Yahwist', he continues, 'through the
primary line of the patriarchs also leads up to the events of the exodus from Egypt and the conquest of the land. In both cases, the function of the antiquarian tradition is to articulate the corporate identity
of the group encompassed by the genealogical tradition.' This
'Western' influence upon the Yahwist, he concludes, 'goes a long way
to explain the genealogical framework which is the structure upon
which the authors of Genesis have built'; it is 'in the Greek national
antiquarian tradition, in its early historiography, that one finds the
clue to the problem of [the] form [of Genesis]'.

Thus both the Yahwist and the Deuteronomist can be described as
authors and historians in every sense in which these terms apply to
ancient Greek writers such as Herodotus. The Deuteronomistic corpus, divested of secondary additions, is a 'literary work of superb
accomplishment, with a remarkably uniform style and outlook'. In
genre it is a work of ancient historiography wholly comparable to that
of ancient Greece. Its author's purpose was above all to communicate
through his story of the people's past a 'sense of their identity—and
that is the *sine qua non* of history writing'.[34] The Deuteronomist was
Israel's first historian, he argues. The Yahwist wrote subsequently in
the exilic period and composed his narrative as a prologue to the
Deuteronomist's work by extending the history back in time to the
beginning of the world (p. 361).[35]

V

Van Seters rejects the distinction drawn by many students of ancient
historiography between the 'antiquarian tradition' and the 'true historian' such as Thucydides. 'The difference, for the ancients,' he
argues in his *Prologue to History*, (p. 96), 'was primarily one of subject
matter'. Much of the ethnographic material of Herodotus's history,
for example, is antiquarian in form and character. Similarly, with
regard to the Yahwist's narrative, although 'the presence of etiologi-
cal myths and legends may argue against its usefulness for modern

[33] Ibid. 22.   [34] Van Seters, *In Search of History*, 359.
[35] See also Van Seters, *The Life of Moses*.

historiography, that fact does not vitiate its place within the ancient genres of antiquarian "research" (*historia*)' (p. 328).

Few will agree, however, with such a view, and most will regard the claim that the Yahwist engaged in *historia* as a misuse of the word employed by Herodotus to describe the task and the method he adopted, which were crucially different from anything that preceded him in ancient Greece and from the work of either the Yahwist or the Deuteronomist.[36] By *historia* 'enquiry' Herodotus, who coined the word,[37] meant primarily travel and the active pursuit of data and a critical assessment of sources, whether written or oral. More frequently he uses the verb (*historein*) 'denoting precisely the activity of questioning, enquiring, researching'.[38] It was the development of this critical attitude towards recording events and the development of appropriate methods that characterized Greek historiography.[39] Before this there was an interest in the past, as the writings of Homer show, and in genealogical speculation, as the work of Hesiod illustrates. The art of historical narration in the Greek historians was also indebted to the epic narrative tradition stretching back to Homer. But there is no continuity between either Homer or Hesiod and what is specific in Greek history writing—the critical attitude towards sources and to the recording of events.

This attitude began in the late sixth century and arose from a revolution in thought involving a 'rebellion against tradition, the search for new principles of explanation, the rise of doubt as an intellectual stimulus to new discoveries'.[40] At this time it came to be believed 'that a systematic criticism of historical tradition is both possible and desirable, and that a comparison between different national traditions helps to establish truth'.[41] Herodotus and his successors wrote about contemporary or near contemporary events, for example about the Persian Wars of the recent past (Herodotus) or, in the case of Thucydides, the contemporary Peloponnesian Wars. Though the choice of subjects was determined by the importance of the events,

[36] For a fuller discussion of this see my 'Story and History in the Old Testament', in S. E. Balentine and J. Barton (eds.), *Language, Theology, and the Bible: Essays in Honour of James Barr* (Oxford 1994), 135–50.

[37] For a discussion of the word see John Gould, *Herodotus* (London 1989), 9–12; S. Hornblower, *Thucydides* (London 1987), 8–25.

[38] Gould, *Herodotus*, 9.

[39] Cf. A. Momigliano, 'The Herodotean and the Thucydidean Tradition', *The Classical Foundations of Modern Historiography* (Berkeley 1990), 30.

[40] Ibid. 31.   [41] Ibid 34.

the reliability of sources was an additional motive, and reliability was determined by enquiry and question and cross-examination of sources and eyewitnesses.

Such an approach to sources, this 'enquiry' and cross-examination of what is recorded, seen, or heard, is a far cry from the work of either the Yahwist or the Deuteronomist whose writings are devoid of the sort of critical assessment and evaluation of sources which is such a feature of the quest and writings of the Greek historians from Herodotus onwards. Unlike Herodotus, the Old Testament writers do not express their own opinion as to the truth or reliability of the sources they collected. Rather, for them it was a matter of 'thus did the Lord say and thus did He do on behalf of his people or against them'. It is not that the gods were irrelevant to Herodotus. But there is a world of difference between his critical attitude towards reports of divine intervention in history and what the Old Testament writers believed and wrote. He expressed caution when recording the testimony of others about divine intervention, demanding additional weight of evidence, or declining to identify the particular god concerned, or using *oratio obliqua*, or offering alternative explanations.[42] What he wrote may be characterized as 'a multi-subjective, contingency-oriented account' of events and their outcome;[43] 'he wanted to know how everything happened, what had followed what, and what had influenced what. So he showed how the Persian Empire grew up, how Sparta and Athens became powerful, and how it was various chance motives, some of them highly personal, of individual leaders which in a very complicated interaction caused the Ionian conflict with the Persians'.[44] By contrast, for the Deuteronomist the downfall of Israel was brought about by Yahweh who rejected his apostate people. The Assyrians and Babylonians were merely the instruments of his will. That is, what happened to Israel and Judah was not the result of the changes and chances of history, the outcome of the decisions of men, or of power struggles among nations, in other words a sequence of events caused by many different subjects which met as chance would have it. Neither the Deuteronomist nor the

---

[42] See most recently John Gould, 'Herodotus and Religion', in S. Hornblower (ed.), *Greek Historiography* (Oxford 1994), 91–106.

[43] C. Meier, 'Historical Answers to Historical Questions: The Origins of History in Ancient Greece', *Arethusa*, 20 (1987), 41–57. Cf. Gould, *Herodotus*, ch. 4, 'Why Things Happen'.

[44] Meier, 'Historical Answers', 48.

Yahwist can be seriously considered as having sought to compose an accurate 'record' of past events, and it does not seem that the past was the motivation for their endeavours, even in those narratives which may be regarded as providing historically useful information.

Herodotus described the task he set himself thus: 'Here are set forth the enquiries [*historiēs*] of Herodotus of Halicarnassus that men's action may not in time be forgotten nor things great and wonderful, accomplished whether by Greeks or barbarians, go without report, nor especially the cause of the wars between one and the other.' By contrast, the writers of the Pentateuch and of the Deuteronomistic corpus sought to describe to their nation the ways of God in promise, fulfilment and judgement by which means Israel might be brought to think about its present and future as the people of God.[45] That they employed literary techniques which were used also by Greek historians may be so. But both their method and their objectives were very different. In short, their writings are not the result of *historia*.

What of the supposed influence of the so-called Greek 'antiquarian tradition' upon the Yahwist? A serious difficulty is surely of knowing how the Yahwist, living as an exile in an alien land, could have acquired access to this 'Western tradition' represented by works such as *The Catalogue of Women*. The difficulty is not adequately met by Van Seters's general statement in his *Prologue to History* that 'the exilic period was a time when Judaean intellectual traditions were open to strong foreign influence' (p. 332). We know of no Babylonian sources of the exilic period which show any knowledge of such texts or of their influence. Nor, indeed, does Van Seters claim the latter, since part of his case is that the combination of the 'Eastern' and 'Western' traditions 'reflects the Yahwist's historiographic skills' (p. 330). There is evidence of the presence of Greeks acting as official scribes in the Persian administration *c.*500 BC,[46] but not earlier in the

[45] R. Smend has drawn special attention to the prominence of aetiology and paradigm as a primary motivation of the authors of the Pentateuch and Deuteronomistic corpus. See his *Elemente alttestamentlichen Geschichtsdenkens*, Theologische Studien, 95 (Zürich 1968). Cf. J. Barr, 'Story and History in Biblical Theology', in *The Scope and Authority of the Bible*, Explorations in Theology, 7 (London 1980), 7–8, originally published in *JR* 56 (1976), 1–17; 'Historical Reading and the Theological Interpretation of Scripture', in *The Scope and Authority of the Bible*, 36.

[46] See David M. Lewis, 'Persians in Herodotus', in M. H. Jameson (ed.), *The Greek Historians: Literature and History* (Stanford, Calif. 1985), 101–17, and 'The Persepolis Tablets: Speech, Seal and Script', in A. K. Bowman and G. Woolf (eds.), *Literacy and Power in the Ancient World* (Cambridge 1994), 17–27.

sixth century and during the Babylonian period. Whilst it might have been possible therefore for a Jewish exile writing in Babylon to have been influenced by Babylonian religious and mythological lore, the suggestion that he would also have had access to, or come under the influence of, Greek 'antiquarian' texts during the sixth century is egregiously speculative. However the Yahwist's work is to be classified, neither the genre of ancient Greek *historia* nor the so-called Greek 'antiquarian tradition' provide a credible analogy.

VI

Rose's minutely detailed study attempts to show that the Yahwist wrote his narrative subsequent to the Deuteronomistic History and as a prologue to it. His method is novel. Historically the source analysis of the Pentateuch has begun with Genesis, and it has been on the basis of the results achieved from a study of this, the first book of the Pentateuch, that theories of the composition of the Pentateuch as a whole have been formulated. Rose proposes in *Deuteronomist and Yahwist* an approach that begins at the end, that is, with the final book of the Pentateuch, Deuteronomy, and with the occupation of the land as the thematic end of the Hexateuch (pp. 18 f., 320). He chooses a series of texts in Deuteronomy and in the narratives of the conquest in Joshua and compares them with passages in the Tetrateuch which are in some way related to them. Three main groups of texts are discussed: (a) narratives concerning the occupation of the land (Josh. 2–6) and related texts in the Tetrateuch; (b) narratives concerning the Canaanites and their relationship with Israel (Josh. 9–10; Gen. 34); and (c) the introductory chapters of the Deuteronomistic History in Deuteronomy 1–3 and related texts in Exodus, Numbers, and Joshua.

In virtually all instances Rose concludes that the Tetrateuch texts usually ascribed to JE were composed later than related texts in the Deuteronomistic corpus. Two examples only from the many he discusses can be mentioned here. The first comprises the narratives concerning Caleb in Numbers 13–14, Deuteronomy 1: 19–46, and Joshua 14: 6–15 (pp. 264–94). Rose argues that an ancient settlement tradition centring on the boldness of Caleb—the name Caleb itself suggests a sort of 'daredevil' figure (pp. 264 f.)—who was a zealous devotee of Yahweh through whose fearless leadership the powerful city of Hebron was conquered lies behind these much later narratives. Among them, he suggests, the narrative in Joshua 14: 6–15 still reflects most clearly something of the old tradition: though a story of land allocation by Joshua rather than of conquest, the conquest tradition is still reflected in the reference to the Anakim, to the great and fenced cities, and to Caleb's confidence that Yahweh will be with him enabling him to drive them out; the *scopus* of the story is the faithfulness of Caleb who 'followed wholly after Yahweh' when others were fainthearted, and who is rewarded by the possession 'forever' of the land he gains. The story, Rose concludes, is not based upon either Numbers 13–14 or Deuteronomy 1: 19 ff. Rather, its author was directly dependent upon the ancient Caleb tradition.

By comparison, Rose argues, the narrative Deuteronomy 1: 19–46 reflects a 'demilitarized' and theological use of the tradition: the role of Moses rather than Caleb is emphasized; Moses is portrayed as the encourager whilst Caleb is mentioned only late in the story; the focus is upon the faithless response of the people and the rejection of them and their generation in punishment of this; the process of 'demilitarization' of the tradition is also reflected in the emphasis upon faith in Yahweh who alone ensures victory: the people will come to nought if they place their confidence in their own might and in the strength of their weaponry. The role of the spies is in this way pushed into the background.

Rose then argues that the commonly accepted view that the original narrative in Numbers 13–14, which can still be discerned after the removal of the later priestly reworking of it, was presupposed and used by the authors of Deuteronomy 1: 19 ff. cannot be sustained. This J narrative in Numbers is no longer a story proper about Caleb, as in Joshua 14: 6 ff. Neither is it primarily concerned with the faithlessness of the people, as in Deuteronomy 1: 19 ff. Rather, it reworks the old tradition into a story about the spies, more specifically a 'theological' story the effect of which is to distance the spies even more than in Deuteronomy from their strictly military role. Rather, returning from the land laden with the signs of its fruitfulness, the spies have become witnesses to the richness of the land which Yahweh in his faithfulness has promised to his people. According to Rose, where the narratives in Numbers and Deuteronomy display literary similarities, this is not because they are in some way interdependent, but arose from the use by their respective authors of a common tradition (p. 282).

Rose maintains that a similar result is achieved from an examination of the narrative in Exodus 18 (usually ascribed to E) and the parallel J text in Numbers 11 and the further parallel in Deuteronomy 1: 9–18. Though the narrative in Exodus 18 describing the institution, at the suggestion of Jethro, of judicial helpers for Moses reflects an ancient, even pre-monarchic, tradition, it is a late composition. In comparison, however, the story in Deuteronomy 1 is later and Numbers 11 later still and displaying a further development of the institution as described in Exodus 18. As in the case of the Caleb stories, where Exodus 18, Numbers 11, and Deuteronomy 1: 9 ff. show similarities, these are for the most part to be explained as deriving from the dependence of their authors upon a common tradition.

On these grounds Rose argues that the J(E) material in the Tetrateuch was composed after the Deuteronomistic History. Theologically it also sought to counter the theology of the Deuteronomists (pp. 325 f.). Here Rose adopts a view close to that of his mentor H. H. Schmid according to whom the centre of the Yahwist's theology is the proclamation of Yahweh's 'indestructible nevertheless' to his wayward and faithless people. Rose focuses upon the theme of Israel's 'murmuring'. Deuteronomistic theology too knows of Israel's failure before Yahweh as expressed in a theme such as this. But whereas the Deuteronomists, at least at the stage in the development of the Deuteronomistic corpus represented in the texts analysed by Rose, still held out hope that Israel could choose to obey and be faithful to Yahweh, in the Yahwist's theology there is complete disillusion of any possibility of Israel's faithfulness to Yahweh. At the hands of the Yahwist, Rose argues, the period of the wandering in the wilderness is no longer characterized by occasional failures and offences; rather, the people are depicted as being fundamentally incapable of being the human partner of God's work of salvation. Hence, in the Yahwist's theology Israel's future depends solely upon the grace of Yahweh whose freely bestowed salvation was archetypally manifested in the exodus (p. 325). This does not mean that the Yahwist sought to displace the Deuteronomistic History. Rather, according to Rose, as a prologue to the latter, the Yahwist's theology of Yahweh's faithfulness towards Israel provided the theological 'key' for the interpretation of the whole of God's dealing with his people from creation to the exile, that is, the theological key to the history recorded in Genesis–2 Kings (p. 327).

VII

Clearly, if Rose's and Van Seters's conclusions are correct it turns our usual conception of the stages in the composition of the Pentateuch upside down, and substantiates the 'paradigm' noted earlier according to which there never was an independent Tetrateuch but that the (pre-P) narrative in Genesis–Numbers was composed instead as a prologue to the Deuteronomistic History, extending the story of Israel back from the eve of the settlement to the patriarchal age and providing also a primeval history beginning with creation. We shall examine in some detail one of Rose's 'test' cases in Chapter 6 and comment further on Van Seters's conclusions in this regard. Here two general questions may be asked.

A main difficulty which Rose's conclusions run into is the question how and where the traditions which he believes to lie behind the narratives he discusses were transmitted. How and where was the ancient Caleb tradition, for example, which according to Rose both the Deuteronomist author and the author of Numbers independently drew upon, transmitted? Where and how was the ancient tradition concerning Jethro and the institution of 'judges' to assist Moses preserved and handed down, and what was its function? In both instances the period of transmission would have been, *ex hypothesi,* centuries. How are we to imagine such traditions to have been transmitted over so protracted a period? Were they handed down as independent stories, or did each belong to a complex of oral tradition? Why were such traditions not committed to writing until such a late stage in Israel's history? These questions are not raised by Rose. The very asking of them, however, raises doubts about the credibility of his hypothesis.[47]

Credulity is all the more strained when the conclusions reached on the basis of the texts examined are extended to the J(E) material in the Tetrateuch as a whole. On Rose's hypothesis we must presume that only an amorphous collection of traditions or, indeed, since he offers no discussion of this, perhaps scattered traditions existed which it fell to the Yahwist in the exilic period, and subsequent to the composition of the Deuteronomistic History, to collect and shape

---

[47] See the apt comments by A. H. J. Gunneweg, 'Anmerkungen und Anfragen zur neueren Pentateuchforschung', *ThR* 48 (1983), 237 f. Cf. N. Lohfink's review of Rose's work in *ThPh* 57 (1982), 276–80, esp. 277 f.

into the first Tetrateuch. This in turn raises the further question of what complex or complexes of traditions the author of the retrospect of the wilderness wanderings in Deuteronomy 1–3 was evidently able to presume on the part of his readers or hearers. What accumulated lore or story of the journey from Horeb was there, such that this author could expect his readers and listeners to know what happened 'at that time'? The nature of the opening chapters of Deuteronomy as a retrospect on the plains of Moab seems naturally to point to some such narrative of events of preceding years as JE offers.[48] I shall argue later that neither Rose nor Van Seters has made the case for his view that the Deuteronomistic narratives he examines were composed before their parallels in the Tetrateuch.

VIII

This is an appropriate stage at which to comment on Hermann Vorländer's contribution, *The Origin of the Jehovistic History*.[49] He devotes the larger part of his book to arguing that JE was unknown to any of the writings of the pre-exilic period (pt. 1, pp. 23–284).[50] It derives instead from the exilic/post-exilic period and thus from a time 'when there was throughout the entire ancient Near East a special interest in the past' (p. 368): 'Israel's interest in its own history was apparently stimulated by the rich historical tradition of Mesopotamia, with which Israel in exile became familiar' (ibid.). Further, outside the Tetrateuch, he argues, a use of the past and a theological interpretation of history first appear in the exilic period; Ezekiel and Deutero-Isaiah are examples of how intensive such a concern became at that time. Following Schmid, therefore, Vorländer dates the origin of JE in proximity to the writings of the Deuteronomistic 'school' and regards JE also as the work of a 'school' on the analogy of the latter.

---

[48] See the comments of N. Lohfink, 'Deutéronome et Pentateuque: État de la Recherche', in Pierre Haudebert (ed.), *Le Pentateuque: Débats et Recherches*, Lectio Divina, 151 (Paris 1992), 35–64, esp. 52 ff. Cf. p. 58, 'Dt 1–3, mais aussi les récits d'Horeb du Deutéronome, son trop visiblement une relecture de choses connues, et non une élaboration originale' ('Deuteronomy 1–3, and also Deuteronomy's account of the Horeb, are very obviously a retelling of something already known, and not a first draft').

[49] *Die Entstehungszeit des jehowistischen Geschichtswerkes*.

[50] Cf. also Whybray, *The Making of the Pentateuch*, 48 f.

The major part of Vorländer's book is concerned with contesting the view that some of the contents of JE are referred to in the prophetic literature of the pre-exilic period, for example the passage concerning Jacob in Hosea 12: 4–6, the reference to the destruction of Sodom and Gomorrah in Isaiah 1: 9, the mention of the exodus in Amos 9: 7 and Hosea 13: 1, and the mention of the wandering in the wilderness in Hosea 2: 16 f. and Amos 5: 25. He ranges over the main JE narrative sections of the Tetrateuch—the primeval history, the patriarchal narratives, the exodus narrative, the stories of episodes during the wilderness period, and the Sinai pericope—and concludes that references to them in the pre-exilic prophetic literature are either late, secondary additions to these prophetic collections, or reflect oral tradition but not the narrative compositions of the Yahwist or Elohist. The same is true of texts in the Former Prophets; here too texts mentioning major figures such as Moses, Aaron, and Joshua cannot with any certainty be dated in the pre-exilic period or where they can be so dated—for example the notices about Moses' father-in-law Hobab in Judges 1: 16, 20; 4: 11—are manifestly independent of the JE narratives. Likewise, none of the patriarchs Abraham, Isaac, or Jacob is mentioned in the sayings that can be regarded as authentically from the pre-exilic prophets.

Like Rose and others, therefore, Vorländer argues that though the substance of much of the Pentateuch was known in the pre-exilic period, it was not brought together into the form of JE until a much later period.

Vorländer's argument in this section of his book is an argument from silence and suffers from all the disadvantages of such an argument. It does not follow, for example, that even if Hosea 12: 4–6 does not presuppose the Jacob–Esau narrative in Genesis 27–36* the latter did not exist at that time. Neither Hosea, Isaiah, Micah, nor Amos refer to each other. Nor, except for Isaiah, do the books of Kings mention any of these prophets. Neither is Jeremiah mentioned in the final chapters of Kings narrating the last turbulent years of the kingdom of Judah in which he played such a role. But few would seriously question that these prophets were active in the periods in which the books bearing their names place them. The New Testament provides a similar example. None of the four Gospels yields any hint of the existence of the letters of St Paul, but manifestly this cannot be interpreted as meaning that St Paul's letters post-date them.

Vorländer contends that his argument from silence is no more inadmissible than Wellhausen's argument that P could not have existed in the pre-exilic period since the peculiar institutions and cultic laws it contains are unattested in the literature of the pre-exilic period (pp. 278 f.). But Wellhausen's argument concerning P was by no means an argument from silence, for the case argued by him was (and remains) not merely that there are no references to the peculiarly priestly and cultic institutions of P in the pre-exilic literature, but that the cultic and priestly practices and institutions which the pre-exilic literature records and narrates are at odds with what it set out and demanded in P's legislation.

There is space here to consider only one of the sections of JE which Vorländer discusses: the Jacob–Esau narrative in Genesis 27–33*. He focuses largely on whether this narrative is presupposed by the references to Jacob in Hosea 12: 4–6 and various other (mostly exilic or post-exilic) texts which mention this patriarch, concluding that it is not (pp. 68–77). Whether or not this is so, however, there are strong reasons for doubting, against Vorländer and others, that such a narrative would have been composed or compiled during the exilic period.

It is well known that among other features this story displays a marked 'aetiological' element in its description of Jacob and Esau as the ancestors of Israel and Edom respectively. Van Seters writes of this:[51] 'The rivalry of Jacob and Esau is especially noteworthy because it grows directly out of the larger genealogical structure. The story of their birth reflects, predictively, the later relations of the two peoples.' If, however, it is part of the intention of this story of Jacob and Esau to reflect the rivalry between the two states of which they are the ancestors, this makes an exilic setting for its composition improbable. At the end of the narrative and as part of the resolution of the plot, Jacob upon his fearful return from Mesopotamia bows to Esau, seven times no less, as does his entire household, addressing him as 'my lord' and designating himself as Esau's 'servant' (Gen. 33). It is difficult to believe that an Israelite writer of the exilic period would have composed a narrative that describes Jacob, that is, Israel bowing before Esau, that is, Edom, which at that time became one of Israel's most hated enemies, perhaps indeed its most hated enemy, and whose name for centuries thereafter would remain a byword for the most detested of the enemies of the Jewish people. Neither the

---

[51] 'The Primeval Histories of Greece and Israel Compared', 18.

reconciliation between the two brothers nor Jacob's obeisance to Esau whom he had wronged is a likely theme of an exilic writer. A pre-exilic origin of such a narrative surely remains much the more plausible view.

Other recent studies, whilst also arguing an exilic background to the composition of the pre-P Tetrateuch, seek to avoid the difficulty such a narrative poses by arguing that an exilic author employed *written* sources from the pre-exilic period. This is most notably so in the case of Blum's work which, as we have seen, makes full allowance for extensive pre-exilic sources in his early post-exilic K^D, and also of Levin's study *The Yahwist*.[52] My next chapter provides a discussion of the work of these two scholars and will also offer further observations on the research outlined in the present chapter.

---

[52] *Der Jahwist* (Göttingen 1993).

6

New Proposals Concerning the First Tetrateuch and its Sources

Two substantial studies of the origin of the pre-Priestly Tetrateuch must now receive our attention, Christoph Levin's *The Yahwist*,[1] and Erhard Blum's *Studies in the Composition of the Pentateuch*.[2] They have in common with the research outlined in the foregoing chapter that they too date the composition of the 'first Tetrateuch' to the exilic and early post-exilic period respectively. They differ from them, however, in seeking to uncover the earlier, pre-exilic written sources employed by the author(s) of this work which, they argue, were substantial. As we shall see, they also differ strikingly from each other.

I

Levin takes as his starting-point the insight of earlier research that literary unevenness in J is evidence of different stages of its growth (variously described as J^1, J^2, or J^a, J^b, etc.). He argues that this insight was fully justified, but that the evidence must be interpreted differently, that is, not in terms of the growth in stages of an original J narrative at the hands of successive J writers and editors, but of the distinction between pre-Yahwistic sources (J^Q) and the contribution of the Yahwist proper. According to Levin, the Yahwist is correctly understood, therefore, as a redactor (J^R) who selected, arranged, combined, and supplemented inherited narratives and narrative complexes in accordance with the message he wished to convey. That is, he fully accepts the conclusions of other recent studies which point to

---

[1] C. Levin, *Der Jahwist*, FRLANT 157 (Göttingen 1993). Though more narrowly based, H.-C. Schmitt's monograph *Die nichtpriesterliche Josephsgeschichte*, BZAW 154 (Berlin 1980) provides another example of this approach. He argues along similar lines to Winnett for a so-called 'late Yahwist' who worked in the exilic period but employed earlier, pre-exilic sources.

[2] Blum, *Studien zur Komposition des Pentateuch*.

the original independence of such pericopae as the primeval history, the Abraham–Lot 'cycle' of stories, the Joseph 'novel', etc. In this respect, the Yahwist's 'eclecticism' may be compared with that of the Deuteronomistic historian who likewise collected a mass of written sources from which to select. In terms of the history of research, Levin's conclusions concerning the work of the Yahwist thus combine a 'fragment theory' with a 'supplementary theory'; the Yahwist is both collector and redactor.

Levin argues that the Yahwist's narrative began with the creation story in Genesis 2 and ended with the story of Balaam in Numbers 22–4*, thus narrating a history of Israel from the creation of mankind up to the threshold of the settlement in the land but not including an account of the entry into Canaan. Ranging over this extensive narrative, he isolates sources from the redactional additions to, and reshaping of, them by the Yahwist himself. The Yahwist's narrative was subsequently supplemented by a non-Yahwistic editor (J^S). (Taken together, $J^Q + J^R + J^S$ comprise JE of the Documentary Theory.) A later redactor (R) combined 'JE' with P. The siglum R^S stands for further additions after 'JE' and P were combined.

Levin argues that the audience to which the Yahwist addressed his narrative were the exiles. But unlike Schmid, for example, he does not locate the Yahwist's 'message' in one predominating theme. Rather, he believes the Yahwist's narrative to be shot through with a concern for the exiles, both in the selection he made from inherited materials and in the redactional additions he made to it.[3]

The absence of a narrative of the entry into Canaan is already an indication of this. Though confirmed by promises, the occupation of the land is reserved for the future. The Yahwist thus describes Israel as being on a journey full of hope (p. 415). The exodus itself, described in the revelation at the burning bush as a saving act of the future for Moses and the generation in bondage at that time, can now also, in this much later period of exile, be a sign of hope, of a new exodus for the generation to whom the Yahwist addressed himself. The depiction of the patriarchs as 'strangers and sojourners' is a further indication of the historical and social setting of Israel to which the Yahwist addressed his narrative (pp. 415–17). Indeed, the history of the patriarchs may be described as a 'history of sojourning (*Fremdlingschaft*)' (p. 416)—Hagar in the wilderness (Gen. 16), Lot

---

[3] See his chapter 'Die Botschaft des Jahwisten', 414–35.

in Sodom (Gen. 19), Abraham's servant in Aram-naharaim (Gen. 24), Isaac in the land of the Philistines (Gen. 26), Jacob in Haran (Gen. 28–32), Joseph in Egypt (Gen. 37–50) where also Jacob himself and his sons join him later, Moses in Midian (Exod. 2). Even Abraham, when he arrived in Canaan, is described as being in a 'land of sojourning'. The condition of being 'strangers and sojourners' is depicted in various ways. 'Strangers' live as people of lesser rights among an indigenous population from which they differ both ethnically and in religion. They face a double hazard: an exterior one, which can range from deprivation of material and legal rights to physical violence, and an interior danger of loss of self-esteem which can express itself in loss of one's ancestral religious affinities and loyalties. What the native population thinks and practises inevitably makes claims upon the sojourner in its midst, and it takes greater self-confidence and the constraints of kinship relationships to refuse to participate in worship of the indigenous gods.

Other features of the selection of sources and redactional additions to them by the Yahwist likewise point to an exilic setting for both author and audience. The loss of land itself is a burden, even a curse, that the exiles have to bear, since there is an anthropological bond between mankind and land, as the creation narrative itself and other related stories in Genesis narrate (pp. 417 f.). Family life, pervasively portrayed in the Yahwist's narrative, was also especially important for an exiled community; the less the individual knew himself to be in harmony with the larger, indigenous population among whom he lived, so much the more important was life in, and the support of, family and kindred (p. 418). Endogamy, which is so emphasized in the patriarchal stories, is also obviously a significant aspect of ethnic communities living among an alien people (pp. 418 f.). The close bond between exiles is further evidenced in the moral sphere, specifically in the stories of peace-making and reconciliation among the patriarchs (pp. 419 f.). According to Levin, even the legitimation of a double standard of morality in some of the Yahwist's narratives is indicative of an exilic setting. The narratives of the despoiling of the Egyptians by the Israelite women (Exod. 3: 22; cf. 12: 35–6), of the defeat of Pharaoh and his army in the Sea, or of the destruction of Sodom would have had peculiar relevance for people living in the threatening environment of exile amongst a numerous and powerful indigenous population, inspiring them to confidence in the power of their own God to defend them (p. 420).

Levin similarly argues that the prominent notion of the 'God of my/our/your fathers', to which Alt drew special attention, would have had peculiar relevance for the exiles (pp. 420–2), as also would the theme of the God 'who goes with' his people (p. 422). This conception of Yahweh as being ever present with his servants is at one with the larger religious claim that Yahweh is 'the God of Heaven' (Gen. 24: 7) or 'the God of Heaven and Earth' (Gen. 24: 3). Indeed, were one to summarize the message of the Yahwist in a sentence it would be 'Yahweh, the God of Israel, is the God of Heaven and Earth; the God of Heaven and Earth is the God of Israel' (p. 425). That is, at the hands of the Yahwist 'the God of Israel and Judah shed the trappings of an ancient Near Eastern national deity to become the One God of the World' (p. 425). That the very title 'God of Heaven' is otherwise attested in the Old Testament in literature only from the Persian and Hellenistic periods also points to a late period for the work of the Yahwist (pp. 423 f.). A further prominent theme of the Yahwist, and again one that would have been of self-evident significance to the exiles, is that of blessing for Israel. Indeed, one may justifiably describe the Yahwist's narrative as a 'history of blessing', announced to the first forefather of the nation (Gen. 12: 2–3), continued in his descendants, testified to by the nations, and uttered (in fear) by the Moabites on the eve of the settlement (Num. 22: 3) and by Balaam who could only bless and not curse (Num. 24: 5–6, 9).

Levin writes of the special character of the Yahwist's theology within the Old Testament. The Yahwist does not acknowledge the distance between Yahweh and his people that arose with, and characterized, the preaching of the prophets and influenced the Deuteronomistic theology. His background is not therefore the prophetic religion of the Old Testament. Rather, the religious tradition which he adopted and employed in the late period in which he wrote was the 'folk religion' of the pre-exilic period, as various of the themes of the narrative mentioned above indicate. For example, the prominent theme of divine blessing has its roots in this religious tradition, and the various formulae in which we encounter it (the prayer for blessing 'blessed be so-and-so by Yahweh', the expression of praise 'blessed be Yahweh . . . ', the salutation 'I bless you through Yahweh') are now all attested in extra-biblical inscriptions from the monarchical period. Even the Aaronite Blessing was known in Jerusalem from at least the mid-seventh century BC (p. 415). Such 'folk religion' did not form the stuff of literature, when no particular circumstances made this necessary. But in the altered circumstances brought about by the exile, the Yahwist found in this older folk religion a ready source for the message he wished to convey.

As to a more precise date and the location of the Yahwist, Levin accepts the usual view that his work was already known to the Deuteronomist historian and also to Deutero-Isaiah (pp. 432 ff.). On the other hand, the Yahwist both presupposed and intended his work as a counter to Deuteronomy, specifically to its demand for centralization of the cult which he rejected. The exiles' need to worship Yahweh and to know his presence with them made it necessary to dispense with the Deuteronomic law of centralization. Thus, to counter this central demand of Deuteronomy, the Yahwist described Abraham as having built altars at the various stopping places of his wanderings, at Shechem and between Bethel and Ai, as also at the Oaks of Mamre, 'calling upon the name of Yahweh' at each of them. He even dared describe the founding by Jacob of the sanctuary at Bethel—the location later of the sin of Jeroboam the son of Nebat, singled out in the Deuteronomistic corpus as the arch-villain of Israel's history. The altar law in the 'book of the covenant', which was later incorporated into the Yahwist's narrative and was similarly anti-Deuteronomic in intention, is fully in keeping with this in legislating for a multiplicity of sanctuaries where Yahweh may be worshipped. Levin concludes, therefore, that the Yahwist lived and wrote among the exiles and may have been among those deported from Judah in 597 or 587.

II

It is to Levin's credit that he has attempted to account for a feature of J which, if it was composed after Deuteronomy, demands explanation, viz. why its author would have described the legitimation of a multiplicity of sanctuaries in the face of Deuteronomy's law of centralization of the cult. Winnett's explanation of this is scarcely adequate when he argues that the Yahwist anticipated the Priestly author in that, though he refers to the erection of altars at various locations, he does not describe the patriarchs as having offered sacrifice at them. It is difficult to see what difference the omission of specific references to offering sacrifice makes, however, since the very fact that altars were erected seems naturally to imply that sacrifices were offered, or at any rate were intended to be offered at them, whilst the Priestly legislation, like Deuteronomy, recognizes the legitimacy of only one place of sacrifice.

Neither is Levin's argument convincing, however. There is no ring of controversy in the narratives recording the erection of altars by the patriarchs, and the most natural reading of them is that they were in part intended to legitimize, or record the legitimization of, different major sanctuaries in Israel as having been founded by patriarchal figures. In this respect, these narratives correspond with the law in the book of the covenant—whether or not this collection was originally part of J—in allowing for a multiplicity of sanctuaries (Exod. 20: 24). It is worth recalling Wellhausen's observations on this issue:[4]

At every place where they take up their abode or make a passing stay, the fathers of the nation, according to this authority [JE], erect altars, set up memorial stones, plant trees, dig wells. This does not take place at indifferent and casual localities, but at Shechem and Bethel in Ephraim, at Hebron and Beersheba in Judah, at Mizpah, Mahanaim, and Penuel in Gilead; nowhere but at famous and immemorially holy places of worship. It is on this that the interest of such notifications depends; they are no mere antiquarian facts, but full of the most living significance for the present of the narrator. The altar built by Abraham at Shechem is the altar on which sacrifice still continues to be made, and bears 'even unto this day' the name which the patriarch gave it. On the spot where at Hebron he first entertained Jehovah, there down to the present day the table has continued to be spread; even as Isaac himself did, so do his sons still swear (Amos viii. 14; Hos. iv. 15) by the sacred well of Beersheba, which he digged, and sacrifice there upon the altar which he built, under the tamarisk which he planted. The stone which Jacob consecrated at Bethel the generation of the living continues to anoint, paying the tithes which of old he vowed to the House of God there . . . [T]hese legends glorify the origin of the sanctuaries to which they are attached, and surround them with the nimbus of venerable consecration. All the more as the altars, as a rule, are not built by the patriarchs according to their own private judgement wheresoever they please; on the contrary, a theophany calls attention to, or at least afterwards confirms, the holiness of the place . . . All that seems offensive and heathenish to a later age is here consecrated and countenanced by Jehovah Himself and His favoured ones,—the high places, the memorial stones (maççeboth), the trees, the wells.

More generally, a flaw in the case Levin seeks to make for an exilic dating of the Yahwist is that many of the features he cites as evidence

---

[4] *Prolegomena*, 31–3; Eng. trans., 30–2.

of this author's message to the exiles were already present in his supposed sources from the pre-exilic period. Levin argues that, though
this is so, the Yahwist's theological and religious purposes motivated
and guided his selection of the sources he employed. But this is to beg
the question, for it is only on the hypothesis that the Yahwist wrote
during the exilic period that one can then conclude that this or that
earlier source or motif he adopted was intended to convey a message
to the exiles. The stories he narrates and the various theological and
religious notions they contain do not in themselves point to an exilic
setting, however much they may have been a source of hope, confidence, and courage to the exiles. It makes no essential difference when
Levin argues that the Yahwist's redactional additions to the sources
he employed in order to emphasize aspects of them are evidence of an
exilic setting, for the setting he claims as the background to such
emphasis is itself part of the hypothesis. In short, the supposed use
the Yahwist made of his sources and the message he wished to
convey by means of them depend on the hypothesis that he was an
exilic writer; they cannot at the same time be used as a basis for the
hypothesis.

Levin, like Winnett, claims that at the hands of the Yahwist 'the
God of Israel and Judah shed the trappings of an ancient Near
Eastern national deity to become the One God of the World' (p. 425).
Van Seters, arguing that the larger world of the diaspora is evident
throughout the Yahwist's work, likewise claims that this 'called for a
transformation from a national religion of the land of Israel to a
world religion in which the chosen people and the Promised Land
continued to have a destiny beyond the crisis of the state's demise';[5]
hence, at the hands of the Yahwist 'the national religion of the
prophets is given universal scope' (p. 191). Winnett saw further evidence of this in the Yahwist's concept of sin which is no longer understood as 'a nationalistic affair, the apostasy of the nation from
Yahweh, as it was to the eighth-century prophets'; rather, for the
Yahwist sin 'is a universal, human phenomenon'. Van Seters similarly
argues: 'It is no longer the particular ethic of a national code reflected
in Deuteronomy but a universal morality that is in view, and this constantly informs the Yahwist's perspective throughout Genesis.
Yahweh is both the creator of all humanity but also its judge. If the
DtrH corresponds to the nationalistic, prophetic view of Israel's

---

[5] Van Seters, *Prologue to History: The Yahwist as Historian in Genesis*, 332.

history up to the exile, then the Yahwist is more akin to the broader universalist concerns of Second Isaiah' (p. 330).[6]

Certainly, though there is no explicit statement of it as a theological principle, the Yahwist's understanding of God and his relationship to the world is universalist: Israel's God is creator and is in sovereign control of the nations, providentially protecting the patriarchs and their descendants, whether in the land of Canaan or outside it, and delivering them from bondage in Egypt. It is striking also that no mention is made of the gods of other nations, not even of the Egyptian gods. Nor, unlike Deuteronomy and the Deuteronomistic corpus, is there any polemic against other gods. It seems, indeed, on the usual interpretation of the text, that at an early time in the history of the world all humankind 'called upon the name of Yahweh' (Gen. 4: 26).

Contrary to the claims of these scholars, however, such universalism is by no means a development of the exilic period. It is already well in evidence in the pre-exilic period. It is the presupposition of Amos's oracles against the nations (Amos 1–2), and of his statement concerning Yahweh's providential guidance of nations other than Israel in chapter 9: 7. Deities other than Yahweh are not mentioned a single time by this prophet. H. W. Wolff puts the matter succinctly:[7]

No Baal competes with Yahweh for Israel's affections as we find the situation to be in Hosea. But neither is there a god apart from Yahweh responsible for foreign nations (1: 3–8, 13–15; 2: 1–3; 3: 2; 9: 7). It is astonishing how unproblematic this is for Amos, and that he therefore offers no polemic against any cult of foreign gods. That Yahweh is the only God of Israel and of the world of nations is not a theme of his message but its self-evident presupposition.

The same universalism is well in evidence also in the preaching of Isaiah of Jerusalem. One has only to recall this prophet's preaching of Yahweh's 'work' and 'purpose' which is set in the widest possible historical context, universal history.[8] This 'work' and 'purpose' was predetermined long ago (Isa. 22: 11; cf. 27: 26), and thus 'enfolds the

---

[6] Cf. also H. Vorländer, *Die Entstehungszeit des jehowistischen Geschichtswerkes* (Frankfurt am Main 1978), 359.

[7] H. W. Wolff, *Dodekapropheten: Joel und Amos*, BKAT, XIV/2 (2nd edn., Neukirchen-Vluyn 1975), 122; the quotation is from the Eng. trans., *Joel and Amos* (Philadelphia 1977), 101.

[8] See G. von Rad, *Theologie des Alten Testaments*, ii. *Die Theologie der prophetischen Überlieferungen Israels* (5th edn., Munich 1968), 168 ff.; Eng. trans. (from the 1st edn., Munich 1960), *Old Testament Theology*, ii. *The Theology of Israel's Prophetic Traditions* (Edinburgh 1965), 161 ff.

whole realm of world history as it was understood at that time; and the way in which the great world empires who were proudly strutting about on this very stage of history came into collision with God's plan is one of the great themes to which Isaiah returned again and again':[9]

> The LORD of hosts has sworn:
> As I have planned it, so shall it be,
> and as I have purposed it, so shall it stand,
> to break Assyria in my land;
> upon my mountains will I trample him under foot . . .
> this is my purpose, resolved concerning the whole earth;
> this is the hand, stretched out over all the nations.
> For the Lord of hosts has resolved it, and who can annul it?
> His hand is stretched out, and who will turn it back?
>
> (Isa. 14: 24–7. Cf. also 10: 5–19)

The evidence of such texts as these in Amos and Isaiah places a question mark also against the argument of Schmid and Rose that the theme of Yahweh's control of history and thus of the destiny of his people was an issue specific to the exilic period during which, in their view, the Yahwist wrote his narrative. The stories of the 'murmuring in the wilderness' as illustrative of Israel's lack of faith in Yahweh, notwithstanding the manifest effectiveness of his actions on his people's behalf in history, may well have struck home to exiles whose faith wavered in the face of the fate that had befallen them and their homeland at the hands of the might of Babylon. Similarly, the theme of Yahweh's sovereign control of history would assuredly have found anxious and expectant ears in these same circumstances. It coincides with an important aspect of the message of Jeremiah, Ezekiel, Deutero-Isaiah, and the Deuteronomistic authors. But neither the crisis this theme addresses nor the theological claims it makes concerning Yahweh were new in the exilic period, even if the crisis intensified at that time. The texts cited above are sufficient evidence of the belief in the operation of Yahweh's sovereign will in history at a much earlier time in the pre-exilic period. As for this kind of crisis, it is found already in the situation in which both Isaiah and Hosea prophesied in the changing world of the eighth century when Israel found itself caught up in the superpower struggles of the ancient Near East, and abandoned trust in Yahweh's power in favour of an engagement

---

[9] Von Rad, *Die Theologie des Alten Testament*, 169; Eng. trans., 162.

in the *Realpolitik* of the time (cf. for example Hos. 7: 11; 8: 9; Isa. 7: 1–7; 30: 1–5; 31: 1–3).

Further, it is surely to be concluded that since Hosea, Amos, and Isaiah independently declared or at least presupposed a belief in Yahweh's sovereign control of history, such a belief was by their time an integral feature of Israelite religion. Quite apart from this, however, general considerations concerning the nature of ancient Near Eastern religions, including Israelite religion, as grounded in a 'theology of creation', fundamental to which was the notion of a divinely willed and established world order over which the creator deity or deities exercised control, render it probable that belief in Yahweh's sovereign control of the affairs of the world was an axiom in Israelite religion from at least an early period if not from the beginning.[10] In short, 'universalism' with its related theme of Yahweh's control of history and of his people's destiny is as much a theme of the pre-exilic period as of the exilic period or later. It offers no evidence that the Yahwist was necessarily an exilic thinker and writer.

Against all who would date J(E) to the exilic period, the general character of J also ill fits an exilic background, and the evidence suggests that the historical circumstances in which the Yahwist wrote it were different from and earlier than those of the sixth century. What is strikingly absent in J when compared with the literature of the exilic period is any indication that Yahweh has abandoned his people and that they have been given into the hands of other nations; the *dies irae* that so palpably forms the background and in large measure the subject of this literature is not discernible in J. The contrast with Deuteronomy is particularly telling, since it too, like the Yahwist's narrative, relates to the Mosaic period. Here it is narrated that already on the plains of Moab before Israel entered the land the shadow of the cataclysm of exile was present (e.g. Deut. 4: 25–8; 28: 36, 64; 29: 27; 30: 1–5); that is, exile and loss of the land, Yahweh's judgement upon his people in the catastrophic events of the sixth century, are here already known and addressed. There is nothing resembling this in J; there are no *ex eventu* warnings or foreboding of this cataclysm, no sense of a break in the relationship between Yahweh and Israel necessitating a new beginning beyond present judgement.

---

[10] H. H. Schmid has been especially concerned to establish this. See, for example, his *Altorientalische Welt in der alttestamentlichen Theologie* (Zürich 1974). Vorländer's claim (*Enstehungszeit des jehowistischen Geschichtswerkes*, 29–44) that the belief in Yahweh as creator was unknown in Israel until the exilic period is incredible.

Rather, for the Yahwist, in the narratives of the 'murmuring in the wilderness', the issue seems to have been Israel's ungrateful lack of trust notwithstanding Yahweh's proven, unbroken, and continuing commitment to his people. A setting before the exile is surely indicated, and, as we have seen, there is sufficient evidence that such lack of trust addressed by the Yahwist was already known in the pre-exilic period.

Put differently, if the Yahwist's narrative derives from an exilic author it is the only literature from that period that does not reflect the trauma of exile and the dire question of the future of Israel as the people of Yahweh, issues which preoccupy the known literature of the exilic period. What a contrast there is in this respect between J and this literature—the Deuteronomistic History, the books of Jeremiah and Ezekiel, and Deutero-Isaiah. What predominates in them is the theme of theodicy; they may, indeed, be described as theodicies. By contrast there is no element of theodicy in the Yahwist's narrative at all commensurate with the scale of the disaster with which the known literature of the exilic period wrestles.

III

I turn again to the monumental contribution by Blum whose analysis of the composition of the patriarchal narrative in Genesis 12–50 we considered earlier. His study of the patriarchal complex in Genesis 12–50 was followed by a detailed study of the remaining books of the Tetrateuch.[11] Together both volumes offer the most comprehensive and detailed study of the composition of the Pentateuch as a whole in recent years. His conclusions differ markedly from the other works we have examined in this and the preceding chapter.[12] He abandons the conventional sigla J, E, JE, and the literary sources they designate. Instead he argues that two main stages can be discerned in the composition of the Pentateuch, the first the D-Komposition (K^D),

---

[11] *Studien zur Komposition des Pentateuch.*

[12] William Johnstone, *Exodus*, Old Testament Guides (Sheffield 1990), has argued independently a view similar to Blum's. He also finds two main stages of redaction in Exodus, the first representing a 'D-version', and the second a 'P-edition'. The authors of the 'D-version' incorporated earlier source materials, but these are quite generally stated ('legal, folk, institutional and the like' (p. 81)) and there is no mention of the conventional Documentary sources J, E, JE. The 'P-edition' is the work of redactors of the earlier 'D-version', and P never existed as an independent source.

and the second the P-Komposition (K^P). K^D is the work of editors who worked under the influence of the Deuteronomistic authors and after their composition of the Deuteronomistic History. He dates K^D to the generation immediately following the return from exile. K^P is the work of later Priestly writers who edited K^D.[13] Once again it is impossible within the space here available to give any impression of the wealth of detail offered by Blum's analysis. The following summary offers only a broad outline.

The authors of K^D inherited two main narrative complexes, an edition of Genesis 12–50* from the exilic period, which itself was a reworking and expansion of an earlier patriarchal narrative from the late pre-exilic period, and a narrative which may be described as a 'Life of Moses' from his birth to his death, that is from the bondage to the end of the period of the wandering in the wilderness. (Thus, though he agrees with Rendtorff that the patriarchal history in Genesis 12–50* was originally independent of the other main literary complexes of the Pentateuch, Blum rejects his view that these other complexes were also composed independently of each other.)[14] This 'Life of Moses' was composed in the pre-exilic period sometime after the fall of the Northern Kingdom in 722 BC. It is to K^D that we owe the promise texts in Genesis which connect the patriarchal history with Exodus and the remainder of the Pentateuch (Gen. 15; 22: 15–18; 24: 7; 26: 3bβ–5, 24*; Exod. 13: 5, 11; 32: 13; 33: 1; Num. 11: 12; 14: 16, 23). K^D was composed subsequent to the Deuteronomistic History, but its distinctive literary nature rules out the notion currently favoured by a number of other scholars that it was consciously composed as a sort of 'prologue' to that corpus.[15]

In Exodus Blum finds evidence of the hand of the K^D authors in 3: 1–4: 18 with which he associates a number of other texts in chapters 1–14.[16] He regards Exodus 3: 1–4: 18, the story of the call of Moses at the holy mountain, as an insertion into the surrounding narrative. He rejects the usual source analysis of this passage, arguing that with the exception of 4: 13–16, which is at odds with 3: 18, it is a compositional unity. A number of other texts are in one way or another related to this passage. Thus the content of 14: 31 shows similarities with 4: 31 which is part of the sequel to the story of the commissioning of Moses in 3–4, especially 3: 16–17 and 4: 1–9. Exodus 5: 22–6:

---

[13] See below, Ch. 7.　　[14] *Studien zur Komposition des Pentateuch*, 215 ff.
[15] Ibid. 164 n. 276.　　[16] Ibid. 9–43.

1 shows links with 3: 8, 10, 19b; 11: 1–3 is also bound to 5: 22–6: 1, and 11: 1–3 and 12: 25–36 are linked to 3: 21–2. Exodus 12: 21(25)–27 and 13: 3–16 are related to 10: 2 and pick up elements in chapters 3–4. Blum describes these passages as together forming a 'composition layer' which gives the bondage-exodus narrative a unified theological scheme. He does not regard the 'layer' as entirely a free composition of the author responsible for it, but finds evidence that this author reworked already existing, written narrative texts (cf. pp. 208–18). He identifies elements of an earlier basis for K^D's work even in chapters 3–4, as well as in 5: 22–6: 1; 12: 21–7; 14.

In considering the authorship of this 'composition layer', Blum draws special attention to the parallels between Exodus 14: 13, 31 and the Deuteronomistic text 1 Samuel 12: 16–18, and concludes that Exodus 14 is also from a Deuteronomistic author. As further support for his conclusion that this 'layer' is from a Deuteronomistic author, he cites with approval H. H. Schmid's conclusions concerning Deuteronomistic influence upon the composition of the call of Moses in Exodus 3–4.

Blum finds evidence of the work of K^D in the Sinai pericope in Exodus 19–24, 32–4 (pp. 45–99). With the exception of 34: 11–26, all of chapters 33–4 are attributed to the K^D 'composition layer', together with 32: 7–14. These conclusions are then the basis for including a number of passages in Numbers and Deuteronomy which show connections with the Sinai pericope: Numbers 11–12, Deuteronomy 31: 14–15, 23; 34: 10–(12). Since Exodus 24: 12–15a, 18b prepares the way for 32: 1 ff., it too is from K^D. So also are Exodus 19: 3b–8 and 20: 22. Since the 'seventy elders' play a part in the K^D narrative in Numbers 11, the reference to them in Exodus 24: 9 is from K^D. With the exception of some minor additions by a Priestly editor, therefore, Exodus 24: 1–2, 9–11 is from K^D. This passage frames vv. 3–8 which originally belonged to an older narrative of the book of the covenant. The analysis is extended to the narratives of the wandering in the wilderness. He concludes that K^D began with Genesis 12: 1–3 and concluded with a narrative of Israel's sojourn in the wilderness. There is no sign of the work of K^D in Genesis 1–11. Blum argues that the primeval history is a creation of the Priestly author who also utilized some older written tradition.[17]

[17] Ibid. 278–85. Cf. also his 'Israël à la montagne de Dieu: Remarques sur Ex 19–24; 32–4 et sur le contexte littéraire et historique de sa composition', in A. de Pury (ed.), *Le Pentateuque en Question*, 271–95 (esp. 293). See also F. Crüsemann, 'Die

IV

Though he dates the work of K^D and thus, with the exception of the primeval history, the formation of the first Tetrateuch proper to the early post-exilic generation, Blum traces the beginnings of the formation of the literature to much earlier periods. He thus avoids some of the difficulties that arise for a view such as that of Van Seters or Rose who 'concertina' the composition of the formative stage in the creation of the Tetrateuch to the exilic period, leaving the pre-exilic period apparently void of any literary activity resembling the narratives of the Tetrateuch, a literarily thoroughly 'deforested' terrain, as one critic of their work has put it.[18] For the same reason, Blum's conclusions do not run into the difficulty raised for an exilic dating of the Yahwist by a narrative such as that about Jacob and Esau which, as suggested earlier,[19] is unlikely to have been composed by an exilic author.

Blum has been described as a 'new Wellhausen'.[20] Such is the detail of his analysis that, if it can be sustained, it would offer a comprehensive theory of Pentateuchal origins that would displace Wellhausen's presentation of the 'New Documentary Theory'. It is obviously radically different in its conclusions from those argued by Wellhausen. The stages in the formation of the Pentateuch suggested by Blum—early written traditions, Deuteronomy, the Deuteronomistic History, K^D, K^P—and the 'paradigm' his study advances is correspondingly different: an originally independent Tetrateuch (K^D) composed subsequent to Deuteronomy and the Deuteronomistic History and only secondarily combined with the latter.

In examining and discussing Blum's arguments and conclusions, it must first be acknowledged that there are passages in the Tetrateuch which show some affinity with the style and some of the interests of Deuteronomy and the Deuteronomistic corpus of literature. They

Eigenständigkeit der Urgeschichte. Ein Beitrag zur Diskussion um den "Jahwisten"', in J. Jeremias and L. Perlitt (eds.), *Die Botschaft und die Boten. Festschrift für Hans Walter Wolff zum 70 Geburtstag* (Neukirchen-Vluyn 1981), 11–29; and R. Rendtorff, 'L'histoire biblique des origines (Gen 1–11) dans le contexte de la rédaction "sacerdotale" du Pentateuque', in A. de Pury (ed.), *Le Pentateuque en Question*, 83–94.

[18] Cf. A. H. J. Gunneweg's sharp comments in 'Anmerkungen und Anfragen zur neueren Pentateuchforschung', *ThR* 50 (1985), 112.

[19] See above, Ch. 5, p. 159 f.

[20] See J. L. Ska, 'Un nouveau Wellhausen?', *Biblica*, 72 (1991), 252–63 (esp. 257).

have been variously appraised, however. Whilst some attribute them to a Deuteronomic or Deuteronomistic redactor, others more cautiously have described them as insertions in the style of the Deuteronomist.[21] They have attracted renewed study in more recent years,[22] but as far as I am aware Blum's work represents the first systematic study of the Deuteronomistic elements in the Tetrateuch.

Two main issues arising from Blum's work require discussion: first, do the passages in the Tetrateuch which he assigns to Deuteronomistic authors constitute the systematic 'composition layer' that he suggests? Can we speak of a 'Deuteronomic Tetrateuch'? Secondly, to what period are such passages to be dated? Is the claim justified that they are the work of an early post-exilic author and presuppose the Deuteronomistic History? We saw earlier that Rose has offered a detailed study of the relationship between duplicate narratives in 'JE' and the Deuteronomistic History on the basis of which he has concluded that, contrary to the conventional view, the latter corpus was composed before the former. Though Blum disagrees with some of the details of Rose's conclusions, he is in broad sympathy with them. Before considering further Blum's conclusions, it will be helpful at this stage to return to Rose's arguments. It is beyond the space here available to discuss all the examples examined by Rose. His analysis of the well-known narrative in Numbers 13–14 and its parallel in Deuteronomy 1: 19–2: 1 provides a convenient example, especially since Blum is in substantial agreement with the conclusion he reaches.[23] These narratives have also been discussed by Van Seters in his recent study of Exodus and Numbers, and I begin with some observations on his presentation of the issues.

Though his arguments are differently based, Van Seters arrives at the same conclusion as Rose on the priority of the account in Deuteronomy 1 over that in Numbers 13–14.[24] According to Van

[21] Most notable among these is Martin Noth in his *Überlieferungsgeschichte des Pentateuch*.

[22] Notably C. H. W. Brekelmans, 'Die sogenannten deuteronomischen Elemente in Genesis bis Numeri. Ein Beitrag zur Vorgeschichte des Deuteronomiums', SVT 15 (1996), 90–6; 'Éléments Deutéronomiques dans le Pentateuque', *Recherches Bibliques*, 8 (Bruges 1967), 77–91; N. Lohfink, *Das Hauptgebot. Eine Untersuchung literarischer Einleitungsfragen zu Dtn 5–11*, Analecta Biblica, 20 (Rome 1963), 121–4. Cf. more recently M. Vervenne, 'The Question of "Deuteronomic" Elements in Genesis to Numbers', in F. García Martínez, A. Hilhorst, J. T. A. G. M. van Ruiten, and A. S. van der Woude (eds.), *Studies in Deuteronomy in Honour of C. J. Labuschagne*, SVT 53 (Leiden 1994), 243–68 where further bibliography is also provided.

[23] Blum, *Studien zur Komposition des Pentateuch*, 177–81.

[24] *The Life of Moses*, 370–9.

Seters, the association of Caleb with the story of the spies in Deuteronomy 1 is secondary. The abrupt reference to Caleb in verse 36 is itself an indication of this, since he is not mentioned as having participated in the events narrated earlier. Originally, he had no part in the story of the spies here narrated. It was the Yahwist who, taking up the story in Deuteronomy 1, worked Caleb into his narrative in Numbers 13. Van Seters argues that J, on the basis of the reference to the Anakim in Deuteronomy 1: 28 (cf. Josh. 15: 14), combined the Caleb tradition about the conquest of the Hebron region, the oldest version of which is contained in Joshua 15: 14–19, with the story of the spies in Deuteronomy 1, making Caleb one of the spies, substituting his encouragement of the people for that of Moses and making him an exception to the judgement. Once Caleb was associated with the spy story, the account in Deuteronomy had to be edited to include Caleb as an exception also (Deut. 1: 36).

He argues that the abrupt introduction of Caleb in Numbers 13: 30 is itself indicative of the secondary association of the tradition concerning him with the story of the spies. In the J narrative in Numbers 13, Caleb, who is introduced 'out of the blue', and the statement that 'he hushed the people for Moses' (Num. 13: 30) come too soon 'before the people have reacted to the report and begun to grumble' (p. 375). Since at this point, the Deuteronomist (Deut. 1: 29) narrates that Moses himself spoke to calm the people, it is clear that in the J account Caleb has been substituted for Moses, who makes no response in this narrative. Numbers 13: 30 is thus of key significance for Van Seters's view, for it is here that he finds the clues that this narrative was partly derived from that in Deuteronomy 1 and that its author was responsible for combining the tradition of Caleb with that of the spies narrated there.

Van Seters translates the opening phrase of Numbers 13: 30 *waya-has cālēb 'eth hā'ām 'el mōšeh* as 'Caleb hushed the people for Moses'. Like him, some other commentators have suggested that Caleb's intervention at this stage is premature, since the people have not yet said anything, and that the verse originally had a different context in which the people had already murmured. G. B. Gray, for example, adopted this view and suggested that the opening phrase is an ellipse for 'and Caleb stilled *the murmuring of the* people *against* Moses'.[25] There is nothing implausible, however, about Caleb's sudden appear-

[25] G. B. Gray, *A Critical and Exegetical Commentary on Numbers*, ICC (Edinburgh 1903), 151.

ance at this stage. The author had no reason for mentioning him prior to this juncture in the story, but the negative report of the spies is now countered by him, and appropriately so, since he was one of them, as verse 31 states. Caleb's intervention is in turn countered by a further outburst of discouragement from the other spies (v. 31).[26] In this way the scene is fully set for the murmuring and rebellion of the people. Nor is there any need to regard Caleb's action here as premature. It does not require undue literary licence to understand his words as implying alarm on the part of the people as they listened to the adverse report of the spies.

The main weakness in Van Seters' argument is his translation of the preposition *'el* as 'for' in the opening phrase of Numbers 13: 30 *wayahas cālēb 'eth hā'ām 'el mōšeh* which he renders 'But Caleb hushed the people *for* Moses' (p. 375). Such a translation of *'el* is inadmissible in Biblical Hebrew, and Van Seters offers no defence of it. The translation presupposes the theory he wishes to argue and thus the text is made to support the theory rather than to test it. A translation such as that offered by the Authorized Version and Revised Version 'And Caleb stilled the people *before* Moses' or the Revised Standard Version 'Caleb quieted the people *before* Moses' more accurately renders the Hebrew preposition.

Turning to the narrative in Deuteronomy 1, Van Seters concedes that the reference in verse 1: 36 to Caleb presupposes the narrative in Numbers, since in Deuteronomy Caleb is indeed introduced 'out of the blue' and is not mentioned in any of the actions described earlier in the narrative and, unlike the narrative in Numbers (cf. Num. 13: 31), is not directly associated with the spies. The reference to him in Deuteronomy 1: 36 is thus what is sometimes referred to as a 'blind motif', that is, some unexplained action or detail in a narrative that assumes consciously or unconsciously that an earlier account is known,[27] in this instance the story in Numbers 13. So also, however, is Deuteronomy 1: 28 in which the people describe discouraging words of their 'brethren' about the possibility of entering the land and which cannot be regarded as a secondary insertion into this chapter. Who these 'brethren' are is clear only because we have the

[26] Van Seters (*The Life of Moses*, 375) writes that in 'J the spies report essentially what they have been asked to do in Moses' commission so that it cannot even be called a negative report'. It is difficult to see how such a claim can be justified in view of the discouraging report of the other spies in verse 31 to Caleb's endeavour to encourage the people in the preceding verse.

[27] Cf. Van Seters, *Abraham in History and Tradition*, 163.

account in Numbers 13, since in Deuteronomy the spies are recorded as having given only a positive report about the land. Without the story in Numbers, we would have to surmise that 'brethren' refers to the spies mentioned earlier in the narrative in Deuteronomy rather than to some other group among the people, and we are left also to suppose that they gave their discouraging report, not to Moses, but surreptitiously to the people.

Van Seters' hypothesis thus yields rather tortuous consequences for reading the story in Deuteronomy 1. These are avoided, however, if the account in Deuteronomy presupposes the J narrative in Numbers 13–14. Deuteronomy then reads like a retrospect of an earlier record of the events described, which it has reshaped for its own purposes (see below), and such elements in the narrative as the people's report of the discouraging words of the spies (v. 28) as well as the announcement of divine favour to Caleb (v. 36) may then be regarded as 'blind motifs' fully understandable in the light of the earlier account in Numbers. Such a view of the relationship between these parallel narratives has the advantage of being simpler for our understanding of both stories. A somewhat more expansive consideration of the differences between the two narratives supports such a conclusion.

I draw attention again to Suzanne Boorer's study *The Promise of the Land as Oath: A Key to the Formation of the Pentateuch*. Of Rose's handling of individual texts such as Deuteronomy 1: 19–46 and the non-Priestly text of Numbers 13–14 she has made the apt observation that his approach of focusing on the 'points of contact' between these texts along the lines of the use of specific words and motifs is at the expense of first 'analysing each of the texts as a whole, their structure, the interrelation of their parts, and their overall intention, and then comparing them in order to discern the most probable direction of change'.[28] She continues (397 f.):[29]

The danger in Rose's approach, that neglects to consider first the texts as a whole, is that the nuance of the motifs focused on may be misinterpreted if not first seen within their contexts as a whole, and such motifs may not be important within the central concerns of the text as a whole. For example, the primary issue in Deut. 1: 9–2: 1* and the non-P text of Num. 13–14 is not correlative with the position of the spies and Yahweh but has to do with the

---

[28] Boorer, *The Promise of the Land as Oath*, 397.
[29] See also the observations by L. Perlitt, 'Deuteronomium 1–3 in Streit der Exegetischen Methoden', in N. Lohfink (ed.), *Das Deuteronomium. Entstehung, Gestalt und Botschaft* (Leuven 1985), 156.

rejection of the land by the people. The threads Rose has used, as guide through the labyrinth of these texts, such as Caleb, the spies, and Caleb the spy, as lexical items leave out the broader concerns of the texts. To draw general conclusions with regard to the relative levels of these texts on such a narrow basis as these individual 'points of contact', isolated from consideration of the concerns of the texts as a whole, cannot be justified and must be criticized despite Rose's attempt to defend himself against such criticism.

Boorer shows convincingly that the evidence remains strong, against Rose, that the author of Deuteronomy 1–3 most probably knew the pre-P texts in the Tetrateuch to which Rose refers, and that therefore the JE narrative of the Tetrateuch was composed before the Deuteronomistic History. For example, there are compelling reasons for believing that Deuteronomy 1: 19–2: 1* was dependent upon the non-P narrative in Numbers 13–14* including the secondary expansion of this narrative in 14: 11b–23a.[30]

The similarities between the two narratives are obvious: they both follow the sequence: exploration of the land, response of the people to the report of the spies, Yahweh's consequent judgement upon the people, and their final rebellion ending in defeat. The differences are more striking, however, and are most reasonably explained on the basis that the author of Deuteronomy 1: 19–2: 1* wrote after the narrative in Numbers 13–14* and adapted it for his own theological purposes.

For example, the report of the spies in Deuteronomy 1: 25 is solely positive: 'The land which the Lord our God is giving to us is good'. The hazards the land holds for any who would enter it are unmentioned. In Numbers, by contrast, both the goodness and the dangers of the land are reported together: the land flows with milk and honey, but its inhabitants are strong, its cities fortified and great, and the sons of Anak are there. It is not until Deuteronomy 1: 28, however, that its author mentions the hazards of the land, and then with two differences. First, the dangers that lie in the land are more

---

[30] Boorer, *The Promise of the Land*, 386–98. The following observations are dependent upon her arguments. She isolates Numbers 13: 17b–20, 22–4, 27–8, 30–1; 14: 1aβb, 4, 11a, 23a–4, 25b, 39–45 as belonging to an original J narrative. A later editor has added 14: 11b–23a (pp. 332–56). She finds the original narrative of Deuteronomy 1: 19–2: 1 to comprise vv. 19–20, 22–30, 31b–6, 39aβb–45; 2: 1 (pp. 370–86). For the priority of the Numbers text over Deuteronomy 1: 19ff. see also A. D. H. Mayes, *Deuteronomy*, New Century Bible (London 1979), 125–33. (In his later study *The Story of Israel between Settlement and Exile* (London 1983), 145–9, he abandons this in favour of Rose's view.)

emphasized than in the Numbers text: the people are 'greater and taller' (cf. Num. 13: 28 'strong'); the cities are 'great and fortified to heaven' (cf. Num. 13: 28 'fortified and very large'); as in Numbers 13: 28, the sons of Anak are also there. Second, and more significant, unlike Numbers 13: 28, the report of the dangers of the land does not come directly from the lips of the spies but from the people (Deut. 1: 28) and is cast as a rumour that has arisen and circulated separately from the formal report of the spies. It seems that the author of Deuteronomy 1: 19–2: 1* has separated the positive element in the report of the spies from the negative in order to portray the people's response in the worst possible light. Whereas the narrative in Numbers provides a reason for the people's fearful response to the report of the spies, in Deuteronomy their ungrateful response follows a wholly positive report of the spies concerning the land that Yahweh is giving them and is thus thrown into sharper relief as mistrust of Yahweh. In this way Yahweh's good gift of the land is highlighted and Israel's lack of faith underscored. On this basis it seems likely that of the two narratives, Deuteronomy 1: 19–2: 1* is the later. 'The most probable direction of change is from portraying Yahweh's land as having drawbacks (Num. 13: 27–8) and hence the people's rejection of the land as being somewhat reasonable (Num. 13: 31; 14: 1aβb, 4) to portraying Yahweh's land as all good (Deut. 1: 25) and thus portraying the people's rejection of the land as solely due to the fault of the people themselves (Deut. 1: 26–8). Thus, Deut. 1: 25–8 would appear to be the later account in comparison with Num. 13: 27–8, 30–1; 14: 1aβb, 4' (Boorer, 389).

This conclusion is further supported by a consideration of the significance of the exodus and wilderness motifs in Deuteronomy 1: 27, 30, 31b, 33 and Numbers 14: 13–14, 16, 19b. The latter verses belong to a passage (Num. 14: 11b–23a) which is usually assigned to a secondary editor and in style and tone shows affinities with the Deuteronomic literature. The motif of the guidance by fire and cloud in v. 16 forms part of Moses's intercession where it is argued that if Yahweh abandons his people, the nations will interpret this as due to his inability to fulfil what he had begun on behalf of his people in the exodus. In Deuteronomy 1: 33, however, this motif is employed to accentuate the rebellious nature of the people's response to the report of the spies, for here it is they and not foreign nations who make the claim that Yahweh has abandoned them. Further, whilst according to the narrative in Numbers 14: 13–14, 16 the foreign nations explain the demise of Israel on the grounds that Yahweh was unable to fulfil his intentions for them, the author of Deuteronomy describes Israel as accusing Yahweh, not of inability to fulfil his intentions, but of hating them and having had malice aforethought in bringing them from Egypt into the wilderness to have them destroyed at the hand of foreigners. Here again, therefore, it seems most likely that the Deuteronomist has reshaped the narrative in Numbers to portray the people in the worst possible light (see Boorer, 390 f.). It is evident that the author of Deuteronomy 1: 19–2: 1* probably knew and used not only the original J narrative in Numbers 13–14* but also the secondary expansion of it in 14: 11b–23a.

Boorer's conclusion, exemplified by this 'test case' of a comparison of Numbers 13–14* with Deuteronomy 1: 19–2: 1*, has obvious implications for the views of those, including Blum, who argue that the pre-P Tetrateuch was composed after the Deuteronomistic History. With this conclusion in mind we may now examine another passage, in this instance one that is of key importance for Blum's thesis of the work of his proposed author K^D, the narrative of the call and commissioning of Moses in Exodus 3–4.

V

As we have seen, Schmid argues that this narrative displays a number of the features of the call-visions and role of the writing prophets from Isaiah onwards. Blum accepts this, and finds that other elements in the narrative not only provide additional evidence of the late dating proposed by Schmid but also of specifically Deuteronomistic influence on its composition.[31]

It may be asked, however, to what extent Moses is cast as a prophet in this narrative and in the plagues stories that follow later. He shares with the prophets the role of Yahweh's messenger, but there does not seem to be a concern on the part of the author of the narratives to employ the stereotyped formulae employed of the prophetic messengers.[32] Like some of the prophets, for example Amos, he is an

---

[31] *Studien zur Komposition des Pentateuch*, esp. 32–5.

[32] See the comments by F. Langlamet in his review of Schmid's *Der sogenannte Jahwist* in *RB* 84 (1977), 622 f. Gunneweg has commented that the only thing the prophets have in common with the figure of Moses in the bondage narratives is that they are all commanded to 'go and speak'! ('Anmerkungen und Anfragen zur neueren Pentateuchforschung', *ThR* 48 (1983), 234.)

intercessor (Exod. 5: 22; 8: 28; 9: 28). But this is not an exclusively prophetic activity. His prophetic authority is vindicated by signs (4: 2 ff.). Nowhere, however, is the word 'prophet' (*nābī'*) used of him in Exodus 3–4 or throughout Exodus 1–14, and the task laid upon him is surely unlike that of the writing prophets. It seems rather that in these narratives Moses is primarily portrayed as Yahweh's agent in the deliverance of Israel from bondage in Exodus 1–14. The specifically prophetic element in the depiction of his role in these chapters in Exodus is at best secondary to this role. In this respect, as many have observed, his commissioning resembles that of the 'deliverers' Gideon (Judges 6: 11b–17) and Saul (1 Samuel 9: 1–10: 13) and shares most of the features of the form employed in these two texts.[33]

According to Van Seters,[34] Exodus 3 draws on two streams of literary tradition. On the one hand in language and structure the narrative follows the pattern of the commissioning of a deliverer as described in these two texts, both of which he regards as Deuteronomistic creations that are unrelated to the origins of the prophetic call narratives. On the other hand, he argues, although the literary form of the commissioning of a deliverer has been employed, the deliverer in the case of Exodus 3–4 has been 'transformed' into a prophet. For this purpose, the author has drawn upon the call narratives of classical prophecy, particularly that of Jeremiah.[35]

Against Van Seters, it is surely unlikely, however, that the narrative of the commissioning of Saul in 1 Samuel 9: 1–10: 13 is a Deuteronomistic composition. The juxtaposition of pro- and anti-monarchical narratives in 1 Samuel 8–12 has long been the subject of discussion, and it remains a matter of debate as to how the Deuteronomist intended this pericope to be understood. The probability remains, however, that the Deuteronomists were responsible for the anti-monarchical narratives, whether or not they took up an earlier anti-monarchical tradition in Israel. It is inherently unlikely that they created such a pro-monarchical and, one might add, a pro-Saul story as 1 Samuel 9: 1–10: 13. This popular tale about the youth who

---

[33] See W. Richter, *Die sogenannten vorprophetischen Berufungsberichte: Eine literaturwissenschaftliche Studie zu 1 Sam 9, 1–10, 16; Ex. 3f. und Ri 6, 11b bis 17*, FRLANT 101 (Göttingen 1970). Schmid notes Richter's work (*Der sogenannte Jahwist*, 19 ff.) but does not give sufficient weight to his insights into the 'call' narratives of Judges 6 and 1 Samuel 9. Cf. the comments by F. Langlamet in his review of Schmid (see previous note).

[34] *The Life of Moses*, esp. 41–6.

[35] Cf. also Blum, *Studien zur Komposition des Pentateuch*, 33.

was sent to find his father's lost donkeys but instead found a kingdom has all the hallmarks of a popular, pro-Saul story which may well have originated contemporarily with the reign of Israel's first king. If this is so, then the genre of the commissioning of a deliverer was known in Israel from much earlier periods than Van Seters allows.

Since there is no evidence before the narrative in Isaiah 6 of the adaptation and use in prophecy of the form of these narratives about Gideon and Saul, Schmid questions the plausibility of regarding the narrative in Exodus 3–4 as the first to do so. He suggests that it makes better sense to see this narrative as reflecting the form as it was more fully developed in classical prophecy from the eighth century onwards.[36]

The question arises, however, whether there need be any direct dependence of any of these call narratives, including those of Gideon and Saul, upon other similar narratives. At a general level they reflect a well-attested tradition in the Old Testament of the call and enabling of agents of Yahweh who seem, and feel themselves to be, unlikely candidates for the office or task to which they are summoned, or who for whatever reason protest the inappropriateness of Yahweh's choice of them. Gideon and Saul protest that they are from insignificant families; David, in the well-known narrative of his anointing (1 Sam. 16: 1–13), is the last of Jesse's sons to be paraded before Samuel, having been fetched from minding the sheep (cf. 2 Sam. 7: 8), and is preferred over his older brethren, for 'the Lord sees not as man sees; man looks on the outward appearance, but the Lord looks on the heart' (v. 7); upon succeeding his father David, Solomon says of himself that he is 'but a little child' and no leader of people and so asks for the wisdom necessary to rule; Moses protests his incompetence as an orator; Isaiah is filled with a sense of the 'uncleanness' of his lips; Jeremiah objects that he is but a youth and does not know how to speak. There is nothing in the account of Jeremiah's call to suggest that it depended in any way upon that of Isaiah, and even the elaborate call vision of Ezekiel cannot be said to be directly dependent upon earlier call narratives. Does it not seem more likely that such call narratives reflect a common tradition and that there is no need to attempt to define any one of them as a prototype of the form which in any case is used more or less flexibly from one to another?

Exodus 3–4 itself provides some support for such a conclusion. It is claimed by Schmid, Van Seters, Blum, and others that its composition has been influenced by the narrative of the call of Jeremiah. But there are distinctive differences between the accounts in Exodus 4: 10–12 and Jeremiah 1: 4–10, and the resemblances between them are superficial. Jeremiah protests that he is 'but a youth' and does not 'know how to speak'. Moses says that he is not an 'eloquent speaker' (lit. 'a man of words') but rather is 'slow of speech and of tongue'. Yahweh 'puts forth his hand and touches' Jeremiah's mouth and 'puts' his words in Jeremiah's mouth. In Exodus 4 Yahweh promises that he will be 'with' Moses' mouth and 'will teach' him what to say. The inability that each declares upon being called is differently expressed, and the divine means of overcoming the lack of confidence is also different in each case. The only word they have in common is 'mouth', and, given that one of the main tasks each has to undertake is to speak, this is scarcely a basis on which to claim that the one account has influenced the other. There are no compelling reasons for believing that the narrative in Exodus 3–4 was influenced by the description of Jeremiah's call. There is no reason to doubt that it was composed independently, employing a form that was known in Israel from an early time.

Other details focused upon by Schmid as evidence of the influence of the classical prophets upon the composition of Exodus 1–14 are no more persuasive. The motif of the 'hardening' of the Pharaoh's heart (Exod. 4: 21) is surely different from the notion of the 'hardening' of Israel's heart in the call narrative of Isaiah 6 (cf. Schmid, 35 f.).[37] There is no reason to believe that either of these texts influenced the other. Similarly, neither the expression 'I will stretch out my hand' in Exodus 3: 20 nor the phrase 'with a strong hand' (which in any case is here used of the Pharaoh and not of Yahweh) in 3: 19 warrant the suggestion (p. 35) that they may have been influenced by the Deuteronomistic fondness for describing 'the strong hand' of Yahweh in the events of the exodus.[38] Neither does the role of Moses as intercessor necessarily presuppose the intercessory role of some of the classical prophets. Among the latter, Amos was the first to perform such a role. But it can scarcely be supposed that such intercession was first practised by him. There does not seem to be any compelling reason for believing that the portrayal of Moses as intercessor is a necessarily late construction.

[37] Gunneweg, 'Anmerkungen und Anfragen zur neueren Pentateuchforschung', 234.

[38] See J. M. Roberts, 'The Hand of Yahweh', *VT* 21 (1971), 244–51. Cf. the comment by Langlamet, *RB* 84 (1977), 624.

Blum draws attention to some further features of Exodus 3–4 which he believes to reflect Deuteronomic/Deuteronomistic influence. He suggests (p. 33) that the promise in Exodus 3: 21b—'when you go forth, you shall not go empty-handed (ריקם)'—reflects the Deuteronomic requirement for the release of Hebrew slaves (Deut. 15: 13): 'when you set [a slave] free, you shall not send him forth empty-handed (ריקם)'. But should so much be based upon the one word that these two texts have in common (ריקם)? The purpose of the 'borrowing' of jewellery and other items is to 'plunder', 'despoil' (נצל) the Egyptians (Exod. 3: 21–2; 11: 2–3; 12: 35–6) whom Yahweh will delude into being well-disposed towards the Israelites.[39] As Childs points out,[40] a closer analogy to what is described in these texts is provided by 2 Chronicles 20: 25 where the Israelites take spoils (the same verb, the piel of נצל , is used) from a defeated army after they had defeated them in war.

Blum finds further evidence of the influence of Deuteronomy upon this narrative in the 'sign' promised to Moses in Exodus 3: 12 (p. 34). The sign is in the nature of the case *post factum* and as such, Blum suggests, reflects the criterion prescribed in Deuteronomy 18: 21 f. for discerning between true and false prophets. But the difference between the two texts renders this comparison questionable. In Deuteronomy the sign of a false prophet is the non-fulfilment of the word he had declared to the people. In Exodus, however, the context of the sign is Moses's own questioning of his capability for the task which he is summoned to undertake and therefore of the authority of the call he has received: 'Who am I that I should go to Pharaoh and bring the Israelites out of Egypt?'. The promise of the sign is evidently given to reassure Moses—'Behold I will be with thee (עמך) and this will be a sign to *thee* (לך) that I have sent thee (שלחתיך)'— and does not ostensibly have anything to do with the people's doubting the credentials of Moses.[41]

Blum does not suggest, however, that Exodus 3: 1–4: 18 is simply a creation of the author of KᴰKᴰ. Two prominent features of the narrative derive from earlier tradition: (a) the description of the theophany at the 'burning bush' which, he suggests, may have once belonged to an aetiological story of Sinai as a holy place, since the word 'bush'

[39] For a discussion of the various issues involved in this story, see B. S. Childs, *Exodus*, OTL (London 1974), 175–7.
[40] Ibid. 77.
[41] For the different ways in which this 'sign' has been understood see ibid. 56–60.

(s^eneh) seems to be a play upon 'Sinai'; and (b) the revelation of the divine name Yahweh to Moses, since the tradition of Yahweh's self-revelation to Israel 'in Egypt' is apparently already attested in Ezekiel 20: 5 and still earlier in Hosea 12: 10; 13: 4, whilst the same word-play *Yahweh/'ehyeh* in Exodus 3: 14 may also be intended in Hosea 1: 9 (w^e'*ānōkī lō 'ehyey lākem*).[42]

In so far as Moses is portrayed as a prophet-deliverer in Exodus 1–14, this tradition too is older than Deuteronomy and the Deuteronomistic writings, and is already referred to in Hosea 12: 13:

> By a prophet the Lord brought Israel up from Egypt
> And by a prophet he was preserved.

The tradition is more fully developed in Deuteronomy which portrays Moses as the first and greatest of a line of prophets whom Yahweh promises to raise up (18: 15–19)[43] and summarizes his achievement thus (34: 10 ff.):

There has not arisen a prophet since in Israel like Moses, whom the Lord knew face to face; in all the signs and the wonders, which the Lord sent him to do in the land of Egypt, to Pharaoh, and to all his servants, and to all his land; and in all the mighty hand, and in all the great terror, which Moses wrought in the sight of all Israel.

These texts in Deuteronomy serve only to underline, however, the difference between Exodus 3–4, which does not employ the word 'prophet' for Moses, and their much more overt and developed notion of Moses as the archetype and paragon of the prophetic office. Given that the depiction of Moses as a prophet-deliverer was already known as early as the mid-eighth century BC, does it not seem more probable that the narrative of the call and activity of Moses in Exodus 1–14 was composed before rather than after the Deuteronomistic History (including Deuteronomy 34: 10 ff. which clearly presupposes the narrative in Exodus 1–14) with its more developed notion of, and emphasis upon, the prophetic office of Moses?

---

[42] *Studien zur Komposition des Pentateuch*, 40 ff.

[43] On the portrayal of the prophets in the Deuteronomistic History as successors of Moses, see my *Preaching to the Exiles: A Study of the Prose Tradition in the Book of Jeremiah* (Oxford 1970), 45 ff.

VI

Other passages regarded by Schmid as showing the influence of the Deuteronomistic corpus and attributed by Blum to his proposed K^D 'composition layer' create, in my opinion, a similar unease. For example the structure of such narratives as Exodus 15: 22–5a; 17: 1bβ–7; Numbers 11: 1–3; *11: 4–32; *12: 1–15; 21: 4b–9 describing (a) an offence by Israel, incurring (b) God's anger and punishment, followed by (c) plea/intercession for help, and (d) deliverance, is by no means necessarily due to the influence of its well-known use in the Deuteronomistic literature. There is nothing so distinctive about the notion of adversity interpreted as divine punishment because of an offence, followed by a plea or intercession for deliverance, and an understanding of subsequent relief from the adversity as a sign of divine forgiveness, that necessitates attributing its original conception and coinage to a Deuteronomistic author or, indeed, to any single author. Lament, confession, and intercession in the face of adversity interpreted as divine punishment followed by a new turn of events perceived as forgiveness was surely a common phenomenon in ancient religions. For example, the experience seems to underlie the opening lines of Mesha's inscription from the mid-ninth century BC celebrating Chemosh's deliverance of Moab from foreign oppressors at whose hands he is said to have previously punished his people on account of some unnamed offence.[44] In the Old Testament it is found with all or most of the elements of the structure in such passages as Hosea 5: 15–6: 3; 14: 1–7; Amos 7: 1–3, 4–6. Consider, for example, the 'murmuring' incident narrated in Numbers 11: 1–2 and compare it with Amos 7: 4–6:

And the people complained in the hearing of the Lord about their misfortunes; and when the Lord heard it, his anger was kindled, and the fire of the Lord burned among them, and consumed some outlying parts of the camp. Then the people cried to Moses; and Moses prayed to the Lord, and the fire abated. (Num. 11: 1–2)

---

[44] Bertil Albrektson provides a number of examples of the common interpretation of adversity and deliverance as the action of the god(s) in ancient Near Eastern societies. See his *History and the Gods: An Essay on the Idea of Historical Events as Divine Manifestations in the Ancient Near East and in Israel*, Coniectanea Biblica, Old Testament Series 1 (Lund 1967), esp. chs. 2 and 6.

Thus the Lord God showed me: behold, the Lord God was calling for a judgement by fire, and it devoured the great deep and was eating up the land. Then I said, 'O Lord God, cease, I beseech thee! How can Jacob Stand? He is so small!' The Lord repented concerning this: 'This also shall not happen,' said the Lord God. (Amos 7: 4–6)

According to Blum, Numbers 11: 1–3 and the story of the making of the 'bronze serpent' in 21: 4b–9 are compositions of K^D forming an inclusio framing a significant section of the narrative of Israel's journey from Sinai to the borders of the land of Canaan (pp. 123 f., 135). The note in 2 Kings 18: 4 is relevant for an understanding of Numbers 21: 4b–9, since both passages refer to one and the same cultic object which was evidently housed and venerated in the Jerusalem temple from an early time: 'And he [Hezekiah] broke in pieces the bronze serpent that Moses had made, for until those days the people of Israel had burned incense to it; it was called Nehushtan'. That a Deuteronomist should describe Moses as having manufactured such a cultic image can only mean that the tradition about it is of older, pre-Hezekian origin. Numbers 21: 4b–9 reflects the same tradition but apparently knows nothing of the shadow cast by the Deuteronomist over its use in the Jerusalem cult. According to Blum in his *Studien zur Komposition des Pentateuch* (pp. 122 f.), however, this does not mean that the Numbers text is older than the record in 2 Kings 18: 4. He argues that what is missing in Numbers 21: 4 ff. is an expected allusion to what became of the object; that is, the story does not appear to be an aetiology of any subsequent cultic use of the object in Israel. This is provided, however, in the note in 2 Kings 18: 4 and, according to Blum, it was because this note already existed that the K^D author was able to include, without any aetiological reference, the episode narrated in Numbers 21: 4 ff. as part of his 'composition layer'.

The argument is scarcely conclusive, however. Indeed, the reverse of it surely makes better sense. The narrative in Numbers 21: 4b–9 can be understood without a knowledge of 2 Kings 18: 4. If we did not possess the latter we might speculate as to whether the Numbers text conceals a reference to an ancient Israelite liturgical practice or cult of which all trace has disappeared. Be this as it may, however, the story in Numbers 21: 4b–9 is fully comprehensible in its context: the bronze model of a serpent made by Moses at the command of God saved the people from death from the plague of snakes. To understand 2 Kings 18: 4 properly, however, requires a story such as

Numbers 21: 4 ff. One has only to ask how the Deuteronomistic author of 2 Kings 18: 4 would have expected his readers to understand this note about an idolatrous cultic object the origin of which is attributed to no less a figure than Moses but without comment concerning the purpose for which he made it as distinct from how it came to be used in Israel's worship. Does it seem likely that an oral tradition about the origin of this cultic object, said to have been destroyed in the late eighth century, was still extant as late as the exilic and early post-exilic period and thus at hand, first to provide a necessary gloss on the otherwise enigmatic reference in 2 Kings 18: 4 to the role of Moses in its origin and manufacture, and subsequently to be taken up by the author of Numbers 21: 4b–9? Who would have preserved such a tradition and why, so long after the disappearance of the cultic object the origin of which it described? Does it not seem more likely that the narrative in Numbers was already known both to the author of 2 Kings 18 and to his readers at the time?

A further passage may be considered here, especially since it very probably derives from the period to which Blum assigns the work of his proposed author K^D, that is, Exodus 19: 3b–8. Coming at the beginning of the Sinai pericope, it is regarded by Blum as a key text in the K^D 'composition layer'. He associates it closely with the ceremony described in 24: 3–8, seeing this ceremony as effecting what is announced in 19: 3b–8—the consecration of Israel as 'a kingdom of priests' and a 'holy nation'.[45] Both of these texts are in turn associated with the narrative of the origin of the priesthood of the Levites in Exodus 32: 25–9 (pp. 54 ff.). According to Blum, the 'investiture of a separate priestly office marks the end of the "general priesthood" announced in Exodus 19: 6 and effected in 24: 3 ff. With the "Fall" because of the "golden calf" Israel lost its innocence, so to speak, and was no longer invested with the same standing as previously' (p. 56).

The presence of some Deuteronomistic vocabulary in Exodus 19: 3b–8 is generally acknowledged.[46] For example, the phrase 'you have seen' (v. 4a) or similar expressions (e.g. 'what your eyes have seen'), when used of what God has done on Israel's behalf, is especially characteristic of the Deuteronomistic corpus (cf. Deut. 4: 3, 9; 10: 21 f.; 11: 7; 29: 1; Josh. 23: 3); the imagery in v. 4b ('I bore you on eagle's wings') is similar to that in Deuteronomy 32: 11, a Deuteronomistic

---

[45] *Studien zur Komposition des Pentateuch*, 51 f., 92 f.
[46] See especially L. Perlitt, *Bundestheologie im Alten Testament*, WMANT 36 (Neukirchen-Vluyn 1969), 190 ff.

addition to Deuteronomy; the description of Israel as Yahweh's 'peculiar possession' (*s^egullāh*, v. 5b) is found in Deuteronomy 7: 6; 14: 2; 26: 18; in Deuteronomy also Israel is described as a 'holy people'—the fact that Exodus 19: 6 uses the phrase 'holy nation' (*gōy*) indicates not a non-Deuteronomistic hand but only that its author wrote against the background of the exile when Israel found itself exiled amongst the nations (cf. the use of *gōy* for Israel in the late Deuteronomistic passage Deut. 4: 6–8).

There are, however, several strikingly non-Deuteronomistic features of the text which give it a distinctive and, indeed, unique stamp in the Pentateuch and which are without parallel in the Deuteronomistic corpus. Its depiction of Israel as a 'kingdom of priests' and 'a holy nation (*gōy*)', with the implied concept of the role of Israel as a priestly nation witnessing to the holiness of Yahweh among the nations, has no background in Deuteronomistic theology. These two striking descriptions of the vocation of Israel probably reflect the emergence of such a concept in prophecy from the exilic period onwards. Thus, as Perlitt has observed, with Israel's vocation 'you shall be to me a holy nation' may be compared Ezekiel 36: 23: 'When they see that I reveal my holiness through you, the nations (*haggōyīm*) will know that I am the Lord, says the Lord God'. Israel's status as Yahweh's 'kingdom of priests' is close to Isaiah 61: 5: 'you shall be named priests of the Lord and ministers of our God', and the expression 'all the earth is mine' (v. 5b) echoes Deutero-Isaiah (cf. for example Isa. 42: 5). The combination of Deuteronomistic, priestly and prophetic elements and terminology that characterizes this passage points to an author of the late exilic or early post-exilic period and thus the period to which Blum assigns the work of K^D. But these same striking theological features of the text are unparalleled anywhere in the Deuteronomistic corpus, and the passage cannot be described straightforwardly as 'Deuteronomistic'.

There is surely also reason to be uneasy about the significance Blum attaches to Exodus 19: 3b–8 in relation to the story of the investiture of the Levites in Exodus 32: 25–9. On such an understanding of these two texts, significant trends in exilic and early post-exilic prophecy concerning Israel's future as the people of Yahweh are reduced, so to speak, in Exodus 19: 3b–8 and reported as something that might once have been but which Israel's apostasy aborted forever, and both this text and Exodus 24: 3–8 become merely a foil for the narrative of the ordination of the Levites in Exodus 32: 25–9. It is generally agreed that Exodus 19: 3b–8 is an insertion into this context, and there is much to be said that part of its purpose was to interpret the ritual in Exodus 24: 3–8 as the 'consecration' of Israel.[47] But is it not more likely that the high vocation it declares to be Israel's is a promise that points beyond the events of Sinai, notwithstanding Israel's apostasy, just as, for example, the promise of blessing for the nations in Genesis points beyond the immediate events being narrated?

What emerges from a consideration of these selected texts is that the passages ascribed by Blum to his 'composition layer' K[D] probably do not all belong on the same level. Thus, whilst it may be agreed that Exodus 19: 3b–8 is from the late exilic or early post-exilic period, there are good reasons for believing that Numbers 14: 11b–23a is earlier than the parallel narrative in Deuteronomy 1: 19–2: 1 and thus pre-dates the Deuteronomistic History. The narrative of the call and commissioning of Moses in Exodus 3–4 is also most probably pre-Deuteronomic. Further, there are no compelling reasons for assigning such passages as Exodus 15: 22–5a; 17: 1bβ–7; Numbers 11: 1–3; *11: 4–32; *12: 1–15; 21: 4b–9 to a Deuteronomic or Deuteronomistic writer. In short, it does not seem likely that these various texts derive from a systematic reworking by one and the same author of an earlier narrative of the events of bondage, exodus, and the wandering in the wilderness. There was no 'Deuteronomic or Deuteronomistic Tetrateuch'.

I refer again to Suzanne Boorer's study of the texts in Exodus and Numbers centring upon the oath promising the land to Israel. She has made a good case for the view that although these texts are editorial additions to an underlying narrative and are dependent upon Genesis 15, they were probably not all added at the same time. For example, although Exodus 32: 13 and 33: 1 and the secondary units to which they belong (32: 7–14 and 33: 1–3) probably derive from the same hand, Numbers 14: 23a, which belongs to the secondary unit 11b–23a, shows signs of being from a later editor. Thus, whilst Exodus 32: 7–14 resolves the ambiguity in Exodus 32: 31–4, which seems to announce punishment for all the people whilst envisaging the continuation of the nation, Numbers 14: 11b–23a weaves these two accounts into a coherent text with its own distinctive argument and intention. In this way the portrayal of Yahweh's decision in

---

[47] See also my *God and His People: Covenant and Theology in the Old Testament* (Oxford 1986), 172–4.

Numbers 14: 20–3a is quite different from, and more complex than, his decision in Exodus 32: 14 where he simply reverses his initial decision to disown, destroy, and replace his people. In Numbers 14: 20–3a there is a more complex interaction of forgiveness and judgement. This contrast, together with other differences between the two passages, is plausibly explained by seeing the Numbers passage as later than Exodus 32–4 including the secondary addition to it of Exodus 32: 7–14.[48] On the other hand, Numbers 14: 11b–23a is probably earlier than Deuteronomy 9: 12–14, 26–9 which seems to use elements not only from Exodus 32–4 but also from the text in Numbers 14 (Boorer, 363–8). The retrospect to Numbers 14: 11b–23a in Numbers 32: 7–15, however, is probably from a later editor, and is probably also later than Deuteronomy 9: 12–14, 26–9 (pp. 415–25).[49] It may be added that Boorer's findings that these passages are not all on the same level from a compositional point of view is surely nothing more than we would expect, since it is now generally agreed that the Deuteronomistic corpus itself shows evidence of the work of more than one stage of Deuteronomistic redaction.

VII

At the outset of the survey of modern research in this and the preceding two chapters, I outlined four main 'paradigms' of how the Pentateuch was composed, two of them relating to research of the past, and two of them to the main proposals that have emerged from research during the past thirty years or so. The latter two are:

(1) The Pentateuch is the creation of a Deuteronomic redactor who combined originally independent tradition complexes, arranging them sequentially into a history of Israel from the patriarchs to the settlement, a Priestly writer subsequently adding the primeval history.

(2) There never was an independent Tetrateuch. Rather, the pre-P Tetrateuch was composed after and perhaps as a 'prologue' to the Deuteronomistic History, extending the story of Israel back from the eve of the settlement to the patriarchal age and providing also a primeval history beginning with creation. A Priestly editor subsequently incorporated much additional material.

---

[48] For details see Boorer, *The Promise of the Land*, 331–63.
[49] See also Blum, *Studien zur Komposition des Pentateuch*, 112.

Neither of these two paradigms carries conviction. Rendtorff's theory, represented by (1), that the Pentateuch is the result of an editorial 'stitching' together of a number of originally independent tradition complexes, has gained little following among scholars.[50] Blum has supported it only to the extent of regarding the patriarchal complex in Genesis 12–50 as having its own history of composition before being integrated with the remaining sections of the Pentateuch.

The second paradigm has found wider support. Yet it too, as we have seen, has serious drawbacks. At the hands of most who argue it, it is associated with a late dating of the Yahwist's narrative. But though there are elements in this narrative which may be dated as late as the exilic period or even later, most of it is more plausibly dated to an earlier, pre-exilic period. There is little in it that is incompatible with a pre-exilic origin, and some features of it cannot plausibly be attributed to an exilic setting. For example, the narrative of Jacob's reconciliation with Esau, as we saw earlier, is unlikely to have been composed in the exilic period. Similarly, the stories of the founding of major sanctuaries by the patriarchs and thus the legitimization of major cultic centres of the pre-exilic period are more plausibly derived from that period than from the exilic or early post-exilic period. We saw also, against Rose's conclusions, that there are compelling reasons for regarding a narrative in the Deuteronomistic History such as Deuteronomy 1: 19–2: 1* as later than, and a development of, its parallel in Numbers 13–14*, including the later addition in Numbers 14: 11b–23a, and not vice versa, and thus an indication that the composition of the Tetrateuch began before that of the Deuteronomistic History. In addition, the general character of the pre-Priestly Tetrateuch sits ill alongside that of the known literature of the exilic period. Again as we have seen, the *dies irae* that so palpably forms the background and in large measure the subject of this literature—the books of Jeremiah and Ezekiel, Isaiah 40–55, and most notably the Deuteronomistic corpus—is absent from JE.

---

[50] See, for example, the critical responses to it in *JSOT* 3 (1977) by R. N. Whybray, 'Response to Professor Rendtorff', 11–14; Van Seters, 'The Yahwist as Theologian? A Response', 15–19; N. E. Wagner, 'A Response to Professor Rolf Rendtorff', 20–7; G. E. Coats, 'The Yahwist as Theologian? A Critical Reflection', 28–32; R. E. Clements, 'Review of R. Rendtorff, *Das überlieferungsgeschichtliche Problem des Pentateuch*', 43–5, and more recently R. N. Whybray, *The Making of the Pentateuch*, 205–10; J. Blenkinsopp, *The Pentateuch*, 23–4; Van Seters, *Prologue to History: The Yahwist as Historian in Genesis*, 17–18, 20–1, 284–6.

By positing substantial pre-exilic literary compositions as sources employed by his proposed post-exilic author K^D, Blum avoids such difficulties as these. His work has also the merit of reinforcing the view, until recently relatively unquestioned, that the Old Testament preserves a substantial body of literature from the pre-exilic period, a period which, indeed, can be looked upon as the classical period of Hebrew literature. In this, as in other ways, he has rightly been described as 'a moderate, a mediating figure, in the current debate'.[51] Further, the comprehensiveness of his research has done more than any other recent study I know to yield a 'synchronic' understanding of the literature at each stage of its emergence and of its final form.[52]

As we have seen, however, his theory has its own difficulties, for whilst some of his K^D passages can confidently be ascribed to Deuteronomistic writers, others are less convincingly so described, and in any event even those passages that can be so described may not have derived from the same author or the same period. Some may derive from a period as late as Blum suggests—the early post-exilic period—but others are more plausibly dated to a time prior to the composition of the Deuteronomistic History. In short, the evidence does not support the notion of a systematic Deuteronomistic editing of the Tetrateuch, much less the view the the first Tetrateuch was the work of a Deuteronomistic author.

VIII

The critique offered in the foregoing chapters of contemporary research suggests that the composition of the Tetrateuch/Hexateuch reaches back into the pre-exilic period. At the same time, it has reinforced the view that the work of composition and redaction continued, so that we can speak, as did earlier scholars, of the necessity of retaining something of a supplementary hypothesis. This process continued into the post-exilic period when, as still seems most likely, the Priestly material was incorporated. It reinforces also what C. R. North wrote in his judicious assessment of the state of research in 1951: 'the history of any one of the "documents" may well be as com-

---

[51] G. I. Davies, 'The Composition of the Book of Exodus: Reflections on the theses of Erhard Blum', in M. Fox (ed.), *Texts, Temples and Tradition: A Tribute to Menaham Haran* (Winona Lake, Minn. 1977), 77.

[52] See below, Ch. 9.

plicated as the history of the whole Pentateuch'.[53] Not all that can be attributed to J, for example, was written at one sitting, so to speak. Rather, as North put it, the 'gauge' of J is broader in the pre-exilic period than in the subsequent period.

One might also recall a memorable description by von Rad which, though he applied it to the entire process from the earliest oral stages in the transmission of the traditions and literature to the final form of the Hexateuch, is applicable to the written stages themselves:[54]

No doubt the Hexateuch in its complete and final form makes great demands upon the understanding of its readers. Many ages, many men, many traditions, and many theologians have contributed to this stupendous work. The Hexateuch will be rightly understood, therefore, not by those who read it superficially, but only by those who study it with a knowledge of its profundities, recognising that its pages speak of the revelations and religious experiences of many different periods. *None of the stages in the age-long development of this work has been wholly superseded; something has been preserved of each phase, and its influence has persisted right down to the final form of the Hexateuch.* Only a recognition of this fact can prepare one to hear the plenitude of the witness which this work encompasses.

Such an insight has surely been too often forgotten in recent new 'solutions' of the problem of the Pentateuch which have tended to telescope the composition of this manifestly complex literature into one or two stages. In this way, in my opinion, they have made no advance upon the Documentary Theory which they seek to discard. In the final two chapters that now follow, therefore, I shall argue that more of that theory can still carry conviction than has been conceded in recent years and that, granted its shortcomings, it remains the most comprehensive among all those that have recently been advanced as its replacement.

[53] C. R. North, 'Pentateuchal Criticism' in H. H. Rowley (ed.), *The Old Testament and Modern Study* (Oxford 1951), 48–83 (the quotation is from p. 81).
[54] Von Rad, *Das formgeschichtliche Problem des Hexateuchs*, 85; Eng. trans., 77 f.

7

Renewed Debate about P

Amidst the diversity of recent new theories of the origin and composition of the Pentateuch, support has remained strong, as we have seen, for the notion of a 'Yahwist' author whose work spanned all or most of the narrative of the Hexateuch. Increasingly, however, this has been denied in the case of E and P which, according to the Documentary Theory, were also originally independent narrative sources similar to J. The origin of the Elohist passages and fragments is closely related instead to the emergence of the Yahwist's narrative, whether as a stage on the way to it or as editorial supplements to it. The Priestly material, which is more expansive than E, is likewise regarded as the work of an editor or editors of an already formed Pentateuch or Hexateuch. That is, Wellhausen's 'book of the four covenants' (Q), or, as others termed it, the Priestly *Grundschrift* (P^G), never existed.

Such an assessment of these 'strata' in the Pentateuch is not new. As we have seen, the original independence of P was already questioned soon after the publication of Wellhausen's *Composition of the Hexateuch* and it has remained debated ever since. The origin of E as an originally discrete source narrative has likewise been frequently challenged. In recent research, however, the case against the Documentary Theory of these two sources has gained momentum and fresh arguments have been added.

This assessment of these 'strata' in the Pentateuch must now receive our attention, since it not only strikes at the foundation and rationale of the Documentary Theory but is also important for the viability of most of the new theories outlined in the preceding two chapters. On the principle that an analysis of the Pentateuch should begin with the text we possess, the completed Pentateuch, and work back from there, I shall begin with the Priestly material. The question of the E fragments will be considered in Chapter 8.

I

Throughout the period since Wellhausen's work on the composition of the Pentateuch the dominant view has been that there once existed an independent Priestly narrative which began with the account of creation in Genesis 1 and continued its narration up to at least the period immediately prior to Israel's settlement in Canaan. That not all of the material which we can label P belonged to that original narrative has also been widely agreed, though opinions vary in detail as to what material, especially in the extensive legislation contained in the account of the revelation at Sinai in Exodus 19–Numbers 10, was incorporated by way of secondary accretions, whether before or after the combination of P with the older Pentateuchal sources. The original Priestly narrative or *Grundschrift* was usually designated by the siglum P^G to distinguish it from the supplementary Priestly materials added secondarily to it and usually referred to as P^S (= P supplementa).

Throughout this same period, however, a minority view has persisted that P^G never was an independent narrative, and that the material assigned to it is best explained as deriving from an editor who reworked the older sources incorporating a mass of additional material, some from sources which he inherited and some composed by himself. Such a view was argued in the latter part of the nineteenth century by, for example, S. Maybaum and A. Klostermann, earlier this century by J. Orr, B. D. Eerdmans, M. Löhr, P. Volz, subsequently by I. Engnel.[1] In still more recent years it has been freshly argued by, for example, F. M. Cross, J. Van Seters, R. Rendtorff, J. Vermeylen,

---

[1] S. Maybaum, *Die Entwickelung des altisraelitischen Priesterthums* (Breslau 1880); A. Klostermann, *Der Pentateuch* (Leipzig 1897; 2nd edn. Leipzig 1907); J. Orr, *The Problem of the Old Testament* (London 1905); B. D. Eerdmans, *Alttestamentliche Studien*, i. *Die Komposition der Genesis* (Giessen 1908); M. Löhr, *Untersuchungen zum Hexateuchproblem*, i. *Der Priesterkodex in der Genesis*, BZAW 38 (Giessen 1924); P. Volz, 'Anhang. P ist kein Erzähler', in P. Volz and W. Rudolph, *Der Elohist als Erzähler: ein Irrweg der Pentateuchkritik?*, BZAW 63 (Giessen 1933), 135–42; I. Engnell, *Gamla Testamentet. En traditionshistorisk inledning*, i (Stockholm 1945); 'Moseböckerna', *Svensk Bibliskt Uppslagsverk*, ii (2nd edn., Stockholm 1962), cols. 152–65; Eng. trans., 'The Pentateuch', *Critical Essays on the Old Testament* (London 1970), 50–67. For a discussion of the earlier debate see J. Skinner, *A Critical and Exegetical Commentary on Genesis* (Edinburgh 1910, 2nd edn., 1930); *The Divine Names in Genesis* (London 1914); C. R. North, 'Pentateuchal Criticism', in H. H. Rowley (ed.), *The Old Testament and Modern Study* (Oxford 1951), 48–83.

S. Tengström, E. Blum, R. N. Whybray, M. Vervenne.[2] Of these the comprehensive discussion by Frank Moore Cross, for many years Professor of Hebrew at Harvard and one of the most distinguished American Old Testament specialists of this century, has been widely influential. I shall begin with a review of his work, and then turn to the still more recent study by Erhard Blum who, though building upon Cross's conclusions, has introduced some fresh considerations. Sven Tengström's detailed discussion of the *tōlᵉdōth* passages must also be singled out for special consideration.[3]

---

[2] The more recent works referred to are: F. M. Cross, *Canaanite Myth and Hebrew Epic* (Cambridge, Mass. 1973), 293–325; Van Seters, *Abraham in History and Tradition* (1975); Rendtorff, *Das überlieferungsgeschichtliche Problem des Pentateuch* (1977); J. Vermeylen, 'La formation du Pentateuque à la lumière de l'exégèse historico-critique', *RTL* 12 (1981), 324–46; S. Tengström, *Die Toledothformel und die literarische Struktur der priesterlichen Erweiterungsschicht im Pentateuch*, Coniectanea Biblica, Old Testament Series, 17 (Lund 1981); Blum, *Die Komposition der Vätergeschichte* (1984), and *Studien zur Komposition des Pentateuch* (1990); Whybray, *The Making of the Pentateuch* (1987). A helpful bibliography of recent work is contained in M. Vervenne, 'The "P" Tradition of the Pentateuch. Document and/or Redaction?', in C. Brekelmans and J. Lust (eds.), *Pentateuchal and Deuteronomistic Studies*, Bibliotheca Ephemeridum Theologicarum Lovaniensium, 94 (Leuven 1990), 67–90. Though his article was prepared before the publication of Blum's volume of 1990, Vervenne's suggestion concerning the origin of P (see esp. p. 88) approximates to Blum's which is outlined below. Vervenne also provides additional bibliography to what is referred to here (see esp. p. 73 n. 18).

[3] Defences of the view that P was originally an independent narrative have come from, for example, E. W. Nicholson, 'P as an Originally Independent Source in the Pentateuch', *IBS* 10 (1988), 192–206; J. A. Emerton, 'The Priestly Writer in Genesis', *JTS* NS 39 (1988), 381–400; N. Lohfink, 'Die Ursünden in der priesterlichen Geschichtserzählung', in G. Bornkamm and K. Rahner (eds.), *Die Zeit Jesu. Festschrift für Heinrich Schlier* (Freiburg 1970), 38–57; Eng. trans., 'Original Sins in the Priestly Historical Narrative', in *Theology of the Pentateuch: Themes of the Priestly Narrative and Deuteronomy* (Edinburgh 1994), 96–115; 'Die Priesterschrift und die Geschichte', SVT 29 (Leiden 1978), 189–225; Eng. trans., 'The Priestly Narrative and History', in *Theology of the Pentateuch*, 136–72 (see esp. n. 31); S. McEvenue, *The Narrative Style of the Priestly Writer*, Analecta Biblica, 50 (Rome 1971); P. Weimar, 'Struktur und Komposition der priesterschriftlichen Geschichtsdarstellung', *BN* 23 (1984), 81–134, and 24 (1984), 138–62; id., *Untersuchung zur Redaktionsgeschichte des Pentateuch*, BZAW 146 (Berlin 1977); V. Fritz, 'Das Geschichtsverständnis der Priesterschrift', *ZThK* 84 (1987), 426–39; E. Zenger, *Gottes Bogen in den Wolken: Untersuchungen zu Komposition und Theologie der priesterschriftlichen Urgeschichte*, WMANT 57 (Stuttgart 1983); K. Koch, 'P–Kein Redaktor! Erinnerung an zwei Eckdaten der Quellenscheidung', *VT* 37 (1987), 446–67; J. Hughes, *Secrets of the Times: Myth and History in Biblical Chronology*, *JSOT* Supplement Series, 66 (Sheffield 1990). Additional bibliography is provided in M. Vervenne, 'The "P" Tradition', esp. p. 71 n. 15.

II

Cross begins with an analysis of the Priestly 'tradent's' theology (pp. 295–300). As edited by this tradent, history from creation to Moses is 'periodized' into four ages, those of Adam, Noah, Abraham, and Moses. Each period after creation is marked by a covenant, and this system of covenants, reaching its climax at Sinai, constitutes P's main theological concern. The first is the Noachic covenant (Gen. 9: 1–17), a covenant made by Elohim, God, with all flesh, that is, a universal covenant. The second covenant, made with Abram (17: 1–27), is 'at once deeper and narrower than the Noachic. More is revealed to fewer. *'Ēlōhīm*, "God", now revealed himself by his more intimate and precise epithet *'Ēl Šadday*' (p. 296). Abram receives the new name Abraham together with the blessing 'I will make thee exceedingly fruitful . . . and kings shall come forth from thee'. The sign of this covenant, and also its law, is circumcision. This Abrahamic covenant is then extended to Isaac (Gen. 17: 21; 21: 4) and subsequently more fully to Jacob (Gen. 35: 9–13). Though both of these first two covenants remain valid, however, each is provisional, a stage on the way to God's ultimate covenant and ultimate self-disclosure—the revelation at Sinai and the covenant made there with Moses and Israel. Its 'prologue' is set out in Exodus 6: 2–9 where God's proper name, Yahweh, is finally disclosed. 'This gives the sequence *'Ēlōhīm, 'Ēl Šadday, Yahweh* in the Priestly schema of covenants, the general appellative, "god", the archaic epithet, "'Ēl Šadday", and the unique proper name "Yahweh."' (p. 298). This prologue also renews the promise of the land, but now places it within the context of a new and central theme: 'I am Yahweh, and I will bring you forth from under the burdens of Egypt . . . and I will take you to be my people and I will become your God and you shall know that I am Yahweh . . . and I will bring you into the land' (vv. 6–8). The blessing of the covenant is expressed in its appropriate place in the list of blessings at the close of the covenant formulary (Lev. 26: 9). The sign of the covenant is the sabbath (Exod. 31: 13, 16 f.). That God may 'tabernacle' among his people—this was the purpose of this covenant, expressed most decisively in Leviticus 26: 11–13 and Exodus 29: 45–6, and the elaborate cultic requirements prescribed in the making of this covenant were 'the device contrived by Yahweh to make possible his "tabernacling" in Israel's midst, which alone could make full the redemption of Israel' (pp. 299–300).

Such a well-defined and carefully executed theology does not imply, however, that P was originally an independent narrative. According to Cross, P is most aptly described as a 'systematizing expansion of the normative JE tradition in the Tetrateuch' (pp. 294–5); the editor responsible for it was primarily concerned to supplement JE upon which he imposed 'framing elements', at the same time adding theological formulae and an occasional discrete document until reaching the description of the revelation at Sinai where he incorporated a mass of material.

In Genesis this editor framed the J account of the primeval history and the JE patriarchal history by means of a series of superscriptions employing the rubric 'these are the generations (*tōlᵉdōth*) of ...'. This formula was secondarily derived from an originally independent source 'The document of the generations of Adam', which has been preserved in 5: 1–32 and 11: 10–26. It is employed on ten occasions (2: 4; 5: 1; 6: 9; 10: 1; 11: 27; 25: 12; 25: 19; 36: 1; 37: 2) and in each case is a superscription. That this series never formed part of an independent P narrative is evidenced especially by Genesis 2: 4a which cannot be related to the preceding Priestly story of creation but is clearly a P editorial heading to the exclusively J narrative of creation and the 'fall' in 2: 4b–4: 26. Its occurrence in 6: 9 is similarly an editorial heading to the flood story which has been 'completely rewritten by P' (p. 303).

As for narrative material, one is struck by its paucity in the P passages in Genesis. Apart from chapter 23, the bulk of the P material here consists of the blessing and covenant passages (9: 1–17; 17: 1–22; 28: 1–9; 35: 9–13; 48: 3–7), none of which can properly be called a narrative, and most of which depend directly on a parallel JE narrative.

Cross goes on to suggest that 'perhaps the most persuasive evidence that the Priestly strata of the Tetrateuch never had existence as an independent narrative source comes from its omissions' (p. 306). He draws particular attention to the absence of a P account of humanity's sin and rebellion in the time before the flood. Apart from Genesis 2: 4a, there is no P material in chapters 2–4. P's summary statement in 6: 13 'The end of all flesh has come before me, for the earth is filled with violence through them', must presuppose 'a knowledge of concrete and colourful narratives of the corruption of the creation. Otherwise, it has neither literary nor theological force' (p. 306). The P statement in Genesis 9: 6, 'He who spills man's blood, his blood shall be spilled by man', as well as the entire Priestly scheme of divine covenants must also presume a description of man's primeval rebellion and sin. The paradox to which the generally accepted theory gives rise of an originally independent Priestly narrative which contained no account of this rebellion and sin is removed when P is seen instead as a tradent whose work incorporated the J narratives in Genesis 2–4.

Other narrative traditions absent from 'the putative P narrative' in Genesis are the story of Abraham's faithfulness in Genesis 22, the thrice-told tale of the patriarch and his wife in the court of a foreign king (12: 10–20; 20: 1–17; 26: 1–14), the search for a wife for Isaac and the discovery of Rebekah (ch. 24), the rivalry between Esau and Jacob for their father's blessing (ch. 27), Jacob's vision at Bethel (28: 10–22), the entire Jacob–Laban cycle (chs. 29–33), the tale of Dinah and Shechem (ch. 34), and the Joseph narrative (37: 2b–47: 26 [50: 26]). 'What remains makes poor narrative indeed' (p. 307).

The result is the same when one turns to Exodus and Numbers. If possible, indeed, P here 'has even a lesser claim to being a narrative source' (p. 307); nor does it cease to depend on JE. Further, what is missing from the P material in these books, if it was an originally independent document, is no less striking than in the case of Genesis (pp. 317–21). For example, nothing is narrated about the birth of Moses, or of the episodes during his youth in Egypt or of his flight to the desert, whilst without the accompanying JE material concerning his death, nothing of the circumstances of it or of the place of his burial is narrated. But the most 'stunning omission' of all from the alleged P narrative source is an account of the covenant ceremony at Sinai, 'the climax to which the entire Priestly labour has been directed' (p. 318).

It is not by chance that the P tradent poured his traditions into the Sinai section until it dwarfed all his other sections and indeed his other periods. The climactic blessing of Leviticus 26: 9, 11–13a stresses most clearly the supreme meaning of the covenant at Sinai, Yahweh's tabernacle in Israel's midst and thereby his covenant presence with his people . . . In looking to the darkness of exile and beyond, the last words of the peroration of Leviticus 26 [vv. 44 f.] made Yahweh's purpose clear (and the purpose of the Priestly hand which added this summary to the Holiness Code)'. (pp. 318–19)

It is 'beyond credence' that P had no tradition of the covenant ceremonies at Sinai or that he had no covenant at all there. 'Either the Priestly tradent had the tradition and a redactor has removed it in combining P with JE, or he relied on the Epic tradition, especially the

E tradition of Exodus 24: 1–8 for the narrative of the covenant rites. In our view, the latter alternative fits far more easily with the evidence' (p. 320).

III

Erhard Blum concurs with Cross's main conclusions that the Priestly 'layer' in the Tetrateuch never existed as an independent source. Rather, it derives from a Priestly writer's revision and supplementation of K^D which resulted in the Pentateuch substantially as we have it (K^P).[4] The case against regarding P as an originally independent source is especially strong in Genesis: the short P additions to the stories about Isaac, Jacob, and Joseph, for example, cannot have derived from an independent narrative source; the *tōlᵉdōth* texts have been employed as a framework for the older narrative; and the longer 'theological texts' (17; 27: 46–28: 9; 35: 9–15; 48: 3–7), which stand in some tension with, or are doublets of, older narratives, not only show a knowledge of the latter but were designed and inserted as corrections of them.[5] In the remainder of the Tetrateuch, P is also best understood as a reworking of K^D. Thus, small additions have been inserted at Exodus 15: 19; 20: 11; 24: 1, 9 (the references to Aaron, Nadab, and Abihu); 31: 18; 32: 15–16; 34: 29–35. Likewise, other short passages were composed with their present contexts in mind (Exod.1: 1–5, 7, 13–14; 2: 23aβ–25; 11: 9–10; 12: 1–10, 28, 37a(?), 40–2, 43–51; 13: 1, 20. With Cross, Blum also argues that what is left out is a telling indication that P was never an independent narrative. For example, there is nothing in P about Moses before his sudden appearance in Exodus 6: 2.[6]

However, Blum argues a more complex understanding of the nature and origin of the P material in the Tetrateuch than Cross, as the title of his discussion indicates: 'The Priestly layer: neither "source" nor "redaction"' ('Die priesterliche Schicht: weder "Quelle" noch "Redaktion"').[7] Rejecting the view that P derived from an originally independent source, whilst at the same time regarding the description 'redactional' as an inadequate description of the nature of this material, he employs the description 'compositional' as a more

---

[4] Blum, *Studien zur Komposition des Pentateuch*, 229–85.
[5] Ibid. 229 f. Cf. also Blum, *Die Komposition der Vätergeschichte*, 420–58.
[6] *Studien zur Komposition des Pentateuch*, 230 f.   [7] Ibid. 229.

accurate appreciation of the intention and achievement of the writer responsible for its inclusion. In this way he attempts to explain those features of P which stand in tension with, or are doublets of, narratives in the older source(s) and have thus been viewed as strong evidence in favour of the view that P was an originally independent narrative source. The following examples illustrate the case he seeks to make.[8]

(1) The narrative of the call of Moses in Exodus 6 offers evidence of the tension between P's theology and that of K[D], especially the well-known contradiction—so important for the Documentary Theory—between its statement that God has not hitherto been known by the name Yahweh and the use of this name in Genesis. The general principle advanced by Blum to explain the relationship between P and the older context into which it has been worked is that the P writer, though preserving the substance of the tradition he inherited (K[D]), endeavoured to give it a new interpretation by means of reformulations of traditions which he inserted into it.[9] As a result of such interpolations the narrative was henceforth understood differently. On this basis, for example, the statement concerning the revelation of the divine name in Exodus 6: 3 meant that readers/listeners henceforth made the necessary corrections mentally when reading Genesis where the name Yahweh is already employed. That is, the older narrative was not altered, but Exodus 6: 3 gives a 'binding interpretation' of it.[10]

Blum argues that such a 'compositional' understanding of the origin and nature of P accounts also for the continuity that exists between the P passages in Exodus 1–7 (1: 1–5, 7; 2: 23–5; 6: 2–7: 13). He concedes that these passages themselves form a continuous narrative, but this does not necessarily mean that they once belonged to an independent Priestly source.[11] The abrupt introduction of Moses in Exodus 6 itself weighs against this. According to Blum, the Priestly author had this continuity in mind, as well as the coherence of the revised narrative he sought to create on the basis of K[D], when composing the passages. He suggests that it is possible that the

---

[8] For the following observations on Blum's view of P I am indebted to Graham Davies, 'The Composition of the Book of Exodus: Reflections on the theses of Erhard Blum', in M. Fox (ed.), *Texts, Temples and Tradition: A Tribute to Menahem Haran* (Winona Lake, Minn. 1996), 71–85.

[9] *Studien zur Komposition des Pentateuch*, 235. Cf. *Die Komposition der Vätergeschichte*, 270.

[10] *Studien zur Komposition des Pentateuch*, 235.   [11] Ibid. 240.

'compositional texts were not immediately written into the [K^D] text, but were first conceived "for themselves" (of course with knowledge of the tradition which was to be reworked)'.[12] Blum argues that all this explains how these Priestly passages are so closely related to the surrounding narration.[13]

(2) The plague narrative in Exodus 7–11 shows the same 'compositional' revision and supplementation by the Priestly writer.[14] The texts ascribed by Blum to P here are 7: 19–22*; 8: 1–3, 11–15; 9: 8–12, 22–3, 35; 10: 12–13a, 21–3, 27; 11: 9–10, and thus include parts of the passages about the seventh, eighth, and ninth plagues of hail, locusts, and darkness (9: 22–3, 35; 10: 12–13a, 21–3, 27) which are usually assigned to E. Blum points to various features of these texts that give the impression of an originally independent narrative:[15] the first four plague episodes stand out as a coherent and rounded narrative; like the K^D narrative, the P material here also has a distinctive profile and narrative progression; the plagues of gnats (כנים) and boils (שחין), which are entirely from P, seem to parallel those of flies (ערב) and pestilence (דבר) in the older narrative K^D(J). Once again, however, this does not justify the conclusion that this material derives from an originally independent Priestly narrative such as is posited by the Documentary Theory. First, he argues that what he identifies as P sections concerning the plagues of hail and locust and darkness 'lean on' the K^D narrative and cannot therefore have existed apart from it; second, P contains a reference to the destruction of the first-born but does not describe its enactment—Exod. 11: 4–8 and 12: 29–33 are K^D—and thus also presupposes the older narrative; and thirdly, the theme that as a result of Yahweh's actions the Egyptians will 'know' that he is the Lord in the P text 7: 5 is not referred to in the stories of the plagues, but only in K^D and in the P account of the crossing of the sea (14: 4, 18). That the K^P elements at the beginning of the plagues cycle duplicate some of the older K^D narrative shows, not that they derive from an originally independent Priestly source, but only that K^P here made use of an already existing and already partly shaped Priestly tradition ('partiell vorgeprägte (priesterliche) Überlieferung' (p. 251)). In short, the work of K^P is best explained by understanding

---

[12] *Studien zur Komposition des Pentateuch*, 241 f.

[13] He cites with approval the observations concerning this by J. L. Ska, 'La place d'Ex 6, 2–8 dans la narration de l'exode', *ZAW* 94 (1982), 530–48, and M. Greenberg, 'The Thematic Unity of Exodus III–XI', *World Congress of Jewish Studies* (Jerusalem 1967), 151–4.

[14] *Studien zur Komposition des Pentateuch*, 242–56.   [15] Ibid. 250.

it as 'neither source nor redaction'; rather, it is a well-crafted 'composition' which in addition to reworking K^D also occasionally incorporates other already existing narrative material.

(3) Blum discusses the narrative of the destruction of the Egyptians at 'the sea' in Exodus 14 as a further example of the complex nature and origin of the P material in the Tetrateuch.[16] He accepts the usual division of this narrative into two sources (P and his K^D), each relatively complete in itself and offering its distinctive description of the events. Once again, however, this does not mean that the P story derives from an originally independent P narrative source. That this story did not originate with the Priestly writer is clear from the reference in v. 15a to Moses's 'crying to the Lord', since there is no allusion to this earlier.[17] Rather, we have here a further example of P's adoption of an already existing story which he has used for his revision and supplementation of K^D.[18] This inherited tradition has been skilfully worked into the K^D narrative so that the peculiar emphasis of each contributes to the description of the deliverance of Israel and of the might of Yahweh. Here also, therefore, P is best understood as a 'composition layer' rather than deriving from a Priestly narrative source or from a supplementer.

IV

It is well known that in the source analysis of the Pentateuch the flood story in Genesis 6: 5–8: 22 has been regarded as particularly cogent evidence of the secondary combination by an editor of two originally independent narratives, J and P. For this reason critics of the Documentary Theory have devoted special attention to this story. All the more surprising, therefore, is Cross's bald statement that it has been 'completely rewritten by P'. In spite of many attempts to challenge it, the evidence in favour of the two-source theory of the composition of this narrative remains compelling.[19] The evidence is well known and need be only briefly stated here. First, there are discrepancies and contradictions. In J a distinction is maintained between

---

[16] Ibid. 256–62.   [17] Ibid. 260 f.
[18] He argues (263–71) a similar conclusion in the case of the P narrative of rebellion in the wilderness in Numbers 16.
[19] For a detailed discussion see J. A. Emerton, 'An Examination of Some Attempts to Defend the Unity of the Flood Narrative in Genesis', pt. 1, *VT* 37 (1987), 401–20, and pt. 2, *VT* 38 (1988), 1–21.

clean and unclean animals, the clean entering the ark by sevens, the unclean by twos (7: 2; cf. 8: 20), whilst in P one pair of every animal without distinction between clean and unclean enters (6: 19f.; 7: 15–16). In J the flood is brought about by forty days of rain which began seven days after the command to enter the ark, and the waters of the flood subside after forty days (7: 4, 10, 12; 8: 6). In P a partially different cause of the flood is described—'the fountains of the great deep (*tᵉhom*) burst forth, and the windows of the heavens were opened' (7: 11; 8: 2)—and the chronological scheme is also different: the waters increase for one hundred and fifty days and the entire duration of the flood is one year (7: 6, 11, 13, 24; 8: 3b, 4, 5, 13a, 14). Secondly, there is much repetition of commands and statements, and although some of this may be explained in terms of literary style, not all of it can plausibly be so accounted for, but provides supporting evidence for the two-source theory.[20] Not duplicated in P, however, is the J record of the offering of a sacrifice by Noah after the flood (8: 20), and it seems clear that the reason for this is that P reserved all offering of sacrifices until the consecration of Aaron and his sons as priests at Sinai.[21]

In the face of this evidence, it is difficult to comprehend how it can be claimed that a Priestly tradent has 'completely' rewritten the flood story. How can it be said to have been 'completely rewritten' when so much of the older story has been retained?[22] And why would such a tradent have endeavoured to change so much of his supposed source and still have left it to tell so much of its own story, a story so manifestly at odds with what he himself evidently believed, and to some extent in flat contradiction of it? Volz, acknowledging such a difficulty, suggested that the older J narrative had by the time of P acquired an authority which made dispensing with it impossible.[23] If this was so, however, why did this editor nevertheless venture to change and contradict it in the ways indicated above? In short, it remains the more plausible explanation of the discrepancies, contradictions, and repetitiveness of this story to see them as arising from a conflation by an editor of two originally separate and distinctive narratives.

---

[20] See Emerton, 'An Examination', pt. 1, 411–13.
[21] See also R. E. Friedman, *The Exile and Biblical Narrative* (Chico, Calif. 1981), 82.
[22] See also the comments of Emerton, 'The Priestly Writer in Genesis', 397.
[23] Volz, 'P is kein Erzähler', 141.

Unconvincing also is Cross's argument concerning the absence from P of a narrative of humanity's primeval rebellion which, he maintains, would have been a necessary presupposition of such a statement as that in Genesis 6: 11–12 which speaks of the corruption of the world that had originally been 'good' in God's eyes (Gen. 1: 31). It is likely that the Priestly author knew the stories of J in Genesis 2–4. But Genesis 6: 11–12 does not suggest that he had these stories directly in mind in composing what he here states, and there is no reason why he should not have said succinctly what was self-evident to his audience—the presence of sin and 'violence' in the world—without explaining it or composing an accompanying 'myth' or aetiology about its origin. Lohfink has shown that the Priestly author by no means overlooked this matter, but treated it differently from the Yahwist's account.[24] He makes the case that the Priestly statement in Genesis 6: 11—'Now the earth was corrupt in God's sight, and the earth was filled with violence'—'contains an entire doctrine of sin', and he goes on to illuminate other texts in which P relates this 'doctrine' to Israel and its leaders.

A more general observation may here be made concerning the significance attached by Cross to P's 'omissions' and the paucity of P passages in Genesis. The weakness of such an argument, as Lohfink has pointed out,[25] is its assumption that an independent Priestly narrative would necessarily have narrated everything in the older source (JE). Cross's statement that the P material in the Tetrateuch is 'nothing like the narrative of saga' is justified, but shows only that its author did not intend to write 'saga' and that what he wrote was different from the older sources, not that it could not have been conceived and composed as an independent source.[26]

Some of P's omissions are readily explicable on other grounds. The consistency with which, for example, stories reflecting what has aptly been termed the 'all too human'[27] behaviour of ancestral figures are not represented in P may be because its author studiously avoided a retelling of them: such are, for example, the stories about Noah's

[24] 'Die Ursünden in der priesterlichen Geschichtserzählung', 38–57; Eng. trans., 96–115.
[25] 'Die Priesterschrift und die Geschichte', 189–225; Eng. trans., 'The Priestly Narrative and History', 136–72 (see esp. n. 31).
[26] See also the comments of Emerton, 'The Priestly Writer in Genesis', 392 f. For an analogy to P, Emerton points to the work of the Chronicler who left out much that was in Samuel and Kings but wrote more fully on some subjects.
[27] R. Smend, *Die Entstehung des Alten Testaments* (Stuttgart 1978), 54.

drunkenness and those reflecting the doubtful morality of the patriarch and his wife in a foreign court, and the story of Jacob's treach-
erous deceit of Esau. In the case of Genesis 28: 10–22 it is possible
that the Priestly author wished to avoid such a cult-foundation story,
just as elsewhere he avoids those stories in which patriarchal figures
build altars and thus found sanctuaries. Thus in his account of God's
appearance to Jacob at Bethel in Genesis 35: 6a, 9–13 he makes no
mention of the building of an altar, in contrast to what is stated in the
older material in 35: 1, 3, 7.

The main reason, however, for the literary structure of P arises
from its author's distinctive theology. His main emphasis is upon the
foundation of the theocratic community of Israel at Sinai; this, as
Cross himself states, dwarfs all that precedes. And to this end, it
seems, only that is narrated of the periods preceding which is theologically required as *praeparatio*: the story of creation concluding
with the hidden foundation of the sabbath, the flood narrative concluding with the Noachic covenant, the covenant with Abraham and
its extension to his descendants, the purchase of the burial place from
Machpelah signalling faith in the divine promise of the land, a story
of Jacob's acquisition of wives from his parents' kin thus securing the
racial purity of the coming 'congregation', the bondage in Egypt—all
this placed within a genealogical framework—the call of Moses and
the revelation of the divine name Yahweh to him and the promise to
deliver Israel from the burdens of the Egyptians, a plague narrative
and the escape from Egypt. In short, what emerges from the literary
evidence is a coherent and well-executed theology within an appropriately structured literary presentation even though in the process of
redaction some of the constituents of the latter have been left out.[28]

As in past debates about the character of P, the sequence of the
names employed for God also merits more significance than Cross is
willing to concede. In the P passage Exodus 6: 2–9, which duplicates
what is narrated in the older material in Exodus 3, God declares that
he had revealed himself to the patriarchs as El Šadday and not by his
name Yahweh which is now made known for the first time to Moses.
The sequence, to which Cross himself draws attention, Ēlōhīm—'Ēl
Šadday—Yahweh, is thereby completed, and it seems that such a
sequence was of some importance for the writer responsible for P; it
points to ever increasing degrees of revelation culminating in God's

[28] See further, Fritz, 'Das Geschichtsverständnis der Priesterschrift', 426–39. Cf.
Emerton, 'The Priestly Writer in Genesis', 396–8.

actions on behalf of Israel under Moses and the crowning meeting between Yahweh and his people at Sinai. Under this new name, God intends to deliver his people from the burdens of the Egyptians and finally make them his own in fulfilment of the promise made to the forefathers (vv. 7–8). It is difficult to see, as older commentators pointed out, how the Priestly writer of Exodus 6: 2–9 could have been merely an editor or supplementer of the older Pentateuchal material which up to this stage flatly contradicts what is here narrated.

This calls for comment on Blum's suggestion concerning the significance of Exodus 6: 3 which, he argues, is a 'key' whereby 'the whole preceding presentation, including its recalcitrant, "unharmonised" components, is given a binding interpretation'.[29] It seems very doubtful, as Graham Davies has pointed out, 'whether such a strategy could have succeeded or have been expected to succeed by the Priestly author, especially when the "key" follows the texts which have to be so "interpreted". The combination of the new Priestly passages [in Genesis] with the older material could not but serve to blur the important distinctions which the Priestly author wanted to make'.[30] But the statement in Exodus 6: 3 is comprehensible on the basis that it derives from an originally independent P narrative that has been secondarily worked into the older sources by a scribe.

Reference to Exodus 6: 2–9 leads us to Cross's argument concerning P's handling of the Sinai covenant of which, he believes, this passage is the 'prologue'. Assuming that the making of the covenant at Sinai was, as he maintains, crucially important for P, is it not still somewhat strange that he did not compose an account of his own of the making of this covenant, just as he carefully set out the Noachic and Abrahamic covenants earlier?

That no P account proper of the making of the covenant at Sinai exists is most probably because, as many scholars have argued, the Priestly author consciously rejected this tradition and instead subsumed the revelation at Sinai and the institution of the theocratic community and its cult there under the covenant with Abraham which was all-important for this author.[31] For P, Israel at Sinai

[29] *Studien zur Komposition des Pentateuch*, 235.

[30] Davies, 'The Composition of the Book of Exodus', 81.

[31] See e.g. W. Zimmerli, 'Sinaibund und Abrahambund: Ein Beitrag zum Verständnis der Priesterschrift', *THZ* 16 (1960), 268–80, repr. in *Gottes Offenbarung. Gesammelte Aufsätze zum Alten Testament* (Munich 1963), 205–16; *Grundriss der alttestamentlichen Theologie* (Stuttgart 1972), 45–7; Eng. trans., *Old Testament Theology in Outline* (Edinburgh 1978), 55–7; R. E. Clements, *Abraham and David* (London 1967), 74–7.

'stands in the covenant of Abraham';[32] what happened at Sinai was a 'discharging of the earlier pledge of grace'.[33] In contrast to the covenant described in, for example, Exodus 24: 3–8 or the book of Deuteronomy, P sets out 'a conception of Israel's covenant relationship to God which is unbreakable', that is, the Abrahamic covenant which is 'everlasting' and 'is not subject to any conditional element of law'.[34] Far from being 'beyond credence', therefore, P's omission of an account of the covenant at Sinai belongs to a coherent theological intention, indeed 'kerygma'. And this too strengthens the view that the material in question once constituted an independent narrative giving expression to a distinctive and independent theology.

V

One of the most prominent elements in the Sinai pericope places a serious question mark against Blum's particular understanding of the origin and nature of his proposed 'composition layer' K[P]. Like Cross, he too regards the description of the events at Sinai as the crowning climax of the Priestly writer's work of 'composition', comprising as it does thirteen chapters in Exodus as well as Leviticus and substantial parts of Numbers.[35] It has often been pointed out, as Davies comments, how contradictory P's provisions are to features of the older texts relating to the events at Sinai. They are such, indeed, as to provide some of the strongest evidence that P derives from an originally independent narrative source rather than from the hand of a supplementer. Davies (p. 83) has put succinctly the difficulty that arises for Blum's view as follows:

According to P it is exclusively Aaron and his descendants who are to be priests in the full sense (Exod. 29; cf. Lev. 8–10) and the Levites occupy an inferior position. In the older narrative [Exod. 32] Aaron is an idolater and the Levites by their zeal for pure religion 'ordain themselves for the service of the Lord' (Exod. 32: 1–6, 21–9).[36] It is surely inconceivable that P could have allowed this chapter to stand in the middle of the tabernacle chapters, in his 'holy of holies'.

[32] Zimmerli, *Gottes Offenbarung*, 213. [33] Ibid. 215.

[34] Clements, *Abraham and David*, 75.

[35] *Studien zur Komposition des Pentateuch*, 293–332.

[36] As Davies points out ('The Composition of the Book of Exodus', 83 n. 52), the idiom used in 32: 29 of the Levites (מלאו ידכם היום ליהוה) is exactly the same as that used in 29:9 of Aaron and his sons alone.

Some further observations about Blum's view of P may appropriately be made at this stage. First, and remaining with the Sinai pericope, it seems very unlikely that the references to Nadab and Abihu
in Exodus 24: 1, 11 derive from P. In favour of Blum's view is the fact
that it is only in a priestly passage elsewhere in the Pentateuch that
these two figures are mentioned (Lev. 10: 1–2). When they are mentioned in this text, however, it is as the two disobedient sons of Aaron
whose misdemeanour earns death. This makes it improbable that P
would have included them in the description of the remarkable vision
of God on the holy mountain rather than Aaron's other sons Eleazar
and Ithamar, who became the ancestors of the legitimate priesthood.
It is more probable that the mention of Aaron, Nadab, and Abihu
belongs to an older tradition preserved in Exodus 24.[37]

The sudden appearance of Moses in the P narrative in Exodus 6 is
not the problem Blum believes it to be for the notion of P as an originally independent source. As Davies points out, the contents and
position of the passage which Blum cites to show this (Exod. 6:
14–25)[38] indicate that it was included mainly to introduce Aaron.
Moses, however, would scarcely have needed an introduction since by
the time of the Priestly author his place could be assumed to be well
known, just as it could be assumed by the authors of Deuteronomy
(whichever of the various introductions one chooses as the original
beginning of this book, 1: 1; 4: 44; 5: 1).[39]

A more general argument frequently advanced by Blum is that the
P passages have been so smoothly worked into their contexts as to
warrant the conclusion that they were deliberately designed with
these contexts in mind. As Davies observes (p. 80), however, such
smoothness of fit need not be surprising, since the subject-matter was
the same in P and, further, the Priestly writer may well have known
the older version. The smooth fit of the P passages may therefore just
as plausibly be explained as the work of an editor working material
from an independent Priestly source into the older narrative as that
such passages were composed *ad hoc* for insertion into it.

More fundamentally, however, Blum surely concedes too much in
the interest of the case he seeks to argue, and some of his observations
on the nature of the P material appear to support rather than counter

---

[37] For a discussion see E. W. Nicholson, 'The Antiquity of the Tradition in Exodus
XXIV 9–11', *VT* 24 (1974), 77–97.

[38] *Studien zur Komposition des Pentateuch*, 231.

[39] Davies, 'The Composition of the Book of Exodus', 80.

the theory of the original independence of P. As we have seen, he allows that there is continuity between some sequences of passages giving the impression that they derive from a continuous narrative, for example, the P texts in Exodus 1–7 (1: 1–5, 7; 2: 23–5; 6: 2–7: 13); this, indeed, is what the Documentary Theory maintains.[40] He argues, however, that the Priestly editor of K^D had this continuity in mind, as well as the coherence of the expanded narrative he sought to create, when composing the insertions he wished to make. Blum suggests that it is possible that the 'compositional texts were not immediately written into the [K^D] text, but were first conceived "for themselves" (of course with knowledge of the tradition which was to be reworked)'. This surely comes close, however, to conceding that the Priestly narrative existed independently of the older narrative before being inserted into it. Davies's comment is apt: 'If we consider the extent of the Priestly materials involved not just in Exodus but also elsewhere in the Pentateuch, it is very difficult to believe that the Priestly author was able to do this entirely in his head, and a separate written composition becomes almost inevitable' (p. 81). When we add to this, for example, the contradiction between P's theology of the step-by-step revelation of the divine name, culminating in the announcement to Moses in Exodus 6: 3, and what is described in much of Genesis, it surely seems likely that P was originally composed as an alternative narrative of Israel's origins and was intended to replace it as the standard account.

There are difficulties too with Blum's explanation of the Priestly texts in the plagues narrative. His assignment of the 'non-J' sections of the seventh, eighth, and ninth plagues of hail, locusts, and darkness (9: 22–3, 35; 10: 12–13a, 21–3, 27) to his Priestly writer K^P is questionable. As Davies points out, in a number of ways these passages differ from the pattern of the other plague stories in P, for example, by the fact that Aaron is not involved in them. The older argument that they derive from a source independent of either J or P remains the more plausible view. They scarcely provide a secure basis on which to argue the nature and origin of the P material in this cycle. Sounder method surely requires that one should proceed on the basis of those Priestly elements at the beginning of the cycle, and these, as Blum concedes, have the appearance of deriving from an independent source which in part duplicates the older narrative of the plagues. To

---

[40] For a recent discussion see W. H. Schmidt, 'Plädoyer für die Quellenscheidung', *BZ* n.F. 32 (1988), 3–5.

claim that they derive only from a short, 'partly shaped priestly tradition' presupposes his theory rather than leading to it.[41] At the least,
the distinctive features and profile of the P stories at the beginning of
the cycle are just as compatible with the Documentary Theory's
understanding of them as deriving from an originally independent
source. Here too the observation made above concerning other P passages which have the appearance of deriving from an existing source
is valid—that Blum is forced to concede more than is desirable from
the point of view of his thesis that P is 'neither source nor redaction'.

VI

We turn now to Cross's understanding of Genesis 2: 4a as a superscription to what follows and not, as generally believed, a conclusion
to the preceding creation story. In this he has received support from
the Swedish scholar Sven Tengström who has, however, gone further
and argued that the whole of this verse is from a P redactor.

To consider first Tengström's view: against the generally accepted
understanding of v. 4b as the beginning of the J narrative of creation,
he argues (a) that the use of the verb עשה 'made', as against ברא
'created' in v. 4a, is not necessarily an indication that it derives from
J rather than from P, since the latter elsewhere employs עשה as an
alternative to ברא ; (b) that the divine name Yahweh in v. 4b may be
a gloss prompted by the use of this name in the narrative that follows;
and (c) that syntactically the J narrative could have begun at v. 5; such
a beginning, indeed, would reflect the sort of beginning found in
other ancient Near Eastern creation stories, for example *Enuma eliš*
(pp. 54–5). Genesis 2: 4 as a whole, therefore, derives from a Priestly
editor and acts as a superscription to what follows, just as elsewhere
the *tōleᵈōth* formula functions as a superscription. As such, this verse
heads the narrative that follows to the end of Genesis 4 which the
Priestly editor understood as the story of the 'generations' of the first
humans after the creation narrated in Genesis 1. Viewed in this way
the verse means something like 'These are the generations of heaven
and earth (who lived) when these (heaven and earth) were created, at
the time when Yahweh-God made heaven and earth' (p. 57).

[41] See Davies, 'The Composition of the Book of Exodus', 80. I must refer the reader
to Davies for other pertinent observations he makes on Blum's conclusions concerning
P in this cycle.

Several considerations render such a view improbable. First, and most obvious, unless other compelling reasons can be found, there are no grounds for regarding the name Yahweh in v. 4b as a gloss. Tengström himself acknowledges this (p. 54). Second, the order 'earth and heaven' in v. 4b is the reverse of this phrase in v. 4a—unless we change the former with the Samaritan text and the Syriac version to 'heaven and earth'—and the definite article employed with both words in v. 4a is not used in v. 4b. These differences, which cannot seriously be explained in terms of a desired literary effect, are surely odd if both parts of the verse are from the same hand. Third, the phrase וכל שיח השדה טרם יהיה בארץ 'And every seed of field before it was in the earth' (v. 5) would read strangely as the beginning of the story that follows and would be quite uncharacteristic of Hebrew narrative art. From a literary and syntactical point of view v. 4b remains the more likely beginning of this narrative, functioning as a protasis to a following apodosis, even though it is disputed whether the latter begins at v. 5 or v. 7. Further, if a comparison is to be made with the opening words of the Babylonian creation story *Enuma eliš* ('*When* on high the heaven had not been named . . . '),[42] Genesis 2: 4b '*In the day when* Yahweh-God made earth and heaven . . . ' provides a more obvious parallel than the opening words of v. 5 which does not resemble the opening words of *Enuma eliš*.

For these reasons the generally accepted division of Genesis 2: 4 between P and J remains the more plausible analysis of this much debated verse. Is v. 4a nevertheless a superscription to what follows, as Cross argues, or a conclusion to what precedes? On either view it is peculiar in this context. If it is a conclusion it departs from the use of the *tōlᵉdōth* formula which elsewhere is a superscription, and it has also to be understood 'metaphorically'[43] as applying to the generation of 'heaven and earth' rather than to humans, or as carrying some such generalized meaning as 'story of origins' rather than its usual connotation 'genealogy', 'family tree'.[44] On the other hand, if it is a superscription it also differs, necessarily so, from its use elsewhere by being unable to mention the names of the ancestors of the persons in the narratives that follow, since Adam had no ancestors. Further, 'the

---

[42] See Tengström, *Die Toledoth formel und die literarische Struktur*, 72 n. 61.

[43] Cf. S. R. Driver, *An Introduction to the Literature of the Old Testament* (Edinburgh 1913), 6.

[44] G. von Rad, *Das erste Moses, Genesis* (5th edn., Göttingen 1958); Eng. trans., *Genesis* (London 1961).

generations of the heavens and the earth' is surely a somewhat strained description of Adam and the other persons mentioned in Genesis 2–4.

In short, there are difficulties for either view, and such are the verse's peculiarities that it is a weak basis on which to argue that P was a redactor rather than an author. Even if it is conceded, however, that it is a superscription to what follows, and thus an editorial addition, it does not constitute evidence that P as a whole in the Pentateuch is the work of an editor rather than from an originally independent narrative, for in arguing that the P material was worked into the older JE material the Documentary Theory also allowed for the possibility that the Priestly editor(s) responsible for this may have on occasion inserted comments, linking passages, etc. which he felt necessary.

VII

Tengström argues that the remaining *tōlᵉdōth* passages in Genesis likewise provide evidence that P is the work of a redactor rather than the author of an originally discrete narrative. But these passages are a doubtful basis for such a view. It seems in fact that in the case of at least some of them one's assessment of the relation of the P material to the older sources depends on the view one already holds of the nature of P.

An example is provided by Tengström's discussion of Genesis 10. His source analysis of this chapter is the standard one, the J material being vv. 8–19, 21, 24–30, the P sections vv. 1–7, 20, 22–3, 31, 32, the P material thus forming the framework. According to Tengström this framework is not the work of a redactor employing an already existing independent P narrative; rather, it was P himself, understood as an editor, who has constructed it and incorporated the J material into it. He offers two arguments in support of this. First, the structure of the subdivisions is the same in both J and P (p. 23):

(a) a statement of the genealogical descent of the people/ancestors, followed by

(b) a statement of their settlement and geographical 'spread'.

An example of this structure as employed by P is provided by vv. 2–5 (a = vv. 2–4; b = v. 5. Cf. v. 32). Examples in J are vv. 8–12 (a = vv. 8–9; b = vv. 10–12); vv. 15–19 (a = vv. 15–18a; b = vv. 18b–19); vv. 26–30 (a = vv. 26–9; b = v. 30). That both J and P use the same structure, he argues, is best explained on the assumption 'that the author of the P material employed the older material as the model for his own contribution' (p. 23). But the conclusion that Tengström draws from this observation does not necessarily follow. That is, it does not follow that P was necessarily an editor rather than an author; it is just as possible that he was an author who adopted the form from J in composing his own independent narrative which (or some of which) was subsequently combined by an editor with the older J narrative. Alternatively, the conclusion is equally warranted that both the Yahwist and the P author independently employed a common form.

Tengström's second argument is as follows. In v. 6 P lists the sons of Ham (Cush, Egypt, Put, Canaan), but in v. 7 expands only on Cush and not upon Canaan, as one expects, since it is mentioned last in the list. A genealogy of Canaan is, however, given in the J passage later in the chapter (vv. 15–19), and the conclusion cannot be avoided, Tengström contends, that the reason P did not expand on Canaan at v. 6 was because he reserved such expansion to the J passage which he, working as an editor, incorporated later in the chapter (pp. 23–4). It is clear once again, however, that what Tengström describes is capable of an alternative explanation, namely that a redactor combining originally independent P and J passages chose J's genealogy in vv. 15–19 rather than P's (assuming the latter contained one).

The same holds also in the case of the material relating to Arpachshad in 10: 22–3 (P), 24–30 (J), and 11: 10–16 (P). In 10: 23 P expands upon the descendants of Aram, even though, according to Tengström, we expect him to expand instead upon Arpachshad whose line leads to Abraham (11: 10–13). Arpachshad's line is, however, given in the immediately following J passage (10: 24–30) which has the sequence Arpachshad, Shelah, Eber, and Peleg, exactly as in P's genealogy in 11: 10–16. 'The only probable assumption here is that the author of the P material in chapter 11 depended upon the J section in chapter 10' (p. 24). Once again, however, it is only an assumption that P was bound to expand upon Arpachshad at 10: 22 f. and that, since what follows concerning this ancestor is from J, P was therefore an editor who utilized J instead of composing his own material for this genealogy. It could equally well be that P did not here expand upon Arpachshad's line because he wished to reserve this for chapter 11. Alternatively, if the assumption be granted that P was bound to expand upon Arpachshad after 10: 22 f., the presence of the

J material in vv. 24–30 could again equally well be accounted for as the work of a redactor combining an originally independent P narrative with J and at this point choosing J's genealogy. Further, if P at 11: 10–16 was dependent upon J's genealogy in 10: 24–30, why should it necessarily follow from this that he was an editor? It is equally possible that he was an author who used J in composing his own independent narrative. Here too, therefore, one's assessment of the relation of the P material to the older source depends on the view one already holds of the character of P. In short, taken by itself, the material in Genesis 10 and 11 settles nothing in the issue under discussion.

In my opinion, what is evident of the genealogies in Genesis 10 and 11 is the case also in the genealogical passages throughout that book. It seems clear that material from both JE and P has been combined by a redactor, in ways creatively so. Tengström's monograph is a valuable contribution for its exposition of the function of these genealogies in Genesis. But it is clear also that these passages by themselves are an insufficient basis on which to determine whether this redactor was P himself rather than one who combined an already existing P source with JE.

A further argument adduced by Tengström remains to be briefly considered. It arises from the absence of a P narrative of the conquest in the book of Joshua where, according to the view currently generally accepted, P is represented by only a small number of sporadic texts. Tengström shares this view. He rejects Noth's well-known claim that P in the Tetrateuch is disinterested in the settlement in the land and that the so-called P texts in Joshua are merely secondary insertions in the style of P. Rather, he argues, the P editor of the Tetrateuch looks to the settlement as a fulfilment of God's promises to Israel, and relies upon the book of Joshua for the account of this. The P texts in Joshua evidence this. Since, however, these texts are clearly of an editorial nature, they offer additional support for the view that P was an editor of the Hexateuch rather than the author of an independent narrative (pp. 14–15).

A discussion of the composition of the book of Joshua is beyond the scope of the present study. This much may be said, however, in response to Tengström's claim. It may be conceded that such P material as there is in Joshua is editorial and not derived from an originally independent source. But there are obvious differences between this material and P in the Tetrateuch. Unlike the latter, in Joshua P does not form the framework of the narrative; rather, it is set within the Deuteronomistic framework. Such differences render the P texts in Joshua inadmissible as a basis on which to draw conclusions concerning the origin of the P material in the Tetrateuch.

VIII

The minority view, already argued by August Dillmann in the debate following Wellhausen's *Composition of the Hexateuchs*, that P predates Deuteronomy has continued to find favour. It was extensively argued earlier this century by Yehezkel Kaufmann in his multi-volumed history of Israelite religion.[45] More recently it has found support among a number of Jewish scholars.[46] But their arguments have found no support among scholars at large, whether those who regard P as an originally independent source or those who regard it as the result of Priestly editing of the Pentateuch.

Moshe Weinfeld, for example, has argued that the divergencies between the two 'schools', D and P, 'stem from a difference in their sociological background rather than from a difference in their chronological setting', and regards their writings 'as concurrent rather than successive documents' (p. 180). Further, all the indications are that, far from being later than Deuteronomy, 'it was the deuteronomic school that incorporated and redacted Priestly tradition'. For example, Deuteronomy 4 employs a number of Priestly idioms,[47] and other passages in the Deuteronomistic corpus similarly show a knowledge of P (pp. 180ff.). The passages he cites, however, are usually regarded as late additions to the Deuteronomistic literature.[48] At best, therefore, they might indicate a late exilic origin for P, a date favoured by many scholars.

[45] Y. Kaufmann, *The Religion of Israel from its Beginnings to the Babylonian Exile* (in Hebrew), i–viii (Jerusalem 1937–56); abr. and Eng. trans. by Moshe Greenberg, London 1960.
[46] M. Weinfeld, *Deuteronomy and the Deuteronomic School* (Oxford 1972), 179–89; A. Hurvitz, 'The Evidence of Language in Dating the Priestly Code: A Linguistic Study in Technical Idioms and Terminology', *RB* 81 (1974), 24–56 and *A Linguistic Study of the Relationship between the Priestly Source and the Book of Ezekiel: A New Approach to an Old Problem, Cahiers de la Revue Biblique*, 20 (Paris 1982); M. Haran, *Temples and Temple Service in Ancient Israel* (Oxford 1978); Z. Zevit, 'Converging Lines of Evidence Bearing on the Date of P', *ZAW* 94 (1982), 481–511.
[47] Weinfeld, *Deuteronomy and the Deuteronomic School*, 180 n. 3.
[48] On Deuteronomy 4 see A. D. H. Mayes, 'Deuteronomy 4 and the Literary Criticism of Deuteronomy', *JBL* 100/1 (1981), 23–51. He suggests (p. 50) that a

Weinfeld also draws attention to cultic and other regulations in P which are attested already in pre-exilic texts. Dating the composition of P to the late exilic or early post-exilic period, however, does not mean that its authors spun it out of thin air. That they took up traditions and cultic ordinances from earlier times need not be questioned. The main difficulty with Weinfeld's view is that there is no evidence that the theocratic and hierocratic understanding of Israel as the 'congregation' of Yahweh with the distinctive sacral and cultic institutions so characteristic of P was known in the pre-exilic period. He offers no discussion, for example, of the difficulty in reconciling P's understanding of the priesthood with what we know of pre-exilic practice and of how also it is to be understood in relation to Ezekiel 44.[49]

Menahem Haran's view represents a position midway between that of Wellhausen and Kaufmann, but the result is so strange as to strain credulity.[50] He argues that P was composed as early as *c.*700 BC in the reign of Hezekiah, but that it belonged at this stage to the 'semi-esoteric' priestly circle in Jerusalem who composed it as an idealistic, utopian depiction of what they conceived Israel to be: 'The utopian, imaginary prospect of the tribes of Israel assembled in right-angle formation around a lavishly adorned tabernacle enthralls P's authors from a distance in time and space and against this backdrop they give full expression—so full as to make the prospect at times unrealistic—to their legal aspirations and theological concepts. However, they content themselves merely with giving a shape to the utopian perfection and are oblivious of the contemporary reality, in that they make no explicit demands that it be changed.'[51] The work remained strictly within the circle responsible for it and was preserved as the special possession of that circle. It was not until the time of Ezra that it came out 'into the daylight': 'That is to say, until the time of Ezra the priestly source, to all intents and purposes, is non-existent—after Ezra it takes on a dominant role in the life of Israel and as part of the holy Torah it pertains to the foundations of communal life.'[52] Thus

---

number of distinctive features of this chapter may be due to the influence of the prophets of the exile rather than to P.

[49] See above, Ch. 1, pp. 20–1.

[50] In addition to the work cited in n. 46, see also M. Haran, 'The Law-Code of Ezekiel XL–XLVIII and its Relation to the Priestly School', HUCA 50 (1979), 45–71; id. 'Behind the Scenes of History: Determining the Date of the Priestly Source', *JBL* 100/3 (1981), 321–33.

[51] 'Behind the Scenes of History', 328.   [52] Ibid. 324.

Kaufmann was correct in his view that P was of pre-exilic origin, but 'it is perfectly clear that there is also truth in the view represented by Wellhausen, namely, that before Ezra one can in no way detect P's impression on historical reality'.[53] The comment is justified that to regard a source as having been in existence for three centuries or so before it was made known outside the group by whom it was composed and transmitted is scarcely convincing when compared with the case made by the Documentary Theory for the origin of P.

Finally, Avi Hurvitz in arguing for a pre-exilic origin of P has drawn attention to its use of many words well-attested in pre-exilic Hebrew. Once again, however, this is not necessarily evidence that P was composed in the pre-exilic period. Such vocabulary may be due to the use of traditional terms in priestly circles. Further, against Hurvitz, Robert Polzin's study of syntax has shown persuasively that P's language differs from that of pre-exilic writings and has the appearance of being a transitional stage in the development to Late Biblical Hebrew, as represented by the books of Chronicles.[54] His findings thus tend to support a sixth-century date for the composition of P.

It remains a valuable contribution of these studies, however, especially those by Haran and Weinfeld, that they show that the Priestly material in the Pentateuch was not spun out of thin air in the exilic or post-exilic period, but embodies more ancient tradition, especially laws. In addition, the fresh emphasis they place upon the distinctiveness of the Priestly material which in turn suggests an equally distinctive scribal group lends credence to the view that such writers are more likely to have formulated their vision of Israel as an autonomous narrative rather than blend it in with an earlier narrative with whose ethos and portrayal of Israel it differs so markedly.

John Emerton has reminded us that in the matter of whether P was an originally independent narrative 'we are dealing with what are at best probabilities rather than certainties'.[55] Recent study has confirmed this, highlighting, though not for the first time, passages which may be more plausibly explained as redactional addition by an editor

[53] 'Behind the Scenes of History', 327. Cf. also Haran, *Temples and Temple Service in Ancient Israel*, p. v: 'it was only in the days of Ezra . . . that P's presence became perceptible in historical reality and began to exercise its influence on the formation of Judaism'.

[54] R. Polzin, *Late Biblical Hebrew: Toward an Historical Typology of Biblical Prose* (Missoula, Mont. 1976).

[55] 'The Priestly Writer in Genesis', 384.

rather than deriving from an independent narrative. It remains a strong probability, however, that there was originally a independent source P, that its authors knew JE and may have designed their narrative partly as a corrective to it, perhaps in some places polemically so, [56] but intended it primarily to set out their distinctive vision of Israel as the 'congregation' of Yahweh. Whether it was composed in the exilic or post-exilic period is difficult to determine; there are arguments in favour of both of these proposed dates. It is unlikely that it was composed earlier than the exile, though this does not mean that it does not contain elements of tradition from much earlier periods. It was secondarily combined with JE. Before this it may have been supplemented with additional Priestly material. Further similar material was added subsequent to its combination with the older corpus. The redactors who worked both it and additional Priestly lore into JE may also have added comments and passages of their own composition. Thus, against Blum's proposal that P was 'neither "source" nor "redaction"', the older view that it derives both from a source and redactional work remains the more plausible view.

This does not mean, however, that there have not been important gains in the recent study of the Priestly material in the Pentateuch. Tengström's study sheds light upon the use of the genealogies in the structure of the P editing of JE. Blum's study is especially significant, for whilst I do not accept that he has made a case for the origin of P simply as a 'compositional layer', his work contributes significantly to a more subtle understanding of the work of the Priestly redactors of the Pentateuch, and to a 'synchronic' reading of the final form of the text.[57] Future studies of the Priestly redaction of the Pentateuch will surely have to take their starting point from his work.[58]

[56] See R. E. Friedman's lively argument for this in 'The Recession of Biblical Source Criticism', in R. E. Friedman and H. G. M. Williamson (eds.), *The Future of Biblical Studies: The Hebrew Scriptures*, Society of Biblical Literature Semeia Studies (Atlanta 1987), 81–101.
[57] See also William Johnstone's study of the Priestly redaction of the Sinai pericope in 'Reactivating the Chronicles Analogy in Pentateuchal Studies, with Special Reference to the Sinai Pericope in Exodus', *ZAW* 99 (1987), 16–37.
[58] See also below, Ch. 9.

8

The Documentary Theory Revisited

According to the Documentary Theory, when the P material is excluded the Tetrateuch comprises mainly the work of the so-called 'Jehovist' but includes also a certain amount of additional material from subsequent redactors, including Deuteronomic editors. It is with this corpus, which as we have seen has been the subject of the most intense debate in recent research, that I am mainly concerned in this chapter.

Following Wellhausen's view, many have seen the Jehovist (R^{JE}) as not merely an editor but also an author who added passages which he freely composed. We have seen, however, that there is currently increasing support for the view of such earlier scholars as Paul Volz that E never was an independent narrative source on the analogy of J, but is rather the work of an editor of J. The fragmentary nature of E, which scholars such as Noth concede, has itself been seen as evidence of this, just as the sparse nature of P in Genesis has been seen by others as evidence that P never was an independent narrative. For obvious reasons, this questioning of E as a separate source has also necessitated a rejection of the well-known criteria on the basis of which the two sources J and E were identified and isolated from one another, that is, differences in style, the variation in the use of the names for God, and the phenomenon of duplicate narratives. Among recent scholars, Whybray has most comprehensively marshalled the arguments questioning these criteria.[1] He has also raised again the question of the credibility of the Documentary Theory as an explanation of how such a corpus of literature as the Pentateuch was composed, claiming that it depends upon implausible notions of how authors and editors in the ancient world would have worked. It will be convenient in what follows to focus upon Whybray's discussion, though the observations of others who share his conclusions will also be noted and considered. I begin with Whybray's claims concerning

---

[1] Whybray, *The Making of the Pentateuch*.

the plausibility of the Documentary Theory in general before considering his arguments and those of others concerning the criteria upon which it is based.

I

Whybray has questioned the general coherence of the Documentary Theory, which he regards as the least plausible of the main traditional solutions to the problem of composition of the Pentateuch (the so-called Fragment and Supplementary Hypotheses). It is, he argues, inherently a much more complex theory than the others which, by contrast, 'envisage relatively simple, and, it would seem, logical processes and at the same time appear to account for the unevennesses of the completed Pentateuch' (p. 18). He suggests that one can easily accept, for example, the rationale of the Fragment Hypothesis that at some stage in Israel's history it was felt necessary to assemble and give a connected form to the various records of the nation's history which had hitherto been transmitted only in fragmentary form. Or one can accept as plausible the main tenet of the Supplementary Hypothesis that a narrative 'history' could once have existed which later editors and authors saw fit to supplement with additional materials (p. 18). But the Documentary Theory is not only much more complicated; it also involves specific assumptions about the historical development of Israel's understanding of its origins. Further, the theory that several similar but not identical works were composed at different times and that the need was later felt to weave these, by stages, into a single work calls for far more elaborate explanations (p. 18).

The incoherence of the Documentary Theory is especially evident, he argues, in the matter of its claims concerning the work of redactors, for the proponents of this theory have to suppose that redactors wantonly destroyed the unity and coherence of the documents with which they worked, and were thus guilty of 'faults of logic and sensitivity' of which these proponents are at such pains to absolve the authors of the documents: 'If the redactors were unconcerned about these things', he writes, 'it is difficult to understand on what grounds the proponents of the hypothesis maintain that the authors of the documents were concerned about them' (p. 19). The more logical conclusion, he argues, is that ancient Israelite ideas of consistency were different from ours, that ancient Israelites were quite indifferent to what we should regard as inconsistencies.

The argument that the Documentary Hypothesis entails accepting that the composition of the Pentateuch is the result of processes involving conflation, inconsistencies, and the like that are nowhere paralleled in the history of literature, whether ancient or modern, is not new. Over a century ago C. M. Mead, for example, argued the implausibility of the documentary analysis of the Pentateuch on the grounds that 'no example of such a "crazy patchwork" can be found in all literature as the one alleged to have been discovered in the Pentateuch'.[2] In more recent times M. H. Segal has expressed the same opinion: [3]

> Hebrew literature, or any other literature the world over, cannot show another example of the production of a literary work by such a succession of recurring amalgamations and such a succession of compilers and redactors centuries apart, all working by one and the same method, as attributed by the [Documentary] Theory to the formation of the Pentateuch.

The issue does not at all depend, however, on what we imagine ancient Israelite ideas of consistency to have been, for there is ample evidence from other ancient sources, as Jeffrey Tigay and others have recently shown,[4] of just the sort of conflation by redactors of originally discrete texts and the retention of duplicate narratives, including the inconsistencies to which such redactional activity can give rise, as the Documentary Theory finds in the Pentateuch. Examples are the conflation in 4QDeut[n] of the motivation for keeping the sabbath in Exodus 20: 11 with that in Deuteronomy 5: 14, and a similar conflation in Codex Vaticanus; Jethro's advice to Moses in the Samaritan Pentateuch which conflates the narrative in Exodus 18: 13–27 with Deuteronomy 1: 9–18; the Samaritan Pentateuch's version of the theophany at Sinai in Exodus 20: 18–26 into which the redactor has fully worked the variant account in Deuteronomy 5: 22–31 as well as Deuteronomy 18: 18–22; a duplicate narrative of the one and the same event in the LXX version of Esther; and the Samaritan Pentateuch's tenth commandment in Exodus 20 which incorporates elements from Deuteronomy 11 and 27.

[2] C. M. Mead, 'Tatian's Diatessaron and the Analysis of the Pentateuch', *JBL* 10 (1891), 44–54 (the quotation is from p. 44).

[3] M. H. Segal, *The Pentateuch: Its Composition and Its Authority, and Other Biblical Studies* (Jerusalem 1967), 4.

[4] J. Tigay (ed.), *Empirical Models for Biblical Criticism* (Philadelphia 1985).

For purposes of illustration two of these examples will suffice, beginning with the Samaritan Pentateuch narrative of Jethro's advice to Moses.[5] The Samaritan text of Exodus 18 is as follows, the translation of the Exodus text in roman type, that of Deuteronomy in italics; the redactor's insertions are underlined:

You shall seek out for yourself from among all the people capable men who fear God, trustworthy men who spurn ill-gotten gain; and set these over them as chiefs of thousands, chiefs of hundreds, chiefs of fifties and chiefs of tens. Let them exercise authority over the people at all times; let them bring every major matter to you, but decide every minor matter themselves. Make it easier for yourself, and let them share the burden with you. If you do this—and God so commands you—you will be able to bear up; and all these people will go home content. Moses heeded his father-in-law and did all that he had said. *Moses said to the people, 'I myself cannot bear the burden of you alone. The Lord your God has multiplied you until you are today as numerous as the stars in the sky. May the Lord, the God of your fathers, increase your numbers a thousand-fold, and bless you as He promised you. How can I alone bear the trouble of you, and the burden, and the bickering! Pick from each of your tribes men who are wise, discerning, and experienced, and I will appoint them as your heads.' They answered and said, 'What you purpose to do is good.' So he took their tribal leaders, wise and experienced men, and he appointed them heads over them: chiefs of thousands, chiefs of hundreds, chiefs of fifties, and chiefs of tens, and officials for their tribes. He charged their magistrates as follows: 'Hear out your fellow men, and decide justly between any man and a fellow Israelite or a stranger. You shall not be partial in judgement; hear out high and low alike. Fear no man, for judgement is God's. And any matter that is too difficult for you, you shall bring near to me and I will hear it.' Thus He commanded them about the various things that they should do.* And they would exercise authority over the people at all times: the major matters they would bring to Moses, and all the minor matters they would decide themselves. Then Moses bade his father-in-law farewell, and he went his way to his own land.

In view of the claim by Whybray and others that the assumptions behind the Documentary Theory of the composition of the Pentateuch are flawed, it is instructive to consider whether the sort of critical analysis applied by scholars to the Pentateuch would uncover discrete sources in this version of Jethro's advice to Moses if we did not possess the Massoretic text of Exodus and Deuteronomy. The redactor who wove the two accounts together made some necessary adjustments, for example omitting elements in the text of Deuteronomy arising from its being cast as a retrospective speech by

[5] See ibid. 61–8.

Moses. As a result, the newly formed version of the story reads smoothly. As Tigay shows, however, the 'pericope is full of signs of compositeness which would have led critics to unravel its components rather accurately' (p. 67). Such an analysis would have drawn attention to inconsistencies in the narrative which suggest that Jethro's proposal and Moses' execution of it are from different sources. Thus (a) Jethro advises Moses to seek out men 'from among all the people' (from the version in Exodus), but Moses asks the people to do the choosing (from Deuteronomy); (b) Moses then takes men not 'from among all the people' but 'the tribal leaders' (from Deuteronomy); (c) Jethro suggests 'capable men who fear God, trustworthy men who spurn ill-gotten gain' (from Exodus), but Moses asks for and appoints 'wise, discerning, and experienced men' (from Deuteronomy); (d) Jethro speaks only of 'chiefs of thousands, hundreds, fifties, and tens' (from Exodus), but Moses adds 'magistrates' (from Deuteronomy). In the manner familiar from the source analysis of the Pentateuch, this unevenness in the pericope would have been explained as probably arising from the use by its author of two originally discrete accounts of the event narrated. Differences in vocabulary would have been cited as providing added support.[6] Thus Jethro uses the verb 'bring' (from Exodus) in referring to the matters of dispute to be brought for adjudication, but Moses uses a different verb 'bring near' (from Deuteronomy); Jethro differentiates between 'major' and 'minor' matters (from Exodus), whereas Moses refers only to any matter that is 'too difficult' (from Deuteronomy). The reversion to the use of the terms 'bring', 'major', and 'minor' at the end of the pericope would have suggested that the redactor had at this point returned to his first source.

Tigay pertinently comments that if we did not possess the two sources employed by the redactor responsible for this pericope, those who question the plausibility of the assumptions of Pentateuchal source criticism might regard such variation in terminology and vocabulary as the author's attempt to avoid monotony. Certainly allowance must be made for an author's desire for variety in composing a narrative, and variation in the terminology and vocabulary must not therefore be regarded as an automatic indication that different sources have been combined in a given passage. But the pericope fully justifies critical attention to such variation as a prima-facie indication

6 Tigay, *Empirical Models for Biblical Criticism*, 67–8.

of compositeness. Thus, for example, a similarly close reading of duplicate passages such as those narrating the flight or expulsion of Hagar (see below) take on renewed credibility in the light of an example such as this pericope in the Samaritan Pentateuch.

The second example is the Samaritan Pentateuch tenth commandment in its version of Exodus 20 which is constructed from Deuteronomy 11 and 27.[7] In the following translation the Massoretic text of Exodus 20 is represented by roman type, material from Deuteronomy 11 by italic, and material from Deuteronomy 27 by bold type. Additions by the Samaritan redactor are underlined. The translation begins with the ninth commandment according to the Samaritan version (the prohibition on coveting):

You shall not covet your neighbour's house; you shall not covet your neighbour's wife, <u>his field</u>, his male or his female slave, his ox or his ass, or anything that is your neighbour's. *And when the Lord your God brings you into the land <u>of the Canaanites</u> which you are about to invade and occupy,* **you shall set up large stones and coat them with plaster. And you shall inscribe upon <u>the stones</u> all the words of this teaching. And, upon crossing the Jordan, you shall set up these stones, about which I charge you this day, on Mount <u>Gerizim</u>. And you shall build an altar there to the Lord your God, an altar of stones. Do not wield an iron tool over them; you must build an altar of the Lord your God of unhewn stones. You shall offer on it burnt offerings to the Lord your God, and you shall sacrifice sacrifices of well-being and eat them there, rejoicing before the Lord your God.** *<u>That mountain</u> is across the Jordan, beyond the west road which is in the land of the Canaanites who dwell in the Arabah—near Gilgal, by the terebinth of Mora, near Shechem.*

Unlike the Samaritan version of the pericope Exodus 18, there is an obvious tendentiousness in the compilation of this passage. Tigay points out that the creation of this commandment as the tenth commandment of the decalogue is not without logic from the standpoint of Samaritan theology, since this law about an altar of uncut stone is thereby brought into the same context as the law in the Massoretic text of Exodus 20: 25 concerning the building of an altar of uncut stone. In this way the Samaritan redactor endowed his religion's central dogma with Sinaitic, decalogue authority (p. 81). In order to do so, however, he had to emend the Massoretic text's provision for a plurality of altars—'in every place where I cause my name to be recorded' (v. 24b)—to provide for only one, central altar: 'in the place

---

[7] See ibid. 78–83.

where I cause my name to be recorded', referring of course to Gerizim.

The passage provides a good example of how redaction and interpolation can cause inconsistencies, for the commandment to build an altar of unhewn stones is then followed a few verses later (v. 24, from the Massoretic text of Exodus 20 though reworded in terms of a central sanctuary) by the command 'Make for Me an altar of earth and sacrifice on it your burnt offerings and your sacrifices of well-being, your sheep and your oxen'. The editor 'could not remove conflicting verses in the original text. But the point of the interpolation was so important for him that he was willing to live with the inconsistency, which he presumably rationalized in some way' (p. 81).

It must be noted finally that the claim is justified, in any case, that Whybray and others have exaggerated the extent to which the Documentary Theory of the composition of the Pentateuch charges the redactors and editors with inconsistency. In not a few instances duplicate narratives read as stories of separate events. Genesis 1 and 2 are more complementary than inconsistent with each other. The duplicate narratives of Abraham and Sarah in the court of a foreign king read as two separate events. The story of Hagar's flight in Genesis 16 and of her expulsion in chapter 21 can be read as two separate episodes, the one before and the other after Ishmael's birth. The Priestly reason for Jacob's departure for Mesopotamia recorded in Genesis 27: 46–28: 5 can be read as an additional reason to that described in the J narrative in chapter 27: 41 ff.[8]

II

The Documentary Theory stands or falls by the credibility of the well-known criteria on the basis of which it is argued: differences in style as an indication of the composite nature of the literature, the variation in the use of the names for God, and the phenomenon of duplicate narratives. It is not surprising therefore that the new directions and theories currently being proposed have included a fresh critique

---

[8] The narrative of the flood in Genesis 6: 5–8: 22, on the other hand, is notorious for inconsistencies arising, as most scholars agree, from the conflation of the J and P narratives. In the case of these two narratives, there could have been no question of a redactor understanding or presenting them as recording separate events, since there could not have been two floods.

of these criteria. Once again Whybray has conveniently marshalled the arguments and the following discussion will focus upon his work, though the views of others who share his conclusions will be noted and discussed where appropriate.

(1) Stylistic variations as an indication of different sources

Caution is required in the use of this criterion. Stylistically speaking, the Yahwist and Elohist sources are written in a Hebrew vernacular which, in the absence of other criteria, would not enable us to differentiate reliably between them.[9] In the case of the P material, Whybray has gone so far as to claim it has no distinctive narrative style of its own, and that some of the narratives usually attributed to it might with equal plausibility be assigned to J, for example the P sections in the plagues pericope in Exodus 7–11 (p. 61). In the case of P, caution is also called for.[10] The probability that its authors, like the authors of J and E, took up much traditional material warns against expecting a rigid uniformity in style or linguistic usage. The evidence from style and vocabulary is stronger for some passages than for others, and in any event a list of favourite words and phrases cannot be used mechanically in determining whether a passage belongs to P. In addition, it is widely accepted that the Priestly material in the Pentateuch was not written down at one sitting by one author, and that much of it has been added secondarily and over a protracted period of time. The observation made by Emerton is well taken that there are some places where the evidence is strong for ascribing a passage to P, some where it is weaker, and some where the evidence is insufficient to justify a confident conclusion.[11] Allowing for such caution, however, his own careful analysis of a number of key passages (Gen. 1: 1–2: 4a; 6–9; 17; 23) reaffirms the probability that these and some smaller, related passages belong together and derive from a Priestly author.

An observation of a more general nature may be added. Such passages display in various ways an unmistakable family resemblance to the Priestly legislative sections in the Tetrateuch which is lacking in the JE material. Thus, the creation narrative in Genesis 1: 1–2: 4a, the P elements in the flood story, the narratives of the covenants with

[9] Cf. Noth, *ÜGP* 20–1; Eng. trans., 21.
[10] For the following observations I am indebted to J. A. Emerton's judicious treatment of these issues in 'The Priestly Writer in Genesis', 381–400.
[11] Ibid. 391.

Noah and Abraham, and other P narratives contain a range of distinctive religious, cultic, and theological motifs and interests which relate them intrinsically to the Priestly legislation but which are absent in the JE material. The stylistic features of the narratives have always been but a secondary argument for attributing them to P in comparison with these more substantial features which link them to the Priestly legislation and render any attempt to dissolve the distinction between these narratives and JE highly questionable. The evidence remains strong, as I argued in the previous chapter, that these passages once belonged to an independent Priestly narrative.

(2) The variation in the names for God

There has scarcely been a time since Wellhausen when the criterion of the use of different names for God in Genesis and its explanation on the basis of the statements in Exodus 3 and 6 has not been challenged. Blum has recently devoted an Excursus to it,[12] pointing out among other things that, contrary to what is often supposed, Elohim is a noun rather than a proper name, and that accordingly this means that the Yahwist could have employed it as an alternative to the proper name Yahweh, thus rendering the use of this criterion invalid for differentiating an Elohistic source from a supposed J source. Still more recently Walter Moberly has discussed the issue at some length.[13] He acknowledges that both Exodus 3: 13–15 and 6: 2–7 portray 'the name YHWH as newly revealed to Moses and hitherto unknown' (p. 36). He argues, however, that 'it is perfectly intelligible that a writer who holds that the name YHWH was first revealed to Moses should none the less feel free to use it while telling the story of Israel's forebears' (p. 70). This means that 'Gen 12–50 conveys the perspective of the Yahwistic storytellers, who are retelling originally non-Yahwistic traditions in a Yahwistic context, and as they appropriated the stories for Yahwism, so they tend to use the familiar name of their God' (p. 70). His thesis is therefore that all the Pentateuchal writers, including the Yahwist, 'share a common tradition that the divine name was first revealed by God to Moses, and yet all feel free to use the divine name where they consider appropriate in the patriarchal stories' (ibid.). Genesis 4: 26, which has been a key text in the debate, is not evidence

---

[12] Blum, *Die Komposition der Vätergeschichte*, 471–5.
[13] R. W. L. Moberly, *The Old Testament of the Old Testament*, Overtures to Biblical Theology (Minneapolis 1992).

that its author (J) believed that the name Yahweh had been known from primeval times. It is the writer's own use of what for him was the name of the only God, and it is a 'misunderstanding of the nature of the text to interpret it as showing that the writer thought that people actually knew God specifically as YHWH' (p. 69). Understood in such a way, therefore, Genesis 4: 26 does not contradict the statements in either Exodus 3: 13–15 or 6: 2–7. Further, since the very term 'Yahwist' was coined because this author was assumed on the basis of this text to have believed that the name Yahweh had been known since primeval times, in contrast to what the authors of Exodus 3: 13–15 and 6: 2–7 believed, its use should now be abandoned (p. 177).

Such a conclusion does not take us far, however. Even assuming that Moberly's conclusion concerning Genesis 4: 26 is correct, sooner or later the question arises whether the statements in Exodus 3: 13–15 and 6: 2–7 are reflected in the preceding narratives of the Pentateuch. That is, the issue is not simply whether the author of the texts in Genesis employing the name Yahweh nevertheless shared the same understanding of the revelation of that name as the authors of these two texts in Exodus, but whether these authors shared his free usage of the name Yahweh before the decisive revelation to Moses which they record. Thus we are inevitably brought back to the stubborn phenomenon that whilst some narratives in Genesis reflect the usage characterized by Genesis 4: 26, others seem to remain in line with what is stated in Exodus 3 and 6 by refraining from using the name Yahweh before the revelation to Moses described in these latter two passages.

One can agree with Blum that the use of the name Yahweh cannot be employed as an *a priori* argument for source division. But, as Sean McEvenue has recently pointed out, this has never been the case,[14] and advocates of the Documentary Theory have recognized that it is not one hundred per cent trustworthy, since names could in some instances have been changed in the course of the transmission of the text.[15] The probability, against both Blum and Moberly, that P was originally an independent author whose theology incorporated as an important feature the notion of the revelation of the name Yahweh to Moses strengthens the view that the author of Exodus 3 held a similar view and that this could accordingly be expected to be reflected in

---

[14] S. E. McEvenue, 'A Return to Sources in Genesis 28: 10–22?', *ZAW* 106 (1994), 375–89 (see p. 386 and n. 23).

[15] See the comments of Noth, *ÜGP* 23; Eng. trans., 23.

Genesis. In short, the use of the name Yahweh or of the noun Elohim in passages in Genesis is properly regarded as supporting evidence alongside other indications that such passages belong to one source rather than another. This has been the predominant view among the advocates of the Documentary Theory, and I find nothing in recent reassessments of the distribution of the names for God in Genesis 1–Exodus 6 to dislodge a duly cautious use of this criterion.

(3) Duplicate narratives

What of the third criterion, that is, the presence of duplicate narratives? Does this phenomenon provide an adequate basis for literary analysis and point to originally independent literary strata in the Pentateuch? Whybray challenges whether some of the duplicate stories are correctly thus described, for example the creation narratives in Genesis 1 and 2, and argues that the genuine duplicates can be explained otherwise than by postulating that they derive from originally independent sources which have been secondarily combined. An alternative way of accounting for such duplication, he suggests, is to understand it 'as a deliberate literary device'; 'a place must be given to the possibility of literary ingenuity on the part of a single author and to the possibility of deliberate repetition on his part' (p. 76). The two versions of the story of Hagar in Genesis 16 (J) and 21: 9–21 (E) provide an example, for clearly they are '*the same story* told twice with variations, at different points in the total Abraham narrative' (p. 75). The narratives in between them include accounts of the promise of the birth of a son to Abraham and Sarah and of the fulfilment of this promise in the birth of Isaac. 'By placing the story of the miraculous birth of the true heir between the two stories about Hagar and Ishmael,' Whybray suggests (p. 76), 'the author may have intended to draw attention to the way in which God faithfully and effectively overcame, on two separate occasions, the threat to the true succession to Abraham caused by human entanglements and muddle.' That is, the second narrative was not composed and placed in its context by an author or editor working subsequently to the author of chapter 16, but is due to 'literary ingenuity' of the same author and to 'deliberate repetition on his part' (p. 76).

Whilst the two stories are so manifestly similar that they are correctly regarded as duplicates, as Whybray agrees, there are also well-known differences between them that render common authorship unlikely. Characters, functions, and motives are differently portrayed. In chapter 16 it is Hagar's attitude of scorn towards her childless mistress that evokes Sarah's anger; in chapter 21 it is behaviour on the part of the boy Ishmael that rouses Sarah's fury. In the first story Hagar is Sarah's maidservant and at her disposal, whilst in the second she is Abraham's handmaid and concubine over whom he exercises authority. In chapter 16 Hagar is portrayed as a proudly self-sufficient rival of Sarah, whilst in the second account she is a downtrodden and helpless mother. In the first story Hagar flees from her mistress; in the second she is expelled by Abraham at the insistence of Sarah. The stories are from different authors, and it seems likely that the second was originally composed for a different context.[16] Whether or not the editor who juxtaposed it with chapter 16 had in mind some such theological intention as Whybray suggests, in its present context it reads as though the incidents it narrates were separate from and later than those described in chapter 16.

Alternative explanations have been attempted by those who deny that such duplicates derive from an originally independent source and argue that they are editorial additions to an existing text. John Van Seters has dealt extensively with the problem[17] and, indeed, as we have seen, believes that these well-known doublets are the key to understanding the origin and development of the Abraham narrative as a whole, since a study of them will reveal whether these duplicates are based upon independently transmitted oral tradition or whether the one version of a story was presupposed and used by the author of its doublet(s). Making use of Olrik's 'epic laws', he makes a number of observations on the nature of oral composition and contrasts some of its main characteristics with those of written or 'scribal' composition (ch. 7). Turning to the thrice-told tale of the 'ancestress in danger' (ch. 8), narrated of Abraham and Sarah in Genesis 12 and 20 and of Isaac and Rebekah in Genesis 26, he argues that the story in Genesis 12: 10–20 is the earliest and that it corresponds closely to the folk-tale model as exemplified in Olrik's 'epic laws', suggesting that indeed a finer example could scarcely be found to illustrate these laws. On the other hand, such a claim cannot be made for the story in

[16] On Whybray's theory of the composition of the Pentateuch the story in 21: 9–21 cannot have been composed for its present context, since the chronological statements in Gen. 16: 16; 17: 1, 24, 25; 21: 5 make Ishmael a boy of fifteen or sixteen by the time the incident it narrates took place, though the story still describes him as a child who has to be carried by his mother when she flees to the steppe.

[17] Van Seters, *Abraham in History and Tradition*, esp. chs. 8 and 9.

Genesis 20: 1–17. Rather, he argues, it is a literary composition by an author who had before him the narrative in chapter 12 which he has recast for quite specific theological and moral purposes. As for the story as told in chapter 26, neither is it an oral composition; it too is a literary composition by yet another author directly dependent upon both Genesis 12 and 20. Indeed, the Isaac tradition in chapter 26 as a whole is a literary composition worked out by an author using as his sources not old oral tradition, as often supposed, but elements and motifs from the Abraham narratives.

Van Seters argues (pp. 173 f.) that the main purpose of the author of Genesis 20 was to answer important theological and moral issues that are inadequately treated in the earlier story in chapter 12—for example, why God should have punished Pharaoh, who did not know that Sarah was Abraham's wife, and how it was that the king knew that Sarah was the cause of divine displeasure. Genesis 20: 3–7 answers these questions by suggesting that God appeared to the king in a dream and accused him of his fault, and when the king protested his innocence God provided a way by which the consequences of his action could be averted. The author of chapter 20 was also concerned by two other features of the story in chapter 12: the plague brought by God upon Pharaoh's household, a surely unjustified punishment, and Sarah's moral position. The author of the second story specifically states that God prevented the king from touching her. Similarly, the author of chapter 20 exculpates Abraham from the lie recorded in chapter 12 where he asks Sarah to state that she is his sister. In chapter 20: 12 Sarah is described as the patriarch's half-sister.

Earlier, Paul Volz had argued a similar view, suggesting that when an older literary composition such as the Yahwist's narrative was issued in a 'new edition', a parallel recension was occasionally added to a story which for one reason or another was considered objectionable—'as a substitute, as it were, for the old story, so that the new story could be used instead of the old for instruction or for reading in worship services'.[18] But neither Volz nor Van Seters explain why the older 'objectionable' narrative was nevertheless retained in the text, and why the new 'parallel recension' at times deviates so much from the old narrative that it was bound to appear to the pre-critical reader as the report of a new event, not as a variant. Thus, for example, as

---

[18] W. Rudolph and P. Volz, *Der Elohist als Erzähler: Ein Irrweg der Pentateuchkritik? An der Genesis erläutert*, BZAW 63 (Berlin 1933), 23.

Noth pointed out,[19] when Genesis 12: 10–20 takes place at the court of the Pharaoh, and Genesis 20, on the other hand, in the territory of King Abimelech of Gerar, we recognize two different treatments of the same material, but pre-critical readers would have assumed that Abraham acted in a similar fashion on two different occasions. If Genesis 20 were to be a 'substitute' for Genesis 12: 10–20, why should the external circumstances in both instances not have been the same?

Adopting a similar approach to Volz and Van Seters, Samuel Sandmel explained the duplicate narratives as evidence of 'hagadda within scripture', that is, a retelling of a tale that revises an earlier version containing elements that seemed morally or otherwise unworthy to a later editor.[20] The stories about Abraham and Sarah in Genesis 12 and 20 and those of the expulsion of Hagar in Genesis 16 and 21 are examples. Similarly, the reason given by the Priestly writer of Jacob's journey to Paddam-aram in Genesis 27: 46–28: 5—so as to marry a kinswoman and not a foreigner, as Esau had done (26: 34–5)—was to counter the rather less noble reason for his flight from Esau narrated in 27: 41 ff.(J). In answer to the question why the author of the doublets, whilst seeking to counter the moral shortcomings of the earlier stories, nevertheless left the latter in the text, Sandmel argues that this was because of a disinclination on the part of the authors of the doublets to expunge even an objectionable narrative from the source they were editing. 'The redactors turn out to have counterbalanced the disinclination to expunge by adopting what we may call a process of neutralizing by addition. The haggada item once added, meant to the redactor that that which he was emending had the same meaning as that which was the result of the emendation. The Abraham of Genesis 20 thus determines the character of the Abraham of Genesis 12: 10–20' (p. 120).

This is scarcely an advance on Volz's explanation, however, and the same objection is apt here also. The ancient reader would surely have understood doublets such as the story of Abraham and Sarah in the court of Abimelech in Genesis 20 and of the expulsion of Hagar in Genesis 21 as different events from those described in chapters 12 and 16 respectively. In any event, it is difficult to comprehend how a story such as Genesis 12: 10–20, if it was felt to be morally objectionable, could be 'neutralized' by a new narrative inserted rather later in the sequence of narratives relating to the patriarch.

[19] Noth, *ÜGP* 22–3; Eng. trans., 22–3.
[20] S. Sandmel, 'The Haggada Within Scripture', *JBL* 80 (1961), 105–22.

Van Seters seeks a different motivation for the composition of the doublet in Genesis 21 of the expulsion of Hagar which he regards as the work of the Yahwist, the earlier story in chapter 16 being attributed to a pre-Yahwistic stage in the composition of the Abraham narrative as a whole (ch. 9). Whilst the story in chapter 16, when some secondary additions have been deleted, has the form of an 'anecdotal folktale' exemplifying, like chapter 12: 10–20, Olrik's epic laws of folklore (pp. 192 ff.), one cannot find in its doublet in 21: 8–21 a single example of these laws (p. 198). Rather, 21: 8–21 is 'a literary composition drawing its material from chap. 16, but written for its own distinctive purpose and concern' (p. 200). He argues that the clue to its author's purpose lies in the two themes that are central to the story and closely related to each other: Israel inheriting the land, and Abraham's offspring becoming a great nation (pp. 200 ff.). Israel's inheritance of the land in J 'is tied to the expulsion (*grš*) of non-Israelites. The theme of expulsion dominates the first scene, and the divine approval given to this action indicates its importance' (p. 201). The second theme is the promise that Abraham's son Ishmael will become a great nation: 'God's blessing and providence extends beyond Israel to also include those who are expelled.'

There are two difficulties with such a view. First, though the verb 'to expel, drive out' (*grš*) is employed (21: 10), it is surely implausible to equate the 'expulsion' of Hagar and her child, Abraham's son, with the 'driving out' of the inhabitants of the promised land. Certainly the story has for part of its purpose the aetiology of the origin of the Ishmaelites as descendants of Abraham. But they cannot be regarded as having ever been counted among the indigenous inhabitants of the land of Canaan, none of whom is conceived of as genealogically related to Israel. Rather, the 'expulsion' of Hagar is more correctly understood on the analogy, not of the 'driving out' of the indigenous inhabitants of the land, but of the origin of and allocation of land to other descendants of the patriarch—the Edomites, Aramaeans, Ammonites, and Moabites.

Secondly, the same theme of the promise concerning Ishmael's descendants is found also in chapter 16: 10. Van Seters acknowledges this but regards this verse as an addition by the author of the story in chapter 21: 9–21 to whom he attributes several other editorial insertions in chapter 16 (vv. 7b, 11c, 13–14). If, however, the editor who placed the story in chapter 21 in its present context was also its author, why then would he have felt it necessary to edit the narrative in chapter 16 so that it makes the same promise he narrates in chapter 21? Or, put alternatively, if the author of 21: 9–21 also freely edited chapter 16, why did he feel it necessary to compose a separate narrative instead of working the desired themes into chapter 16? In short, is the duplicate in chapter 21 not better understood as having been derived by an editor from an independent source and placed in its present context? It is sufficiently different from the story in chapter 16 to read as a separate incident.

III

It is time to draw some conclusions concerning the pre-Priestly Tetrateuch.

(1) Though the view that E derives from an originally independent narrative has its modern champions,[21] the trend in recent research, as we have seen, is to reject this and to regard E either as a stage on the way to J or, more usually, as additions to J. In my opinion, the reasons in favour of the two-source theory remain compelling. The presence of duplicate narratives is best explained by such a theory; alternative explanations of this phenomenon are unconvincing. Further, though for the reason suggested by Noth the criterion of the use of divine name is not one hundred per cent reliable, neither can it be ignored as a special feature of the E material and an indication of a distinct theology of the revelation of the name Yahweh to Moses in Exodus 3. In addition, a range of distinctive theological and religious features characterize the E passages in the Pentateuch, and these also support the understanding of this material as deriving from a source which had its own literary and theological outlook and intention.[22]

Among those who accept that E was an originally independent source, there is a tradition of caution about the extent of E in the

---

[21] See especially, H. W. Wolff, 'Zur Thematik der elohistischen Fragmente im Pentateuch', *EvTh* 29 (1969), 59–72; reprinted in his *Gesammelte Studien zum Alten Testament* (2nd edn., Munich 1973), 402–17; Eng. trans., 'The Elohistic Fragments in the Pentateuch', in W. Brueggemann and H. W. Wolff (eds.), *The Vitality of Old Testament Traditions* (Atlanta 1978), 67–82; A. W. Jenks, *The Elohist and North Israelite Traditions*, Society of Biblical Literature Monograph Series, 22 (Missoula, Mont. 1977); H. Klein, 'Ort und Zeit des Elohisten', *EvTh* 37 (1977), 247–60. Cf. also W. H. Schmidt, 'Plädoyer für die Quellenscheidung', *BZ* n.F. 32 (1988), 7–9. See also R. E. Friedman's contribution noted below.

[22] For a recent presentation of these, see A. W. Jenks' monograph referred to in the preceding footnote.

Pentateuch which, ironically, may have contributed to the current growing tendency to reject this view. S. R. Driver already expressed reserve in delineating E in the Pentateuch. He was critical of the ease with which some scholars distinguished between J and E and wrote that he could not 'hold the particulars, even in the Book of Genesis, to be throughout equally assured',[23] concluding, however, that if 'minuter, more problematic details be not unduly insisted on, there does not seem to be any inherent improbability in the conclusion, stated thus generally, that "JE" is of the nature of a compilation, and that in some parts, if not so frequently as some critics have supposed, the independent sources used by the compiler are still more or less clearly discernible' (p. 117).

A 'minimalist' tendency was later adopted by Martin Noth, who, though he held to the theory of an originally independent E source, believed that much of it was lost when it was combined with J, since the redactor made J the basis and framework and incorporated only selected material from E. Noth insisted that we cannot therefore assume the preservation of a continuous narrative of both J and E. Attempts 'to demonstrate at any cost a continuous narrative in the case of both the J and E strands have led to impossible literary-critical dissections of self-contained narrative units which, not without justification, have evoked the criticism of Volz, Rudolph and others'.[24] As a corollary of this Noth argued that one must presume in favour of the unity of a passage unless there are compelling reasons for regarding it as the result of a combination of J and E; indeed, 'Volz and Rudolph unquestionably deserve the credit for having wrested from customary literary criticism the literary unity of many a beautiful story' (ibid.). When in doubt about the composition of a passage, therefore, one must decide in favour of J rather than E. Noth thus gave his imprimatur to the view that E is only preserved in fragments, and this has, in my opinion, contributed to the growing tendency recently to reject E altogether as an originally independent source.

A 'maximalist' view of E in the Pentateuch has more recently been re-argued, though briefly, by Richard Friedman in a lively and, indeed, timely article defending the importance of source criticism and the results it can achieve in the face of a growing tendency to abandon it as outmoded, the 'failure of a fiction', as one scholar has

---

[23] Driver, *An Introduction to the Literature of the Old Testament*, 117.
[24] Noth, *ÜGP* 24; Eng. trans., 24.

described it.[25] Friedman suggests that if those who share Noth's view would fairly read Exodus first rather than Genesis, where E is less represented, 'they would have to conclude that E is the more complete source' (p. 91). He finds two continuous narratives, J and E, and describes them as alternative versions of the shared national traditions of patriarchs, exodus, Sinai/Horeb, and wilderness sojourn. He traces E to northern Israelite Levitical circles, and J to non-priestly, pro-Davidic circles in Judah. After the fall of the Northern Kingdom in 722 BC, the two sources were combined in Judah. He argues that the preservation in JE of E's polemic in Exodus 32 against the Aaronites evoked a response from the Jerusalem priestly establishment in the form of the Priestly source.[26]

It needs to be restated that there is nothing inherently implausible in the idea of two such independently composed sources such as J and E, each with its own particular religious and theological character, just as Deuteronomy has also its own distinctive nature and purpose. There remain difficulties with Friedman's view. There are, for example, signs that neither the J nor E material is all of one piece, and he has not considered the possible contribution of the redactor (R^{JE}) who combined them and whom many have regarded as an author as well as an editor (see below). Nevertheless, his call for a new attempt at a synthesis of the results of Pentateuchal source analysis[27] is all the more welcome at a time when new and untried theories are already being approvingly cited as though we have irrevocably moved on to a better and more comprehensive understanding of the composition of the Pentateuch than the older theory offered.

(2) The recent attempts to date the origin of JE to the exilic period are not persuasive, and the older view which dates it substantially to the pre-exilic period remains much more plausible. Various features and aspects of the narrative are unlikely to have had an exilic background for their composition. As I suggested earlier, it is difficult to imagine, for example, an exilic writer describing Jacob's obeisance to Esau in Genesis 33. The description of the legitimization of the major sanctuaries and holy places of Israel, which the patriarchs are described as having established or on the site of which they received

[25] R. E. Friedman, 'The Recession of Biblical Source Criticism', in R. E. Friedman and H. C. M. Williamson (eds.), *The Future of Biblical Studies: The Hebrew Scriptures*, The Society of Biblical Literature Semeia Studies (Atlanta 1987), 81–101.
[26] See also R. E. Friedman, *The Exile and Biblical Narrative* (Chico, Calif. 1981).
[27] Friedman, 'The Recession of Biblical Source Criticism', 98 f.

divine revelations, is also more plausibly read against a pre-exilic background than an exilic. Further, none of the main theological features of the corpus is necessarily of exilic origin; for example, belief in Yahweh's sovereign control of history or that his will embraces a universal morality beyond a narrow 'nationalistic' notion of sin are well in evidence in the pre-exilic period. The general character of this corpus also ill fits an exilic background, and the evidence suggests that the historical circumstances in which it was composed were different from, and earlier than, those of the sixth century. As we saw earlier, what is strikingly absent in JE when compared with the literature of the exilic period is any indication that Yahweh has abandoned his people and that they have been given into the hands of other nations; the *dies irae* that so palpably forms the background and in large measure the subject of this literature is quite absent in JE. The difference in this respect between this corpus and the Deuteronomistic History, which is so directed to interpreting the disaster of exile, is itself strong evidence of the improbability that they were composed at the same time. We have seen in addition that the attempt, most notably by Rose and Van Seters, to place the composition of passages in the Deuteronomistic literature prior to that of parallel passages in the Tetrateuch is unconvincing. The paradigm according to which the pre-P Tetrateuch was composed as a 'prologue' to the Deuteronomistic History does not carry conviction.

That there are passages in the pre-Priestly Tetrateuch that derive from the exilic period may be agreed. It is possible, for example, that the divine promise-speeches in Genesis and related passages in Exodus and Numbers, or some of them, are as late as the exilic period. We have noted other passages also in the course of the discussion in the foregoing chapters which may readily be ascribed to an exilic or even post-exilic hand. Such passages are but one indication of what scholars have long since recognized: that the literary prehistory of the final form of the Pentateuch was much too complicated to permit a theory offering an understanding of how the whole emerged to solve in any mechanical manner all individual problems. The reverse of this is equally valid, however, for neither should such passages become the basis for conclusions concerning the whole. Rather they illustrate the truth of C. R. North's statement referred to earlier, that 'the history of any one of the "documents" may well be as complicated as the history of the whole Pentateuch'.[28] Or, to adapt a

[28] C. R. North, 'Pentateuchal Criticism', in H. H. Rowley (ed.), *The Old Testament and Modern Study* (Oxford 1951), 81.

further observation by North, the conclusion is warranted that the 'gauge' of the pre-Priestly Tetrateuch is broader in the pre-exilic period than in the subsequent period.

(3) Some of these secondary passages in the pre-P Tetrateuch show affinities with Deuteronomy and the Deuteronomistic corpus. Nineteenth- and early twentieth-century scholars found evidence of a Deuteronomic redaction of JE for which they employed the siglum R^D. Though some found extensive evidence of the work of this redactor in Genesis, Exodus, and Numbers,[29] most confined the contribution of R^D within much narrower limits, arguing that other passages showing affinity with the style of D can be explained on the grounds that the Jehovist was an immediate forerunner of the Deuteronomic authors, if not indeed a member of the Deuteronomic 'school', or that the authors of Deuteronomy derived some of their vocabulary from JE (see below). As Mark Vervenne has pointed out, however, twentieth-century scholarship until recently has not given 'much attention to the complicated question of the "deuteronomic" elements in Genesis–Numbers. The occurring of dt passages or fragments in these books was simply accepted without any further argumentation or discussion'.[30] One probable reason for this is that, largely under the influence of von Rad's study of the Yahwist in 1938, emphasis became focused upon the original documentary sources of the Tetrateuch, J and E, rather than upon their subsequent combination and redaction and the possible theological intentions of the editors responsible for it.

As the foregoing chapters have shown, however, attention has recently shifted heavily to the nature and extent of Deuteronomic influence and Deuteronomic redaction on these books and with dramatic results. Thus, H. H. Schmid finds Deuteronomistic influence virtually omnipresent in 'the so-called Yahwist', and Blum attributes the creation of the first Tetrateuch (K^D) to Deuteronomistic writers. In my view these results are flawed in two ways. First, Blum has treated the materials as being virtually all on the one level, whereas the evidence suggests that they probably entered the narrative at different stages of transmission and redaction. Secondly, more is

---

[29] Notably Colenso (see above, Ch. 1, p. 23). For a brief history of the discussion see M. Vervenne, 'The Question of "Deuteronomic" Elements in Genesis to Numbers', in F. García Martínez, A. Hilhorst, J. T. A. G. M. van Ruiten, A. S. van der Woude (eds.), *Studies in Deuteronomy in Honour of C. J. Labuschagne*, SVT 53 (Leiden 1994), 246–51.
[30] Vervenne, 'The Question of "Deuteronomic" Elements', 248.

claimed for these redactors than is warranted. Whilst earlier commentators may have underestimated the contribution of Deuteronomic editors to the Tetrateuch, the reverse is now the case and all or most passages which can be shown to be expansions of, or insertions into, an underlying narrative are attributed to a Deuteronomic or Deuteromistic redactor. The critique of Blum's arguments in Chapter 6 above, especially his claims concerning such a key narrative as the call of Moses in Exodus 3–4, cast doubt upon the notion of a 'Deuteronomic Tetrateuch'.

(4) At the heart of the matter is the question of what is meant by 'Deuteronomic' or 'Deuteronomistic'.[31] The term Deuteronomistic may be applied, for example, to Joshua chapter 1; it focuses upon a central theological theme of Deuteronomy: obedience to the Torah. Thus Wellhausen correctly described this chapter as 'purely deuteronomistic' ('rein deuteronomistisch').[32] But should the presence alone in a passage in the Tetrateuch of words and expressions familiar also in the Deuteronomistic corpus automatically lead to the designation of that passage as 'Deuteronomistic'? For example, whilst Wellhausen described Joshua 1 as 'purely Deuteronomistic', he attributed Numbers 14: 11b–23a to the Jehovist, even though the latter contains words and expressions familiar also in the Deuteronomistic literature.[33] Is this passage correctly described as from the Jehovist or from a Deuteronomistic editor?[34]

The relationship of the Jehovist to the authors of Deuteronomy was much discussed in earlier Pentateuchal research. For example, Holzinger raised the question whether the two redactors were one and the same, commenting that the

relationship [between R^{JE} and R^D] is so marked that it is frequently difficult to decide whether a secondary passage is to be ascribed to R^{JE} or a Deuteronomistic editor . . . It must be asked whether, given this evidence, it

---

[31] The following comments are prompted by N. Lohfink's perceptive article 'Gab es eine deuteronomistische Bewegung?', in W. Gross (ed.), *Jeremiah und die 'deuteronomistische Bewegung'*, BBB 98 (1995), 313–82 (see esp. 317 ff.).

[32] Wellhausen, *Die Composition des Hexateuchs*, 117.   [33] Ibid. 102.

[34] S. Boorer, *The Promise of the Land as Oath*, 332–8, concludes that the passage has 'close affinity with both Dtr and non-P/non-Dtr material, especially in Exodus, material that is traditionally regarded as earlier than Dtr' (p. 338). She too, therefore, refrains from describing the passage simply as 'Deuteronomistic'. Noth, *Das vierte Buch Mose, Numeri*, Eng. trans., *Numbers, in loc.* describes the passage as being 'strongly permeated by deuteronomistic conceptions and turns of phrase' and therefore 'an extensive late addition'.

is not altogether simpler to identify R^JE with R^D, and thus combine the two redaction stages J + E and JE + D into one single stage J + E + D.[35]

His own conclusion was that two stages of redaction rather than one remains the more probable explanation of the evidence, but that the relationship between the redactions was such that they derived from the same 'school'.[36] He saw a gradual process of redaction from R^JE to R^JED.[37] Earlier, Wellhausen had also pointed to a close relationship between the Jehovist and the authors of Deuteronomy, but without identifying them.[38]

S. R. Driver likewise drew a distinction between the two redactions, but explained the relationship between them differently. Surveying JE, he differentiated between passages which (a) '*approximate* in style and tone to Deuteronomy', suggesting that 'these are, no doubt pre-Deuteronomic', and (b) others 'with a *strong* Deuteronomic colouring' which 'will have been written under the influence of Dt., and be post-Deuteronomic'.[39] Driver's explanation of this phenomenon was, not that the Jehovist was to be identified with R^D, but that the authors of Deuteronomy adopted stylistic features including words and phrases from JE. Thus, in his commentary on Deuteronomy he wrote that there are

certain sections of JE (in particular Gn. 26: 5; Ex. 13: 3–16; 15: 26; 19, 3–6; parts of 20: 2–17; 23: 20–33; 34: 10–26), in which the author (or compiler) adopts a parenetic tone, and where his style displays what may be termed an approximation to the style of Dt.; and these sections appear to have been the source from which the author of Dt. adopted some of the expressions currently used by him.[40]

A more recent writer, Moshe Weinfeld, from who has come one of the most important studies of Deuteronomy in recent years, lends support to Driver's approach:

The main characteristic of deuteronomic phraseology is not the employment of new idioms and expressions, because many of these could be found in the earlier sources and especially in the Elohistic source. Indeed, it would be nonsense to say that all of a sudden in the seventh century a new vocabulary and new expressions were created ... What constitutes the novelty of the deuteronomic style therefore is not new idioms and new expressions, but a specific

[35] Holzinger, *Einleitung in den Hexateuch*, 490.   [36] Ibid. 491.   [37] Ibid. 491.
[38] Wellhausen, *Die Composition des Hexateuchs*, 73 f., 79, 85 f., 94, 115.
[39] S. R. Driver, *Exodus* (Cambridge 1911), pp. xvii–xviii.
[40] S. R. Driver, *Deuteronomy* (Edinburgh 1895), pp. lxxvii–lxxviii.

jargon reflecting the religious upheaval of this time . . . what makes a phrase deuteronomic is not its mere occurrence in Deuteronomy, but its meaning within the framework of deuteronomic theology.[41]

He goes on to list the main themes of this theology including, for example, the struggle against idolatry, the centralization of the cult, the worship of Yahweh alone, observance of the Torah and loyalty to the covenant, inheritance of the land.

(5) A growing number of scholars in recent years have focused attention anew on passages in the Tetrateuch which are pre-Deuteronomic but display affinities in style and vocabulary with the Deuteronomic literature. They employ the term 'proto-Deuteronomic' for such passages, but acknowledge their close relationship with the contribution to the Tetrateuch of the so-called Jehovist R[JE].[42] In my view this is a line of investigation that should now be pursued, but I prefer to focus it upon the contribution of the Jehovist, understanding by this term, however, not an individual redactor and author but a 'school' of scribal theologians who engaged in a creative reworking of older sources and traditions in the late pre-exilic period and continuing perhaps into the exilic period, and whose work was presupposed by, and influential upon, the authors of Deuteronomy and the Deuteronomistic History.

The narrative of the oath to Abraham in Genesis 15* and the promise speeches related to it in Genesis can plausibly be attributed to this stage of redaction. So too may the allusions to the oath to the fathers in Exodus and Numbers. The inclusion of the notion of a covenant at Sinai may also be due to these redactors. If such a notion was already known to Hosea,[43] there is no need to attribute its incor-

---

[41] M. Weinfeld, *Deuteronomy and the Deuteronomic School* (Oxford 1972), I. N. Lohfink also ('Gab es eine deuteronomistische Bewegung?') rightly cautions against too free a usage of the term 'Deuteronomic' when assessing passages which show some usage of the vocabulary of these writers.

[42] See above, Ch. 6 n. 22. Vervenne ('The Question of "Deuteronomic" Elements') provides extensive bibliography of the discussion this approach has generated.

[43] E. W. Nicholson, *God and His People: Covenant and Theology in the Old Testament* (Oxford 1986), 179–88. Hosea 8: 1 is usually regarded as Deuteronomic or Deuteronomistic. But some of its phraseology is unparalleled in the Deuteronomistic corpus. Lohfink has argued persuasively ('Gab es eine deuteronomistische Bewegung?', 326 ff.) that, for example, passages in Amos usually ascribed to a Deuteronomistic editor are pre-Deuteronomic and may, indeed, have been a source for the Deuteronomistic writers. In my opinion, Hosea 8: 1 perhaps provides a further example of this.

poration into the Sinai tradition to Deuteronomic editors.[44] Consideration should also be given to the possibility that the stories of rebellion in the wilderness focusing upon lack of faith in Yahweh's control of history (Exod. 15: 22–5a; 17: 1bβ–7; Numbers 11: 1–3; *11: 4–32; *12: 1–15; 21: 4b–9) derive from such redactors. As we saw earlier, there is no need, with H. H. Schmid and others, to confine the emergence of this theme to the crisis brought about by the exile, however much it intensified then. It is already known in the last century and a half or so of the pre-exilic period and is addressed both by Hosea in northern Israel and by Isaiah in Jerusalem (cf. Hos. 7: 11; 8: 9; Isa. 7: 1–7; 30: 1–5; 31: 1–3). The background of the power and imperial domination of Assyria and of the sporadic challenge to this by Egypt, and the political involvement—ultimately catastrophic—in the superpower struggles of the time both by the northern Israelite state and by Judah was certainly one in which the theme of Israel's loss of trust in Yahweh reflected in the 'murmuring' stories could readily have found expression. The suggestion that such authors may also have contributed significantly to the narrative of apostasy and renewal in Exodus 32–4 should also be taken seriously.[45] In short, in my view the recent renewed focus upon the so-called 'proto-Deuteronomic' or, as I still prefer, Jehovistic redactional elements in the Tetrateuch merits continued study. *That is, we should adopt an approach similar to that of H. H. Schmid but with the significant difference that the sort of creative redactional reworking of tradition which he attributes to the 'so-called Yahwist' should instead be considered as the work of the 'so-called Jehovist'.*

(6) This should include a further neglected issue in recent research, namely the question whether the JE material, including the work of the Jehovist, included an account of the settlement. We have become accustomed since the publication of Noth's work on the Deuteronomistic History to accepting that the Pentateuchal sources J and E, or the work of the Jehovist, are no longer extant beyond the end of Deuteronomy.[46] That is, the older view according to which these

---

[44] The description of the covenant ritual in Exodus 24: 3–8 is unlikely to be from a Deuteronomic hand, since the making of the covenant by such ritualistic means is foreign to these authors for whom, it seems, the covenant was made rather by pledged word. For a discussion of this passage see my *God and His People*, 164–78.

[45] See the discussion along these lines by C. Begg, 'The Destruction of the Calf (Exod. 32, 30/Dt 9, 21)', in N. Lohfink (ed.), *Das Deuteronomium. Enstehung, Gestalt und Botschaft* (Leuven 1985), 208–51.

[46] See above, Ch. 3, s. III.

sources contained a narrative of the settlement which can be isolated in the book of Joshua, and that therefore we can speak of a Hexateuch, has been abandoned. That these sources originally contained settlement narratives was not questioned. According to Noth they were omitted by the redactor who combined JE with P, which contained no such narrative and into the framework of which JE was worked. There has been powerful opposition to Noth's view, most notably from von Rad and Mowinckel.[47] It can be said, however, that Noth's view has commanded majority support, and has been strongly defended, though with some important modifications, in recent years by, for example, Graeme Auld.[48]

In a review of Auld's monograph, Graham Davies has called for a fresh testing of Noth's theory.[49] He draws attention to observations by F. Langlamet who finds continuity in vocabulary between Joshua 1–12 and the older Pentateuchal sources.[50] Against Langlamet, Auld stressed Noth's insistence on the need for substantive connections between texts in Joshua and the older Pentateuchal narrative. Davies urges that this challenge should be freshly taken up, and he offers as the beginnings of a response some evidence of just such substantive connections between Joshua 1–12 and the older sources of the Pentateuch. Thus, geographically, he points out, the stories of Rahab and the crossing of the Jordan, with their reference to Shittim as the point of departure (2: 1; 3: 1), are connected with Numbers (cf. 25: 1) rather than with Deuteronomy, which never mentions Shittim and describes the encampment east of the Jordan in quite different ways (1: 1(?); 3: 29; 4: 46; 28: 69; 34: 1, 6, 8). He points out also that the title 'Moses' minister' given to Joshua in 1: 1 'presupposes a relationship which is not apparent in Deuteronomy, but only in Exodus (24: 13; 33: 11) and Numbers (11: 28)' (p. 211). The investigation of such possible connections between elements in Joshua 1–12 and the older sources in the Tetrateuch should now receive fresh investigation.

[47] For von Rad's, see above, Ch. 3. Mowinckel dealt with the problem especially in his *Tetrateuch–Pentateuch–Hexateuch. Die Bericht über die Landnahme in den drei altisraelitischen Geschichtswerken*, BZAW 90 (Berlin 1964).

[48] A. G. Auld, *Joshua, Moses and the Land: Tetrateuch–Pentateuch–Hexateuch in a Generation since 1938* (Edinburgh 1980).

[49] G. I. Davies, Review of A. G. Auld, *Joshua, Moses and the Land*, JTS NS 33 (1982), 209–13.

[50] F. Langlamet, *Gilgal et les Récits de la Traversée du Jourdain*, Cahiers de la Revue Biblique, 11 (Paris 1969); 'Josué, II, et les Traditions de l'Hexateuque', *RB* 78 (1971), 5–17, 161–83, 231–54; 'La Traversée du Jourdain et les Documents de l'Hexateuque', *RB* 79 (1972), 7–38.

(7) Finally there remains the question of the dating of the Jehovist's two main sources, the Yahwist and Elohistic narratives. Earlier scholars characteristically attempted to determine this on the basis of the presence of the influence of classical prophecy upon J and E or lack of it. Thus Wellhausen found evidence of this influence in E, but less in J, which he therefore regarded as displaying a less advanced stage in the development of Israelite religion than E. He offered no more precise dating than this, however. Driver on the other hand was less convinced of the influence of classical prophecy beginning with Amos and Hosea, and thus dated both J and E before their time, but did not go beyond assigning both sources to the early centuries of the monarchical period. The appeal of the early dating of the Yahwist suggested by von Rad, which became widely accepted during the middle decades of this century, was that he believed it possible to match this author's theology with a specific cultural setting in early Israel, that is, the supposed 'enlightenment' that emerged during the reign of Solomon. The notion of such an 'enlightenment' finds little support in contemporary Old Testament scholarship, however. Some still favour such an early date for J[51] and E.[52] The criteria for arriving at a precise dating for such sources are lacking, however, and in any case there are sufficient signs that neither source was composed all at one sitting to caution reserve.[53]

As the foregoing chapters have argued, however, there are no convincing reasons for doubting the relative chronology of the sources: that J and E are earlier than Deuteronomy and derive from the pre-exilic period; that their combination and redaction likewise preceded

[51] For example, L. Schmidt, 'Überlegungen zum Jahwisten', *EvTh* 37 (1977), 230–47; W. H. Schmidt, 'Ein Theologe in salomonischer Zeit? Plädoyer für den Jahwisten', *BZ* n.F. 25 (1981), 82–102; Eng. trans., 'A Theologian of the Solomonic Era? A Plea for the Yahwist', in T. Ishida (ed.), *Studies in the Period of David and Solomon and Other Essays* (Winona Lake, Minn. 1982), 55–73; cf. also his 'Plädoyer für die Quellenscheidung', *BZ* n.F. 32 (1988), 1–14; K. Berge, *Die Zeit des Jahwisten: Ein Beitrag zur Datierungjahwistischer Vätertexte*, BZAW 186 (Berlin 1990); S. Tengström, *Die Hexateucherzählung. Eine literaturgeschichtliche Studie*, Coniectanea Biblica, OT 7 (Lund 1976), who argues for an eleventh-century origin of a *Grunderzählung* which he believes can be isolated from Genesis–Joshua.

[52] Jenks, *The Elohist and North Israelite Traditions*, esp. ch. 3, argues a tenth-century origin for E.

[53] For example, the story of Abraham and Sarah in Egypt in Genesis 12: 10–20 is probably a secondary addition to the J narrative. Noth, though not unsympathetic to von Rad's view, concluded that 'discernible concrete references to this [the Davidic-Solomonic] period are lacking, and thus the possibility also must be reckoned with that J is later' (*ÜGP* 249 f.; Eng. trans., 230).

the work of the authors of Deuteronomy and the Deuteronomistic History, though this stage of redaction (R[JE]) may have continued in to the period in which they wrote.

A further task remains to be more fully undertaken. Throughout the debate about the composition of the Pentateuch since Wellhausen there has been one stage in its emergence that has been very largely neglected, that is, the Pentateuch as we have it. Scholars throughout this period have for the most continued to focus upon the sources behind the final form of the text, their composition, the historical setting in which they were composed, and the theological or other intentions of their authors and of the redactors who combined them. Each supposed stage of composition and redactional combination has been the subject of much thought and reflection with a view to understanding what its authors or redactors sought to achieve. But this has usually stopped short of the final stage in the process, the Pentateuch as it lies before us, even though there has been much concentration upon *how* the final form of the text came about. More recently, however, a number of scholars have sought to correct this omission in the study of the Pentateuch, calling for a 'synchronic' approach to reading the text as against the 'diachronic' approach that has prevailed hitherto. The next and final chapter outlines in some more detail this call for a 'final form' interpretation of the Pentateuch and the issues it raises.

9
Understanding the Final Form of the Pentateuch

I

I began this book with the observation that Wellhausen did not regard the investigation of the composition of the Pentateuch as an end in itself. Rather, it was a means to solving a larger and for him more urgent problem—the history and development of Israelite religion from the pre-exilic period to the beginnings of Judaism in the post-exilic period. In the nature of the case therefore his approach was in a manner of speaking 'archaeological'. That is, he was concerned with uncovering earlier from later layers of literary composition and redaction in the Pentateuch in order to reconstruct a picture of the religious traditions, beliefs, and institutions of Israel in the Old Testament period. In short, the Pentateuch was a source for historical reconstruction rather than a literary composition or compilation to be studied and appreciated for its own sake, whether as literature or theologically.

The triumph of the 'New Documentary Theory' as a result of Wellhausen's *Composition of the Hexateuch* led, as we saw, to the further splitting up of the text into subdivisions of J and E (J^1 J^2 J^3; E^1 E^2 E^3, and the like), or to further sources as variously proposed by the advocates of the so-called 'Newest Documentary Theory'. In addition, source analysis of texts at the hands of some was so minutely pursued that single verses were divided between several sources, giving the impression that the text as we have it was put together by a 'scissors and paste' process. In these ways too, much of the further work stimulated by Wellhausen's influential study led further and further away from the text of the Pentateuch to its supposed earlier stages.

The main focus of the new phase in Pentateuchal research inaugurated by Gunkel and the 'history of religions' movement gave further impetus to such a trend. As we saw in Chapter 2, the representatives of this movement endeavoured to penetrate behind the sources to the preliterary stages in their emergence, that is, to the diverse oral and cultic materials which were available to, and collected by, those who gave us the source documents. Traditio-historical research with its quest for the history of traditions, beliefs, and institutions was similarly preoccupied with the preliterary stages. In short, whether at the hands of source critics or of form critics and those concerned with the history of traditions, therefore, the text of the Pentateuch or Hexateuch was merely the starting point for an investigation of problems behind the text or exterior to it, and the text itself was dissected in the interests of the quest for answers to such problems.

The period of research outlined in Chapters 1 and 2 above may thus be characterized as one that *moved backwards* from the text of the Pentateuch or Hexateuch, first to the earlier stages in the composition of the literature and then to the still earlier stages in the history of individual stories or complexes of stories, and of the traditions reflected in them. How the text was put together into its final form was not of course neglected. Attention was given to the work of editors who united the different sources (R^{JE}; R^{JED}; R^{JEDP}). There was little or no attempt, however, to ask how stories or literary complexes from originally discrete sources were to be read and understood when combined with one another. That is, the new context arising from the combination of sources was insufficiently examined to ascertain the effects the redactor may have had in mind in selecting and uniting materials from the sources he had assembled. This omission only underlined the main drive of research—to move backwards from the literature as we have it to its earlier components.

II

Writing in the late 1930s, Gerhard von Rad sounded a protest against the disintegrating and fragmenting effect of Pentateuchal research hitherto, notwithstanding the valuable insights it had yielded into the sources and the information gained concerning the history of Israel, its religion and institutions. He castigated scholars as being guilty of an approach which viewed the Hexateuch as 'a starting-point barely worthy of discussion, from which the debate should move away as rapidly as possible in order to reach the real problems underlying it'.[1] Against such an approach, he sought to direct attention again to the

---

[1] *GS* 9; Eng. trans., 1.

whole which had hitherto been generally ignored in the interests of the parts. As we saw, he found the first Hexateuch to have been the creation of the Yahwist on the basis of an ancient creed-like statement, into the framework of which this author incorporated further traditional materials. In short, von Rad sought to show that '[o]ne plan alone governs the whole'.

In the nature of the case von Rad in his famous monograph was also much concerned with origins. Much of the monograph is devoted to the origin and development of the traditions behind the Yahwist's work. Such a movement backwards from the text was of course essential for the return journey, that is for the movement forward 'from tradition to literature', to the accomplishment of the Yahwist. However, the movement forward from origins to the text was not carried through to anything approaching the totality of the text of the Hexateuch. This of course would have been beyond the scope of what von Rad intended in his short monograph. Here he was concerned primarily with uncovering what he believed to be the plan of the Hexateuch, adding some brief concluding observations concerning the work both of the Elohist and the Priestly writers. Subsequently, however, in his commentary on Genesis, he offered some comments on the exegetical task that arises from the final form of the literature, but before considering these comments Martin Noth's discussion of the matter in his *History of Pentateuchal Traditions* must be brought into the picture.

Noth also, as we saw, quite in keeping with the protest sounded by von Rad, was concerned with the formation of the totality of the Pentateuch. The difference was that, whilst for von Rad the Yahwist played the decisive role in this, for Noth the formative stages had been completed before the Yahwist took up his pen, that is, in the emergence of a *Grundlage* (G). He defined the task of comprehending the formation of the Pentateuch as understanding 'in a manner that is historically responsible and proper, the essential content and important concerns of the Pentateuch—which, from its manifold beginnings, variously rooted in cultic situations, to the final stages in the process of its emergence, claims recognition as a great document of faith'.[2]

Noth's *History of Pentateuchal Traditions* was primarily concerned with the formative, preliterary stages in the creation of the Pentateuch, a task that no one hitherto had attempted. He had much to say about the literary and redactional stages, however, and pref-

[2] *ÜGP* 3 f.; Eng. trans., 3.

aced the book with a invaluable, succinct, and, indeed, vigorous defence of the documentary theory against its latest critics. He also returned at the end of his study to the literary sources and included a chapter under the title 'The Pentateuchal Narrative as a Whole'. What was involved in the creation of the completed Pentateuch, however, he judged to have been 'a purely literary work, one that has contributed neither new tradition-material nor new substantive viewpoints to the reworking or interpretation of the materials. This work issued merely in an addition of sources . . . '.[3] The purpose of those who at different stages combined the sources was simply to augment the tradition-material through addition, first by fitting special E material within the framework of J, and later by working the combined JE into the framework of P. For the period in which the latter was carried out, 'the paramount concern could only be the gathering together of the entire known material of tradition bearing upon the prehistory of Israel'.[4]

Noth asks 'whether the combination of the sources . . . actually did not give rise to something new, which transcended the individual sources and their particular content and put them in a peculiar light, beyond the conscious intentions of the redactors' and thus 'whether this combination has not resulted, perhaps unintentionally, in unexpected narrative connections and theological insights, than merely the sum of the parts'.[5] The most that can be said, however, is that numerous particulars have been determined by the new contexts, for example the time sequence and the localization of individual narratives. But these are relatively minor matters, no more than 'incidental consequences of the uniting of the sources'. Further, the theology of P and that of the older sources 'stand side by side amicably', and '[h]ardly any occasion arose for a conflict between these two or for a synthesis on a higher plane', though sometimes, as in the two creation stories in Genesis 1 and 2, they supplement each other and 'reach a new unity'.[6] All in all, therefore, the final text of the Pentateuch remains 'a compilation in which not only narrative materials but also the theological concerns are juxtaposed and interwoven with one another just as plainly and incongruously as the individual sources had presented them'; the 'conflation of the sources resulted in a very uneven and inorganic whole'.[7]

---

[3] *ÜGP* 268; Eng. trans., 248.   [4] *ÜGP* 269; Eng. trans., 249.
[5] *ÜGP* 270; Eng. trans., 250.   [6] *ÜGP* 271; Eng. trans., 251.
[7] *ÜGP* 269; Eng. trans., 249.

At first glance von Rad, in his commentary on Genesis published in 1956, seems to take us beyond Noth's view of this issue when he states that if

such a carefully considered and often skilful intertwining of both great compositions [JE and P] is more than an obtuse archivist arrangement, then it also places its demands on the exegete. Surely a perceptible failure in our expositions to date is that they renounce every mutual reference from one source to the other by their separated interpretations of the three source documents.[8]

He goes on to describe briefly a way in which, for example, the story from J in Genesis 2 complements that in Genesis 1 from the Priestly source. In the commentary proper, however, the 'failure in our expositions' to which von Rad draws attention remains only partially addressed, and there is the familiar 'separated interpretations of the three source documents'. That is, the move backwards to the originally separate sources was not followed by a move forwards to an exegesis of text in its final form. Yet again, the focus remains on the parts at the expense of the whole. For example, what difference, if any, does it make that the older narrative of a covenant between God and Abraham in Genesis 15 is now followed by the different account of such a covenant from P in Genesis 17? In what way might the redactor have intended them to be understood in the new context in which he placed them in close proximity to one another?

To sum up at this stage: what was missing in earlier exegesis of the Pentateuch was an endeavour to embrace not only the earlier stages in the history of the text such as those represented by J and E, the work of the Jehovist, and P, but the text as it has come to be. There was little or no attempt to ask how stories or literary complexes from originally discrete sources were to be read and understood when combined with one another. That is, the new context arising from the combination of sources was insufficiently examined to ascertain the effects the redactor may have had in mind in selecting and uniting materials from the sources he had assembled.

III

There is a more favourable climate in Old Testament research currently for an attempt to understand the text of the Pentateuch as it

---

[8] Von Rad, *Das erste Buch Moses, Genesis*, 31 f.; Eng. trans., *Genesis*, 40 f.

has come to be, and it is one of the more positive aspects of recent study that this task is now being more seriously undertaken. This has been facilitated by a shift in Old Testament study generally to a holistic, or what is frequently termed a 'synchronic' reading of texts, accompanied by a new appraisal of the literary achievement of the authors.

The term 'synchronic' is usually employed for the endeavour of interpreting a text as a whole irrespective of what history it has gone through to reach its present form, which 'diachronic' study seeks to uncover.[9] Scholars adopting the 'synchronic' approach view a text, for example the Pentateuch, 'as a concerted literary work with its own artistic integrity, composed, as it were, contemporaneously under a unitary creative impulse'.[10] It is for this reason sometimes referred to as 'final form' interpretation. Employed in such a way[11] the term designates the study of the intention and achievement of the final redactor of the Pentateuch and thus the study of the final form of the text.[12] Recent attempts at such an interpretation have been provided by, for example, David Clines and Norman Whybray.

Clines was early off the mark calling for greater attention to the meaning of the final form of the Pentateuch in his monograph of 1978 on the 'theme' of the Pentateuch.[13] He is critical of the preoccupation with an 'atomistic' and 'genetic' approach to texts that has prevailed hitherto. By 'atomistic' he has in mind, for example, studies of individual parts or layers of the text of the Pentateuch such as discussions of the theology of J or E or P.[14] Though such studies have yielded

[9] I am indebted for the following comments to William Johnstone, *Exodus*, Old Testament Guides (Sheffield 1990), 86 f.

[10] Ibid. 87

[11] The term is employed in some circles of modern literary theory for a concern with a text in itself as a literary artefact that is 'the bearer of, indeed *is*, its own meaning and can be appreciated without reference to the purpose or beliefs of the writer, who may become a figure of no more importance for the appreciation of the artefact than is the painter, sculptor or composer for the appreciation of other works of art' (Johnstone, 87).

[12] Allowance is made, however, for some minor secondary additions to the work of the redactor who combined JE with P (e.g. Gen. 14).

[13] D. J. A. Clines, *The Theme of the Pentateuch*, JSOT Supplement Series, 10 (Sheffield 1978).

[14] For example, cf H. W. Wolff, 'Zur Thematik der elohistischen Fragmente im Pentateuch', *EvTh* 29 (1969), 59–72; repr. in his *Gesammelte Studien zum Alten Testament* (2nd edn., Munich 1973), 402–17; Eng. trans., 'The Elohistic Fragments in the Pentateuch', in W. Brueggemann and H. W. Wolff (eds.), *The Vitality of Old Testament Traditions* (Atlanta 1978), 67–82; id., 'Das Kerygma des Jahwisten', *EvTh* 24 (1964), 73–93; repr. in his *Gesammelte Studien zum Alten Testament*, 345–73; Eng.

worthwhile results, they have been at the expense of treating the text as a whole, the text as we have it. By 'geneticism' he means the belief underlying much research that texts can only be appreciated when their origin and growth has been uncovered. Such an approach may suit some subjects, but when

> as in Old Testament studies, the sources and the prehistory of our present texts are for the most part entirely hypothetical, and when, in any case, a work of art, such as a good deal of the Old Testament literature undoubtedly is, yields its significance to the observer as a whole and through the articulation of its parts in its present form, one would have imagined that a genetic approach would not be strongly favoured. But it is, and it must indeed be confessed that many Old Testament scholars know of no other way of doing research in the Old Testament except along such lines. I do not decry such methodology; it is a scientific necessity, even if its firm results turn out to be meagre. But I do protest against the dominance of that approach, and set forth, by way of an alternative approach, the method adopted in this book as a gainful form of employment in Old Testament study. (p. 9)

He therefore calls for, and in this monograph provides an example of, a 'holistic approach to the Pentateuch . . . which goes beyond questions about its (presumed) sources, and enquires about the meaning of the text that now exists' (p. 8). He finds God's promise and its partial fulfilment to be the all-embracing theme of the Pentateuch, including Genesis 1–11, and that which enabled the combination of the originally separate sources.

In a more recent contribution[15] Norman Whybray adopts a similar approach, arguing for a 'synchronic' approach as against a 'diachronic'. That is, 'the Pentateuch in its final form is treated as a "book" which exists in its own right as an artifact with a theme and a message. This approach is distinct from the "diachronic", which is concerned primarily with the history of composition, which may (or may not) have extended over a long period' (p. 135). 'The advantage of using the synchronic approach', he argues, 'is that in this way one is dealing with something concrete that actually exists: the text of the Pentateuch which lies before us. The diachronic method is necessarily speculative' (p. 135). Like Clines, he finds that the 'primary theme

trans., 'The Kerygma of the Yahwist', in W. Brueggemann and H. W. Wolff, op. cit., 41–66. Cf. also more recently R. B. Coote and D. R. Ord, *The Bible's First Historian: From Eden to the Court of David with the Yahwist* (Philadelphia 1989); R. B. Coote, *In Defense of Revolution: The Elohist History* (Minneapolis 1991).

[15] R. N. Whybray, *Introduction to the Pentateuch* (Grand Rapids, Mich. 1995).

. . . is undoubtedly that of the promises made to the patriarchs from Abraham on' (p. 136), and their partial fulfilment.

A fundamental difficulty for the approach of both Clines and Whybray is that it begs the question whether the Pentateuch can be regarded as a work in itself, a ' "book" which exists in its own right as an artifact'. That is, the question is begged whether the Pentateuch is part of a larger work, the Hexateuch, or, indeed, as a finished text is part of a still larger corpus comprising the Former Prophets arising from a combination of an originally independent Tetrateuch with the Deuteronomistic corpus, or whether there was originally a Tetrateuch which was only secondarily combined with Deuteronomy to form the Pentateuch. This is an especially important issue for the conclusion of these scholars, since on the very theme 'promise and *partial* fulfilment' rather than 'promise and fulfilment' depends the relation of the Pentateuch with the book of Joshua.

Whybray's grounds for treating the Pentateuch as a ' "book" which exists in its own right as an artifact', as a 'closed entity' (p. 136), are that the death of Moses recorded in Deuteronomy 34 marks the 'end of an era' and that the book of Joshua 'clearly marks the start of an entirely new age' (p. 2). The difficulty is, however, that one can easily point to other junctures in the Pentateuch that are equally well described as the end of one era or the beginning of another, for example the death of Jacob in Egypt and the end of the patriarchal age, or the birth of Moses and the beginning of a new one. Moses farewell speech on the Plains of Moab, which is the form taken by Deuteronomy, also marks a natural break in the narrative and the end of one era, the wandering in the wilderness, and the advent of a new one, the imminent crossing of the Jordan into the land.

Whybray further defends his 'synchronic' approach on the grounds that a 'diachronic' approach has been shown to be highly speculative and subjective. Commenting on the recent breakdown of the consensus about the Documentary Theory, he writes that 'the complete lack of agreement at the present time about the composition of the Pentateuch should warn the student that theories about the dates of different parts of it are *extremely subjective*' (p. 135; italics mine). William Johnstone has rightly observed concerning this sort of claim in favour of a 'synchronic' over a 'diachronic' approach that 'diachronic study may serve to confirm the confines of the compositional unit, the artistic integrity of which is under study. Without this confirmation, there can be as much of the speculative and subjective in "final form" interpretation as in the attempt to reconstruct origins and development; one may be just as oppressed by the arbitrariness with which passages are delimited by this kind of study and by the impressionism of the "reading" offered by it as by the speculations of old-style literary and form criticism.'[16]

Clines's argument is subject to this same criticism. His reason for regarding the Pentateuch as 'a single literary work . . . an independent work in its own right' (p. 11) is that 'the Pentateuch has been recognized as a literary entity by Jews, Samaritans, Christians and Muslims for somewhere between twelve hundred and twenty-five hundred years. It is for that reason, if for no other, appropriate to ask what the work *is about*, which is to say, more or less: What is its theme?' On this view, therefore, it is the history of the canon that determines that the Pentateuch is a 'single literary work' rather than a consideration of the literary structure, contours, and contents of the work itself. That is, it is not at all the work in *its own right* that leads to the conclusion that it is a single literary work, but the decision to adopt ancient tradition rather than modern critical criteria for determining whether the text is a compositional unit in its own right. Clearly this is just as subjective and even more arbitrary than Whybray's grounds for treating the Pentateuch as a ' "book" which exists in its own right as an artifact'. There is no more justification for delimiting the text on such grounds than there is for accepting the closely associated ancient designation of the text as the *Torah* as a description of what the Pentateuch is 'all about'. If tradition is to be the arbiter in deciding upon the limits of the text, why should the issue of 'what it is all about' be decided on other grounds, that is, modern critical methods? In short, so-called 'diachronic' considerations cannot be so easily evaded if, as Johnstone has rightly put it, the confines of the compositional unit which is under study are to be established.

The text should first be delineated from a critical perspective and for this purpose, against Whybray's strictures, we should build upon the insights of earlier scholars rather than simply jettisoning them. For example, it might be argued that a Deuteronomistic or Priestly redactor consciously created the Pentateuch, working over JE and D or JED. On such a basis we may then seek to understand what this redactor, who gave us the Pentateuch in substantially its final form,

[16] Johnstone, *Exodus*, 89.

intended by his work of redaction. As we shall see, such a critical approach has been adopted by Brevard Childs who in his study of the 'canonical form and function' of the Pentateuch argues that there is internal evidence that the five books of the Pentateuch were seen together as a 'canonical' unit and that there is evidence of a coherent inner relationship in terms of content as well (see below section V).

A further question arises concerning the views of Clines and Whybray, that is, whether the notion of a single 'theme' that will embrace the entire Pentateuch is likely to succeed in the face of the very varied contents of this complex corpus of literature. One can think of a number of themes any one of which might serve heuristically or as a sort of middle point for comprehending in a convenient manner the varied religious, theological, legal, prophetic, priestly, and other instructional materials and genres which the Pentateuch comprises. Theologically too, there are marked differences between parts, the theology of the Joseph story, for example, contrasting with that of the patriarchal stories earlier in Genesis. This polyvalent nature of the Pentateuch means that it is only by a *tour de force* that its varied contents can be subordinated to one supposed overriding theme—unless it is so broadly defined as to be generalized, like the traditional description *Torah* 'Instruction'. Put briefly, is the search for such an overriding theme not destined to run into the same difficulties as the quest for a 'centre' (*Mitte*) once favoured as a way of arranging a 'theology' of the Old Testament as a whole?

The task proper of a 'final form' reading of the Pentateuch will not be fulfilled by identifying possible themes that the different parts may have in common, though this may contribute to our understanding of the whole. What is required is rather a detailed study of the interweaving of the sources to determine what the redactor sought to achieve. We have to enquire how stories or literary complexes from originally discrete sources were intended to be read and understood when combined with one another. What significance do passages newly acquire when juxtaposed with each other in the larger context created by the combination of the sources? To what extent do they supplement each other and 'reach a new unity' or, indeed, to what extent might one passage have been intended to 'gloss' another or modify, qualify, or even counter it? For example, the combination of the P and J stories of creation in Genesis 1–2 has sometimes been viewed as yielding such a new unity, and this raises the possibility that the redactor who combined the two stories may have had other similar creative syntheses in mind when bringing together other texts from his sources.

IV

Claus Westermann in his monumental commentary on Genesis has recognized the task and includes discussions of the achievement of the redactor (R) who combined J with P. He describes Genesis 1–11 as 'a construct of texts that has its own independence and its own individual contribution to make over and above those of J and P. R wants to preserve several points of view of one and the same event and pass them on', and displays an attitude to tradition that 'is more profound and thoroughgoing' than either the author of J or of P.[17] R created out of J and P 'a new, coherent and self-contained narrative' and this was possible because 'R shared with J and P a basic attitude to reality and event'. Hence it is, for example, in the case of the stories of creation, that by combining J and P the redactor 'creates a new tension between creation of the world and creation of humans and allows it to be developed further. When different voices [J, P, and R] in different keys, counterpoised and in harmony, can be heard and preserved, then the presumption is that they have a profound, firm and unshakable sharing in common. This is the reason why one can speak of a theological meaning of the primeval story as a whole.'[18]

Writing of R's work in Genesis 12–36, Westermann comments that the 'work of the redactor consisted, not as classical source criticism understood it earlier, namely, in arranging mechanically a succession of small and tiny fragments out of a number of "sources", but rather in fashioning the two works that lay before him into one whilst allowing each to speak for itself. R achieved this with scarcely any alteration of the wording and by leaving the textual unity undisturbed'.[19] R's hand can be seen in the introductions and conclusions which he constructed in 11: 27–32 and 21: 1–7 for chapters 12–25 and in 25: 19–28 and 35: 1–23 for chapters 25–36. These texts 'impress on the whole a unifying stamp' (p. 698). That R could weave the J(E) and P

---

[17] C. Westermann, *Genesis 1–11*, BKAT (Neukirchen-Vluyn 1966–), 797; Eng. trans., *Genesis 1–11: A Commentary* (London 1984), 600.

[18] Ibid. 798; Eng. trans., 600.

[19] C. Westermann, *Genesis 12–50*, BKAT (Neukirchen-Vluyn 1977–), 698; Eng. trans., *Genesis 12–36: A Commentary* (London 1986), 593.

texts together in such a way as to leave them intact was 'because J consisted mainly of narratives and P mainly of genealogies' (ibid.).

Westermann's exegesis of Genesis 1–11 is more persuasive in its assessment of the contribution of R than what he offers in his study of chapters 12–36. Whilst it is true that P's genealogies lend themselves readily to combination with the older JE narrative, there remain P passages of a different nature and content whose relationship with the older material is more problematic. The 'unifying stamp' which he believes R's introductions and conclusions impress upon the whole does not account for these passages which prima facie stand in some tension with the older material. How is the account of the covenant between God and Abraham in Genesis 17 to be understood alongside the older narrative in Genesis 15 with which it differs in a number of significant ways? Or how, for example, did R intend us to understand P's account of the reason for Jacob's journey to Mesopotamia in Genesis 27: 46–28: 9 which he included alongside the older JE account in chapter 27 with its very different reason for Jacob's flight? Similarly, P's account of the revelation of God to Jacob at Bethel (Gen. 35: 9 ff.) differs in significant ways from the older account of this in chapter 28. What might R have intended by including the former alongside the latter? What does it mean to say in the case of these parallel narratives that each is left to 'speak for itself'? How are they to be reconciled with the statement that R has impressed on his combination of the sources a 'unifying stamp'? Such issues are not satisfactorily considered by Westermann.

V

I turn to the well-known contribution of Professor Brevard Childs of Yale Divinity School whose *Introduction to the Old Testament as Scripture* more than any other single work has enhanced the place of 'final form' interpretation on the agenda of current biblical study.[20] His interest in the final form of the text of the Old Testament arises from his concern to understand how the Pentateuch for example was shaped within the community of faith and of how it functioned for that community, that is, as he terms it, 'the canonical form and function' of the Pentateuch. He writes of how the victory of the historical

[20] B. S. Childs, *Introduction to the Old Testament as Scripture* (London 1979).

critical method has meant that every *Introduction* to the Pentateuch now identifies its task as one of reconstructing the historical development through its various complex stages, and whilst not denying that 'such a historical enterprise is legitimate and at times illuminating', contends that 'the study of the history of Hebrew literature in the context of the ancient Near East is a different enterprise from studying the form and function of the Pentateuch in the shape accorded it by the community of faith as its canonical scriptures' (p. 128). On the grounds that the 'present shape of the Pentateuch offers a particular interpretation of how the tradition is to be understood', he argues that 'the critical task at hand is both to describe the actual characteristics of the canonical shape and to determine the theological significance of that shape' (p. 128).

Childs argues (pp. 128 ff.) that there is internal editorial evidence that the five books of the Pentateuch—the 'five-fifths of the Law' of later Jewish tradition—were seen together as a 'canonical unit'.[21] First of all, it is clear, he suggests, that the five books were seen as separate entities by the final redactor in spite of the obvious continuity of the one story which extended from the creation of the world in Genesis 1 to the death of Moses in Deuteronomy 34. For example, the book of Genesis is structured by means of a repeated genealogical formula which ties the various parts of the book into a unity, and the book closes with the death of the last patriarch. Exodus begins with the nation in Egypt and Exodus 1: 1–5 recapitulates material from Genesis (Gen. 46: 8 ff.) in order to form an introduction to the new book. Similarly, the final chapter of Exodus concludes with the building of the Tabernacle and summarizes the role in the future wanderings of the people. The book of Leviticus continues the same historical setting of Moses' receiving the law at Sinai, but the different approach to the material serves to set the book off from Exodus. Childs quotes with approval J. Milgrom's observation: 'It [Leviticus] is thematically an independent entity. In Exodus, the P code describes the construction of the cultic implements . . . , whereas Leviticus converts this static picture into scenes from the living cult.'[22] Leviticus closes with a clear summary, marking it off from Numbers. In distinction from Leviticus, Numbers 'focuses on the laws of the camp when on the march, thus the military order of the tribes, the census

---

[21] Childs draws support for this from James A. Sanders, *Torah and Canon* (Philadelphia 1972).

[22] J. Milgrom, 'Leviticus', *IDB Supplement* (Nashville, Tenn. 1976), 541.

of the fighting force, and the laws related to the Levites, which are found only in Numbers'.[23] Further, the book begins with a precise date formula which indicates a new section of material and concludes with a summary. Deuteronomy represents a sharp break from what precedes, having both an introduction and conclusion which establishes it as an independent work although it shares the setting on the plains of Moab with the latter part of Numbers.

Beyond such a formal relationship of the five parts of the Pentateuch, however, Childs argues that 'the content of the five books gives additional evidence of an intentional structuring of these books into a purposeful whole' (pp. 130 f.). Thus, it is obvious that the three middle books share the same basic content, which has to do with the giving and receiving of the divine law by Moses at Sinai. In addition, the events at Sinai are preceded and succeeded by the account of the wilderness wanderings which led the people from Egypt to Sinai, and from Sinai to the edge of the promised land.

He acknowledges that it is more difficult to determine the place of the first and fifth books. Genesis differs markedly in style and content from the three middle books; for example, it recounts the history of a family and does not yet speak of the nation of Israel. 'Yet it is also evident', he comments, 'that the patriarchal material has not just been accidentally attached to the story which follows, but is integrally connected. Indeed, the patriarchal stories have been consistently edited in such a way as to point to the future. In spite of a complex development within the tradition of the promise to the patriarchs . . . the continuing thread which ties together the material is the promise of a posterity and a land. Clearly Genesis was conceived of by the final redactor as the introduction to the story of Israel which begins in Exodus' (p. 130).

Finally, Childs argues that whatever its original role was in the development of Israel's law, 'the final editor of the Pentateuch understood Deuteronomy's role as providing a type of commentary to the preceding law. Moreover, the book was given a setting consciously different from the original declaration of the law at Sinai. Some forty years later, to a new generation, Moses interprets the meaning and purpose of the law of Sinai which he had once received in terms of a covenant. Deuteronomy emphasizes the unique role of Moses as mediator and interpreter of the divine will. It is, therefore, fully in

---

[23] Childs, *Introduction to the Old Testament as Scripture*, 129.

order when Deuteronomy closes the Pentateuch with an account of the death of Moses' (pp. 130 f.). From all this Childs concludes (pp. 131 f.):

For the biblical editors the first five books constituted the grounds of Israel's life under God and provided a critical norm of how the Mosaic tradition was to be understood by the covenant people. The fundamental theological understanding of God's redemptive work through law and grace, promise and fulfilment, election and obedience was once and for all established. The story which continued in the book of Joshua was thus qualitatively distinguished from the Pentateuch by the shape given by the canon.

Childs thus seeks to avoid the arbitrary criterion on which both Clines and Whybray delineate the Pentateuch as 'a book in itself'. In addition, however, he eschews their 'theme approach' and instead examines each of the five books to ascertain its place in, and contribution to, the whole.

In considering Genesis he stresses what has frequently been ignored in the exegesis not only of this book but of the remaining books of the Pentateuch and of the Pentateuch as a whole (p. 148):

Above all, it is essential to recognize that the present shape of the book of Genesis is not simply a juxtaposition of independent literary strands which previously had had nothing to do with one another. Rather, the development of the book underwent a complex process of growth and change in which different literary traditions mutually influenced each other in a dynamic interaction within the community of faith. Thus it seems increasingly evident from the close parallelism of sequence that the editors of the Priestly writings were aware of the earlier epic traditions and did not develop their composition in complete isolation as often suggested.

Further, in considering the final redaction of the text, which has woven together the originally discrete sources, it is equally important to investigate the different role assigned to a passage from that which it originally performed.

There is space here for only one example of what Childs has in mind in making this suggestion. Writing of the function of the Joseph narrative in Genesis 37–50, he recognizes the lively contributions to the study of this story from Gunkel onwards, especially von Rad's famous essay in 1953.[24] He then comments: 'However, through the

---

[24] Von Rad, 'Josephsgeschichte und ältere Chokma', SVT 1 (1953), 120–7, repr. in *Gesammelte Studien zum Alten Testament* (Munich 1958), 272–80; Eng. trans., 'The Joseph Narrative and Ancient Wisdom', *The Problem of the Hexateuch and Other Essays* (Edinburgh 1965), 292–300.

whole debate there was little or no attention given to the canonical questions. What is the shape of the final chapters and what is their function within the book of Genesis?' (p. 156). His suggestion is as follows. In Genesis Joseph, the central figure of the narrative in Genesis 37–50, is clearly set apart from the earlier patriarchs, that is, the triad to whom the promises of land and posterity had been directly given. Rather, Joseph becomes the first (Gen. 50: 24) to whom the promise to Abraham, Isaac, and Jacob is reiterated. Since Joseph is not the bearer of the promise in the same way as his forefathers, what then is his role in Genesis? Childs finds one of the keys to an understanding of this in the place assigned to Judah (Gen. 38) and in the inclusion of Jacob's final blessing of his sons in Genesis 49. According to Childs, these, together with the *toledoth* formula in 37: 2 indicate that the redactor intends these closing chapters to deal with the whole family of Jacob. He suggests that the 'blessings of Jacob' also reveal an important perspective of the tradition, namely, that it is from the line of Judah, not Joseph, that Israel's redemption is to come, and he concludes (p. 157):

The point of this last section [of Genesis] seems to lie somewhere in the contrast between the stories of these two sons in relation to the promise. Joseph became the means of preserving the family in a foreign country (50.20), but also the means by which a new threat to the promise of the land was realized. Conversely, Judah demonstrated an unfaithfulness which threatened to destroy the promise of a posterity, which was only restored by the faithfulness of a Canaanite wife. In sum, the final section of the book of Genesis turns on the issue of the threat to the promise which leads inevitably to the book of Exodus.

In the space permitted in an *Introduction* Childs can give only a sketch of the kind of exegesis a proper concern for the final form of the text calls for.[25] The main reservation I have concerns his claim as to the role of the final form of the text in relation to its prehistory. Before commenting to this, however, I draw attention again to Blum's work.

VI

Blum in his two substantial volumes offers a comprehensive analysis of the purpose and effect of the inclusion of P in the older

[25] See also his commentary on *Exodus* (London 1974).

Pentateuchal literature and thus an understanding of the purpose of the redactors who gave us the Pentateuch substantially in its present form. Stated briefly, what the Priestly redactors of the Pentateuch sought to create was a new 'constitution' for the Israel of their time, a law governing the Jewish nation within the context of the Persian empire. The depiction of Israel as the 'congregation' of Yahweh involved the inclusion of the mass of cultic and ritual regulations that so characterize the Priestly material and give the Pentateuch its distinctive nature and form, superimposing upon it P's understanding of Israel. These redactors also modified, supplemented, and in places added material intended to correct or counter features in the traditional source material they inherited.

For example,[26] according to Blum the Priestly passage in Genesis 27: 46–28: 9 narrating the reason for Jacob's departure for Mesopotamia implicitly corrects that given in the older story in Genesis 27, though the latter remains incongruously in the text. Similarly, the Priestly story of the appearance of God to Jacob at Bethel in Genesis 35: 9 ff., he suggests, was intended to correct the older narrative in Genesis 28 which contains a number of unacceptable elements of cultic tradition. In Genesis 17, he argues, the Priestly writer has adopted elements of the J account of God's covenant with Abraham which he has reshaped and supplemented into an account which stands in tension with the older narrative, and in important respects has a different message for its time. As we saw earlier, he suggests that a further example is provided by the Priestly account of the revelation of the divine name to Moses in Exodus 6: 3 which, he argues, acts as a 'binding interpretation' of the older narrative in Genesis according to which the name Yahweh was already known to the patriarchs. To such examples one may add, for example, the way in which the Priestly account of creation complements the older J account with the result that, as various commentators have suggested, both together form a new unity.

Blum's expansive study must command the attention of any future endeavour to understand the intention and achievement of the redactor(s) who gave us the Pentateuch in its final form. His suggestions concerning key passages will require further examination, and the decision as to whether there was an originally discrete Priestly narrative will have a bearing on this, at least in places. For example, his

---

[26] For this and other P passages in Genesis, see Blum's discussion in *Die Komposition der Vätergeschichte*, 420–58.

argument that Genesis 17 was directed at 'correcting' Genesis 15 depends largely upon the contrast between Abraham's trusting response in the latter and his reaction to God's promise as recorded in the former where he laughs at the promise of a son to the elderly Sarah. But the substance of the narrative in Genesis 17 is different from Genesis 15, the latter concerned with the promise of land whilst Genesis 17 centres on the promise of the patriarch's progeny and its future including Ishmael, a topic that is far removed from the promise of land to Abraham's Israelite descendants in Genesis 15. Does Genesis 17 not provide a further example of a Priestly narrative that has been inserted to supplement rather than correct the older narrative? On the other hand the flood story provides an example where the Priestly redactors sought to impose elements of their own distinctively different account of it upon the older narrative, though in this case the result is scarcely a 'new unity' but a somewhat confusing conflation of originally separate stories.

Not least among the merits of Blum's work is that it avoids a pitfall that can beset 'final form' reading of the Pentateuch, that is, harmonization. His results fully allow for the incongruities and unevennesses that characterize the Pentateuch and which, indeed, are the evidence of its composite nature and also of its theological variety. In the same way it also allows for the polyvalent nature of the contents of the Pentateuch and thus avoids the risk of the sort of 'theme' approach favoured by Clines which can create the impression of a coherence of the contents which is in the face of the evidence.

This leads me to a final observation concerning 'final form' reading of the Pentateuch. If at long last in modern Pentateuchal scholarship the final form of the Pentateuch is being given the significance it is manifestly due, it is important not to neglect the insights of earlier research into the diverse stages of the growth of this complex corpus of literature. And here I question one of the central claims made by Childs concerning the role of the final form of the text, that is, what he describes as the 'canonical shape' of the Pentateuch. He quotes von Rad's well-known statement concerning the long process that went into the making of the Hexateuch: 'For no stage in this work's long period of growth is really obsolete; something of each phase has been conserved and passed on as enduring until the Hexateuch attained its final form.'[27] He acknowledges that von Rad

[27] Von Rad, *Das erste Buch Moses, Genesis*, 18; Eng. trans., 27.

was correct in suggesting that the final form of Genesis reflects the layering of tradition in which there has been no attempt to flatten out the diverse material into a monolithic whole. He then comments (p. 157):

> However, von Rad's traditio-historical approach, as a legacy of Gunkel, has failed to reckon seriously with the full implications of the canonical progress on the traditioning process. Above all, the final form of Genesis provides a hermeneutical guide by which to interpret this complex prehistory of the literature. It introduces a critical judgement in emphasizing certain features, subordinating others, and even suppressing some. *To speak of Genesis as scripture is to acknowledge the authority of this particular viewing of Israel's tradition which in its particular form provided a critical theological standard for future generations of Israel.*

Childs' so-called 'canonical' approach raises a series of issues which I cannot discuss here and which, in any event, have been thoroughly considered by James Barr.[28] The words which I have italicized in the quotation above can rightly be regarded as an expression of what Barr has described as 'the strong zealotic legalism'[29] that regards all stages prior to the final text as irrelevant and insists, as Childs does, that the 'particular view of Israel's tradition' which the final form of the text provides is solely relevant for the theological exegete. Thus, if it has been the case that scholarship in the past has been at times preoccupied with the 'original' and the earlier at the expense of the final form of the text, the approach adopted by Childs now seeks to render absolute the latter and to deny the earlier any relevance. If the quest for 'the original' or the earlier is now regarded rightly as inadequate, however, the absoluteness now being accorded the final form reading of the text must also be rejected, for there is no reason, as Barr argues, to suppose that the product of final redaction is in any way more valid or more proper than earlier stages in the emergence of the text. Thus it is perfectly valid and proper for an exegete to seek to understand Genesis 1 apart from Genesis 2 and vice versa, and wrong to impose a stricture which requires that exegesis proper must consider either of these chapters only alongside the other. Similarly, whilst one might accept Childs' suggestions

---

[28] For a full discussion see James Barr, *Holy Scripture: Canon, Authority, Criticism* (Philadelphia 1983). See esp. ch. 4, 'Further Adventures of the Canon: "Canon" as the Final Shape of the Text'. See also the discussion of Childs's work in J. Barton, *Reading the Old Testament: Method in Biblical Study* (London 1984), chs. 6 and 7.

[29] Barr, *Holy Scripture: Canon, Authority, Criticism*, 92.

concerning the function of the Joseph narrative, including the secondary additions to it, within the context of the final form of the
book of Genesis, much is also to be gained from reading the Joseph
narrative as an originally discrete story with its own meaning within
the community of faith to which its author belonged. Originally discrete stories such as Genesis 1 and 2 and the Joseph story may thus
be described as instances of 'disclosure', so to speak, within the life
of the community of faith at different times in its history, unless we
are to believe that the only community of faith that was relevant was
that to which the final redactor belonged and in engagement with
which he carried out his work of redaction.

To concentrate upon the final stage is to foreshorten what was a
long process of reflection, debate, and not infrequently controversy in
the history of the community of faith. The text of the Pentateuch
offers the testimony of many voices at differing stages in the history
of the community of faith that was Israel. In this matter, therefore, I
remain on the side of von Rad whose oft-quoted comment cited by
Childs remains as valid today as it was nearly sixty years ago, and the
truth of which we will neglect to our great loss as students of the
Pentateuch:

The Hexateuch in its present form arose by means of redactors who heard the
peculiar testimony of faith of each document and considered it binding.
There is no doubt that the present Hexateuch in its final form makes great
demands on the understanding of every reader. Many ages, many men, many
traditions and theologies, have constructed this massive work. Only the one
who does not look superficially at the Hexateuch but reads it with a knowledge of its deep dimension will arrive at true understanding. Such a one will
know that revelations and religious experiences of many ages are speaking
from it. *For no stage in this work's long period of growth is really obsolete;
something of each phase has been conserved and passed on as enduring until the
Hexateuch attained its final form.*[30]

[30] Von Rad, *Das erste Buch Moses, Genesis*, 19 f.; Eng. trans., 27.

BIBLIOGRAPHY

ALBREKTSON, B., *History and the Gods: An Essay on the Idea of Historical Events as Divine Manifestations in the Ancient Near East and in Israel*, Coniectanea Biblica, Old Testament Series 1 (Lund 1967).

ALT, A., *Die Landnahme der Israeliten in Palästina* (Leipzig 1925), repr. in his *Kleine Schriften zur Geschichte des Volkes Israel*, I (Munich 1953), 89–125; Eng. trans., 'The Settlement of the Israelites in Palestine', in his *Essays in Old Testament History and Religion* (Oxford 1966), 133–69.

—— *Der Gott der Väter*, BWANT 3/12 (Stuttgart 1929), repr. in his *Kleine Schriften*, i. 1–78; Eng. trans., 'The God of the Fathers', *Essays in Old Testament History and Religion*, 1–66.

—— *Die Ursprünge des Israelitischen Rechts* (Leipzig 1934), repr. in his *Kleine Schriften*, i. 278–332; Eng. trans., 'The Origins of Israelite Law', *Essays in Old Testament History and Religion*, 79–132.

AULD, A. G., *Joshua, Moses and the Land: Tetrateuch–Pentateuch–Hexateuch in a Generation since 1938* (Edinburgh 1980).

BARR, J., 'Story and History in Biblical Theology', in his *The Scope and Authority of the Bible*, Explorations in Theology, 7 (London 1980), 1–17, originally published in *JR* 56 (1976), 1–17.

—— 'Historical Reading and the Theological Interpretation of Scripture', in his *The Scope and Authority of the Bible*, Explorations in Theology, 7 (London 1980), 30–51.

—— *Holy Scripture: Canon, Authority, Criticism* (Philadelphia 1983).

BARTON, J., *Reading the Old Testament: Method in Biblical Study* (London 1984).

—— 'Wellhausen's *Prolegomena to the History of Israel*: Influences and Effects', in Daniel Smith-Christopher (ed.), *Text and Experience: Towards a Cultural Exegesis of the Bible* (Sheffield 1995), 316–29.

BEGG, C., 'The Destruction of the Calf (Exod. 32, 20/Dt 9, 21)', in N. Lohfink (ed.), *Das Deuteronomium. Entstehung, Gestalt und Botschaft* (Leuven 1985), 208–51.

BENZINGER, I., *Jahwist und Elohist in den Königsbüchern*, BZAW 27 (Giessen 1921).

BERGE, K., *Die Zeit des Jahwisten: Ein Beitrag zur Datierung jahwistischer Vätertexte*, BZAW 186 (Berlin 1990).

BLENKINSOPP, J., *The Pentateuch: An Introduction to the First Five Books of the Bible* (London 1992).

BLUM, E., *Die Komposition der Vätergeschichte*, WMANT 57 (Neukirchen 1984).

—— 'Israël à la montagne de Dieu: Remarques sur Ex 19–24; 32–34 et sur le contexte littéraire et historique de sa composition', in A. de Pury (ed.), *Le Pentateuque en Question: Les origines et la composition des cinq premiers livres de la Bible à la lumière des recherches récentes* (Geneva 1989), 271–95.

—— *Studien zur Komposition des Pentateuch*, BZAW 189 (Berlin 1990).

BOORER, S., *The Promise of the Land as Oath: A Key to the Formation of the Pentateuch*, BZAW 205 (Berlin 1992).

BREKELMANS, C. H. W., 'Het "historische Credo" van Israël', *TvT* 3 (1963), 1–11.

—— 'Die sogenannten deuteronomischen Elemente in Genesis bis Numeri: Ein Beitrag zur Vorgeschichte des Deuteronomiums', SVT 15 (1966), 90–6.

—— 'Éléments Deutéronomiques dans le Pentateuque', *Recherches Bibliques*, 8 (Bruges 1967), 77–91.

BRUSTON, C., 'Les Quatre Sources des lois de l'Exode', *Revue de Théologie de Lausanne* (1883).

—— 'Les deux Jehovistes: Études sur les sources de l'histoire sainte', *Revue de Théologie de Lausanne* (1885).

—— 'Les cinq documents de la loi mosaïque', *ZAW* 12 (1892), 177–211.

BUDDE, K., *Die biblische Urgeschichte, Genesis 1–12.5 untersucht* (Giessen 1883).

—— *Die Bücher Richter und Samuel. Ihre Quellen und ihr Aufbau* (Giessen 1890).

CARPENTER, J. E., and HARFORD, G., *The Composition of the Hexateuch* (London 1902).

CHILDS, B. S., *Exodus* (London 1974).

—— *Introduction to the Old Testament as Scripture* (London 1979).

CLEMENTS, R. E., *Abraham and David* (London 1967).

—— Review of R. Rendtorff, *Das überlieferungsgeschichtliche Problem des Pentateuch*, *JSOT* 3 (1977), 43–5.

—— 'Pentateuchal Problems', in G. W. Anderson (ed.), *Tradition and Interpretation: Essays by Members of the Society for Old Testament Study* (Oxford 1979), 96–124.

CLINES, D. J. A., *The Theme of the Pentateuch*, JSOT Supplement Series, 10 (Sheffield 1978).

COATS, G. W., 'The Traditio-Historical Character of the Red Sea Motif', *VT* 17 (1967), 253–65.

—— 'The Yahwist as Theologian? A Critical Reflection', *JSOT* 3 (1977), 28–32.

COLENSO, J. W., *The Pentateuch and Book of Joshua Critically Examined*, 7 vols. (London 1862–79).

CORNILL, C. H., 'Ein Elohistischer Bericht über die Entstehung des israelitis-

chen Königtums in I Samuelis i–xv aufgezeigt', *Zeitschrift für kirkliche Wissenschaft und kirkliches Leben*, 6 (1885), 113 ff.
—— 'Zur Quellenkritik der Bücher Samuelis', *Königsberger Studien* I (1887), 23–59.
—— 'Noch einmal Sauls Königswahl und Verwerfung', *ZAW* 10 (1890), 96–109.
—— *Einleitung in das Alte Testament* (Tübingen 1891).
COOTE, R. B., *In Defense of Revolution: The Elohist History* (Minneapolis 1991).
—— and ORD, D. R., *The Bible's First Historian: From Eden to the Court of David with the Yahwist* (Philadelphia 1989).
CROSS, F. M., *Canaanite Myth and Hebrew Epic* (Cambridge, Mass. 1973).
CRÜSEMANN, F., 'Die Eigenständigkeit der Urgeschichte. Ein Beitrag zur Diskussion um den "Jahwisten"', in J. Jeremias and L. Perlitt (eds.), *Die Botschaft und die Boten. Festschrift für H.-W. Wolff* (Neukirchen-Vluyn 1981), 11–29.
CULLEY, R. C., *Studies in the Structure of Hebrew Narrative* (Missoula, Mont. 1976).
DAHSE, J., *Textkritische Materialen zur Hexateuchfrage*, i (Giessen 1912).
DAVIES, G. I., Review of A. G. Auld, *Joshua, Moses and the Land: Tetrateuch–Pentateuch–Hexateuch in a Generation since 1938*, in *JTS* NS 33 (1982), 209–13.
—— 'The Composition of the Book of Exodus: Reflections on the Theses of Erhard Blum', in M. Fox (ed.), *Texts, Temples and Tradition: A Tribute to Menahem Haran* (Winona Lake, Minn. 1996), 71–85.
DE VRIES, S. J., 'A Review of Recent Research in the Tradition History of the Pentateuch', in SBL Seminar Papers (1987), 459–502.
DEWETTE, W. M. L., *Dissertatio Critico-Exegetica qua Deuteronomium a prioribus Pentateuchi libris diversum alius cuiusdam recentioris auctoris opus esse monstratur* (Jena 1805).
—— *Beiträge zur Einleitung in das Alte Testament*, 2 vols. (Halle 1806–7).
DILLMANN, A., *Die Bücher Numeri, Deuteronomium und Josua* (2nd edn., Leipzig 1886).
DIRKSEN, P. B. and VAN DER KOOIJ, A. (eds.), *Abraham Kuenen (1828–1891): His Major Contributions to the Study of the Old Testament*, OTS 29 (1993).
DRIVER, S. R., *Deuteronomy*, ICC (Edinburgh 1895).
—— *Exodus*, Cambridge Bible for Schools and Colleges (Cambridge 1911).
—— *An Introduction to the Literature of the Old Testament* (9th edn., Edinburgh 1913).
EERDMANS, B. D., *Alttestamentliche Studien*, i. *Die Komposition der Genesis* (Giessen 1908).
EICHRODT, W., *Die Quellen der Genesis von neuem untersucht*, BZAW 31 (Giessen 1916).

EISSFELDT, O., *Hexateuch-Synopse* (Leipzig 1922).
—— *Die Quellen des Richterbuches* (Leipzig 1925).
—— *Die Komposition der Samuelbücher* (Leipzig 1931).
EMERTON, J. A., 'The Origin of the Promises to the Patriarchs in the Older Sources of the Book of Genesis', *VT* 32 (1982), 14–32.
—— 'An Examination of Some Attempts to Defend the Unity of the Flood Narrative in Genesis', pt. 1, *VT* 37 (1987), 401–20, and pt. 2, *VT* 38 (1988), 1–21.
—— 'The Priestly Writer in Genesis', *JTS* NS 39 (1988), 381–400.
—— 'Some Problems in Genesis XIV', SVT 41 (1990), 73–102.
ENGNELL, I., *Gamla Testamentet. En traditionshistorisk inledning*, i (Stockholm 1945).
—— 'Moseböckerna', *Svensk Bibliskt Uppslagsverk*, ii (2nd edn., Stockholm 1962), cols. 152–65; Eng. trans., 'The Pentateuch', *Critical Essays on the Old Testament* (London 1970), 50–67.
EWALD, H., Review of J. Stähelin, *Kritische Untersuchungen über die Genesis* (Basel 1830), in *ThStKr* 4 (1831), 595–606.
FOHRER, G., *Überlieferung und Geschichte des Exodus*, BZAW 91 (Berlin 1964).
FRIEDMAN, R. E., *The Exile and Biblical Narrative* (Chico, Calif. 1981).
—— 'The Recession of Biblical Source Criticism', in R. E. Friedman and H. G. M. Williamson (eds.), *The Future of Biblical Studies*, The Society of Biblical Literature Semeia Studies (Atlanta 1987), 81–101.
FRITZ, V., 'Das Geschichtsverständnis der Priesterschrift', *ZThK* 84 (1987), 426–39.
GEDDES, A., *The Holy Bible or the Books accounted Sacred by Christians and Jews: Otherwise called the Books of the Old and New Covenants: Faithfully translated from corrected texts of the originals with Various Readings, Explanatory Notes and Critical Remarks*, i (London 1792).
GEORGE, J. F. L., *Die älteren Jüdischen Feste mit einer Kritik der Gesetzgebung des Pentateuch* (Berlin 1835).
GOULD, J., *Herodotus* (London 1989).
—— 'Herodotus and Religion', in S. Hornblower (ed.), *Greek Historiography* (Oxford 1994), 91–106.
GRAF, K. H., *Die geschichtlichen Bücher des Alten Testaments* (Leipzig 1866).
—— 'Die sogenannte Grundschrift des Pentateuchs', in A. Merx (ed.), *Archiv für wissenschaftliche Erforschung des Alten Testaments* (Halle 1869), 466–77.
GRAY, G. B., *A Critical and Exegetical Commentary on Numbers*, ICC (Edinburgh 1903).
GREENBERG, M., 'The Thematic Unity of Exodus III–XI', *World Congress of Jewish Studies*, i (Jerusalem 1967), 151–4.
GRESSMANN, H., *Mose und seine Zeit. Ein Kommentar zu den Mose-Sagen*, FRLANT 18 (Göttingen 1913).

—— *Albert Eichhorn und die Religionsgeschichtliche Schule* (Göttingen 1924).

GRUPPE, O., 'War Genesis 6, 1–4 ursprünglich mit der sintflut verbunden?', *ZAW* 9 (1889), 135–55.

GUNKEL, H., *Schöpfung und Chaos in Urzeit und Endzeit. Eine religions-geschichtliche Untersuchung über Gen 1 und Ap Joh 12* (Göttingen 1895).

—— *Genesis, übersetzt und erklärt*, HKAT (Göttingen 1901).

—— *The Legends of Genesis*, trans. by W. H. Carruth of the 'Introduction' to *Genesis, übersetzt und erklärt* (first pub. 1901; repr., New York 1964).

—— 'Die Grundprobleme der israelitischen Literaturgeschichte', *Deutsche Literaturzeitung*, xviii (1906), 1797–1800, 1861–6, repr. in *Reden und Aufsätze*, 29–38; Eng. trans., 'Fundamental Problems of Hebrew Literary History', in his *What Remains of the Old Testament*, 57–68.

—— *Reden und Aufsätze* (Göttingen 1913).

—— *Das Märchen im Alten Testament* (Tübingen 1913); Eng. trans., *The Folktale in the Old Testament* (Sheffield 1991).

—— *What Remains of the Old Testament* (London 1928).

—— 'Literaturgeschichte', *RGG* 3 (2nd edn., Tübingen 1929), cols. 1677–80.

—— 'Sagen und Legenden, ii. In Israel', *RGG* 5 (Tübingen 1931), cols. 49–60.

GUNNEWEG, A. H. J., 'Anmerkungen und Anfragen zur neueren Pentateuch-forschung', *ThR* 48 (1983), 227–53.

—— 'Anmerkungen und Anfragen zur neueren Pentateuchforschung (2)', *ThR* 50 (1985), 107–31.

HARAN, M., *Temples and Temple Service in Ancient Israel* (Oxford 1978).

—— 'The Law-Code of Ezekiel XL–XLVIII and its Relation to the Priestly School', *HUCA* 50 (1979), 45–71.

—— 'Behind the Scenes of History: Determining the Date of the Priestly Source', *JBL* 100/3 (1981), 321–33.

HOFTIJZER, J., *Die Verheissung an die drei Erzväter* (Leiden 1956).

HÖLSCHER, G., 'Komposition und Ursprung des Deuteronomiums', *ZAW* 40 (1922), 161–255.

—— 'Das Buch der Könige, seine Quellen und seine Redaktion', in *Eucharisterion für Gunkel*, I, FRLANT 18 (Göttingen 1923), 158–213.

—— *Die Anfänge der hebräischen Geschichtsschreibung* (Heidelberg 1942).

—— *Geschichtsschreibung in Israel* (Lund 1952).

HOLZINGER, H., *Einleitung in den Hexateuch* (Freiburg 1893).

HORNBLOWER, S., *Thucydides* (London 1987).

HOUTMAN, C., *Inleiding in de Pentateuch* (Kampen 1980); 2nd edn., *Der Pentateuch: Die Geschichte seiner Erforschung neben einer Auswertung* (Kampen 1994).

HUGHES, J., *Secrets of the Times: Myth and History in Biblical Chronology*, *JSOT* Supplement Series, 66 (Sheffield 1990).

HUPFELD, H., *Die Quellen der Genesis und die art ihrer Zusammensetzung* (Berlin 1853).

HURVITZ, A., 'The Evidence of Language in Dating the Priestly Code: A Linguistic Study in Technical Idioms and Terminology', *RB* 81 (1974), 24–56.

—— *A Linguistic Study of the Relationship between the Priestly Source and the Book of Ezekiel: A New Approach to an Old Problem*, Cahiers de La Revue Biblique, 20 (Paris 1982).

HYATT, J. P., 'Were There an Ancient Historical Credo in Israel and an Independent Sinai Tradition?', in H. Thomas Frank and W. L. Reed (eds.), *Translating and Understanding the Old Testament: Essays in Honour of H. G. May* (New York–Nashville 1970), 152–70.

ILGEN, K. D., *Die Urkunden des Jerusalemischen Tempelarchivs in ihrer Urgestalt als Beytrag zur Berichtigung der Geschichte der Religion und Politik*, pt. 1. *Die Urkunden des ersten Buches von Mose* (Halle 1798).

JENKS, A. W., *The Elohist and North Israelite Traditions*, Society of Biblical Literature Monograph Series, 22 (Missoula, Mont. 1977).

JOHNSTONE, W., 'Reactivating the Chronicles Analogy in Pentateuchal Studies, with Special Reference to the Sinai Pericope in Exodus', *ZAW* 99 (1987), 16–37.

—— *Exodus*, Old Testament Guides (Sheffield 1990).

KAISER, O., 'Traditionsgeschichtliche Untersuchung von Genesis 15', *ZAW* 70 (1958), 107–26.

KAUFMANN, Y., *The Religion of Israel from its Beginnings to the Babylonian Exile* (in Hebrew), i–viii (Jerusalem 1937–56); abr. and Eng. trans. under same title by Moshe Greenberg (London 1960).

KENNETT, R. H., 'The Date of Deuteronomy', *JTS* 7 (1905), 161–86.

—— *Deuteronomy and the Decalogue* (Cambridge 1920).

KESSLER, R., *Die Querverweise im Pentateuch. Überlieferungsgeschichtliche Untersuchung der expliziten Querverbindungen innerhalb des vorpriester-lichen Pentateuchs* (unpub. diss., Heidelberg 1972).

KIRKPATRICK, P. G., *The Old Testament and Folklore Study*, JSOT Supplement Series, 62 (Sheffield 1988).

KITTEL, R., 'Die pentateuchischen Urkunden in den Büchern Richter und Samuel', *ThStKr* 65 (1892), 44–71.

—— *Die Heilige Schrift des Alten Testaments*, 4th edn., ed. A. Bertholet (Tübingen 1922).

KLATT, W., *Hermann Gunkel. Zu seiner Theologie der Religionsgeschichte und zur Entstehung der formgeschichtlichen Methode*, FRLANT 100 (Göttingen 1969).

KLEIN, H., 'Ort und Zeit des Elohisten', *EvTh* 37 (1977), 247–60.

KLOSTERMANN, A., 'Beiträge zur Entstehungsgeschichte des Pentateuchs', *Zeitschrift für die gesamte Lutherische Theologie und Kirche*, 38 (1877), 401–45.

—— *Der Pentateuch* (Leipzig 1897; 2nd edn., Leipzig 1907).

KNIGHT, D., *Rediscovering the Traditions of Israel*, SBL Dissertation Series, 9 (Missoula, Mont. 1975).
—— 'The Pentateuch', in D. A. Knight and G. M. Tucker (eds.), *The Hebrew Bible and its Modern Interpreters* (Chico, Calif. 1985), 263–96.
KOCH, K., *Was ist Formgeschichte* (Neukirchen 1964, 2nd edn., 1974); Eng. trans., *The Growth of the Biblical Tradition. The Form-Critical Method* (London 1969).
—— 'P—Kein Redaktor! Erinnerung an zwei Eckdaten der Quellenscheidung', *VT* 37 (1987), 446–67.
KUENEN, A., *Historisch-kritisch Onderzoek*, i (2nd edn., Leiden 1885).
LANGLAMET, F., *Gilgal et les Récits de la Traversée du Jourdain*, Cahiers de la Revue Biblique, 11 (Paris 1969).
—— 'Josue, II, et les Traditions de l'Hexateuque', *RB* 78 (1971), 5–17, 161–83, 321–54.
—— 'La Traversée du Jourdain et les Documents de l'Hexateuque', *RB* 79 (1972), 7–38.
—— review of H. H. Schmid, *Der sogenannte Jahwist*, in *RB* 84 (1977), 622 f.
LEVIN, C., *Der Yahwist*, FRLANT 157 (Göttingen 1993).
LEWIS, D. M., 'Persians in Herodotus', in M. H. Jameson (ed.), *The Greek Historians: Literature and History* (Stanford 1985), 101–17.
—— 'The Persepolis Tablets: Speech, Seal and Script', in A. K. Bowman and G. Woolf (eds.), *Literacy and Power in the Ancient World* (Cambridge 1994), 17–27.
LOHFINK, N., *Das Hauptgebot. Eine Untersuchung literarischer Einleitungsfragen zu Dtn 5–11*, Analecta Biblica, 20 (Rome 1963).
—— 'Die Ursünden in der priesterlichen Geschichtserzählung', in G. Bornkamm and K. Rahner (eds.), *Die Zeit Jesu. Festschrift für Heinrich Schlier* (Freiburg 1970), 38–57; Eng. trans., 'Original Sins in the Priestly Historical Narrative', in his *Theology of the Pentateuch: Themes of the Priestly Narrative and Deuteronomy* (Edinburgh 1994), 96–115.
—— 'Zum "kleinen geschichtlichen Credo" Dtn. 26: 5–9', *ThPh* 46 (1971), 19–39.
—— 'Die Priesterschrift und die Geschichte', SVT 29 (Leiden 1978), 189–225; Eng. trans., 'The Priestly Narrative and History', in his *Theology of the Pentateuch*, 136–72.
—— Review of M. Rose, *Deuteronomist und Jahwist. Untersuchungen zu den Brührungspunkten beider Literaturwerke*, AThANT 67 (Zürich 1981), in *ThPh* 57 (1982), 276–80.
—— *Die Väter Israels in Deuteronomium, mit einer Stellungnahme von Thomas Römer*, OBO 111 (Freiburg 1991).
—— 'Deutéronome et Pentateuque: État de la Recherche', in Pierre Haudebert (ed.), *Le Pentateuque: Débats et Recherches,* Lectio Divina, 151 (Paris 1992), 35–64.

LOHFINK, N., 'Gab es eine deuteronomistische Bewegung?', in W. Gross (ed.), *Jeremiah und die 'deuteronomistische Bewegung'*, BBB 98 (1995), 313–82.

LÖHR, M., *Untersuchungen zum Hexateuchproblem*, i. *Der Priesterkodex in der Genesis*, BZAW 38 (Giessen 1924).

McEVENUE, S. E., *The Narrative Style of the Priestly Writer*, Analecta Biblica, 50 (Rome 1971).

—— 'A Return to Sources in Genesis 28: 10–22?', *ZAW* 106 (1994), 375–89.

McFADYEN, J. E., 'The Present Position of Old Testament Criticism', in A. S. Peake (ed.), *The People and the Book* (Oxford 1925), 183–219.

McKANE, W., Review of Rendtorff, *Das überlieferungsgeschichtliche Problem des Pentateuch*, in *VT* 28 (1978), 379 f.

—— *Studies in the Patriarchal Narratives* (Edinburgh 1979).

MAYBAUM, S., *Die Entwickelung des altisraelitischen Priesterthums* (Breslau 1880).

MAYES, A. D. H., *Israel in the Period of the Judges* (London 1974).

—— *Deuteronomy*, New Century Bible (London 1979).

—— 'Deuteronomy 4 and the Literary Criticism of Deuteronomy', *JBL* 100/1 (1981), 23–51.

—— *The Story of Israel between Settlement and Exile* (London 1983).

MEAD, C. M., 'Tatian's Diatessaron and the Analysis of the Pentateuch', *JBL* 10 (1891), 44–54.

MEIER, C., 'Historical Answers to Historical Questions: The Origins of History in Ancient Greece', *Arethusa* 20 (1987), 41–57.

MILGROM, J., 'Leviticus', *IDB Supplement* (Nashville, Tenn. 1976), 541–5.

MOBERLY, R. W. L., *The Old Testament of the Old Testament*, Overtures to Biblical Theology (Minneapolis 1992).

MOMIGLIANO, A., 'The Herodotean and the Thucydidean Tradition', *The Classical Foundations of Modern Historiography* (Berkeley 1990), 29–53.

MORGENSTERN, J., 'The Oldest Document of the Hexateuch', HUCA 4 (1927), 1–138.

MOWINCKEL, S., *Der Thronbesteigungsfest Jahwäs und der Ursprung der Eschatologie* (Kristiana 1922).

—— *Le Décalogue* (Paris 1927).

—— 'Der Ursprung der Bil'āmsage', *ZAW* 48 (1930), 233–71.

—— *Tetrateuch–Pentateuch–Hexateuch. Die Bericht über die Landnahme in den drei altisraelitischen Geschichtswerken*, BZAW 90 (Berlin 1964).

—— *Erwägungen zur Pentateuch Quellenfrage* (Universitetsforlaget, Trondheim 1964).

NICHOLSON, E. W., *Deuteronomy and Tradition* (Oxford 1967).

—— *Preaching to the Exiles: A Study of the Prose Tradition in the Book of Jeremiah* (Oxford 1970).

—— *Exodus and Sinai in History and Tradition* (Oxford 1973).

—— 'The Antiquity of the Tradition in Exodus XXIV 9–11', *VT* 24 (1974), 77–97.

—— *God and His People: Covenant and Theology in the Old Testament* (Oxford 1986).

—— 'P as an Originally Independent Source in the Pentateuch', *IBS* 10 (1988), 192–206.

—— 'Story and History in the Old Testament', in S. E. Balentine and J. Barton (eds.), *Language, Theology, and the Bible: Essays in Honour of James Barr* (Oxford 1994), 135–50.

NORTH, C. R., 'Pentateuchal Criticism', in H. H. Rowley (ed.), *The Old Testament and Modern Study* (Oxford 1951), 48–83.

NOTH, M., *Das System der zwölf Stämme Israels*, BWANT 4/1 (Stuttgart 1930).

—— *Das Buch Josua*, HAT I/7 (Tübingen 1938).

—— *Überlieferungsgeschichtliche Studien* (Tübingen 1943); Eng. trans., *The Deuteronomistic History*, JSOT Supplement Series, 15 (Sheffield 1981).

—— 'Die "Priesterschrift" und die Redaktion des Pentateuch', in his *Überlieferungsgeschichtliche Studien* (Tübingen 1943), 180–216; Eng. trans., in *The Chronicler's History*, JSOT Supplement Series, 50 (Sheffield 1987), 107–47.

—— *Überlieferungsgeschichte des Pentateuch* (Stuttgart 1948); Eng. trans., *A History of Pentateuchal Traditions* (Englewood Cliffs, NJ 1972).

—— *Geschichte Israels* (Göttingen 1950); Eng. trans., *The History of Israel* (2nd edn., London 1958).

—— *Das zweite Buch Mose, Exodus, übersetz und erklärt*, ATD 5 (Göttingen 1959); Eng. trans., *Exodus* (London 1962).

—— *Das vierte Buch Mose, Numeri, übersetz und erklärt*, ATD 7 (Göttingen 1959); Eng. trans., *Numbers* (London 1968).

—— *Das dritte Buch Mose, Leviticus, übersetz und erklärt*, ATD 6 (Göttingen 1962); Eng. trans., *Leviticus* (London 1965).

NYBERG, H. S., *Studien zum Hoseabuche. Zugleich ein Beitrag zur Klärung des Problems der alttestamentlichen Textkritik* (Uppsala 1935).

OLRIK, A., 'Epische Gesetze der Volksdichtung', *Zeitschrift für Deutsches Altertum und Deutsche Literatur*, 51 (1909), 1–12. An English translation is provided in A. Dundes (ed.), *The Study of Folklore* (Englewood Cliffs, N.J. 1965), 129–41.

OESTREICHER, T., *Das Deuteronomische Grundgessetz* (Gütersloh 1923).

ORR, J., *The Problem of the Old Testament* (London 1906).

OSSWALD, E., *Das Bild des Mose in der kritischen alttestamentlichen Wissenschaft seit Julius Wellhausen*, Theologische Arbeiten, 18 (Berlin 1962).

PEDERSEN, J., 'Die Auffassung vom Alten Testament', *ZAW* 49 (1931), 161–81.

—— 'Passahfest und Passahlegende', *ZAW* 52 (1934), 165–75.

PERLITT, L., *Vatke und Wellhausen. Geschichtsphilosophische Voraussetzungen und historiographische Motive für die Darstellung der Religion und*

Geschichte Israels durch Wilhelm Vatke und Julius Wellhausen, BZAW 94 (Berlin 1965).

—— *Bundestheologie im Alten Testament*, WMANT 36 (Neukirchen 1969).

—— 'Deuteronomium 1–3 in Streit der Exegetischen Methoden', in N. Lohfink (ed.), *Das Deuteronomium. Entstehung, Gestalt und Botschaft* (Leuven 1985), 149–63.

PFEIFFER, R. H., 'A non-Israelite Source of the Book of Genesis', *ZAW* 48 (1930), 63–73.

—— *Introduction to the Old Testament* (New York 1948).

POLZIN, R., *Late Biblical Hebrew. Toward an Historical Typology of Biblical Prose* (Missoula, Mont. 1976).

PROCKSCH, O., *Das nordhebräische Sagenbuch. Die Elohimquelle* (Leipzig 1906).

DE PURY, A. (ed.), *Le Pentateuque en Question: Les origines et la composition des cinq premiers livres de la Bible à la lumière des recherches récentes* (Geneva 1989).

—— and RÖMER, T., 'Le Pentateuque en question: Position du problème et brève histoire de la recherche', in A. de Pury (ed.), *Le Pentateuque en question: Les origines et la composition des cinq premiers livres de la Bible à la lumière des recherches récentes* (Geneva 1989), 9–80.

RENDTORFF, R., 'Der "Yahwist" als Theologe. Zum Delemma der Pentateuchkritik', SVT 28 (1975), 158–66; Eng. trans., 'The "Yahwist" as Theologian? The Dilemma of Pentateuchal Criticism', *JSOT* 3 (1977), 2–10.

—— *Das überlieferungsgeschichtliche Problem des Pentateuch*, BZAW 147 (Berlin 1977); Eng. trans., *The Problem of the Process of Transmission in the Pentateuch*, *JSOT* Supplement Series, 89 (Sheffield 1990).

—— *Das Alte Testament: Eine Einfuhrung* (Neukirchen-Vluyn 1983); Eng. trans., *The Old Testament: An Introduction* (London 1986).

—— 'L'Histoire biblique des origines (Gen 1–11) dans le contexte de la rédaction "sacerdotale" du Pentateuque', in A. de Pury (ed.), *Le Pentateuque en question: Les origines et la composition des cinq premiers livres de la Bible à la lumière des recherches récentes* (Geneva 1989), 83–94.

RICHTER, W., 'Beobachtungen zur theologischen Systembildung in der alt. Literatur anhand des "kleinen geschichtlichen Credo"', in L. Scheffczyk (ed.), *Wahrheit und Verkündigung, Festschrift für M. Schmaus* (Paderhorn 1967), 191–5.

—— *Die sogenannten vorprophetischen Berufungsberichte: Eine literaturwissenschaftliche Studie zu 1 Sam 9, 1–10, 16; Ex. 3f. und Ri 6, 11b bis 17*, FRLANT 101 (Göttingen 1970).

ROBERTS, J. M., 'The Hand of Yahweh', *VT* 21 (1971), 244–51.

ROGERSON, J. R., *Old Testament Criticism in the Nineteenth Century* (London 1984).

—— *W. M. L. de Wette Founder of Modern Biblical Criticism: An Intellectual Biography*, *JSOT* Supplement Series, 120 (Sheffield 1992).

RÖMER, T., *Israel's Väter. Untersuchungen zur Väterthematik im Deuteronomium und in der deuteronomistischen Tradition*, OBO 99 (Freiburg 1990).
—— 'Le Deutéronome: à la quête des origines', in P. Haudebert (ed.), *Le Pentateuque: Débats et recherches* (Paris 1992), 65–98.
ROSE, M., *Deuteronomist und Jahwist. Untersuchungen zu den Berührungspunkten beider Literaturwerke*, AThANT 67 (Zürich 1981).
ROST, L., *Die Überlieferung von der Thronnachfolge Davids*, BWANT 3/6 (Stuttgart 1926); Eng. trans., *The Succession to the Throne of David* (Sheffield 1982).
—— 'Das kleine geschichtliche Credo', in his *Das kleine Credo und andere Studien zum Alten Testament* (Heidelberg 1965), 11–25.
RUDOLPH, W. and VOLZ, P., *Der Elohist als Erzähler: Ein Irrweg der Pentateuchkritik? An der Genesis erläutert*, BZAW 63 (Berlin 1933).
RUDOLPH, W., *Der 'Elohist' von Exodus bis Joshua*, BZAW 68 (Berlin 1938).
SANDMEL, S., 'The Haggada Within Scripture', *JBL* 80 (1961), 105–22.
SANDERS, J. A., *Torah and Canon* (Philadelphia 1972).
SCHMID, H. H., *Altorientalische Welt in der alttestamentlichen Theologie* (Zürich 1974).
—— *Der sogenannte Jahwist: Beobachtungen und Fragen zur Pentateuchforschung* (Zürich 1976).
—— 'In Search of New Approaches in Pentateuchal Research', *JSOT* 3 (1977), 33–42.
SCHMID, HERBERT, *Die Gestalt des Mose: Probleme alttestamentlicher Forschung unter Berücksichtigung der Pentateuchkrise*, Erträge der Forschung, 237 (Darmstadt 1986).
SCHMIDT, L., 'Überlegungen zum Jahwisten', *EvTh* 37 (1977), 230–47.
SCHMIDT, W. H., 'Ein Theologe in salomonischer Zeit? Plädoyer für den Jahwisten', *BZ* n.F. 25 (1981), 82–102; Eng. trans., 'A Theologian of the Solomonic Era? A Plea for the Yahwist', in T. Ishida (ed.), *Studies in the Period of David and Solomon and Other Essays* (Winona Lake, Minn. 1982), 55–73.
—— 'Plädoyer für die Quellenscheidung', *BZ* n.F. 32 (1988), 1–14.
SCHMITT, H.-C., *Die Nichtpriesterliche Josephsgeschichte: Ein Beitrag zur neuesten Pentateuchkritik*, BZAW 154 (Berlin 1980).
SEGAL, M. H., *The Pentateuch: Its Composition and Its Authority, and Other Biblical Studies* (Jerusalem 1967).
SEIDEL, B., *Karl David Ilgen und die Pentateuchforschung im Umkreis der sogenannten Älteren Urkundenhypothese*, BZAW 213 (Berlin 1993).
SIMPSON, C. A., *The Early Traditions of Israel* (Oxford 1948).
SKA, J. L., 'La Place d'Ex 6, 2–8 dans la narration de l'exode', *ZAW* 94 (1982), 530–48.
—— 'Un nouveau Wellhausen?', *Biblica*, 72 (1991), 252–63.
SKINNER, J., *The Divine Names in Genesis* (London 1914).

SKINNER, J., *A Critical and Exegetical Commentary on Genesis* (Edinburgh 1910; 2nd edn., 1930).

SMEND, R., *Die Erzählungen des Hexateuchs auf ihre quellen untersucht* (Berlin 1912).

——'JE in den geschichtlichen Büchern des Alten Testaments', *ZAW* 39 (1921), 181–217.

SMEND, R. (Jr.), *Elemente alttestamentlichen Geschichtsdenkens*, Theologische Studien, 95 (Zürich 1968).

——*Die Entstehung des Alten Testaments* (Stuttgart 1978).

STADE, B., 'Beiträge zur Pentateuchkritik', *ZAW* 14 (1894), 250–318.

STAERK, W., *Das Deuteronomium. Sein Inhalt und seine literarische Form* (Leipzig 1894).

——*Studien zur Religions- und Sprachgeschichte des Alten Testaments*, i (Berlin 1899).

STEUERNAGEL, C., *Der Rahmen des Deuteronomium. Literarkritische Untersuchung über seine Zusammensetzung und Entstehung* (Halle 1894).

——*Die Entstehung des deuteronomischen Gesetz* (Berlin 1895; 2nd edn., 1901).

TENGSTRÖM, S., *Die Hexateucherzählung. Eine literaturgeschichtliche Studie*, Coniectanea Biblica, Old Testament Series 7 (Lund 1976).

——*Die Toledoth formel und die literarische Struktur der priesterlichen Erweiterungsschicht im Pentateuch*, Coniectanea Biblica, Old Testament Series 17 (Lund 1981).

THOMPSON, R. J., *Moses and the Law in a Century of Criticism since Graf*, SVT 19 (Leiden 1970).

TIGAY, J. (ed.), *Empirical Models for Biblical Criticism* (Philadelphia 1985).

TUCH, F., *Commentar über die Genesis* (Halle 1838).

VAN SETERS, J., 'Confessional Reformulation in the Exilic Period', *VT* 22 (1972), 448–59.

——*Abraham in History and Tradition* (New Haven 1975).

——'The Yahwist as Theologian? A Response', *JSOT* 3 (1977), 15–19.

——*In Search of History: Historiography in the Ancient World and the Origins of Biblical History* (New Haven 1983).

——*Der Jahwist als Historiker* (Zürich 1987).

——'The Primeval Histories of Greece and Israel Compared', *ZAW* 100 (1988), 1–22.

——'The So-Called Deuteronomistic Redaction of the Pentateuch', SVT 43 (Leiden 1991), 58–77.

——*Prologue to History: The Yahwist as Historian in Genesis* (Louisville, Ky. 1992).

——*The Life of Moses: The Yahwist as Historian in Exodus–Numbers* (Kampen 1994).

VATER, J. S., *Commentar über den Pentateuch*, i–iv (Halle 1802–5).

VATKE, W., *Die biblische Theologie wissenschaftlich dargestellt*, i. *Die Religion des Alten Testamentes* (Berlin 1835).

VERMEYLEN, J., 'La formation du Pentateuque à la lumière de l'exégèse historico-critique', *RTL* 12 (1981), 324–46.

VERVENNE, M., 'The "P" Tradition in the Pentateuch: Document and/or Redaction?', in C. Brekelmans and J. Lust (eds.), *Pentateuchal and Deuteronomistic Studies*, Bibliotheca Ephemeridum Theologicarum Lovaniensium, 94 (Leuven 1990), 67–90.

—— 'The Question of "Deuteronomic" Elements in Genesis to Numbers', in F. García Martínez, A. Hilhorst, J. T. A. G. M. van Ruiten, and A. S. van der Woude (eds.), *Studies in Deuteronomy in Honour of C.J. Labuschagne*, SVT 53 (Leiden 1994), 243–68.

VOLZ, P., 'Anhang. P ist kein Erzähler', in P. Volz and W. Rudolph, *Der Elohist als Erzähler. Ein Irrweg der Pentateuchkritik?* BZAW 63 (Giessen 1933), 135–42.

VON RAD, G., *Die Priesterschrift im Hexateuch*, BWANT IV: 13 (Stuttgart 1934).

—— *Das formgeschichtliche Problem des Hexateuch*, BWANT 26 (Stuttgart 1938), repr. in his *Gesammelte Studien zum Alten Testament* (Munich 1958), 9–86; Eng. trans., 'The Form-Critical Problem of the Hexateuch', in *The Form-Critical Problem of the Hexateuch and Other Essays* (Edinburgh 1965), 1–78.

—— *Deuteronomium-Studien*, FRLANT 58 (Göttingen 1947), Eng. trans., *Studies in Deuteronomy* (London 1953).

—— 'Josephsgeschichte und ältere Chokma', SVT I (1953), 120–7, repr. in *Gesammelte Studien zum Alten Testament* (Munich 1958), 272–80; Eng. trans., 'The Joseph Narrative and Ancient Wisdom', in *The Problem of the Hexateuch and Other Essays* (Edinburgh 1965), 292–300.

—— *Theologie des Alten Testaments*, i. *Die Theologie der geschichtlichen Überlieferungen Israels* (Munich 1957); Eng. trans., *Old Testament Theology*, i. *The Theology of Israel's Historical Traditions* (Edinburgh 1962).

—— *Das erste Buch Moses, Genesis*, ATD 2–4 (5th edn., Göttingen 1958); Eng. trans., *Genesis* (London 1961).

—— *Theologie des Alten Testaments*, ii. *Die Theologie der prophetischen Überlieferungen Israels* (Munich 1960); Eng. trans., *Old Testament Theology*, ii. *The Theology of Israel's Prophetic Traditions* (Edinburgh 1965).

—— *Das fünfte Buch Mose, Deuteronomium, übersetz und erklärt*, ATD 8 (Göttingen 1964), Eng. trans., *Deuteronomy* (London 1966).

VORLÄNDER, H., *Die Entstehungszeit des jehowistischen Geschichtswerkes* (Frankfurt am Main 1978).

WAGNER, N. E., 'Pentateuchal Criticism: No Clear Future', *Canadian Journal of Theology*, 13 (1967), 225–32.

—— 'A Response to Professor Rolf Rendtorff', *JSOT* 3 (1977), 20–7.

WEEKS, S., *Early Israelite Wisdom*, Oxford Theological Monographs (Oxford 1994).

WEIMAR, P., *Untersuchung zur Redaktionsgeschichte des Pentateuch*, BZAW 146 (Berlin 1977).

——'Struktur und Komposition der priesterschriftlichen Geschichtsdarsstellung', in *BN* 23 (1984), 81–134, and 24 (1984), 138–62.

WEINFELD, M., *Deuteronomy and the Deuteronomic School* (Oxford 1972).

WELCH, A. C., *The Code of Deuteronomy: A New Theory of its Origin* (London 1924).

WELLHAUSEN, J., *Geschichte Israels*, i (Berlin 1878), pub. in subsequent edns. under the title *Prolegomena zur Geschichte Israels* (Berlin 1883); Eng. trans.. *Prolegomena to the History of Israel* (Edinburgh 1885).

——*Die Composition des Hexateuchs*, in his *Skizzen und Vorarbeiten*, ii (Berlin 1885).

——*Die Composition des Hexateuchs und der Historischen Bücher des Alten Testaments* (Berlin 1889).

WEST, M. L., *The Hesiodic Catalogue of Women: Its Nature, Structure, and Origins* (Oxford 1985).

WESTERMANN, C., 'Arten der Erzählung in der Genesis', *Forschung am Alten Testament* (Munich 1964), 9–91.

——*Genesis 1–11*, BKAT (Neukirchen-Vluyn 1966–); Eng. trans., *Genesis 1–11: A Commentary* (London 1984).

——*Genesis 12–50*, BKAT (Neukirchen-Vluyn 1977–); Eng. trans., *Genesis 12–36: A Commentary* (London 1986).

WHYBRAY, R. N., 'Response to Professor Rendtorff', *JSOT* 3 (1977), 11–14.

——*The Making of the Pentateuch: A Methodological Study*, JSOT Monograph Series, 53 (Sheffield 1987).

——*Introduction to the Pentateuch* (Grand Rapids, Mich. 1995).

WILLIAMSON, H. G. M., Review of J. Van Seters, *The Life of Moses: The Yahwist as Historian in Exodus–Numbers*, in *VT* 45 (1995), 431 f.

WINNETT, F. V., *The Mosaic Tradition* (Toronto 1949).

——'Re-examining the Foundations', *JBL* 84 (1965), 1–19.

WOLFF, H. W., 'Das Kerygma des Jahwisten', *EvTh* 24 (1964), 73–93, repr. in his *Gesammelte Studien zum Alten Testament* (Munich 1964), 345–73; Eng. trans., 'The Kerygma of the Yahwist', in W. Brueggemann and H. W. Wolff (eds.), *The Vitality of Old Testament Traditions* (Atlanta 1978), 41–66.

——'Zur Thematik der elohistischen Fragmente im Pentateuch', *EvTh 29* (1969), 59–72; repr. in his *Gesammelte Studien zum Alten Testament* (2nd edn., Munich 1973), 402–17; Eng. trans., 'The Elohistic Fragments in the Pentateuch', in W. Brueggemann and H. W. Wolff (eds.), *The Vitality of Old Testament Traditions* (Atlanta 1978), 67–82.

——*Joel und Amos*, BKAT, 14/2 (2nd edn., Neukirchen-Vluyn 1975); Eng. trans., *Joel and Amos* (Philadelphia 1977).

WRIGHT, G. E. and FULLER, R., *The Book of the Acts of God* (London 1960).

ZENGER, E., *Gottes Bogen in den Wolken: Untersuchungen zu Komposition und Theologie der priesterschriftlichen Urgeschichte*, WMANT 57 (Stuttgart 1983).

ZEVIT, Z., 'Converging Lines of Evidence Bearing on the Date of P', *ZAW* 94 (1982), 481–511.

ZIMMERLI, W., 'Sinaibund und Abrahambund: Ein Beitrag zum Verständnis der Priesterschrift', *ThZ* 16 (1960), 268–80; reprinted in his *Gottes Offenbarung. Gesammelte Aufsätze zum Alten Testament* (Munich 1963), 205–16.

—— *Grundriss der alttestamentlichen Theologie* (Stuttgart 1972); Eng. trans., *Old Testament Theology in Outline* (Edinburgh 1978).

AUTHOR INDEX

Kaiser, O. 142
Kaufmann, Y. 218, 219, 220
Kennett, R. H. 48
Kessler, R. 106
Kirkpatrick, P. G. 140
Kittel, R. 45 f.
Klatt, W. 32
Klein, H. 237
Klostermann, A. 18, 47, 197
Knight, D. 31, 32, 35, 50, 54, 88
Koch, K. 101, 198
König, E. 14
Kuenen, A. 9, 10, 12, 13 f., 14 f.

Langlamet, F. 181, 182, 246
Levin, C. 98, 132, 160, 161–5, 166 f.,
   167–9
Lewis, D. M. 152
Lohfink, N. 89, 91, 127, 157, 175, 198,
   207, 242, 244, 245
Löhr, M. 47, 197

McEvenue, S. E. 198, 231
McFadyen, J. E. 91 f.
McKane, W. 118
Maybaum, S. 19, 46 f., 197
Mayes, A. D. H. 16, 90, 179, 218
Mead, C. M. 224
Meier, C. 151
Milgrom, J. 261
Moberly, R. W. L. 230 f.
Momigliano, A. 150
Morgenstern, J. 44
Mowinckel, S. 49, 52 f., 246

Nicholson, E. W. 15, 16, 48, 89, 150,
   186, 191, 198, 211, 244, 245
North, C. R. 91 f., 194 f., 197, 240
Noth, M. 14, 46, 53, 54, 55, 58–60, 66,
   68, 73, 74–88, 88–90, 96, 99, 103 f.,
   106, 121 f., 134, 175, 222, 229, 231,
   235, 237, 238, 239, 242, 245 f., 247,
   251 f.
Nyberg, H. S. 51

Oestreicher, T. 48
Olrik, A. 134 f., 140, 233, 236
Ord, D. R. 254
Orr, J. 47, 197
Osswald, E. 8

Pedersen, J. 50 f., 52, 67
Perlitt, L. 50, 90 f., 178, 189 f.

Pfeiffer, R. H. 44
Polzin, R. 220
Procksch, O. 12
Pury, A. de 90, 91

Rad, G. von 46, 47, 53, 54, 55, 60,
   63–74, 75 f., 76, 79, 83, 86, 88–90, 96,
   97, 103, 104, 130, 145, 168, 169, 195,
   214, 241, 246, 247, 250 f., 253, 263,
   266 f., 268
Rendtorff, R. 95–131, 172, 173, 174,
   193, 197
Reuss, E. 4 f., 9
Richter, W. 89, 182
Roberts, J. M. 184
Rogerson, J. R. 4, 5, 7, 8, 11
Römer, T. 90, 91, 127
Rose, M. 98, 132, 138, 140, 146, 153–7,
   158, 169 f., 174, 175, 178 f., 193, 240
Rost, L. 46, 71
Rudolph, W. 49, 73, 238

Sanders, J. A. 261
Sandmel, S. 235
Schmid, H. H. 97–8, 132, 143–5, 146,
   155, 162, 169 f., 173, 181–4, 187–91,
   241, 245
Schmid, Herbert 91
Schmidt, L. 247
Schmidt, W. H. 212, 237, 247
Schmitt, H.-C. 98, 132, 161
Segal, M. H. 224
Seidel, B. 6
Simpson, C. A. 45
Ska, J. L. 174, 204
Skinner, J. 47, 197
Smend, R. 44, 45
Smend, R. (Jr.) 152, 207
Stade, B. 12
Staerk, W. 16
Stähelin, J. 7
Steuernagel, C. 16

Tengström, S. 96 f., 198, 213–15,
   215–18, 221, 247
Thompson, R. J. 8, 11
Tigay, J. 224–8
Tuch, F. 7

Van Der Kooij, A. 9
Van Seters, J. 96–8, 132, 134–43, 146–53,
   156, 159, 167–9, 174, 175–8, 182–3,
   193, 197, 233–7, 240

INDEX OF SCRIPTURE REFERENCES

Psalms (*cont.*):
135	65
136	65
136: 16	83

2 Chronicles:
20: 25	185

Isaiah:
1: 9	158
6	183, 184
7: 1–7	170, 245
10: 5–19	169
14: 24–7	169
22: 11	168
27: 26	168
30: 1–5	170, 245
31: 1–3	170, 245
40: 9–10	137
41: 8	141
41: 8 f.	129
41: 8 ff.	137
42: 5	190
51: 2	129, 141
54: 1–3	138
61: 5	190

Jeremiah:
1: 4–10	184
2: 2	129
2: 6	83

Ezekiel:
20: 5	129, 186
33: 23 ff.	141

36: 23	190
40–8	20
44	219
44: 6–16	20

Hosea:
1: 9	186
2: 16 f.	158
4: 15	166
5: 15–6: 3	187
7: 11	170, 245
8: 9	170, 245
11: 1	129
12: 4–6	158, 159
12: 10	129, 186
12: 13	186
13: 1	158
13: 4	186
14: 1–7	187

Amos:
1–2	168
1: 3–8	168
1: 13–15	168
2: 1–3	168
2: 10	83
3: 2	168
5: 5	15
5: 25	187
7: 4–6	187 f.
8: 14	166
9: 7	158, 168

Habakkuk:
3: 3 ff.	65